# THE BOUVIERS
## Genealogical Table

| First Generation | Second Generation | Third Generation | Fourth Generation |
|---|---|---|---|

Anne Bouvier*

Eustache Bouvier
(1824-1866)

John Vernou Bouvier III
(1891-1957)
m.—Janet Norton Lee

Michel Bouvier
(1792-1874)
m. (1)—Sarah Anne Pearson
m. (2)—Louise C. Vernou

Thérèse Bouvier
(1826-1918)
m.—Jon. Patterson, Jr.

Elizabeth Bouvier
(1793-1872)
m. (1)—Noël Baudichon
m. (2)—Etienne Bouchard

Elizabeth Bouvier
(1829-1886)
m.—Joseph E. Dixon

Eustache Bouvier*

Louise Bouivier, R.S.C.J.
(1831-1902)

Anne-Julie Bouvier*

Eustache Bouvier*

Emma Bouvier
1833-1883)
m.—Francis A. Drexel

Louise Bouvier Drexel
(1863-1945)
m.—Edward Morrell

William Sergeant Bouvier
(1893-1929)
m.—Emma Louise Stone

Jean-François Bouvier
m. (1)—Marie Poissonié
m. (2)—Marguerite Lauissat

Zénaïde Bouvier
(1835-1914)

Catherine Bouvier*

Alexine Bouvier
(1837-1914)

Eustache Bouvier
(1799-1817)

Mary Howell Bouvier
(1841-1931)

John V. Bouvier, Jr.
(1865-1948)
m.—Maude Sergeant

Edith Ewing Bouvier
(1895-1977)
m.—Phelan Beale

John Vernou Bouver
(1843-1926)
m.—Caroline Ewing

Rose Pélagie Bouvier
(1830-1922)
m.—Pierre Barry

Josephine Bouvier
(1845-1847)

Elizabeth-Rose Bouvier*

Caroline Bouvier
(1867-1869)

Louise Bouvier
(1833-1898)

Michel Charlès Bouvier
(1847-1935)

Maude Reppelin Bouvier
(b. 1905)
m.—John E. Davis

Anasthasie Bouvier
(1834-?)

Joseph Alexander Bouvier
(1852-1856)

Michelle Caroline Bouvier
(1905-1987)
m. (1)—Henry C. Scott
m. (2)—Harrington Putnam

\* died in infancy

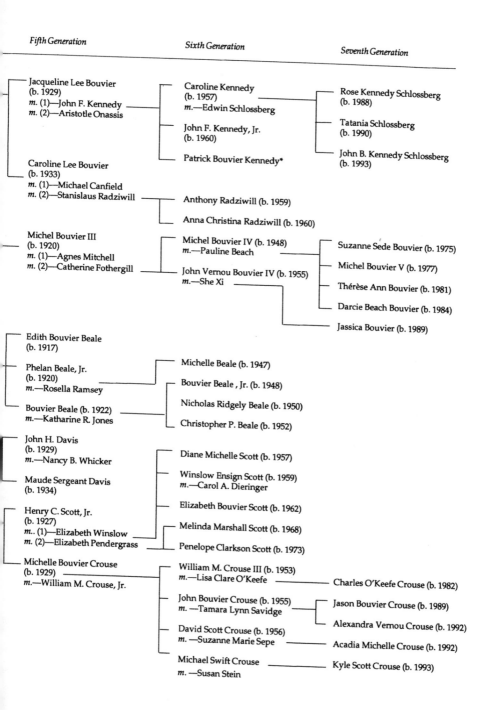

*Fifth Generation*

*Sixth Generation*

*Seventh Generation*

Jacqueline Lee Bouvier
(b. 1929)
*m.* (1)—John F. Kennedy
*m.* (2)—Aristotle Onassis

Caroline Kennedy
(b. 1957)
*m.*—Edwin Schlossberg

Rose Kennedy Schlossberg
(b. 1988)

John F. Kennedy, Jr.
(b. 1960)

Tatania Schlossberg
(b. 1990)

Patrick Bouvier Kennedy*

John B. Kennedy Schlossberg
(b. 1993)

Caroline Lee Bouvier
(b. 1933)
*m.* (1)—Michael Canfield
*m.* (2)—Stanislaus Radziwill

Anthony Radziwill (b. 1959)

Anna Christina Radziwill (b. 1960)

Michel Bouvier III
(b. 1920)
*m.* (1)—Agnes Mitchell
*m.* (2)—Catherine Fothergill

Michel Bouvier IV (b. 1948)
*m.*—Pauline Beach

Suzanne Sede Bouvier (b. 1975)

John Vernou Bouvier IV (b. 1955)
*m.*—She Xi

Michel Bouvier V (b. 1977)

Thérèse Ann Bouvier (b. 1981)

Darcie Beach Bouvier (b. 1984)

Jassica Bouvier (b. 1989)

Edith Bouvier Beale
(b. 1917)

Phelan Beale, Jr.
(b. 1920)
*m.*—Rosella Ramsey

Michelle Beale (b. 1947)

Bouvier Beale , Jr. (b. 1948)

Bouvier Beale (b. 1922)
*m.*—Katharine R. Jones

Nicholas Ridgely Beale (b. 1950)

Christopher P. Beale (b. 1952)

John H. Davis
(b. 1929)
*m.*—Nancy B. Whicker

Diane Michelle Scott (b. 1957)

Maude Sergeant Davis
(b. 1934)

Winslow Ensign Scott (b. 1959)
*m.*—Carol A. Dieringer

Henry C. Scott, Jr.
(b. 1927)
*m..* (1)—Elizabeth Winslow
*m.* (2)—Elizabeth Pendergrass

Elizabeth Bouvier Scott (b. 1962)

Melinda Marshall Scott (b. 1968)

Penelope Clarkson Scott (b. 1973)

Michelle Bouvier Crouse
(b. 1929)
*m.*—William M. Crouse, Jr.

William M. Crouse III (b. 1953)
*m.*—Lisa Clare O'Keefe

Charles O'Keefe Crouse (b. 1982)

John Bouvier Crouse (b. 1955)
*m.* —Tamara Lynn Savidge

Jason Bouvier Crouse (b. 1989)

Alexandra Vernou Crouse (b. 1992)

David Scott Crouse (b. 1956)
*m.* —Suzanne Marie Sepe

Acadia Michelle Crouse (b. 1992)

Michael Swift Crouse
*m.* —Susan Stein

Kyle Scott Crouse (b. 1993)

# THE BOUVIERS

## From Waterloo to the Kennedys and Beyond

John H. Davis

National
Press
Books

Washington, D.C.

**Library of Congress Cataloging-in-Publication Data**

Davis, John H., 1929-
The Bouviers:
from Waterloo to the Kennedys and beyond
by John H. Davis
416 pp., 156 x 22.5 cm.
Expanded edition of: The Bouviers: portrait of an American family. 1969.
Includes index.
ISBN 0-915765-84-5: $24.95
1. Bouvier family.
2. United States—Biography.
I. Title.
CT274.B694D38  1993
929'.2'0973—dc20
93-8036
CIP

*To my mother*
*Maude Bouvier Davis*
*who first told me the story of the Bouviers*

"In the first generation thee must do well,
in the second marry well, in the third breed well,
then the fourth should take care of itself."

QUAKER FORMULA ON THE WAY TO FOUND A
FAMILY

"It is not observed in history that families improve with
time. It is rather discovered that the whole matter is like
a comet, of which the brightest part is the head; and the
tail, although long and luminous, is gradually shaded into
obscurity."

GEORGE WILLIAM CURTIS

"Look: the constant marigold
Springs again from hidden roots.
Baffled gardener, you behold
New beginnings and new shoots."

ROBERT GRAVES

# Preface and Acknowledgments

THIS BOOK WAS FIRST CONCEIVED WHEN I WAS A BOUVIER GRAND-child spending my summers at the family estate in East Hampton. The Bouviers had always fascinated me, even when I was a child, and when I grew into my teens I gradually formed the ambition of writing a book about them some day. Not an insignificant stimulus to that ambition was my grandfather's wishful history of the family, *Our Forebears*. At nineteen, when Grandfather Bouvier died and his East Hampton estate was emptied of his possessions, I saved many family documents from destruction, with the thought that one day I might be able to use them in the book. Subsequently college, service in the Navy, a Fulbright scholarship in Italy, other writing efforts, and my first full-time job forced me to set aside the project—which turned out to be fortunate since I was not ready, intellectually and emotionally, to do justice to the subject until much later.

When I turned thirty, I finally began working on the book, casting it in the form of a novel about the rise and fall of an American family of Southern French descent. I intended to develop one member of the family as the personification of its finest qualities and worst failings; his career would both represent the height of the family's fortunes and pave the way for the family's downfall. I was living in Italy at the time I began writing, benefiting in objectivity from my removal from the family scene. As the book progressed, however, extraordinary things began happening to one of the living Bouviers, and soon a potential subplot began unfolding which, if developed, promised eventually to dominate the book. After attending the inauguration of President Kennedy, I stopped writing and resumed observing. Then came the assassination and the subsequent transformation of Jacqueline Bouvier Kennedy, at thirty-four, into a national folk heroine. By now the novel I had planned and half written had paled before reality. And it was impossible to recast it to include a personage who had become First Lady of the United States and had seen her husband murdered beside her; the facts behind the fictional names and events would be too transparent.

I now had to call a spade a spade and write the true history of the Bouviers. But to do that required absolute honesty. A writer does no service to the dead by lying about them or side-stepping their failings. Yet, as a member of the family, I was reluctant to be too honest. My problem was finally resolved with the help of a good friend, Gustav Herling, the Polish writer and exile, who forcefully advised me at a café in Rome to write a straight, nonfictional account of the family that would tell their story exactly as it was. My obligations to history, he emphasized, were far more important than any narrow concern I might have for family vanity. I then began what turned out to be two years of research on the Bouviers.

I would first like to acknowledge the research conducted by Sally Shepherd. Among her more important discoveries were the article in the *Philadelphia Record* concerning Alexine Bouvier's rejection by "Prince Vallerie"; the contract between Henrietta Graff, the Misses Mary, Zénaïde, and Alexine Bouvier, and the Syrian dragoman, Antonio Macklouf; and the description in Auguste Bouchard's *Livre de Raison* of the Misses Bouvier's visit to their French relatives in Pont-Saint-Esprit. Ms. Sheppard also provided me with material on Los Olivos, California, and the business affairs of M.C. Bouvier.

Others who contributed important research were Paul Hamon of Grenoble, who uncovered the origins of the Bouviers in Savoie; Yves Chassin du Guerny of Nîmes, who did most of the work on the families of Elizabeth, Jean-François, and Pélagie Bouvier and discovered their descendants in France today; Francis J. Dallett of the American Museum of Britain, who did the pioneer research on Michel Sr., and wrote the first serious study of his career as a cabinetmaker; Webster M. Christman III of Philadelphia, who produced valuable information from the Girard Archives; and Linda Barker, a former student of mine in Italy, who traced back the origins of several families the Bouviers married into, and helped gather background material on Philadelphia society and the New York Stock Exchange in the nineteenth century. In am deeply indebted to all these people.

In addition to these contributions, I would also like to acknowledge, with gratitude, the encouragement and counsel my friend and agent, Carl Brandt, has given me since I abandoned the novel and decided to write a nonfictional account. His insistence on an objective, unwhitewashed treatment of the family was just as emphatic as Gustav Herling's and has strongly influenced the ultimate character of this book.

To my original publisher, Roger W. Straus, Jr., and my editor, Henry Robbins, further debts of gratitude are due. The climate of warm cooperation Mr. Straus provided contributed greatly to my peace of mind while I was writing the book, and in Mr. Robbins I was fortunate in having an adviser whose moral support was unfailing and whose suggestions for improving the manuscript were guided by a rare combination of practical sense and literary taste. I am also very grateful to my copy editor, Carmen Gomezplata, for her careful reading of the text and her many judicious suggestions toward refining it.

For access to their archives and help in finding source material in them, I wish to thank the following organizations: The Historical Society of Pennsylvania, and specifically one of its librarians, Mr. Anthony Roth; The French Benevolent Society of Philadelphia; The American Philosphical Society in Philadelphia (custodians of the Girard Archives on microfilm); The Archives Départementales du Gard; and the Sisters of the Blessed Sacrament, Cornwells Heights, Pennsylvania. To Sister Francisca of the latter organization a particular debt of gratitude is due. With patience, perseverance, and generosity she uncovered, over a period of many months, and put at my disposal, an invaluable collection of early Bouvier documents and photographs, including Emma Bouvier's "Journal of a Trip to Europe" in 1853 and many letters of Louise Bouvier Morrell and Mother Katharine Drexel.

For help in typing the manuscript I wish to thank Tammy McCabe, Joanne Luther, Rose Magid, Marjorie Wenzler, Linda Barker, and my wife. To my wife, also, go my thanks for her many perceptive suggestions for improving the text.

Finally, a very special debt of gratitude goes to the many members of the Bouvier family in the United States and in France who provided me with information, documents, letters, and photographs for the book. Among their many contributions I wish to acknowledge, with a deep sense of obligation, the extremely important one made by my mother, Maude Bouvier Davis, and her twin sister, Michelle Bouvier Putnam. It was chiefly owing to their efforts that the Bouvier family papers were preserved and eventually turned over to me. And it was they who first stimulated my interest in the history of the Bouviers.

For this new, updated edition, containing five new chapters, I would like to thank Joel Joseph, president of National Press Books, for commissioning the edition and Alan Sultan, vice president, for overseeing, with perspicacity, the editing of it. I also want to thank Talia Greenberg, the hands on editor, for her many perceptive suggestions for improving the manuscript. To Dan Peragine, my agent for this edition, I want to express my gratitude for his finding a house willing to re-publish the book. Lastly my deep appreciation goes to Sohodra Nathu, who provided me with helpful editorial advice and much needed encouragement to see the projection through to completion.

JOHN H. DAVIS

*New York*
*April 1993*

*Note*

While members of the Bouvier family in America and France have provided me with information for this book, the interpretation of Bouvier family history it contains is wholly my own and does not reflect the views of any member of the family but myself. To preserve the integrity of my viewpoint, I have not allowed any member of the family to read the manuscript before publication.

J. H. D.

# Contents

# PART ONE

## Comet from Pont-Saint-Espirit

FOUNDING AN AMERICAN
FAMILY

[1815-1874]

# I

BY 8:30 THE BATTLE WAS OVER AND WATERLOO WAS ON ITS WAY TO becoming a synonym for final defeat. Napoleon's Imperial Guard had first recoiled a half hour before, now it was in full retreat. What was left of the French Army was scattering into the night. All day the battle had raged. As soon as the usual early-morning fog of Flanders had lifted, 350,000 men had begun a struggle destined to make Sunday, June 18, 1815, one of the watersheds of modern European history. The scene of the fighting was a vast rolling plain twenty miles south of Brussels, sewn with rye, wheat, corn, and barley and interspersed with farm cottages. Throughout the warm, sunny day, terrified peasants had peered through the windows of these cottages at a spectacle they and the world would never forget. With flags and pennants waving, golden eagles glistening in the sun, bagpipes squealing, and drumbeats echoing the cannon and musket, the deadly duels between cavalry, artillery, and infantry unfolded in an interminable series of charges, withdrawals, and countercharges. Infantry would go into square against cavalry and would thereby become vulnerable to artillery. Breaking out of square amidst a hail of shrapnel, grape, and cannon, infantry would then become vulnerable to cavalry and the dragoons and lancers would surge into the broken ranks. And so it went for ten tumultuous hours until at last Napoleon's elite corps, the Imperial Guard, caved in and Wellington's cavalry turned upon the now panic-stricken French, driving them south into the night. At 9:30 the two victorious generals, Wellington and Blücher, met at a farmhouse near a hamlet called La Belle Alliance to decide what to do next. Wellington told the old Prussian that the British were too exhausted to do anything more that night. Whereupon Blücher agreed to take up the pursuit of the French with all the cavalry he could muster.

The retreat led south along the Charleroi road through cornfields silvered by a nearly full moon. The French in their tight white pants, black boots, gold epaulettes, and burnished helmets made a conspicuous target for their pursuers. On several occasions Napoleon, surrounded by the remnants of his Imperial Guard, attempted to rally his dwindling army as it fled before Blücher's cavalry, but the French no longer had the will to fight. With the Prussian drums dinning in their ears, the French soldiers fled through Flanders in near total disorder. To surrender, to falter, was to die. The Prussian cavalrymen were merciless to the vanquished. The wounded who managed to crawl into farmhouses and barns were bludgeoned to death. Soldiers overtaken on the road or in the cornfields were cut down by saber and bayonet. The Prussians' drums were as relentless as their swords. There was no escaping their persistent demand for blood. Before long, Napoleon's army began disintegrating. Although a fairly large number of men remained with the Emperor, for the most part it was each Frenchman for himself. Napoleon had the reputation of being a squanderer of human life in warfare. The soldiers whose lives he so recklessly risked repaid their commander's faith in their willingness to die for his ambitions by exclaiming "Vive l'empereur" before they breathed their last. Of the 125,000 men Napoleon had brought onto the field of battle at Waterloo, 40,000 remained there and along the avenue of retreat forever. Of the 85,000 who escaped, at least 5,000 died before reaching their homes in France. Those who were fortunate enough to survive had to manage their return home as best they could.

One of the survivors was a twenty-three-year-old infantryman from the Rhône Valley by the name of Michel Bouvier. He had gone down to defeat with Napoleon's forces at least once before— at the battle of Toulouse in April 1814, when Wellington had overcome Soult. Not long after that, the Emperor abdicated, Louis XVIII reentered Paris, Napoleon was exiled to Elba, and Michel had to go back to his native village of Pont-Saint-Esprit. He remained there until shortly after the return from Elba on March 1, 1815, when, as a volunteer, he rejoined Napoleon for the reckless Hundred Days that had just ended so disastrously.

Exactly what happened to Michel between the end of the battle and his departure for America two and a half weeks later is not known, but with the aid of a few unassailable facts of French history and some reasonable assumptions about human nature an attempt can be made to reconstruct the probable sequence of events that led him to abandon his country.

The retreat through Flanders continued all night, with Blücher's cavalry never giving up the pursuit. Meanwhile peasants, thieves, and deserters had begun scouring the battlefield and line of retreat, plundering the dead and wounded, often killing the wounded if they offered resistance. Among the scavengers and looters were many women. They often met face to face with other women searching among the corpses for their dead husbands and with priests administering the last rites to those still able to receive them. Some 62,000 men had lost their lives. In one area of three square miles, 5,000 soldiers lay dead.

During the night Napoleon had to abandon part of the imperial treasure. When the Prussians discovered it, the peasants of the region learned of its existence and a furious fight broke out over leather pouches containing diamonds, gold, and silver that made their finders fortunes. By nine in the morning of June 19 the Emperor had crossed the French border. Once on French soil, Napoleon attempted to rally the troops which had remained with him. The attempt failed, and the army broke up once and for all. Napoleon, still accompanied by the remnants of his ever faithful Imperial Guard, headed for Paris while the bulk of his army scattered to the four winds.

It was at this time, on the morning of June 19, that, we may assume, young Michel Bouvier began his trek south to reach his home in Pont-Saint-Esprit.

Pont-Saint-Esprit is a small village on the Rhône in ancient Languedoc about seventy miles from the Mediterranean. To get there Michel had to travel about six hundred miles. Crossing the French border near the Oise River, he probably headed south through Lorraine along the Meuse, picking up the Saône north of Dijon. The Saône flows to Lyons, where it joins the Rhône. From Lyons, the Rhône Valley descends due south to Valence, Montélimar, and Pont-Saint-Esprit. The journey probably took a little over a week.

While ex-infantryman Michel was making the long trek home, events in Paris moved swiftly. The Emperor Napoleon reentered the capital on June 21, three days after his defeat. Still undaunted, he talked of forming a new army to hurl against the forces that had just defeated him. But what little power remained to him was fast slipping through his hands. While he called for new recruits, more supplies, and a renewed effort, many ministers and members of the Chamber of Deputies called for his abdication. Finally, on June 23, after several passionate appeals to the dwindling loyalty of his supporters, followed in each case by a renewed demand for his withdrawal, he accepted the inevitable and abdicated. The provisional government that took over capitulated to the allies. Whereupon the allies, whose armies had already entered France, announced that all who had joined the Hundred

Days were criminals liable to immediate arrest. The arrests and prosecutions would begin as soon as the allies assumed control of the government. The news sent Napoleon's supporters into a frenzy. It was only a matter of days before the British and the Prussians would occupy Paris. Napoleon's older brother, Joseph, immediately made preparations to leave for the United States, hoping to take his brother with him. Thousands of Waterloo veterans began planning their escapes.

It was probably on the way to Pont-Saint-Esprit that Michel Bouvier first learned he was a criminal, and the news no doubt spurred his efforts to reach his family. When he finally did, his anguish must have been unbearable. All was in turmoil as a confused France awaited the allied occupation and the inevitable restoration of Bourbon tyranny.

The restoration was not long in coming. The allied armies occupied Paris on July 6 and 7 and immediately began hunting down the veterans of the Hundred Days. One of the first to be captured was Marshal Ney, who eventually met his end in the Luxembourg Gardens before a firing squad. The formal Second Restoration took place on July 8, when Louis XVIII, who as an unyielding believer in the Divine Right of Kings had, in his own opinion, never ceased to reign, reentered Paris in ceremonial splendor. Soon the royalist La Bourdonnaye, speaking in the Chamber of Deputies, was demanding in behalf of the king the imprisonment, torture, and execution of all who had participated in the Hundred Days, thus reinforcing the allies' proscription. "Learn how to shed a few drops of blood to spare a torrent of it," he shouted. And the arrests proceeded in earnest. A White Terror broke out in the South which even the government was soon unable to control. For a few weeks, throughout the Midi, to be a veteran of Waterloo meant death.

When Michel Bouvier reached his native village, he had no time to lose. His life depended on making a rapid decision as to where he would go to escape the royalists and acting upon that decision immediately. We can imagine the scene with his parents. The Bouviers of Pont-Saint-Esprit were a modest family of artisans, petite bourgeoisie. Michel's father, Eustache, fifty-six at the time of Waterloo, was a *menuisier ébéniste*, a cabinetmaker, and his three sons, Michel, Eustache, and Jean-François, were apprentices in his shop. His forty-nine-year-old Provençal wife, the former Thérèse Mercier, kept house, and a twenty-two-year-old daughter, Elizabeth, had recently been married. The family was not poor, but it certainly was not rich. The Bouviers lived simply in a small, three-story stone house—the shop below, the living quarters upstairs—on a narrow street in the heart of a village of two thousand inhabitants.

According to family tradition, Eustache Bouvier had fought in the War for American Independence under Rochambeau and had witnessed the surrender of Cornwallis at Yorktown in 1781, returning to France with his regiment shortly thereafter. Assuming the tradition is true, although it has never been substantiated, young Michel's problem was most likely solved by his father. Go to America. There liberty had not been extinguished. There the victory Rochambeau and Lafayette, and Eustache Bouvier, had helped bring about still lived. If Michel had participated in a defeat, his father had participated in a triumph. The Bouviers had always been lovers of liberty, foes of arbitrary privilege, exaggerated wealth, and the monarchy. Go to America. Young Michel accepted the advice, and his mother and sister silently resigned themselves to losing him, perhaps forever. After collecting his things and accepting what little money his father was able to spare, after taking a last look at the Rhône, at Pont-Saint-Esprit, the family shop, his home, he bid his family goodbye and hurried to Bordeaux, where, around the tenth of July, he boarded a ship for New York. Joseph Bonaparte, laden with jewels from the imperial treasury, was to follow him shortly thereafter. Barely three weeks had elapsed since Waterloo.

On July 15, as Michel Bouvier neared the mid-Atlantic, Napoleon, who had also hoped to escape to America, was forced to surrender to the British and was soon on the *Bellérophon* sailing toward final exile on Saint Helena.

ONCE AT SEA, MICHEL MUST HAVE FELT RELIEVED BY THE SUDDEN calm. For four months he had been living at a reckless pace, staking his future on Napoleon's last-ditch attempt to revive the Empire. And from Waterloo to his departure from Bordeaux, he had been in a feverish race with death. Now he was on the Atlantic and the pounding of cannon, the crackling of musket, the hoofbeats accompanying his long flight, had given way to the creaking of yardarms, the cries of gulls, and the vast emptiness of the sea on a warm summer day. The calm must have been welcome, yet an invitation to thought. And the thoughts that stirred in Michel's head could not have been comforting. He was leaving home, family, country, perhaps never to return. And the future held nothing but uncertainty.

During the long, uneventful hours at sea his mind must have wavered between thoughts of what he was leaving and imaginings of what lay ahead. Leaving his family and his village must have been particularly painful. The French at this time were deeply attached to their homes and their families. In spite of recent political and social upheavals, this was still a traditional society. One was born, one worked, one died in one's village. Sons worked at the trade of their fathers. Daughters emulated their mothers and married the men their families selected. The same house remained in the family for generations.

Michel had probably spent most of his youth in his father's furniture shop; we know he was a qualified *menuisier-ébéniste* when he arrived in the New World. Apprenticed to the craft at an early age, he probably had no schooling other than what his father had given him in the shop. And so he spent his youth, with his younger brothers and the other helpers, among sawhorses and door frames, Provençal chaises and écritoires, under the constant scrutiny of his father, midst incessant hammering, with sawdust always in his hair . . . Other than the shop there was the river. A diary of a trip to Europe he took with three of his daughters in 1853 indicates that Michel had spent much of his youth swimming, boating, and fishing in the Rhône. The great river washed the eastern side of the village and was spanned by the eighteen-arched Bridge of the Holy Ghost, built in 1265 by *les frères pontifes*. From the bridge, the only access to the village from the east, one had a magnificent view of the river as it flowed down from the north, as blue as the sky, through the vineyards that produce the celebrated Côtes du Rhône. The shop, the village, the Rhône, and his parents' house at 41 Grande Rue: this was what Michel was leaving. His mother took care of a family of six with the help of a young housekeeper by the name of Louise Perboz. Five of Thérèse Bouvier's nine children had died in infancy, two named after her husband and three after her mother. Thérèse's father, Joseph Mercier, was a hatter, and her mother, Anne Trintignant, was the daughter of a potter. Both grandparents were living in Pont-Saint-Esprit at the time of Michel's departure, and presumably the potter's kiln and the hat shop had rounded out his world.

It was a world his family had arrived in fairly recently, for Michel was the last of a succession of Bouviers who, for one reason or another, had been compelled to leave their birthplaces. His father was born and raised in Grenoble, the son of François Bouvier, an ironmonger, whose Montagnard father, Georges, had come from a hamlet of 101 inhabitants in the Alps of Savoy called les Mazures de Champlaurent. In this isolated community situated 3,000 feet above sea level, which had been Italian territory for most of its history, Georges Bouvier owned "a house, a barn, meadows, orchards, and a chestnut grove" and worked at the trade of charcoal burner. Georges's father and grandfather, both small landowners from neighboring villages, had also been charcoal burners, and it may be that the Bouviers had worked at this occupation in various localities in the mountains of Savoy for centuries.

Whether Michel knew where his itinerant ancestors originally came from and how long they had been on the move is questionable. That he thought about them at all on his way to America is even more improbable. When at sea he thought about the past, it was probably the most recent past, the events that had placed him on a frigate bound for New York: Napoleon, Waterloo. What if Napoleon had won? And won again, as he would have had to do, for the allies had resolved that if he won in Flanders they would fight him again? If he had won, and won again, Napoleon would have become master of Europe, would have unified the Continent, and his followers, far from being criminals, would be ruling provinces, commanding regiments, occupying choice offices in the Tuileries.

Michel and his fellow Bonapartists' arrival in the United States on August 6 must have been a relief. The four-week voyage had given them ample time to ponder their plight. Now they could release their tensions in the great adventure of making their way in the New World. We may picture Michel as his ship entered New York Bay. He was a short, stocky man, five feet six, with the powerful neck, arms, and shoulders of one who works with his hands. His face was broad, his complexion swarthy: he had the long, arched eyebrows of a Latin, wide-apart blue eyes, a rather heavy nose, and a firm, protruding chin, features that have since appeared in nearly all his descendants. The New York that unfolded after his ship passed Staten Island must have seemed disappointingly unspectacular on that warm August day. The United States was only thirty-nine years old at the time and its financial and industrial capital was not New York but Philadelphia. New York was a modest port city of 33,000 inhabitants, spanning the southern tip of Manhattan Island. It boasted no buildings the equal of some of those Michel was familiar with in France, like the Cathedral of Bordeaux, or the Hôtel de Ville at Lyons. And then across the Hudson all he could see were a few hamlets scattered through what no doubt seemed a total wilderness. A monotonous landscape, as flat as the bay that washed it, extending westward to a horizon as unbroken as the one he had been gazing at for the past four weeks. A panorama lonely and desolate, yet full of promise. The land awaited men like ... Did Michel pay himself the compliment? More than likely his mind was occupied by more immediate concerns. The ship would soon dock. He would have to get his things together and perhaps cope with customs officials. Would they speak French? Where was he going to spend the night? Where would he find his first job?

# III

MICHEL BOUVIER'S FIRST TWO YEARS IN THE UNITED STATES REMAIN almost a total mystery. The first record of his presence in America, , following his arrival, is an entry in a ledger indicating he deposited $536 in the Girard bank in Philadelphia in the summer of 1817. Where and how he earned the $536 is not known, but there are indications that he earned the money as a carpenter in New York City. For in 1816 and 1817 his two brothers, Eustache, sixteen, and Jean-François, eighteen, were successively listed in the military-recruitment rolls of Pont-Saint-Esprit as *menuisiers*, "habitant New-Yorck," leading us to assume that Michel, in all probability, started out working as a carpenter in the city and eventually persuaded his brothers to join him.

While Michel prospered in New York, saving at least $536 in two years, his brothers, it appears, fared badly. Since Eustache was no longer in the military-recruitment rolls after 1817 and was later entered in the civil register of Pont-Saint-Esprit as *morte enfant*, it may be assumed that he died within a year of his arrival in the United States. As for Jean-François, he eventually abandoned whatever hopes had prompted him to follow his older brother, and returned to France. His American adventure, however, may have lasted seven years, for it is not until 1825 that we hear of him again, this time on the occasion of his marriage, at twenty-seven, to a girl from Podensac, near Bordeaux. Remaining in France, and an artisan for the rest of his life, Jean-François would be the distant spectator of his brother's gradual transformation from French artisan to American businessman, as Michel, settling permanently in Philadelphia in 1817, pursued the dream that had eluded his brothers.

A haven of refuge for persecuted peoples who chose to be guided by "the inner light of conscience": such was to be Philadelphia as envisioned by its founder, William Penn. When Michel Bouvier arrived there, it had been a haven for the French for over three decades. Whether conscience or mere circumstance had brought them is a question we shall not raise. Suffice it to say that many French who had fought in the War for American Independence settled in Philadelphia after the British surrender, instead of returning to their native soil. Then, after the French Revolution, a stream of royalist émigrés arrived, including the

Vicomte de Noailles, who founded the colony of Azyl near the city. In 1793, six hundred French refugees from Santo Domingo turned up after an outbreak of yellow fever. And in 1796 several hundred French arrived from Haiti, along with many Negroes, after the revolt of Toussaint L'Ouverture. Now the Bonapartist exiles were flooding in, chief of whom was Joseph, Napoleon's brother and ex-King of Naples and Spain, a man who would set Philadelphia society on its ear.

The haven Joseph Bonaparte and Michel Bouvier arrived in, one with a fortune, the other with $536, had been the capital of the colonies during the Revolutionary period and the capital of the United States from 1790 to 1800. Now, upon the transfer of the government to Washington, it had become the financial center of the new nation. The Bank of the United States was located there. And the Bank of Stephen Girard. The city boasted a vigorous industrial life at the time: its weavers, wheelwrights, glass blowers, merchants, shipowners, and shipbuilders had made it the most prosperous in America. Although ample opportunities existed for individual advancement, its social order was still far from democratized: wealth and social standing were concentrated in a small segment of its 45,000 inhabitants and that segment was reluctant to admit newcomers. Physically it was a city of red-brick-paved streets, red-brick houses with white, gray, green, or red shutters, and red-brick public buildings like Independence Hall. In keeping with Penn's intention that it be a "greene countrie towne . . . always wholesome," the city was full of gardens, trees, and public parks.

Not much is known about Michel Bouvier's early years in Philadelphia, but a good deal is known about the two men who were to advance his career there, Joseph Bonaparte and Stephen Girard. In contrast to many of his descendants, Michel was a petitioner most of his life who had to cultivate the mighty to survive.

It was only natural that the first power he looked to was Joseph Bonaparte. Both were veterans of the Hundred Days, although Joseph's role in that madness had been minimal. He had remained in Paris, ostensibly to keep the political situation under control, while his brother charged off to defeat at Waterloo. Artful at slipping out of embarrassing situations, he had made good his escape under an assumed name, with a sizable portion of the imperial treasury, two weeks after Michel's exit and one week

jewels, Joseph's crown and rings from his reign as King of Spain, the crown, rings, and jewels in which Napoleon himself was crowned. And another secret panel behind which lay Napoleon's state papers. And a sliding bookcase at the end of the room, which led into the count's "summer sleeping room," his dressing and bathing room, and summer studio. All the curtains, canopies, and upholstery in these chambers were of light blue satin trimmed with silver. Each room had an enormous mirror reaching from ceiling to floor. On the ceiling over the massive "summer" bed hung another immense mirror. And the walls were covered with costly oil paintings, principally depicting young females, nude. *Mon dieu!* Michel's imagination could not have resisted conjuring scenes appropriate to those surroundings. It is quite possible that he himself fell in love at Point Breeze. There is but the slenderest evidence to support the conjecture: he was to give one of his daughters the uncommon name Zénaïde. Zénaïde Bonaparte was a beautiful young woman of twenty-three when Michel first met her at the estate. Her husband, who later became a renowned ornithologist, spent most of his time bird-watching in the surrounding countryside. Did she take a fancy to the young French cabinetmaker during his many trips to the estate and urge her father to do all he could for him? An enormous gulf separated the two young people. Michel was an artisan, a man who worked with his hands; she was the daughter of an ex-king. If love did spring up between them, it was bound to be the kind neither could requite. Michel, in later years, took to naming his children after people who had helped him get started in the New World. Was the only way he could thank Zénaïde for her love or support to name a daughter after her?

From the secret summer chambers a stairway led to the great reception rooms and halls on the first floor. Massive Empire furnishings. In every room, statues of Napoleon. Then the picture gallery, with much of the loot Napoleon's wars had garnered for his family: Raphael Mengs's "Nativity of Our Savior" was the chef d'oeuvre of the collection. Among the other works of art were seven Murrilos, two Canalettos, a Velázquez, a couple of Rubens—"Two Lions and a Faun," "Lion Caught in a Net"— some battle scenes by Antonio Tempesta, a "Scene Near Naples" by Vernet, "The Triumphal Entry of an Eastern Emperor" by an anonymous Italian, Canova's bust of Napoleon and Princess Pauline, a Venus Victrix, some Medici vases, portraits of Joseph and his wife in their royal robes as King and Queen of Naples, Napoleon in his imperial robes, the Crowning of Napoleon. Michel must have been dazzled. He who had come close to dying for the Emperor, he who had been forced to leave his country because of loyalty to the great Napoleon, was now in the Emperor's brother's gallery gazing upon his busts and portraits. It was ironic: to profit from his loyalty to Napoleon, he had had to come to America.

And so in 1818 Michel went to work for Joseph Bonaparte. And the following year he had enough money to open his own shop. Then, in 1820, something happened that gave his career sudden, unexpected impetus: Point Breeze burned down. It had to be rebuilt and refurnished and Michel was selected to superintend the job. There followed three years of trips back and forth between the shop in Philadelphia and Bordentown, during which he also supervised the construction of the *maison du lac*. Perhaps Michel stayed for long or short periods at Point Breeze. It was during the rebuilding and refurnishing of Joseph's estate after the fire of 1820 that Michel produced one of the few pieces of his furniture that still exists today, a secretary-desk which Bonaparte later presented to Governor Peter Vroom of New Jersey and which is now in the Philadelphia Athenaeum. The desk shows that Michel at twenty-eight was already a highly skilled craftsman, capable of turning out a minor work of art. It is particularly noteworthy in its use of veneers, thin layers of highly finished, costly wood used to coat the desk's surface. Michel was to become noted for his ability to handle veneers and he eventually became a manufacturer of them for use in mass-produced furniture. Another surviving piece from this period is a magnificent carved golden eagle which Bonaparte gave Michel as a reward for his labors and which is now in the possession of one of his great-granddaughters.

A year after Point Breeze burned down, Napoleon died at Saint Helena and the Bonapartists' hopes of restoring the Empire died with him. Michel Bouvier was still a French subject, having made no effort so far to become an American citizen. No doubt he half intended to return to France once the political seas had calmed and there was no risk to his life. But now Napoleon was dead. And Michel was beginning to get along in America. Was there any point in returning to France? He was drifting into that limbo of indecision and non-identification with his native country that all exiles know to be the first stage in acquiring a new identity. But he had plenty of time to decide. He was only twenty-nine, and he was still a bachelor. There was nothing yet to tie him definitively to the New World.

His independence, however, did not last very long. Two years after Napoleon's death, he took the first step binding him to the country he had adopted. He got married. His wife's name was Sarah Anne Pearson. She was the daughter of a Mrs. Goodfellow, who ran a cooking school and wrote a well-known cookbook, and the step-daughter of William Goodfellow, a clockmaker originally from Scotland for whom Michel may have made clockcases. Whether it was Mrs. Goodfellow's cooking, Mr. Goodfellow's clocks, or Sarah Anne's charms that brought the two together is uncertain. The couple were married on June 4, 1822, and exactly two years later to the day, they had a son, whom they named Eustache, after Michel's father and late brother. Four Eustaches in the family had died young, three born to his father, one to his sister, and so it must have gratified Michel to know that his Eustache would carry on the name. Time, however, would prove Eustache to be the antithesis of his hardworking father and grandfather and a source of keen disappointment for Michel.

A year after his son's birth Michel applied to become a United States citizen. That same year, 1825, he was made a senior warden of Masonic Lodge N. 160, known as "La Reconnaissance," and he moved his business to 91 South Second Street, advertising his premises as a "cabinet and sofa warehouse." It was after the move that Michel made the most important sale of his ten year old career as a Philadelphia cabinet maker. He sold twenty-four chairs and a conversation table to the White House under President John Quincey Adams for $352.00. By now he had established himself, albeit on a modest scale, and was probably looking for new worlds to conquer. He was still far from rich, however, and still eons removed from the socially elite of Philadelphia. His ten years in America had seen him establish himself as a cabinet-maker, but that was no higher a plane of existence than his father already enjoyed in Pont-Saint-Esprit. Or his brother, Jean-François, who after his marriage had settled in Bordeaux and opened a cabinet shop of his own. Still petite bourgeoisie, Michel had nothing on his immediate horizon to hint at the financial and social success in store for him.

The following year, in fact, brought tragedy to his life for the first time since he had emigrated to the New World. Five months after giving birth to a daughter, who was named Thérèse after Michel's mother, his young wife died. The loss must have been very hard on the thirty-four-year-old cabinetmaker. Alone now, with two young children to bring up, and no family nearby to comfort him, he must have felt the pressures on him multiplying. There was no turning back now. As a fledgling American citizen, he could not have permitted himself to return to France. He had no choice but to go on with renewed determination and keep a watch for any chance that might come his way. It wasn't long before a chance came, in the person of Stephen Girard.

# IV

STEPHEN GIRARD, AMERICA'S FIRST SELF-MADE MULTIMILLIONAIRE, was the most powerful man in Philadelphia during the years 1810 to 1830. Born in a suburb of Bordeaux in 1750, the son of a French sea captain, he had spent an adventurous youth sailing back and forth between France and the West Indies with his father, and in his early twenties had himself become the owner and master of a small ship. On a trip to New York in May 1776, at the beginning of the Revolution, a British blockade squadron forced him to seek port in Philadelphia. Shortly thereafter, upon being smitten, so the story goes, by a beautiful girl he spied drawing water from a well, he decided to cast his lot with the struggling colonies, settling in Philadelphia and embarking on a money-making career that was to have no equal in the haven city. For Michel Bouvier, Girard must have been encouraging testimony to the extraordinary financial success it was possible for a French immigrant to achieve in the New World. That success had resulted, in part, from a most advantageous marriage. A year after landing in Philadelphia, the twenty-seven-year-old Girard married Polly Lum, beautiful daughter of a prosperous shipbuilder, and the girl he had seen drawing water from the well. Subsequently, Mr. Lum built a ship for his son-in-law, the *Water Witch*, which literally launched his career.

Other ships followed, magnificent high-masted schooners with elaborately carved figureheads and shining fittings, which Girard—a devotee of French letters—named *Rousseau, Voltaire,* and *Montesquieu.* As a sea captain, the one-eyed, sharp-featured Girard earned a reputation for being imperious, shrewd, and iron-willed. These qualities he later brought to his career as a merchant prince. Gradually building up a huge trade with France, China, and the West Indies, he had earned a fortune by the time he was fifty. Thereupon he entered on a third career, that of banker and financier, a career that was paralleled by his adopted city, for it was during Girard's banking days that Philadelphia made the transition from seaport to inland manufacturing and financial center. By 1810 Girard was rich enough to purchase one million shares of the new Bank of the United States. Two years later, during the War of 1812, he established the Bank of Stephen Girard and literally underwrote his adopted country by subscribing, along with John Jacob Astor and David Parrish, to ninety-five percent of the federal government's war loans of over sixteen million, thus guaranteeing the young nation's precarious credit at a critical moment in its history. He was known for his wit as well as his business acumen. Joseph Bonaparte, at a dinner he gave in Girard's honor, informed the one-eyed banker that he wished to buy a certain tract of land within the corporate limits of Philadelphia and asked Girard to help with the transaction. Girard asked Bonaparte what he was willing to pay for the property. "I'll tell you," Joseph replied, letting his vanity, as usual, get the best of him. "I will cover the block from Eleventh to Twelfth and from Chestnut to Market with silver half dollars." Girard pondered for a second, then said slowly, "Very well, monsieur le comte . . . if you will stand them up edgeways."

Girard, who remained an atheist all his life, died in 1831. He left the bulk of his colossal estate to the City of Philadelphia, with the stipulation that the money be used to finance a better police system, effect various municipal improvements, lessen taxation, and to found a college for orphan boys on whose grounds no "minister of religion" would be permitted to set foot. Girard's relatives, with whom he had quarreled all his life and whom he left only token legacies, contested the will in 1836. They were represented by Daniel Webster in 1844 and lost their case. Girard College opened in 1848, without any minister of religion setting foot on its soil. It is still in operation today.

The earliest records of Michel Bouvier's career in Philadelphia are in the college archives. They attest that even though Michel had won important commissions from a man as influential as Joseph Bonaparte, he was still forced to accept very humble jobs as well. For example, on January 22, 1828, Girard paid Bouvier twenty dollars for "furnishing cloth and silk for tables" and ten dollars for "repairing, polishing and putting knobs on Secretary." A bill dated 1829 has Michel receiving one dollar from Girard on July 28 for "repairing sofa," a dollar fifty on August 26 for "polishing dining room table," and fifty cents on September 1 for "taking down and putting up bed." Since Girard's home needed no new furnishings, Michel was probably retained only for maintenance, repairs, and odd jobs. Records indicate, however, that he made a "music stand and chair" in 1831 for Girard's grandniece, Caroline Lallemand, for which he received forty-two dollars. Bouvier at the time never missed a chance to earn an extra dollar if he could help it and probably performed numerous other services for Girard. After the financier's death, Michel billed his executors for coal and in 1833 he billed them for the hire of a furniture van and laborers to move furniture. Girard must have helped Michel in many other ways, for Michel's obituaries mentioned his association with the banker as having been most influential in advancing his career. With patrons like Bonaparte and Girard recommending him, jobs and commissions from Philadelphia's new rich began pouring into his shop.

It was while he was in the occasional employ of Girard that Michel met Louise Vernou and married her. He was thirty-six, a widower with two children, and she had just turned seventeen. Very likely they first met at some function at St. Augustine's Church, parish for both families and a center of Catholic social life frequented by German, Irish, and French immigrants. They were married at St. Augustine's on May 29, 1828, the year Jackson was elected President, and they went to live in a small house on Front Street, in a section of the city that overlooked the Delaware River wharfs. Three years later they moved to a larger place, a three-story brick house on the same street.

Louise Vernou was to play an important role in Michel's life. Besides bearing him ten children, she was to be an immense help to him socially and a powerful spur to his ambitions. Not much is known about her family. However, a legend has come down to us about her parents which may contain a scrap or two of truth. In 1898, one of Louise Vernou Bouvier's unmarried daughters wrote a sixty-one-page account of an episode in her grandparents' lives which she published under the title *Our Grandmother's Story*, using the pseudonym Jeanne d'Outre-Mer. According to this quaintly written story, Louise's mother was born Elizabeth Clifford Lindsay, daughter of a Revolutionary officer, Colonel William Alexander Lindsay, and his wife, Elizabeth Clifford. Elizabeth Lindsay was brought up in an exclusive section of Philadelphia and as a child was "smiled upon" by Martha Washington, whose husband was a friend of her father's. As a teenager she went to live with a wealthy, childless aunt on Third Street, near Walnut, and soon fell in love with a young Creole, Francis Savoy, who was in Philadelphia on business at the time. It wasn't long before Elizabeth and Francis were married and left for Santo Domingo, where Savoy owned a large plantation. Elizabeth was only fourteen; her husband was in his early twenties. The date: sometime in the early 1790s.

Santo Domingo for the Savoys and other colonists like them was an idyllic paradise of sunshine, flowers, mint ices, jewels, lace dresses, and elegant fetes with servants catering to every wish. Then suddenly, without apparent warning, it all came to an abrupt end: the servants turned the tables on their masters. Toussaint L'Ouverture, on becoming commander-in-chief of the island's armies, declared himself master of the entire country, disowned the sovereignty of France, and styled himself the "Bonaparte of Santo Domingo." Whereupon his new subjects ran wild. A band of insurgents invaded Savoy's plantation, captured Francis, and set fire to his house. Elizabeth somehow escaped to "the summer cottage" and was left there undisturbed for a time. Anxious hours went by. Then Antoine, her faithful servant, arrived to tell her to flee into the forest, where the other white settlers had fled, for surely the insurgents would be back and would find her. He did not tell her that in the meantime her husband had been bludgeoned to death and his head displayed on the parapet of a bridge. Elizabeth fled into the forest and eventually found a hut containing a crude bed piled with stinking rags. She crawled under the bed to hide and was soon startled by the eruption of a band of Negro soldiers into the hut, calling, "Leper, come forth!" The rags on the bed stirred and, to Elizabeth's astonishment, a leper did come forth. "Is there anyone else in this hut?" the soldiers asked. "No, no one," mumbled the leper.

After the soldiers left, Elizabeth crawled out from under the bed. The leper urged her to run for her life. She waited a few minutes, pitying the disfigured wretch, then dashed off. She had gone only a few paces when she heard the leper call, and looking back, saw him limping toward her, carrying her purse on a stick.

On returning her purse, the leper offered to guide her through the forest, and she accepted. After a while they met a "forlorn band of old men, women and children" and joined them. For ten days "these outcasts wandered the forest," then suddenly a party of insurgents came upon them.

Their capture was described in detail in *Our Grandmother's Story:*

Delicate women and children, and aged persons of both sexes, were dragged by their bloodthirsty captors over ditches and sharp rocks, over flinty stones and roots and burning sands, through brushwood and thorny briars, to a neighboring town. Those who were too old or too feeble to keep up with the others were ruthlessly murdered, even in the presence of their own children. Some were abandoned by the wayside to die. If a mother stopped for an instant to give nourishment to her child the infant was torn from her arms, and its brains dashed out against the nearest tree or rock.

Of our Grandmother's satin slippers and silken stockings not a shred remained. Her cut and bleeding feet were swollen and discolored with bruises. Her long luxuriant hair, of which her young husband had been so proud, was matted and tangled. Her skin was burned and discolored, and her eyes so swollen from weeping and sleeplessness she could hardly see. The blacks had torn the earrings from her ears and the slits remained open and bleeding and intensely painful. In this pitiable plight she and the others who had survived the journey were crowded into a church, which had been converted into a prison.

While she was in prison, a white officer who had joined the Negro cause came to inspect the captives. He turned out to be a cousin of her husband's and he informed her that Francis was dead and then contrived her escape. For three weeks she stayed with him, then boarded an American vessel bound for Philadelphia. But when she arrived and hurried to her parents' house, she found nobody. Both her mother and father had died. So had her rich aunt, who had changed her will and left all her money to another relative. The yellow-fever epidemic of 1793 had taken her entire family. Widowed, orphaned, friendless, and penniless, she was in difficult straits until a deliverer came along in the person of John Vernou, described in *Our Grandmother's Story* as "one who had escaped from his dear native France with a price on his head." The story concluded: "It was but natural that such hearts should harmonize. He was an émigré driven from home by the French Revolution, and she a refugee despoiled and driven from her adopted land by the Insurrection."

So much for the family legend. How much of it is true? We have little to go on. No record of John Vernou's marriage to Elizabeth

Lindsay has been discovered, but baptismal records of three of their children have been found and in one of them Elizabeth is referred to as Elizabetta Lenzy and in the other as Elizabeth Alexander. Was she the daughter of Colonel William Alexander Lindsay, friend of George Washington's and officer in his army? We cannot be certain, for the record of her birth has disappeared. And who was John Vernou? Later generations of Bouviers proudly identified him as Jean de Vernou, émigré son of Marie-Cèsar-Antoine de Vernou, Baron de Bonneuil, Lieutenant of Cavalry of the Comte de Provence, but this illustrious ancestry has never been substantiated. In the Philadelphia directory of 1801 he was listed as "hairdresser" and later as "perfumer," trades French refugees typically engaged in, but would a member of the notoriously proud French nobility, no matter how impoverished, adopt the then unprestigious trade of hairdresser? At the time of the marriage of his daughter Louise to Michel Bouvier he was listed as "perfumer and segar maker," and his final career, it appears, was that of tobacco merchant. Nothing more is known of him except that he left a very modest estate to his wife, advising her, among other things, to take very good care of the family perfume and tobacco store.

If *Our Grandmother's Story* is reasonably accurate, then Michel Bouvier married a most aristocratic girl—financially no catch, but as blue-blooded as they came in Philadelphia in those days, the daughter of a French nobleman and the granddaughter of one of Washington's officers. Descriptions of her in later years, when she had herself become a grandmother, tend to confirm her alleged background, if only through inference: a book about the family of one of her sons-in-law, Francis Drexel, declared that she was "as stately a dame as ever graced the Court of Versailles—calm and dignified, with an elegant poise nothing could ruffle." And both the content of her letters and her handwriting attest that she had received a superior education. In any event, marrying Louise turned out to be one of the wisest moves Michel made in a career remarkably free of false steps. Louise appears to have given her hardworking husband the social distinction he lacked. A strong-willed, often imperious woman, she expected much from Michel and no doubt added fuel to his already powerful ambition to succeed, at any cost, in the New World. After he married her, he devoted himself to his work with an energy and determination nothing could deflect, however stubborn the obstacle or crushing the setback—and there were to be plenty of both in his middle years to test his nerve.

Michel's business at the time of his second marriage was located at 91 South Second Street, opposite the new Bank of Pennsylvania. At this address he maintained his "cabinet and sofa warehouse," where he made and sold furniture and conducted a number of other, sideline activities as well. A highly skilled craftsman, he turned out what might be loosely described as late Empire or early Victorian furniture: chairs, cabinets, dressers, bedsteads, clockcases, paneling, floors, tables, secrétaires, and étagères. Skillful in the use of veneers, he would face his secrétaires with one piece of mahogany veneer, the graining perfectly joined for the entire front, frame, and drawers. His saber-legged chairs, which he turned out in considerable quantity, were of extremely simple design, having upholstered seats and gently curving top back rails decorated with mahogany veneers. He also applied these veneers, which came to be his trademark, to the legs and frames of the marble-topped tables and dressers he produced in ever increasing quantity to meet the enormous demand for them after 1830. But handmade furniture was not to be his only line. Like the huge corporations of today, he had to diversify to supplement his income and to hedge against technological changes that would threaten his cabinet-making business. And so, in addition to making individual pieces of furniture, he started a wholesale and retail business in mahogany boards, logs, and veneers for other furniture makers, and in "hair seating" for upholsterers, thus preparing for the not too distant day when mass-produced furniture would replace the handmade variety. With wood scraps abundantly available, he also became a supplier of firewood. And as Pennsylvania anthracite became accepted both as a home fuel and as an industrial fuel, in the late twenties and early thirties he became a coal dealer, a sideline that would one day draw him toward his most daring ventures and gain him the biggest profits of his business career. Since he both made and delivered furniture and mahogany, and was as well a retail coal and firewood dealer, he had to have some means of transportation available and so he bought two drays and a van, which he put to use in still another sideline, moving household goods. He and his assistants were also on call as general household repairmen; and so, in addition to making chairs, tables, and desks, selling mahogany, upholstery, firewood, and coal, and moving household belongings, he also went about "repairing, polishing and putting knobs" on secrétaires and "taking down and putting up" beds.

It was an arduous, exhausting life, but he had no choice. With no capital to fall back on and no influential family connections to help him if he faltered, with two young children to support, and a wife about to give birth, he had to work hard or else. Or else he would wind up like so many other French immigrants, penniless wards of the local French Benevolent Society, of which Michel eventually became a director, or candidates for return to France. We may picture him as he went about his daily tasks. Leaving his modest brick house on Front Street early in the morning, he would be greeted by the usual waterfront bustle and panorama of masts and riggings along the Delaware wharfs. A five-to-ten-minute walk along tree-lined cobblestone streets would take him to his shop and warehouse, where he would plunge into the day's activities, assigning his assistants their various jobs, receiving clients, ordering materials from suppliers, and, when he got the time, working on pieces of furniture himself.

Meanwhile, his wife added to his joys and responsibilities by adding to his family. A year after they were married, the eighteen-year-old Louise gave birth to a daughter, whom she and Michel named Elizabeth, after Louise's mother and Michel's sister. And in 1831 another daughter arrived, whom they named Louise. Still another daughter, Emma, came in 1833, and another in 1835, Zénaïde. Thus, by the time Michel was forty-three, he had one son and five daughters to support, and daughters were expensive in those days of dowries and trousseaus. Of course he had to work hard. Who would feed all those mouths if he didn't? His and his wife's parents had enough to do to keep themselves alive: there was no hope of parental aid from either side. Moreover, his two chief patrons were now gone. Stephen Girard had died in 1831, the year the Pennsylvania Railroad was founded, and Joseph Bonaparte had left for England the same year. Times were changing and were therefore uncertain. The industrial revolution was gathering momentum. Who knew what the future held? Michel only knew he had to work and work hard, and keep a vigilant eye out for every chance that might come his way. Turn out tables, chairs, bedsteads, and secrétaires. Sell as much mahogany and hair seating as he could. Advertise his wares in the daily paper. Expand his firewood and coal business. Not let the drays and the van lay idle for a minute. Get the household-moving business into high gear. If there were no workers available when a job came in, the boss would handle it. And so there would be Michel Bouvier, fifteen years after leaving Pont-Saint-Esprit, now a familiar figure along the Philadelphia waterfront, rattling down Third Street in his van with a load of kindling wood for the Barclay house, after which delivery he would pick up a couple of day laborers and move a houseful of furniture, returning later to his warehouse to order a new shipment of mahogany, sell a supply of hair seating, and put the finishing touches on a music stand for Girard's grandniece. It was a crowded routine, but he thrived on it. How many obstacles had he had to overcome to arrive even this far? The language barrier: learning English hadn't been easy for one whose schooling had been limited largely to learning carpentry in his father's shop. Prejudice against the French and the Catholics: to Philadelphians of the day, anyone who wasn't Quaker, or at least Protestant, and wasn't of English, Scotch, Dutch, or German descent, was suspect. The French in mid-nineteenth-century Philadelphia were a minority group fighting for acceptance. No doubt Michel often felt that the Anglo-Saxon Protestant world was impenetrable.

During his initial struggles to establish a family and a business in America, Michel must have thought frequently of the family he had left behind in Pont-Saint-Esprit. News from home was rare, and when a letter came, it usually communicated an important event, such as a marriage, a birth, a death. Something to start him thinking about the life he had abandoned and the France he had never ceased to love. It took five to six weeks usually for a letter to arrive from Europe, and so important events, especially deaths, had a particularly irrecoverable quality to them. In October 1825 Michel learned that his sister Elizabeth's husband, Noël Baudichon, had died, leaving her with two young children to support and a general merchandise store to look after. Then, in 1827, news came that she had married again. Her new husband was Etienne Bouchard, a grocer who had been helping her with the store. There was also sporadic news from Michel's younger brother, Jean-François, who, after his marriage to Marie Poissonié in 1825, and the opening of his shop in Bordeaux, had a son, whom the young couple had named Michel.

Not all the news these years was good. One day early in December 1828 a letter arrived at the small brick house on Front

Street, informing Michel that his mother, Thérèse Mercier, had died at Pont-Saint-Esprit at the age of sixty-two. No chance to go to the funeral. No way to offer immediate sympathy to his father, brother, and sister. By the time they received his condolences, Thérèse would have been dead two months. Of all the news that reached him from abroad, no doubt the deaths of his parents made him regret leaving France the most. He had hated leaving them and had hoped for a day when he would return to Pont-Saint-Esprit for a visit, rich enough to make up in some way for all they had given him.

It would be several years, however, before Michel's father would succumb. A hardy man, only two generations removed from Alpine Montagnards, Eustache married again a year after his first wife died, and opened a new store. He was seventy-one and his new wife, Louise Perboz, was only twenty-five. The daughter of a gardener from neighboring Bagnols, she had been Eustache's housekeeper for several years and had taken care of his wife during her final illness. It must have given Michel a chuckle to receive word the following year that his seventy-two-year-old father had a daughter by Perboz whom they had named Pélagie. The old man had begun a new business and a new family at an age when most people are forced to renounce both. The new business—a second-hand furniture store in the heart of Pont-Saint-Esprit—prospered, and father and son, separated by four thousand miles, were able to boast to each other by mail of their accomplishments. Who would have the most daughters? For, to everyone's surprise, Eustache had another daughter, Elizabeth Rose, in 1831, and another, Louise, in 1833, and still another, Anasthasie, in 1834, at age seventy-six, his thirteenth and last child. Between father and son, nine daughters had been sired in six years—these in addition to the two daughters each had from his first marriage.

In the meantime, François was keeping busy too. During the 1830s, his Bordeaux cabinet shop prospered, and he also had a daughter, Marie-Adèle, the Bouvier family's fifteenth female child.

Michel and François had a lifetime of furniture and daughter manufacturing ahead of them, but how long would old Eustache continue to produce? Pont-Saint-Esprit, Bordeaux, and Philadelphia had been asking the question for some time. The old man was a phenomenon of nature, as strong and steady as the Rhône.

Would he ever give out? The answer came suddenly, enabling the old *ébéniste* to escape the retirement he had always rebelled against. On May 12, 1835, six months after the birth of his thirteenth child, a heart attack carried him off one afternoon as he was resting in his home before returning to work.

Michel probably received word of it in mid-June. We can imagine his feelings. He had a close relationship with his father. With both parents gone, his ties to France were now considerably weakened. Fortunately, he had spent the last twenty years knotting others securely in their place: nothing could unravel them now.

Eustache Bouvier left an estate valued at 4,100 francs (roughly $12,000 at 1835 rates of exchange), consisting primarily of a three-story house at 41 Grande Rue in Pont-Saint-Esprit and the merchandise, mostly furniture, in his store. According to his will, one quarter of the total estate was to go to his widow, Louise Perboz, and the remainder was to be divided equally among his six surviving children. As it turned out, Michel, Elizabeth, and François renounced their legacies in favor of their three young half sisters. Admittedly, for Michel the sacrifice was not very great. He could easily make in two or three months the equivalent of his total inheritance. For François it was another matter. Raising a family of four on the modest earnings of a cabinetmaker in Bordeaux was not easy. As for Elizabeth, since she had received a dowry of 1,500 francs ($4,400) on her marriage, she felt obligated to give up her share of the estate so that Pélagie, Louise, and Anasthasie would have dowries too when the time came. Before long, the family home was sold, the store merchandise was disposed of at auction, and Louise Perboz Bouvier took her three daughters to live in a farmhouse in the country, where they kept a few chickens and goats and tended a little vineyard. There were no Bouvier males left now in Pont-Saint-Esprit. The future of the clan lay in Bordeaux and Philadelphia, where two family sagas would unfold as different from one another as the destinies of the two nations to which they were tied.

Philadelphia in the late 1830s was in the throes of a new phase of the industrial revolution and Michel Bouvier felt the vibrations keenly enough to decide to do something about it. The application of coal-generated steam power to industry was gaining steadily wider acceptance as it opened up new vistas to manufacturers interested in expanding production. The days were rapidly drawing to a close when manufacturers engaged in a strictly made-to-order business. With the population growing and with new sources of power becoming available, the era of mass production was dawning: woe unto the businessman who did not grasp what was happening. The signals had been blinking regularly since the 1820s, when coal had first become accepted as a fuel. In 1822, only four coal ships a year were leaving Philadelphia. Five years later, 397 ships a year, carrying 39,000 tons, were clearing the Delaware wharfs, and ten years after that, 3,225 vessels, carrying 350,000 tons, were leaving port.

Other sources of power were also being exploited. In 1829 the huge Flat Rock Dam was built on the Schuylkill to harness water power, and in 1836 the first Philadelphia gas works were constructed. During the same period, mill, mine, and rail development proceeded at a rapid pace. There was considerable experimentation with steamboats, and a new wave of immigration swept up the Delaware—mostly Irish and German, along with a few skilled workers from already industrialized England. The population of the haven city—63,000 in 1820—was nearing 100,000 by 1840. The country as a whole was close to universal manhood suffrage as property qualifications for voting were being done away with, and one by one the Western states were entering the Union.

Michel met the challenges generated by the changing times by gradually phasing out his made-to-order furniture business and converting to the production of single elements for the manufacture of furniture on a large scale. Thus, instead of turning out tables, chairs, and desks on order from individual customers, he switched to the manufacture of marble mantels for table and dresser tops and the production of mahogany veneers for all kinds of furniture, installing a four-gang steam-engine saw to cut marble and new machinery to produce veneers. To reduce costs, he became an importer of marble and mahogany for his own use and for wholesale to furniture concerns who were converting to mass production. And so, during the thirties, the highly skilled artisan who with his own hands could turn out an elaborately veneered, eagle-armed Empire chair metamorphosed gradually into an importer and manufacturer several stages removed from the actual making of furniture. It was a bold step, one that many Philadelphia cabinetmakers never made, with ultimately disastrous results for their businesses. It was a step that Michel's brother never made either. The poverty that plagued François Bouvier's descendants for three generations (in marked contrast to the affluence of Michel's progeny) may be partly attributed to the fact that he remained an artisan all his life, whereas Michel gave up the hammer and chisel and became a manufacturer.

One thing the brothers did have in common, however, was a propensity to produce daughters. Between 1837 and 1841, when Michel made the transition from artisan to manufacturer, François added three daughters to his family, including twins; and Michel added two, Alexine and Mary. The year 1837 was an eventful one for Michel: Alexine was born; his father-in-law, John Vernou, died; and Joseph Bonaparte returned to America with the future Napoleon III. Bonaparte reopened Point Breeze and soon Michel was doing odd jobs for him again, helping put the immense estate in order. During Bonaparte's second stay at Point Breeze, which didn't last very long, as family problems soon forced him to return to Europe, Michel turned out the last of his individual pieces of furniture: sturdy mahogany armchairs with upholstered seats, backs, and armrests, the arms terminating in finely carved eagle heads. Several of these late Empire chairs are now in the possession of two of his great-grandsons, Richard D. and Michel Bouvier Patterson of Philadelphia.

In 1838 the first paddle-wheel ocean-going steamer, the *Sirius*, made its maiden voyage from London to New York; Joseph Bonaparte left for England; and Michel Bouvier no longer listed himself as a cabinetmaker but as a manufacturer of veneers and dealer in mahogany and marble. Receipts preserved from that year indicate he had not given up his lucrative sidelines, however—only the production of handmade furniture.

In 1841, the year in which his seventh daughter, Mary, was born, Michel took the first step in his third and final career, the one he made his biggest profits in, that of real-estate speculator. For in 1841, with remarkable foresight, he purchased for $6,500 a lot on the west side of North Broad Street and Stiles Avenue, in what was to become one of Philadelphia's most desirable residential areas, a lot on which he would one day erect a mansion to rival the showplaces of Bonaparte and Girard, where as a young immigrant he had polished dining room tables and taken down and put up beds.

Michel was now fifty years old and a prosperous importer and manufacturer with a thirty-year-old wife, a seventeen-year-old son, and seven daughters ranging in age from infancy to fifteen. The family still lived in the three-story brick house at 80 Front Street which Michel had bought in 1831. Front Street at the time was colorful but not fashionable. From the windows of their home the Bouviers could watch the coming and going of great sailing vessels and the ceaseless loading and unloading of cargo not far from their front doorstep. Commerce had been making steady inroads into the former residential section and eventually the family found itself surrounded by offices, warehouses, and shops.

The household must have been a crowded one. With ten in the family, the children had to double up, and there was no place to play but the street. But it was a close-knit, affectionate family, remarkably free of contention. Michel and Louise were proud of their brood, though its lopsidedness must have worried them a little. One boy and seven girls; and the boy, Eustache, though charming, was not too promising. Michel had had high hopes for his son, but Eustache had too many strikes against him ever to fulfill his father's expectations. For one thing, he had so many sisters fussing over him and spoiling him. Surrounded by little girls as he was growing up, he missed the male companionship and rivalry a brother would have provided. Then, for two years in his early childhood, he had not had a mother. Sarah Pearson died in 1826 and his father did not remarry until 1828; thus, between the ages of two and four, he was at the mercy of housekeepers and other surrogates. And, to make matters worse, he had a father who expected everything from him. He was the only child of Michel's who could carry the Bouvier name into the future, who could perpetuate the success his father had worked so hard and sacrificed so much for. We can be sure that Michel expected his son to continue the business he had founded in the New World. Hadn't he followed in the footsteps of his father, learned his father's trade, helped him in the shop when he was a boy?

But Eustache would have none of it. His father's authoritarianism, his self-made-man cast of mind only made Eustache feel hopeless, inadequate, and rebellious. At seventeen he had already shown signs for some time of the restlessness and instability that would plague him the rest of his life. Dark, wild-eyed, very Latin in appearance, he had inherited the mercurial Provençal blood of his grandmother, Thérèse Mercier, but almost none of the sturdy Alpine traits of the Bouviers or the Scotch strain of the Pearsons. The son of an overbearing, self-made man may respond to his predicament by becoming passive and ingratiating or by remaining at the level of a rebellious child, wild and irresponsible, unable to assert himself steadily at anything. Eustache was to follow the second path.

As for his seven sisters, they were a merry bunch destined to span a broad spectrum of feminine occupations from the religious life to motherhood to spinsterhood. Thérèse was the oldest, fifteen in her father's fiftieth year, a sturdy, affectionate girl whose birth had cost her mother her life. Then came Elizabeth, better-known as Lizzie, the first child to be born to Louise Vernou, and at twelve a very pretty blonde. Louise, ten, and Emma, six, were next. They were to be the thinkers in the family: independent, serious, and intensely religious. Finally there were Zénaïde, Alexine, and Mary—Zenney, Allie, and Moll—in 1841 six, four, and newborn, who would become an inseparable trio, a little family in themselves. Seven girls and one boy. To get all these girls married would cost Michel all his savings. And here was Eustache already showing great promise as a playboy, capable of eating up those savings without any help from his sisters. Although Michel had good reason to be satisfied with his career, there was still something lacking in his success. He needed sons. And he needed money, big money, to get all those daughters decent husbands. If he were to launch a family in America, launch one with momentum to carry it forward for generations, he could not be satisfied with what he had done so far, no matter how spectacular it had been. There was still much to be done. The next thirty years would find him working and producing children as if he had just landed on the Delaware docks.

# $\mathcal{V}$

ONE OF MICHEL'S MOST OUTSTANDING CHARACTERISTICS WAS HIS opportunism. Like all successful businessmen, he had an extraordinary ability to make the best use of each chance that came his way, even if that chance demanded radical changes in his business life. Landing in Philadelphia, a veteran of Napoleon's wars, he found none other than Napoleon's brother lodged in the haven city and wasted no time in identifying himself as a former fighter for the cause. The result: his first important commissions. Stephen Girard was a French émigré from Bordeaux. Michel had made his escape from Bordeaux and his brother had moved there to open a shop. Having something in common with a potentate like Girard—no matter how insignificant—was an entrée Michel would not let slip by without taking advantage of. The result: his next important commissions. Michel's first wife's father made clocks and Michel made clockcases. Michel was a great toiler, but he had no "background" and few social graces. His second wife had the education and savoir-faire he lacked. When coal began to be accepted as a fuel, the firewood supplier quickly became a coal dealer. When the steam engine appeared, he put away his hand tools and turned to mass production. Now, in the 1840s, with the city expanding both in area and in population, and industry demanding more and more coal, he plunged into real estate, buying lots in Philadelphia and its outskirts and immense tracts of potential coal lands in West Virginia. These real-estate operations were carried on in addition to his importing and manufacturing business; indeed, they were made possible by that business. It was the profits from marble and mahogany that he alchemized into land and the land he turned into gold.

In 1841 Michel's real-estate holdings consisted of a three-story brick tenement on South Front Street, on which he was still paying off a mortgage, and a small lot on North Broad Street. By 1854 he had sold the place on South Front Street, bought a mansion on Third Street, razed it, built three brownstones in its place, sold them, added to his lot on Broad Street, built a mansion on it, bought several other lots in and around Philadelphia, and acquired extensive acreage in West Virginia.

These operations were not carried on without struggle. One of the first was with his wife. Louise Vernou had gotten used to the brick tenement on South Front Street, and even though it was not in a very fashionable neighborhood, she had hoped to spend the rest of her life there. But Michel had other ideas. He wanted to live in a more fashionable neighborhood: his pride as a self-made man demanded it. Accordingly, in the spring of 1848, Michel sold his brick tenement on Front Street to one Andrew C. Craige without consulting his wife. Since the house, however, was in both Michel's and Louise's names, Louise eventually had to sign the new deed. Michel's day of reckoning must have dawned the day that deed was presented to her for signature.

In the end, Louise refused to sign the deed and the sale was not immediately consummated. Craige then brought suit against Michel and Louise Bouvier. The case dragged on for a couple of years, then the parties finally came to terms. Michel won his wife over and the house was sold.

In the meantime Michel had added land to the lot he had bought on North Street and had bought the old Mansion House Hotel on Third Street above Spruce, which had once been the elegant William Bingham house, one of the most notable residences in the city before it was damaged by fire in 1823 and again in 1847. Paying $20,250 for the entire property, he promptly demolished the house and built three brownstones in its place, two of which he rented, keeping the third as his next residence. Eventually he sold all three, making a whopping profit on the entire deal. The development was located in what is today known as the Society Hill section and is presently under restoration. At the time of its construction, however, the area acquired another name. For some reason, ornamental shields crossed with batons were placed by the architect over the doors of the three brownstones. The local wits interpreted the batons as bars sinister, the heraldic mark of bastardy, and dubbed the development Bastard's Row—which must have appealed greatly to the strait-laced Louise, who hadn't wanted to move into the neighborhood in the first place. As it turned out, the Bouvier family only lived on Bastard's Row for a little over a year. Third above Spruce was not fashionable enough for the social-climbing Michel and it wasn't long before he moved his family into their final, sumptuous resting place on North Broad Street, the area he had been eyeing since the thirties and buying into since 1841 and which became in the mid-fifties the Fifth Avenue of Philadelphia's new rich.

But that is another story. Before the mansion on North Broad Street came his speculations in West Virginia lands.

How Michel first got interested in these potential coal lands is not known. The first record of his speculations in them dates from April 1847, when he bought from one John Hermon 63,000 acres in McDowell County, West Virginia, for $22,000, paying approximately 35 cents an acre. That same year he developed what one of his children described in a letter as a "valvular" heart condition which made him susceptible to incapacitating attacks that would plague him the rest of his life. Despite the heart condition, however, Michel gradually accumulated a total of 157,000 acres of West Virginia lands, at prices ranging from 35 to 41 cents an acre, 112,350 acres of which he sold to several buyers in March 1853 for $1.12 an acre, making a total profit of about $85,500 on his transactions. Later he sold 36,750 acres of the remaining 45,150 he held to one of his sons-in-law for $65,000 so his total profit amounted to something in the neighborhood of $100,000, a considerable sum in those days, worth $800,000 in today's currency.

While Michel was engaged in these speculations, the California Gold Rush began, the Philadelphia-Pittsburgh railroad was completed, *Uncle Tom's Cabin* was written, and an insignificant event took place on Noodle's Island in Boston Harbor which would have very significant repercussions for the Bouvier family a century later: a young Irish immigrant by the name of Patrick Kennedy arrived, along with several hundred other refugees from the potato famine, and took a first look at those puritan shores whose hostility was to goad his descendants to ambitions far greater than those of Michel Bouvier.

Michel's ambitions at the time, however, were strong enough. Like the Kennedys in Boston, he, a Southern French Catholic, had to struggle against an Anglo-Saxon Protestant establishment in Philadelphia that would have held him down had he not proved himself their equal. Now, thirty-eight years after arriving in America, he *had* proved himself their equal. At least in business. In a single real-estate speculation he made what was then regarded as a modest fortune. And he had started from nothing.

For all his business success, however, Michel never let making money become an end in itself. Maintaining a remarkably balanced sense of the proper relationship of wealth to life, he used money as but a means to promote the welfare of his family, avoiding both the extravagances and the avarice to which the *nouveaux riches* are prone. Michel's eulogists were to emphasize the fact that he found his greatest joys and deepest satisfactions in his home life, that his family, not his work, was the aim and justification of his existence.

Testimony to the happiness of Michel's home life has come down to us from many sources. Among them are two letters Zénaïde wrote her French cousin, François-Louis Baudichon, in the 1860s. In one she described her "chers Parents" as "si bons, si aimable, qu'ils font de notre maison un vrai paradis." And in another she wrote of her father: "Il est toujours gai, et donne la vivacite a n'importe quelle coterie où il se trouve."

Since his family was so important to him, the news he received on March 25, 1843, shortly after his fifty-first birthday, must have delighted Michel beyond words. Finally, after six daughters in a row, his wife had given birth to her first son, whom they named John Vernou, after her father. He was the first of four generations of Bouviers to bear the name.

John Vernou Bouvier's birth coincided with the start of the Great Migration along the Oregon Trail, the first trickle of what was to become by the mid-forties a mighty human river flowing West. The following year Joseph Bonaparte died in Florence, leaving a considerable estate to his children and to his American administrator, Louis Mailliard, who, in turn, gave a tiny scrap of that estate—an Empire clock from Point Breeze—to Michel Bouvier. A year later, at the outbreak of the Mexican War, Michel was presented with his eighth daughter, whom he named Josephine, possibly after his late benefactor. Two years after that, in April 1847, little Josephine died. That same month, the Bouviers had their eleventh child, another son, thank the Lord, whom they named Michel Charles.

With two new sons in the fold, Michel and Louise could now look forward more confidently to the continuance of the family they had founded. At the time of Michel Charles's birth, Eustache was only twenty-three, but already his future appeared dubious, to say the least. A school dropout with a reputation for being "wild," he took little interest in his father's business and had not yet held a job. As it turned out, the future of the Bouvier family was to depend wholly on its last arrivals. From the standpoint of the development of character, John and MC benefitted from the fact that, unlike Eustache, they had each other to compete with, and their seven sisters were too old to be their playmates or their hero worshippers. Furthermore, their father had already arrived financially by the time they were born and so they did not have to live up to quite the expectations Eustache had to contend with as a child with a father who had not yet achieved his economic goals. Also, by the time they were born, Michel was well into his fifties. His tremendous energies had been somewhat depleted and so the boys could grow up without being stampeded. For Eustache had to bear the hurricane force of his young, immigrant father's singleminded ambition to succeed at all cost in the New World. In later years, observers were continually amazed at the differences between Michel's first-born and last-born son. Eustache had a twenty-three-year headstart, yet by the time MC was in his early thirties he had already overtaken him financially and professionally.

As for the seven Bouvier girls, Thérèse, the oldest, in 1848 married Jonathan Patterson, Jr., son of a prosperous merchant, and gave Michel and Louise their first grandchild a little over a year later. The Pattersons, a distinguished old Presbyterian clan, would be one of the more prolific branches of the family. By 1966 there were scores of them living in and around Philadelphia, including a 106-year-old granddaughter of Michel's, Mary Patterson Stuart, and three namesakes, Michel Bouvier Patterson, Sr., Jr., and III. At the time of her sister's marriage to Jonathan Patterson, Jr., Lizzie was nineteen, Louise was seventeen, and Emma was fifteen. Lizzie had just finished boarding school at the Sacred Heart Convent at Eden Hall, where all the Bouvier girls went; Louise was on the eve of her novitiate at Manhattanville; and Emma too was thinking of becoming a nun. Michel did not approve of Louise's religious vocation and vigorously opposed it. At Eden Hall the nuns still tell the story of Louise escaping on horseback from her parents' summer home and taking refuge in the convent. So far as Michel was concerned, she was as errant in her way as Eustache was in his. His staunch middle-class morality could not accept extremes in behavior and aspiration, although his common sense must surely have told him that a family of twelve would inevitably span a broad spectrum of personality. As it turned out, all Michel's daughters were to be zealously, even fanatically, devoted to their religion. Louise became a nun. Emma, whom her father persuaded not to take the veil, was as close to being a nun as a married woman could be. And Zénaïde,

Alexine, and Mary, who remained single, stayed "house nuns" all their lives.

With three sons and seven daughters, one would have thought Michel and Louise would have rested from their labors, but Michel had a family tradition to live up to. Hadn't his father sired his thirteenth child at the age of seventy-five? Accordingly, in 1853, when Michel was sixty and Louise forty-one, the Bouviers had another son, Joseph—Michel's twelfth and last child.

Michel was now at the apex of his career. In March 1853 he completed the sale of his West Virginia coal and timber lands. The profits, we have seen, were immense and the deal soon became legendary in Philadelphia business circles, obscuring Michel's earlier achievements as a craftsman and manufacturer. With plenty of ready cash now available, Michel turned his inexhaustible energies to the task of spending money for a change. There were two things he had been wanting to do for some time: build a home that would be a fitting symbol of his success; and take his family on a trip to Europe that would include a visit to the village on the Rhône he hadn't seen since he had left it thirty-eight years before.

For self-made Michel, erecting an imposing residence in one of Philadelphia's most expensive new sections was the surest way to proclaim his financial success in the New World and to elevate his large family to the social status he so much wanted it to enjoy. Accordingly, not long after he concluded his coal-lands deal, he began building a brownstone mansion on his North Broad Street property: a huge, three-story building in Italian Renaissance style, with over twenty-five rooms, including a chapel and an observation tower, and adjoining stables, greenhouses, and "grapery," the entire complex surrounded by a fenced garden filled with statues and fountains.

With his town house underway, and the return of the Bonapartists to power in France, Michel now felt free to fulfill his second ambition: taking his family to Europe and returning in triumph to his village in Provence—a trip which was to be one of the most moving episodes of his life.

Since his wife was busy looking after her three young sons, and Zenney, Allie, and Moll were considered too immature to make the trip, Michel decided to take only his three eldest unmarried daughters with him, Elizabeth, Louise, and Emma, aged twenty-four, twenty-two, and twenty-one. After the trip was over, the plan was for Louise to remain in France to continue her religious studies at the Sacred Heart Novitiate at Conflans, just outside of Paris.

Of the three sisters who accompanied their father on the trip, the most "natural" was Lizzie, a wholesome, uncomplicated girl, tall, with fair hair, blue eyes, and an even temperament like her mother. Her younger sister Louise was very different. Religion had acquired a total hold on her otherwise independent, nonconformist spirit: everything not related to the Church and its doctrines was of little interest to her. Pious in the extreme, the slender, sharp-featured Louise could think of nothing, once in France, but the Church and was willing to sacrifice sightseeing, amusements, and her father's favor to be in its embrace. Emma, too, was religious, but in an intellectual, rather than emotional, or mystical, way. She was devoted to the Church, but she retained some secular interests, and she had a tendency to rationalize her religious experience. Possessed of an insatiably inquiring mind and a superior intelligence, she became the official chronicler of the trip, diligently keeping a detailed and perceptive diary of the expedition.

The voyage began on July 2, 1853, when the *City of Glasgow*, one of the new British steamers, sailed down the Delaware, bound for Liverpool, to the tune of the "Caliph of Baghdad" played by the ship's band. On the way over—the trip took two weeks—Michel was humiliated by an abscess on his left toe which had flared up shortly after the ship left port. He was humiliated because, according to his daughter, he intended to make new business contacts on the voyage and the abscessed toe made him look ridiculous. Evidently quite conscious of his image, he didn't want potential clients to see him limping around with a bandaged foot. So he stayed in his cabin almost the entire voyage, cursing the fates. When the ship arrived in Liverpool, his foot was no better. On first "putting his abscessed toe to ground," he informed his anxious daughters that it was worse. But he stubbornly refused to see a physician in his Liverpool hotel, confessing to his girls that as an ex-soldier of Napoleon's he had little use for the English and less for their doctors, who he had heard were terrible robbers. Even after several days of nursing his toe in the hotel, while his daughters went sightseeing and church visiting in Liverpool, he still refused to see a doctor. Finally Emma took it upon herself to get one and Louise accepted the responsibility of ushering him into her father's irate, though later grateful, presence. After a couple of days, the toe was well enough to allow Michel to go to London, where he recovered his dignity sufficiently to spend five days showing his daughters the Tower, the British Museum, and St. Paul's.

From London they went to Southampton and boarded a steamer for Calais. Later, as they approached the French coast, Michel stood at the ship's rail. He didn't say anything but Emma detected a look in his eyes of "such gratitude and happiness no words could have done it justice." The next entry in her diary is headed in capital letters: ON FATHER'S NATIVE SOIL!

They battled their way through customs, with Father delighted at the opportunity to swear in French. They got on the train for Paris, with Father fuming about luggage and tickets and talking with everyone in sight. They arrived in Paris on July 27, utterly exhausted, and the following morning Michel breakfasted with his old friend Mr. Mailliard, the late Joseph Bonaparte's administrator, who was living in Paris at the time. After breakfast Mailliard accompanied Michel and his daughters to the Sacred Heart Convent at Conflans, where Louise astonished everyone by announcing she intended to remain there and not continue on the journey. Remonstrances, outrage from her father were to no avail. He had hotel reservations. He had wanted her to see Florence and Rome, wanted her to see his native Pont-Saint-Esprit. She would hear none of it. At Sacré Coeur she would remain. Finally they compromised. She would stay with them until they left Paris, then she would go straight to the convent at Conflans: she definitely would not go on the rest of the trip. That was that. The incident prompted Mailliard to confide to his diary that, despite his attachment to the Church, "her devotion, her abnegation" depressed him.

Michel spent the next three days showing his daughters things he himself had never seen before: Versailles, Napoleon's tomb, some Napoleonic mementos in the Louvre. In the midst of these cultural pursuits a letter arrived from his wife, announcing all was well with the three boys and admonishing her daughters: "Aidez-vous et Dieu vous aidera." Then Michel took Louise to Conflans and the next day, August 4, he set out with the other two girls for his birthplace in the Midi.

By the time they reached Lyons the following day, Michel was beside himself with expectation. Not only had he not seen his village in thirty-eight years; he hadn't seen his brother or sisters either. His oldest sister, Elizabeth, still lived in Pont-Saint-Esprit, as did several of her children. So did his three half sisters, whom he had never met. And his brother François lived not far away, in Nîmes.

Feverish with excitement, Michel and Lizzie and Emma took a steamer down the Rhône from Lyons the morning of August 6 and around 2:00 P.M. finally came in sight of Pont-Saint-Esprit. The village appears from the Rhône as a cluster of towers and church domes to the right of a graceful, eighteen-arched bridge. When he saw it, Michel went "crazy with delight." "How often," he exclaimed, "have I passed the day with my companions along these banks! And the bridge, how well I remember it, with its eighteen arches. O! Seigneur, que je suis heureux! Salut, O jours de mon enfance!" In Emma's words:

> He seemed to excite the sympathy of every one of the passengers and when we landed he forgot to make a bargain with a porter for the carrying of our baggage, so that every poor fellow—five in all—who was at the pier, picked up a trunk, or a bag and followed us to the hotel. The foremost of the band, quite a vieillard, declared that he knew father, and that he was a Bouyer—the patois for Bouvier. We endeavored to persuade him he was wrong but he doggedly maintained his opinion, and when we reached the hotel he threw down his share of the burden, and hurried off, contrary to our desire, to apprise father's family of our arrival. We made a careful toilette, in the meantime papa went out to the barber's and was shaved by the same person who was wont to shave him in the bon vieux temps! And now we started for notre tante. Oh, with what joy did she not welcome her dear brother! And how earnestly she exclaimed as if doubting his identity at this happy moment "mais mon frère, mon cher frère, est-ce vraiment toi!"

Before long the other relatives began arriving. Sister Elizabeth's two sons by her second marriage, Auguste and Victor Bouchard, and her daughter, Thérèse Barry, and her husband. And Michel's three half sisters, Pélagie, Louise, and Anasthasie, and their mother, Louise Perboz. A terrific tumult ensued, in the Latin manner, with everybody talking at once. Michel was ecstatic, with relatives swarming around him, offering him sweets and apéritifs. Emma and Lizzie were overwhelmed with attentions. Finally dinner was ready and some thirteen members of the family sat down to a feast of rich Provençal cooking. By this time Emma was quite overcome. Without explaining in detail, she noted in her diary that she "was unable to eat" and had to "retire in the middle of dinner to one of the upstairs bedrooms."

It is evident from the diary that Emma was not very favorably impressed with the Mediterranean effusiveness of her warm-blooded aunts and cousins. Taking after the Lindsay side of the family, she was rarely effusive over anything, preferring to give simple, factual information about the places she visited. The objective treatment she gives Pont-Saint-Esprit is typical:

> Pont St. Esprit is in classic Languedoc, in the Department du Gard, and has a population of about 3000 souls. The main street is broad and planted with trees and ornamented with a very handsome fountain; the other streets are dark, irregular, narrow and badly paved and are without sidewalks. The pont is supported on 18 grand arches, is 3000 feet long, though disproportionately narrow and somewhat crooked. There are many legends connected with its construction. Some say it received its name from the fact of the Holy Ghost laying the foundation of its piers—a work almost impossible for mortals to accomplish owing to the rapidity of the waters of the Rhône. The truth is Pont St. Esprit was built in the 12th Century by the Brethren of the Bridge, a fraternity established for the protection of travelers.

The next two weeks saw Michel and his daughters sightseeing and visiting relatives in and around Pont-Saint-Esprit; following an itinerary that was to be duplicated, down to the present day, by future generations of American Bouviers visiting the land of their forefathers. On Sunday, August 7, Elizabeth took her by now legendary brother and nieces to church, where they were stared at and fussed over as if they were visiting royalty. After church they went "to the old homestead" and saw the room in which Michel was born and his parents died. Then they walked to "Grandma Bouvier's" farmhouse for lunch with her and Michel's half sisters. In her diary Emma is rather condescending about the farm her young French aunts looked after. Having been brought up in a fine house with servants, and educated in the best schools, she found it hard to accept these Provençal farm girls as relatives. They and Emma and Lizzie were roughly the same age, and all five were descended from Eustache Bouvier, yet there was a world of difference between them.

The area around Pont-Saint-Esprit is sprinkled with charming old villages, Roman ruins, châteaux on the Rhône, monasteries, and shrines, and the Bouvier girls wanted to take them all in. Thus, while Michel remained in the village, visiting with his sisters and looking up old cronies, Emma and Lizzie rode off with their French cousins to see everything worth seeing in the brief time they had. On August 8 the cousins rode to a neighboring village for a *fête votive*. Recalling the lively Provençal dances, Emma temporarily lost her dispassionate objectivity to exclaim that there were dark, handsome men at the fête wearing "clean white blouses with scarlet sashes around their waists," and women carrying "gaily colored handkerchiefs and wearing long gay ribbons in their bonnets." They went "running through the town with tambourines beating and ribbons floating in the breeze with such zest that it was wildly exciting to behold them." The next day Thérèse Barry took Lizzie and Emma to see a medieval castle at Uzès, and the following day the cousins went to a fête at the Carthusian monastery of Valbonne in a wooded valley about six kilometers from Pont-Saint-Esprit. Valbonne fascinated Emma. The girls were not allowed to enter the monastery, whose walls Emma described as "emblematic of the separation of man from a corrupted world." They were greeted, however, by the bearded abbot, Dom Augustin, who later gave them lunch under the trees outside the convent, consisting of potage, omelette, pommes de terre frites, fromage, and vin blanc: it was forbidden to serve meat. After lunch Lizzie, Anasthasie, and Louise gathered flowers and Emma and Auguste Bouchard climbed a hill together to get an overall view of the entire monastery.

On August 12 Michel joined his daughters for a day of sightseeing in nearby Orange. An old Roman town dating from the reign of Augustus, Orange, Emma dutifully noted in her diary, was once "the capital of a principality belonging entirely to the House of Nassau from 1530 to 1705." Wandering around the old town, the family admired the immense Triumphal Arch of Augustus and the ancient Roman theater, two monuments Michel had never seen before, though he had lived in the area for twenty-three years. From Emma's diary we get a few hints of the enormous differences between Michel's and his daughters' minds. Michel had no education to speak of, outside his father's carpenter's shop and the army. It is doubtful that he ever learned to read and write with any facility: his wife, or his clerk, wrote all his letters for him, and after Louise died, his daughter Zénaïde handled his correspondence. He probably knew little history or literature. His daughters, on the other hand, had graduated from one of the best boarding schools in Philadelphia, Eden Hall. Thus, on the way to Orange, Emma noted the nearness of Mont-Ventoux, the mountain Petrarch climbed and then wrote about in his *Ascent of Mont-Ventoux*. She also noted the nearness of Avignon, where the Papacy had been in captivity and where Petrarch had first met his great love, Laura, the beautiful married woman to whom he had dedicated *La Canzoniere*. Vaucluse, where Petrarch had a villa and wrote many of his greatest works, was also nearby.

All this fell on deaf ears so far as her father was concerned. To him Mont-Ventoux was a barren mountain with no timber. He preferred the mountains of West Virginia. Avignon was, in his opinion, a fairly good market town, but commerce there was "slow"—nothing to compare with the market towns of Pennsylvania. After a while Emma gave up trying to get him interested in the rich culture of Provence. It was a culture he and his forefathers had been denied participation in. During the four hundred years between Petrarch and Sade, who was born not far from Pont-Saint-Esprit, the Bouviers had not been high enough on the social scale to have the time or education to bother with impractical pursuits such as history and poetry. It remained for their American descendants to gain an appreciation of what they had for centuries been ignorant of.

The rest of Michel's stay in Pont-Saint-Esprit was taken up with old friends and relatives and Emma and Lizzie had to curtail temporarily their cultural explorations. There were dinners at half sister Pélagie's house, called La Villette. She had married a storekeeper by the name of Pierre Barry and not long after Michel returned to America she and her husband followed him to Philadelphia in the hope of acquiring something of his Midas touch. There were visits to the home of Annette Latour, who had "nursed Papa as a child." There was a fête at the local church in honor of the patron saint of France which the local garrison of five hundred men attended, together with all the notables of the village. In the evenings, before sundown, Michel would often take a walk down the Rhône, usually with a child, one of his nephews, or whoever else might be available at the time, visiting the spots where he as a child had fished and swum and dreamed impossible dreams. It was a good place for dreaming, the Rhône. Looking up the great river, one seemed to see the whole world opening up, as if the river's source were infinity.

On August 16, Michel and the girls paid their farewells to the Bouviers of Pont-Saint-Esprit, after showering them with gifts, and left for Nîmes, where Michel's brother François lived. The road from Pont-Saint-Esprit to Nîmes wound for seventy kilometers through olive-feathered hills, past clumps of prickly-pear cactuses, crumbling stone walls, and an occasional parched vineyard. It was more like a Spanish landscape, very different from the fertile valley of the Rhône. Emma described it in her diary as arid and bare, with the "foliage covered with a kind of powder" (probably road dust). Michel must have been a bit apprehensive over the journey. François had run upon hard times. In view of Michel's extraordinary success, their meeting was bound to be a little awkward.

François Bouvier had never abandoned the trade of cabinet-maker and sculptor in wood, the trade he had learned alongside Michel in their father's shop in Pont-Saint-Esprit. Upon his return from America, he practiced that trade in Bordeaux for twenty years while raising a family of two sons and five daughters. Eventually something went wrong with his marriage and he was separated from his wife, who took custody of the children, and moved to Nîmes. Not much about his life in Nîmes can be pieced together. We have only his addresses. They tell us that he lived and worked in a relatively poor quarter of the city, a crowded section veined with narrow streets and packed with old tenements, mostly inhabited by artisans who worked in their homes. It was an area far removed from the wide boulevards and tree-shaded esplanades where Michel's hotel was located, the area Emma Bouvier was to describe so admiringly in her diary.

Michel and his daughters arrived at the Hôtel de France in the evening, after an entire day on the road, and the long-awaited meeting between the two brothers took place shortly thereafter. Emma did not describe the setting in her diary—we can assume it was the hotel—but she did devote a paragraph, in her usual low-keyed style, to the emotion-laden meeting.

> The meeting between Father and his brother was most tender. When he discovered himself to François, the latter, with a shriek, rushed into his arms and would have stifled him with embraces, but exhaustion soon prevented any further demonstration and he sank powerless into a chair. A more affectionate or more sincere meeting has rarely taken place.

What then passed between the two brothers is left to our imagination. During the next four days Emma does not mention her uncle again except to say occasionally that her father was seeing him. She was much more interested in Roman temples and baroque fountains. Michel and François had not met in over thirty years. Their lives had been very different. The destinies of their children and their children's children would be even more different, until by 1961 the gulf between the two branches of the family would be of boundless proportions. If Emma had the instincts of a novelist, or even a good journalist, she would have sensed the drama that must have swirled around her father and her uncle and given it more space in her diary. But she was young and highly educated. And so, instead of describing successive meetings with François, she dismissed him from her thoughts and devoted her pages on Nîmes to more educational matters such as the fact that the city had 41,000 inhabitants and was famous for its elaborate gardens, magnificent esplanade, swan-filled fountains, Temple of Diana, and ancient Roman arena "purpled with martyr's blood."

On August 8 she and Lizzie visited the Museum of Roman Antiquities and the gardens of La Fontaine while "Father saw his brother." The following day the two sisters went to the Maison Carrée, a temple "erected to the patron of the city who was a grandson of Augustus," while "Father saw his brother." Nîmes had a delightful Gallo-Roman air to it, wrote Emma. It also had a touch of the Spanish. They held bullfights in the ancient arena. There were Roman ruins everywhere. Yet "French elegance was equally pervasive." Les jardins de La Fontaine were filled with the most charming baroque fountains and statues. Meanwhile, "Father saw his brother." What did they talk about—Michel, who would shortly move into his mansion on North Broad Street and marry Emma into one of the wealthiest families in Philadelphia, and François in his little carpenter's shop on the rue des Plantes, separated from his wife and children, facing a future of poverty and neglect? Did Emma ignore the drama because she was ashamed of her uncle, whom she never referred to as such, but always as "Father's brother"? On the morning of August 20, their last day in Nîmes, Emma recorded that she and Lizzie went off to take a last look at the arena purpled with martyr's blood, while "Father said good-bye to his brother." Did Lizzie and Emma say goodbye to their uncle? At 2:00 P.M. the Bouviers left for Marseilles, and François was not mentioned in the diary again. During the next fifteen years sad news of François would sporadically reach Philadelphia. There would be appeals for funds, to which Michel would generously respond. In 1860 Zénaïde would recall, in a letter to one of her Aunt Elizabeth's sons, that Lizzie's meeting with François in 1853 was one of "the saddest moments in her life" and that she had found François's children so different from herself that she could not recognize them as her relatives. Finally, in April 1869, news would arrive from the Hospital of the Poor in Nîmes that François Bouvier had died and had been buried in a pauper's grave.

On the way to Marseilles the Bouviers stopped at Beaucaire, where they admired the splendid castle of Tarascon on the Rhône and Michel took his daughters to a spot where as a boy he had "a serious conflict with the Rhône." From Beaucaire, the route led to Arles, "called by Honorarius the Rome of the Gauls," where there were more Bouviers waiting to greet their rich American relations. They were the children of François, who had gone to Arles with their mother not long after the break-up of their parents' marriage. Among them was Michel's namesake, a twenty-eight-year-old cabinetmaker with three children. It was thirty-four years before Van Gogh would settle in Arles to produce those landscapes and portraits that would make the Rome of the Gauls one of the most familiar and beloved cities in the world. When Michel and his daughters arrived in the vicinity of the city, its cypresses and sunflowers, its golden fields pulsating in the sun, and its blossoming fruit trees were still unexploited, and the Arlesienne was yet to adorn the walls and calendars of thousands of European and American homes. Most likely the Bouviers of

Philadelphia rattled across the canal drawbridge to which the Dutch painter would one day give new life.

Arles, the Queen of the Rhône, the Rome of the Gauls! Emma was ecstatic about the city in her diary, but, again, her relatives got scant treatment. She wrote that Arles was noted for its beautiful women, "descended from the Greek." And she recorded that she and Lizzie went to the Roman arena there also, another one "purpled with martyrs' blood." Father, in the meantime, was "looking up some relatives." These relatives were Emma's first cousins: Michel-Chéri Bouvier, twenty-eight; Marie Bouvier, twenty-four; and Clémence Bouvier, seventeen—children of François Bouvier and his estranged wife, Marie Poissonié. The extent of the differences between this clan and the one Michel established in Philadelphia can be seen from their occupations. Michel-Chéri Bouvier of Arles was a cabinetmaker all his life, whereas his American first cousin, Michel Charles Bouvier, became a millionaire Wall Street banker and stockbroker. Marie Bouvier married a seaman from Toulon by the name of Célestin Solard and had nine children, eight of whom died in infancy. Clémence Bouvier married a porter from Arles by the name of Antoine Chabert and they had eleven children, nine of whom died in infancy. Their American first cousins, Emma and Lizzie, would marry millionaire businessmen, one of whom, Francis Drexel, was to found one of the largest fortunes in America. Just as she had ignored her uncle in Nîmes, Emma never mentioned in her diary meeting her less fortunate cousins while she and Lizzie were in Arles. While Father was off "looking up some relatives," they were off looking up the monuments of the Rome of the Gauls. Michel, however, was to remember the relatives he looked up that day. All of them would be mentioned in his will.

From Arles to Marseilles the road skirted the Camargue, that wild, swampy region where the Rhône flows into the Mediterranean. This is the Mississippi delta of France, and several of François Bouvier's descendants were to settle in its villages. According to Emma's diary, the Bouviers of Philadelphia made no further stops. They headed straight to Marseilles, where they wandered around the Vieux Port the night of their arrival and attended the feast of Notre-Dame du Gard in the cathedral the next morning. Then, the following day, they boarded a steamer for Italy.

The vessel was called the *Capri* and some of its passengers intrigued Emma enough to prompt her to include them in her diary. They were the pretentious "Prince and Princess of Montebello, accompanied by a negro servant and a maid"; and an un-named Spanish count and an equally anonymous Neapolitan countess. The prince and princess were constantly ordering their servants and the shipboard personnel around, "with no regard for their dignity or welfare," and the Neapolitan countess did nothing but "twirl her parasole and air her vanity." "Father," however, "exchanged cards with the travellers." Although Emma usually disapproved of the European nobility she met on her travels, she was evidently fascinated by them, all the same, for she frequently mentioned her encounters with them in her journal. She was the first of several Bouvier females to be alternately repelled and spellbound by titled aristocracy.

In Italy, fleecing tourists is as old a trade as selling rosaries near the Vatican. When the Bouviers arrived in Civitavecchia, Michel was quickly tagged as a likely victim. Emma records the episode in her journal:

> To take us from the steamer to land, a distance of probably a couple of hundred yards, father was charged an exorbitant sum. This exasperated him and he gave the boatman a shower of the most piquant language that an American enragé is capable of bestowing. It was very ludicrous to see father thus talking when no one about him comprehended one word of English, whereas French would have been understood by the time we got to the custom-house. There was another volley of words fired at the porter who valued his part of the performance too highly. Poor papa soon discovered that the demanding of unreasonable prices at Civita Vecchia was epidemic and that even the American Consul was stricken with the disease, as he charged TEN FRANCS to vise our pass-ports to Rome.

Once in Rome, the Bouviers put up at the Hotel d'Angleterre, then one of the finest in the city, not far from the Spanish Steps. They came primarily to see the Pope but since they were not important enough to merit a private audience, yet were already too proud to attend a public one, they went to the Quirinale with some chance acquaintances, the Von Coberghs, who had an entrée with a cardinal, to place themselves

> in such a position, that as the Pope would issue from the palace door for his afternoon drive he could not fail to see us. After waiting some time the Swiss guards, who were in the gallery with us, by a signal from the Captain, ranged themselves in opposite files, and immediately Pius IX stepped forth. He paused as he perceived the Viscountess holding forth her beads which he blessed; he then addressed a few words to us, gave us his benediction and passed on to his coach.

After Rome came Florence, where an incident occurred that gives us another insight into Michel's character and how it differed from that of his daughters. Emma described it.

> After dinner we wandered through the dark streets of Florence, and as good luck (or bad luck as Lizzie and I first thought) would have it we stumbled over a house on the door of which was a tablet announcing that Hiram Powers, Sculptor, resided within. In a moment Father resolved, "sans ceremonie," to call on the great American artist, but we refused to intrude thus abruptly upon our distinguished countryman and remained, patrolling the Via della Fornari, whilst Father made his visit. In a few minutes, however, he issued from the house, called us to him and, turning to a person in the doorway in a brown blouse with a brown paper cap in his hand, said "these are my two daughters, Mr. Powers, who are ashamed to come in and see you without a great deal of formality—letter of introduction etc . . . For my part, I am a plain man without pretensions disregarding all these foolish conventions so hurtful to social intercourse. I beg you will pardon my want of ceremony." Mr. Powers answered that it pleased him highly. He took us into his studio and showed us a cast of the bust of Commodore Vanderbilt.

While in Florence, the Bouviers visited most of the buildings tourists to the Tuscan capital feel obliged to see—the Medici Palace, Or San Michel, the Cathedral and Baptistery, Santa Croce, the Pitti Palace. All of them enthralled Emma, but only one appeared to have meaning for Michel: Santa Croce. For in this church, which contains the tombs of most of the great Florentines, the Bonapartes maintained a chapel, in the crypt of which Joseph Bonaparte was interred. Having been unmoved, it appeared, by the graves of Galileo, Machiavelli, and Michelangelo, Michel was deeply affected at the sight of the tomb of his former benefactor and stayed for some time in silent meditation before it, paying, in Emma's words, "homage to the dear old man he had loved during his life, and whose memory he respects in death."

Although he dutifully escorted his daughters through the city's museums and churches, Florentine culture, it seemed, meant little to "Michel Bouvier, dealer in mahogany and marble." Even though he himself had been something of a sculptor in wood, he was much more interested in plain marble than in the statues Michelangelo and Donatello fashioned out of it. It was therefore a keen disappointment for the girls when Michel announced they would cut short their stay in Florence to visit the great quarries at Carrara. However, children were dutiful and obedient in those days, and so Emma recorded that in spite of her disappointment she was "content to obey her dear parent's wishes."

At Carrara, Michel was in his element. Having imported the quarries' finest marble for over fifteen years, he was delighted to see where the lucrative white stone came from and how it was mined. The girls couldn't have been more bored. Marble quarries—when they could have been feasting their souls on such products of the quarries as the Medici tombs and Donatello's Cantorie. Art, in the end, was not neglected, however. Michel bought a marble fountain at Carrara, in the shape of a shell surmounted by a dolphin, that would have a complicated but traceable history. It was first installed in the garden of the new mansion at 1240 North Broad Street as a bird bath. Later, after Michel died, it found its way to Emma's home, and after she died, her daughter gave it to St. Elizabeth's convent in Cornwells Heights, Pennsylvania, to be used as a piscina or sacrarium in the sacristy of the convent's chapel. It is still there, in the new sanctuary behind the altar.

The trip to Carrara, followed by a brief visit to Pisa, ended the Bouviers' Italian journey.

On their way back to Paris they stopped at Toulouse and Bordeaux. Emma recorded an incident in Toulouse on September

27 that is one of the few surviving references to her father's military career.

> We drove out to the scene of that bloody battle of 1814 between the armies of Wellington and Soult. As we approached the ground, now a ploughed field, father, who fought in the contest, became quite excited and pointed out the positions of the respective armies, related several events connected with the bloody affray, and wound up in regular French style by anathematizing the English for obtaining the victory.

Michel's French bias was to remain in his family, in varying degrees of intensity, during succeeding generations, counter to the dominant American tendency to identify with the English.

There were exceptions, however, to the family bias and Emma was one of them. Remarkably un-Latin in temperament and appearance for one who was only a generation removed from Southern France, she did not really care for the French way of life because it did not revolve around *home* the way life did in America, but around the café, the street, and other public places.

When they got back to Paris, Emma and Lizzie revisited some of the places they had liked at the start of their European trip. Michel, as usual, looked up a relative. The relative this time was eminently presentable and so Emma included him in her diary. He was Michel's sister Elizabeth's twenty-nine-year-old son by her first marriage, François-Louis Baudichon, a career military officer who would one day be decorated with the Legion of Honor. It appears that Michel and his nephew got along very well as they traveled around Paris together, and that Baudichon got along even better with his pretty young cousin Lizzie. Exactly what happened between Lizzie and François-Louis is not known. The puritanical Emma inevitably shied away from writing about communion between the sexes. What is known is that after Michel and his daughters returned to Philadelphia, Lizzie began receiving marriage proposals from her cousin that were to cause quite a stir in the Bouvier household. The barrage of correspondence from Lizzie's sisters was so voluminous that some of the letters have survived to this day.

On October 23, two days before leaving Paris, the Bouviers drove out to the novitiate at Conflans to say a last goodbye to

Louise. While Emma and Lizzie were tearful at the parting, the future Madame Bouvier, Dame du Sacré Coeur, seemed unruffled. She had apparently made great progress in her studies, especially in French, which she would one day teach, and was looking forward to her remaining months in France. So upset, however, were her sisters, who thought they were losing Louise forever, that they returned to Conflans the next day for a second final farewell. "Poor Louise," Emma exclaimed in her journal. Yet Louise considered herself the richest Bouvier of them all. That evening Michel, Lizzie, and Emma left for Le Havre, and the following day, October 20, they boarded the steamer *Franklin* for Philadelphia. Emma's last entry in her journal, written the day the ship sailed up the Delaware, was an ecstatic greeting to "AMERIQUE ADORÉ!"

# *VI*

UPON HIS RETURN FROM EUROPE, MICHEL'S NEXT PROJECT WAS TO GET his mansion on North Broad Street completed. He arrived in Philadelphia in November 1853, and it took a year more of prodding and occasional direct supervision for the place to be ready for occupancy. The Bouvier family, eleven strong, finally took possession on All Saints' Day, 1854, the year of the Consolidation Act, when the central city engulfed its outlying areas and Philadelphia's population shot from 100,000 to half a million. It was a day Michel had been planning for since 1841, when he had first bought the property. No doubt he had been planning for it, in a sense, much longer than that. At an indeterminate point in his life he had conceived the outrageous ambition of rivaling the potentates for whom he had worked as a young immigrant. Ever since then he had been moving toward North Broad Street in an inexorable trajectory. Hadn't the Bonapartes conceived, and then fulfilled, similar ambitions? Corsica, after all, was even more of a backwater than Pont-Saint-Esprit. And hadn't Stephen Girard of Bordeaux risen from next to nothing also? Michel well remembered his early labors in the palaces of those nouveaux nabobs. Perhaps he had felt the first sting of ambition polishing tables at Point Breeze. At any rate, here he was, thirty-nine years after landing on the Delaware docks, in *his* palace, employing young immigrants to polish *his* tables. Now, at last, there was plenty of room for everything and everybody. Separate rooms for Zenney, Allie, and Moll. For Eustache, John, Michel, and little Joseph. For Lizzie and Emma. Rooms for Thérèse and Louise when they came back to visit. Rooms for his servants; he now had a cook, three chambermaids, a coachman, and a gardener. What is more, he could finally entertain in style, the way he had heard Stephen Girard used to. With two large drawing rooms, a library, a gaming room, and a spacious dining room on the first floor, he needn't fear comparison with anybody. And, what was more, he had his own private chapel, where the whole family could attend mass on his wife's inconvenient holy days of obligation. And, thanks to the extra lot he had added to the property in 1844, he also had a garden to stroll in—he had just installed the fountain from Carrara in it—and he had greenhouses and stables and he was going to plant a vineyard so he could make his own wine, the way his father had done in Pont-Saint-Esprit.

Michel was sixty-two when he moved into his new home. It was about this time that he had a portrait photograph taken of himself, copies of which he sent to his relatives in France. One of these copies has survived and now hangs in the home of M. Louis Flandin of Valence, a direct descendant of Michel's sister, Elizabeth. The photo portrays a man of Churchillian resolution—strong-willed, energetic, defiant—a man who has overcome countless obstacles to arrive at his goal, yet is still wary of possible threats to his hard-won status and is a little ill-at-ease in his new role. He is sitting for a portrait, yet one of his fists seems clenched. His mouth is grim, his expression somewhat impatient.

The material success of their American relation, amply displayed and probably vaunted on his recent trip to Europe, inspired Michel's French relatives to see if they could not accomplish similar feats in the New World. Immediately after François-Louis Baudichon opened his barrage of proposals to Lizzie, Pélagie Bouvier, who had married the Spiripontain storekeeper, Pierre Barry, decided to take the bull by the horns and migrate with her husband to Philadelphia. She and Pierre arrived in time to be given temporary quarters at North Broad Street. How Mrs. Bouvier reacted to this intrusion by her French in-laws is not known. Her daughter Zenney was to characterize Pélagie, in a letter to Baudichon, as a "seller of tobacco," whatever that may have meant. Michel apparently did a good deal for the Barrys. He got Pierre a job as a clerk and allowed him and Pélagie to live in style in his house until they got on their feet. A year after they arrived in Philadelphia, the Barrys had a child, whom they named—what else?—Michel.

It was during the late forties that Michel acquired his country estate, Fairview, at Frankford, near Torresdale, about fifteen miles north of Philadelphia. Here the family would spend the hot summer months, moving to the country early in June and returning to the city late in September. Fairview was not far from Eden Hall, where the Bouvier girls had gone to boarding school and where Louise would eventually teach French. The next generation of Bouviers would also maintain summer places in the area, at Torresdale and Cornwells Heights, until in the late nineteenth century five of them transferred to New York and Long Island. Fairview caught fire once and had to be partially rebuilt. During the fire Emma is reputed to have saved her little brother MC's life. In the panic that ensued after fire broke out, the nurse dashed to the baby's cradle and tore out of the house, clutching not the baby but a pillow. Whereupon Emma led some firemen into the inferno to save the child. Certainly it would have been unbearable if little Michel had died. The Bouviers had to wait fifteen years for son John to come along, nineteen for Michel. As it turned out, the last-born son, Joseph, died in 1856 at the age of four. Consequently, with Eustache still showing no promise of settling down, the family's future was to depend wholly on John and MC, thirteen and nine at the time of their brother's death.

With his brownstone town house, his country place, ten children, a remarkable wife, and a thriving business, Michel Bouvier in 1856 had earned his place in the American sun. It was at this time that he began slowly phasing out his marble and mahogany business and concentrating the best of his energies on his third career, that of real-estate speculator. Exactly when he sold his last marble mantels and mahogany veneers is not known. We do know, however, that in 1856, the year Western Union was founded to exploit the telegraph, he was spending a good deal of time "collecting rents" at his office opposite the Pennsylvania Bank and that by 1861 the firm of M. Bouvier & Co. had been dissolved. In the intervening years he bought and sold real estate, moving in and out of the market with a deftness that excited the admiration of the business community. Exercising an uncanny ability to buy cheaply and sell dearly, he gradually accumulated a string of profits that would insure the financial security of his family. Typical speculations included the purchase of a lot in the suburb of Coopersville for $25,000, which he later sold for $40,000. Another lot bought at the junction of the Germantown Railroad and Broad Street for $45,000, he sold to the Pennsylvania Railroad for $75,000. In his manufacturing days he had bought the Callowhill Street wharf for $12,000. Later he sold it to the Reading Railroad for $23,000. There is no need to recite his other transactions. Suffice it to say that by the mid-sixties he had parlayed the $100,000 he had saved from manufacturing and importing into something in the neighborhood of $800,000, and that by the crash of 1873 his assets were worth about a million, or approximately six million in today's dollars.

He brought the same acumen to the more delicate task of selecting husbands for his daughters. Michel sized up prospects with an instinct for financial promise equal to his ability to appraise real-estate values. When a young man by the name of

Francis A. Drexel appeared in the parlor of 1240 North Broad Street one day, around the time of the Lincoln-Douglas debates, to see his daughter Emma, it was as if he had just spotted an undeveloped lot over which he was certain a new railroad would eventually put down its main line. Francis A. Drexel was the son of the banker Francis Martin Drexel, who, starting from scratch like Michel, had built up, in twenty-three years, one of the most prosperous banking businesses in Philadelphia—Drexel & Co.— which his two sons were to expand into one of the most important in the nation, opening subsidiary branches in New York and Paris and founding a family fortune that would eventually make the Bouvier money look insignificant. At the time of his engagement to the twenty-seven-year-old Emma, Frank Drexel, a widower with two children, was already a rich man. It didn't take long for Michel and Louise to give their blessing.

Michel's spectacular rise from cabinetmaker's apprentice in Pont-Saint-Esprit to wealthy manufacturer and real-estate operator in Philadelphia was dramatized by the wedding he gave Emma on April 10, 1860 (the year Lincoln was elected President). The event was described in the Philadelphia papers as one of "unusual social distinction"—which must have made the tongues of older Philadelphia families wag since both the father of the bride and the father of the groom were immigrants from remote European villages.

In those days the reception came before the religious ceremony. Michel and Louise received their many guests in "the splendid mansion of the father of the bride on Broad St." Then the wedding party proceeded "in a long line of magnificently appointed carriages" to the "nuptials at St. Joseph's Church." "The Church was filled and there was a full choir and orchestra in attendance." Afterwards the newlyweds left for a long honeymoon in Europe which included, at the bride's insistence, a visit to Pont-Saint-Esprit. Emma Bouvier Drexel was to become the wealthiest and at the same time the most charitable of all Michel's children. Fate reserved a unique destiny for her and her daughters which was yet to yield the family's most unusual honor.

On April 12, 1861, almost a year to the day after Emma's marriage, Southern guns opened on Fort Sumter in Charleston Harbor, and five days later, after Lincoln issued his first call for volunteers, John V. Bouvier, aged eighteen, enlisted as a private and was subsequently mustered into service, for a three-month tour of duty, in Company G, 2nd Pennsylvania Infantry Volunteers, commanded by Colonel Peter Lyle. Three months later, at the end of his brief service, he reenlisted and was mustered into the 22nd Regiment, Massachusetts. He was then detailed to assist Captain J. M. Sanderson on the staff of General J. B. Wadsworth. On Wadsworth's subsequent recommendations, Bouvier was commissioned second lieutenant in the 80th Regiment, New York Volunteers, and detached to serve as aide-de-camp of General Marsena Patrick, who at the time was in command of the 2nd Brigade, 3rd Division, Department of the Rappahannock. Thus began an anxious three years for the Bouvier family. The Union was in peril and their most promising son had gone to war.

Philadelphia, as the greatest Eastern city near the Mason-Dixon line, had always been closely connected with the South. Even after the attack on Fort Sumter, some pro-Southern Copperhead sentiment persisted. As the war intensified, however, with the Confederates continually drubbing the Union armies, that sentiment slowly petered out and Philadelphia finally resolved its identity crisis by becoming a Northern city once and for all. For the Bouviers, however, there was never any doubt whose side they were on. A considerable family Civil War correspondence has come down to us and it reveals that they were strongly opposed to the South from the very start.

Having their beloved John in the Brothers' War made Michel and Louise very proud and at the same time terribly apprehensive. More than thirty of Louise's letters to John have survived and they show a woman consumed with worry over her son's safety. Her concern was not unfounded. In August 1862 word reached Philadelphia from the War Department that Lieutenant John V. Bouvier had been severely wounded at Groveton, Virginia, during the Second Battle of Bull Run. It had been a bloody fight, with Lee driving Pope through and across the deep gullies of northern Virginia until finally Pope was forced to retire across Bull Run and retreat to the Union fortifications outside Washington. It was during the second night of the battle that Lieutenant Bouvier was shot "clear through the lungs and body, from breast to back, the ball passing within one eighth of an inch of his heart." General Patrick described the action in his diary.

A rebel column filed into the road and challenged me, ordering me to halt—supposing, from their position, they were friends, I answered at the 2nd challenge, "Patrick's Brigade, King's Division, surrender or we fire"—It was Ricketts Rebel Brigade. Bouvier was with me—I think, too, that my orderly, Honesty, must have been near me—we turned and struck spurs to our horses—Instantly a shower of bullets whizzed by us—Poor Bouvier was shot and fell, his horse at the same time being killed under him. Perhaps Honesty was killed too, as the Harris cavalry report finding him dead with seven balls in him but I still hope that he is a prisoner—I rode rapidly through the Orchard, warned the Batteries of their danger and then rode down the Road to see what supporters were in my rear.

Later Patrick described what happened to his wounded aide-de-camp.

I may say here in relation to Bouvier that Capt. Kimball and McClure on Sat. found a nice place for him near Bull Run, with a very neat family of free negroes and leaving two of our guard with him, they left him doing well—on Monday we heard that the Rebels had put Hospital badges on our two men left with him and still having charge of him and that he was doing well.

On hearing the news, Michel, Louise, and Zénaïde hurriedly left Philadelphia and dashed by stagecoach to Fairfax County Court House at Bull Run to see their wounded son. They had hoped and prayed for that son for fifteen years before he was born. Now the doctors informed them that he was in critical condition. Whether they actually saw him is not known. For a week his life hung in the balance, then he slowly began to recover. After spending three weeks in the cabin, he was taken into the house of a family friend, Mrs. James Hoban, in Washington, where he was treated at his own expense. Sixty days later he was back on his feet, was exchanged for a Confederate officer, and rejoined the staff of General Patrick, who had in the meantime been promoted to the post of Provost Marshal General of the Army of the Potomac. Patrick mentioned his return to duty in his diary: "This evening as we were at Dinner who should walk in but Lt. John V. Bouvier looking as fresh and fine as silk—His left lung is ruined but he looks well and says he feels pretty well."

Subsequently, Lieutenant Bouvier left General Patrick's staff and became an aide to General A. E. Burnside, whom he served in the horrendous battle of Fredericksburg in December 1862. Burnside had crossed the Rappahannock in an attempt to march on Richmond, met Lee near Fredericksburg, and was repulsed in what turned out to be a terrible slaughter for the Union forces. During the engagement John Bouvier had charge of "all interviews with the enemy by flag of truce," surviving the battle without a scar.

Burnside had been so thoroughly thrashed by Lee that Union headquarters relieved him of his command. General "Fighting Joe" Hooker was sent to replace him, and Bouvier became aide to General Hooker. The next major clash between Union and Confederate forces occurred at Chancellorsville in early May 1863. On April 30, Hooker chose to confront Lee on the south side of the Rappahannock, was outwitted by the Confederate general in a series of sharp exchanges, and was finally forced to retreat across the river the night of May 5. Again Lee was victorious. During the fighting, which saw the South lose Stonewall Jackson, Lieutenant Bouvier, who again had charge of "interviews with the enemy by flag of truce," was wounded once more, this time in the left side.

Meanwhile a steady flow of letters from Philadelphia had been arriving at John's brigade, many of which have been preserved. They came mostly from his mother and his sister Mary, who signed herself Moll. Michel, Sr., never wrote, probably because he never learned to write in English. Louise was extremely concerned over his wounds (she underlined the word in every letter). Mary was more concerned over the fact that John never sent her a picture of himself in uniform (also underlined) that she could display to her friends at boarding school. Louise was always sending her son and his commanding general packages of food and cases of wine. She sent General Patrick a case of claret in the fall of 1862, and for Christmas of the same year she sent John a package containing a "fine large turkey," a "champagne basket," a "keg of excellent butter," some brandied peaches, "pine apples," "sugar plumb candies," strawberries, ten mince pies, a can of pickled oysters, a fruitcake, some "sugar plumbs from Emma," a pound cake, some "pickels," and a dozen oranges. The package never arrived.

John evidently was not much of a correspondent. Louise and Moll were always begging him to write, continually complaining that lack of news worried them to death. In one letter Louise wrote: "I often stand at the window at night and almost fancy I see you coming up the street. It is then that I raise my heart to God and plead for mercy in your behalf . . . Oh John, I so long to embrace you." At one time Michel, Sr., was so unhappy about one of John's long silences that he went to the War Department in Washington to find out what had happened to his son.

Louise Vernou's letters were not exclusively devoted to family matters. Occasionally she would write her soldier son about broader concerns, such as the draft riots and the conduct of the war.

> . . . You have no doubt heard of the very disgraceful riots that raged in New York City for several days on account of the Draft. The ringleaders of this outrage were undoubtedly rebels. Happily on the arrival of a sufficient military force, the rioters were suppressed but not until they had done great damage to life and Property. Every precaution has been taken in Philadelphia to prevent any difficulty that may arise from the draft here. A large military force with plenty of Cannon stationed throughout the city to fire at once at the commencement of any outbreak. . . I must confess that I was greatly surprised that Lee was allowed to make his escape without any resistance on the part of our army or until it was too late to pursue it. . . I suppose there was good cause for not having annihilated the whole of the Rebel forces. When will this cruel war end and our once happy country be restored to Peace? Peace, that greatest of all blessings. Our poor soldiers, how terribly they have been cut up . . . many thousands have arrived in Philadelphia and hundreds are still lying on the battlefield, fearfully wounded. . .

At all Bouvier family reunions in Philadelphia during the war, toasts would be proposed to John. Louise would write about the gatherings, trying to bring her son up to date on each member of the family. Little Michel, fourteen at the time his older brother was wounded, was "just as mischievous as ever," and spent his time "gaming and fishing." Louise was studying to be a nun at Manhattanville. Emma was very happy with her rich and handsome Frank Drexel, who, she underlined, wanted John *to come into his firm when he got out of the army.* Lizzie, who had recently married a businessman by the name of Joseph Dixon, and Thérèse were happy with their husbands too. Joe Dixon was making a lot of money, giving promise of becoming "a very rich man." Allie, Zen, and Moll were busy around the house, helping Father with his accounts and correspondence and sewing things for the boys in service. And then there was Carrie Ewing, John's fiancée, who of course spent most of her time pining for her hero. The only member of the family Louise never mentioned was Eustache, who was off on one of his get-rich-quick adventures, this time trying to strike gold in California.

Though worried, Michel and Louise were very proud of their fighting son. In one of her letters to the front, Louise wrote:

> I cannot refrain from telling you how proud *you, my beloved boy,* have made *me* and as for your *Father* words are inadequate to express his *delight.* He really thinks our son Jack equals our future Washington.

They had good reason to be proud. By the spring of 1863 Jack had fought in three major engagements, had been wounded in two of them, and had participated in eleven minor battles as well. In March 1863 he had been made first lieutenant. Three months later he took part in his fourth major battle, Gettysburg, on the soil of his home state. During the critical engagement, which saw General G. G. Meade pitted against Lee, Lieutenant Jack acted as communicating officer between Meade and General Patrick. With Meade on Cemetery Ridge the night of July 2, Jack was among the defenders against Lee's final assault the next day, During Pickett's charge Jack's horse was shot out from under him and he was severely injured in the fall. While Pickett's men were being repulsed, he lay immobilized on the battlefield. It wasn't until Lee began his retreat across the Potomac on July 4 that he was finally rescued. Soon his health failed completely and he was compelled to resign from service in October 1863, a year and seven months before Lee surrendered to Grant at Appomattox. Six years later, on February 20, 1869, he was commissioned "Captain, United States Volunteers, by brevet, to rank as such from March 13, 1865, for gallant and meritorious services at the battles of Groveton, Virginia, and Gettysburg, Pennsylvania."

When John returned home in the fall of 1863, he was welcomed by a family that had grown considerably since he had entered military service. Lizzie had two children and Emma had just given birth to a daughter. Thérèse had also added another child to her family. The others were still unmarried. Madame Louise, R.S.C.J., had recently begun her religious profession at Eden Hall. MC at sixteen was showing great promise: he was already helping his father out with his accounts. The inseparable trio, Zenney, Allie, and Moll, were the mainstays of the household. Zenney, at twenty-eight, was her mother's chief helper and her father's secretary. After her mother died, she would run the entire menage. Allie, at twenty-six, was the beauty of the family, indulged by everyone because of her fragile health. And Mary, at twenty-two, had already gained a reputation for her wit and conversational brilliance. Michel's half sister, Pélagie Barry, was no longer in Philadelphia. She had returned to Pont-Saint-Esprit with her son Michel after her husband's unexpected death in May 1863. Never very fortunate in his attempt to establish himself in the New World, Pierre Barry had caught a cold after an afternoon of muskrat hunting, and it developed into a fatal case of pneumonia.

Heading the household at 1240 North Broad Street was, of course, the indomitable Louise Vernou. Michel had made a brilliant choice when, thirty-five years before, he had selected her to bring up Eustache and Thérèse and be the mother of his other children. Her letters reveal a wife and mother of great fortitude and boundless devotion to her family. If she had any faults, they derived from a certain aristocratic pride that was frequently observed in her character. Emma's stepdaughter, Katharine Drexel, recalling afternoons with Grandma Bouvier, referred to her "seated at the library table like a queen on her throne . . . Her sons and daughters adored her and rendered homage by anticipating her every wish and desire." "I do not think," she added, "that Grandma Bouvier ever stooped to pick up a handkerchief she had dropped."

Katharine Drexel also recalled that Grandpa Bouvier was "the direct antithesis of Grandma Bouvier." "He was the typical Frenchman," she observed, "mercurial, emotional and at times irascible." Whereas she was always dignified and composed.

It is to Louise, then, that we must attribute the formation of the aristocratic identity that was to characterize the Bouvier family in future generations. Certainly that identity never came from her husband. Michel was a man of the people, if there ever was one—earthy, direct, unrefined, opportunistic, a bit crude. His function in the family was to *provide*, a function he fulfilled abundantly, while it was up to Louise to teach her children the arts of civilization, to give them a sense of style and an appreciation of the "finer things." In this sphere she succeeded as admirably as Michel did in his. Thus, thanks to Michel's moneymaking and Louise's educating, it took only one generation for a Provençal plebeian to produce a family of American aristocrats. There was something miraculous about it. All of a sudden a wedding of the Philadelphia Bouviers would be referred to in the society columns as one of "unusual social distinction." Yet a generation ago they were hammering out tables and chairs in a remote village in Southern France.

John Vernou Bouvier returned to the B-Hive, as the Bouviers liked to call their mansion on North Broad Street, long enough to line up a job and a wife. Then he was off to seek his fortune in New York. His brother-in-law, Frank Drexel, got him his job, a clerkship in the family banking house of Drexel, Winthrop & Co., 40 Wall Street, at $500 a year. His wife was harder to line up. Not that she was reticent. Carrie Ewing and John Bouvier were very much in love, but both her parents and his disapproved, the Ewings on the grounds that John, with only one lung, would soon make their daughter a widow; the Bouviers on the grounds that their son was not able to support a wife, which he wasn't. Eventually, in order to win his bride, John was compelled to produce written medical opinion that he could survive on one lung. As for Michel and Louise, they were so captivated by Carrie that they also dropped their opposition, resigning themselves to helping support the young couple during the first year of their marriage.

Caroline Ewing was a fine young girl, it seems—tall, slim, with blond hair and blue eyes, a shy smile and a wonderful, even disposition. Her father, Robert Ewing, came from a distinguished Maryland family whose Scotch-Irish founder had arrived in America from Northern Ireland in the early eighteenth century. Settling in what later became Caroline County, near Maryland's eastern shore, James Ewing founded a plantation of several hundred acres called Hamstead, parcels of which he passed on to his two sons, Joseph and James, Jr., along with thirteen Negro slaves. In 1792 James, Jr., married Elizabeth Griffith, daughter of a Revolutionary War officer, Lieutenant James Griffith of the Seventh Maryland Line. Their son, Robert, married Caroline Maslin, also of Caroline County, then moved to Philadelphia, where he became a successful textile merchant and art collector. In his day Robert Ewing cut a dashing figure in Philadelphia society, his home at 1628 Walnut Street becoming a salon of art enthusiasts and a meeting place of gentleman politicians. He dabbled in local politics himself and once ran for the office of sheriff of Philadelphia, losing the election on a recount. Among his acquaintances were Presidents Andrew Jackson and Franklin Pierce. Pierce once offered him the job of Treasurer of the United States Mint, which he declined. His portrait by Thomas Sully, painted in 1831, reveals a man of refinement, elegance, and charm many degrees of gentility removed from the likes of Michel Bouvier. For the Bouviers, Carrie Ewing was a catch. In marrying her, their son would substantially improve the family's social position.

In the letters he wrote his mother from New York in the fall of 1863 and the winter of 1864, John revealed the torment he was going through. He told her that New York was "full of temptations" and "fascinating evils" and the only thing that prevented him from tasting them was his love for Carrie. Carrie was everything to him. She was his Beatrice, the dominant influence in his life. And yet he was in no position to support her. Continually he was forced to write home for money. The competition in the New York financial world was so intense he had no idea when he would be on his feet economically. He was saving every penny he earned, however: he often ate only one meal a day and never spent money on "amusements." He felt very lonely in New York, so far from the B-Hive, but he was going to stick it out because "New York is so much ahead of the Old Quaker City in financial pursuits." His aim, he told his mother, was to make a *fortune* in New York so he could then live where he pleased. Meanwhile he was full of nostalgia for the Army and often felt like chucking the financial world and heading for the nearest recruiting station. His old comrades in arms kept writing him, adding to his regret at having left the service. Early in 1864, General Patrick wrote that he missed his former aide and advanced a pessimistic opinion on the war: "I do not expect to see a Commander placed over the army of the Potomac who could possibly cope with Lee." Then, suddenly, everything seemed to fall into place. John Bouvier left his clerkship at Drexel, went into business for himself as a dealer in foreign currencies, and on October 27, 1864, married Caroline Ewing, using his savings and some help from his father.

The following year was a momentous one. On April 9, 1865, Lee surrendered to Grant at Appomattox. And five days later Lincoln was assassinated. At the time of Lincoln's murder, John and Carrie were living their first year of married life in a two-room apartment in New York. That summer they rented a cottage in Torresdale, near Philadelphia, where on August 12 Carrie gave birth to a son, whom they named John Vernou Bouvier, Jr.

The subsequent jubilation in the B-Hive knew no limits. At last Michel had a grandchild who could carry on his name. He had produced twelve children, but there was not one grandchild with the surname Bouvier until now. As it turned out, John and Carrie had no more sons and Eustache and MC never married, so JVB, Jr., was the only male Bouvier of his generation.

With four of their children married and forming their own families, and the other six showing no signs of ever giving up their bachelorhood, Michel and Louise finally saw their family stabilized as they entered their twilight years.

It was during the late 1860s, a period of unprecedented industrial boom for the reunited nation, that Michel turned his still unspent energies to philanthropy, becoming in 1868, at the age of seventy-seven, the sixth president of the French Benevolent Society of Philadelphia, an important charitable institution of which he had been a director for many years. He had been liquidating many of his real-estate and stock holdings since 1864, putting the money into municipal and corporate bonds. Now he was through with speculating. The work of the French Benevolent Society was to absorb his remaining years. The society had been organized a half century before to aid the many poor French families of the city. As the records of the society disclose, not all the French who emigrated to America in the late eighteenth and early nineteenth centuries were able to make a go of it in the New World. Many of the Bonapartist exiles who had come over with Michel in 1815 had fallen into chronic poverty, as had a good many of the royalist refugees of Asylum. As president of the

French Benevolent Society, Michel directed the organization's bimonthly distributions of charity and presided over its meetings. Often the meetings were held in his home. They were colorful affairs serving also as a kind of forum for the French colony of Philadelphia, during which they told stories of the old days and discussed matters of mutual interest, always ending with a champagne toast "Vive la France!"

A year after he became president of the Benevolent Society, Michel loaned his two sons $4,500 each to buy seats on the New York Stock Exchange. Accordingly, MC, at twenty-two, joined his older brother in New York. Now only three of his children were left in the B-Hive, Zénaïde, Alexine, and Mary, who took care of their parents during their declining years.

Life was ebbing now for Louise and Michel. Their generation was disappearing and it would not be long before they would join those with whom they had begun the journey of life. Francis Drexel, Sr., had died in 1863; Robert Ewing in 1868; François Bouvier in 1869. In March 1872, around the time John D. Rockefeller attained mastery over the oil-refining industry in Cleveland, Michel celebrated his eightieth birthday, surrounded by his vast brood of children, grandchildren, and in-laws. That same year Louise developed a case of what was then called dropsy, which grew steadily worse during the summer months, until by September she was in critical condition. A brief rally, then, on October 5, the end came. She was sixty-one. Michel had scarcely gotten over the initial shock of loss when, a month later, news arrived in Philadelphia that his sister Elizabeth had died in Pont-Saint-Esprit, to be followed, in 1873, by his stepmother.

The year 1873 was one of severe economic depression for Philadelphia and the nation. Michel saw his net worth fall from over a million to $850,000. (It was to counteract some of the adverse psychological effects of the crisis that Horatio Alger began writing his stories of rags to riches success.) The depression, however, did not affect the Drexels adversely, for by 1873 their firm had reached a position of such financial strength that together with Jay Cooke it was able to undertake the refinancing of three quarters of a billion dollars of the national debt. For Michel, 1873 was a year of loneliness and failing health. True, he had Zenney, Allie, and Moll to look after him, but the death of his wife had left an emptiness in his life that they could not fill. To make matters worse, his heart condition had deteriorated. It was time to put his affairs in order, and so, with the same thoroughness, devotion, and attention to detail he had brought to his business and family life for over six decades, he now made provisions for the economic security of those who would survive him, leaving as little as possible to chance or the whims of his trustees and executors.

He displayed his usual insight into character in choosing his executors and trustees. Three of them were professional men of finance: son-in-law Frank Drexel and sons John V. and MC. The fourth was Zénaïde, the most practical of all his daughters, manager of his household since his wife's death. To these executors Michel bequeathed his entire estate in trust for partition among a long list of heirs.

The first thing he instructed them to do was pay his funeral expenses and debts as soon as possible after his decease. Then he turned his attention to the problem of his three unmarried daughters, ordering his trustees to "permit" Zénaïde, Alexine, and Mary to reside in his "dwelling house at 1240 North Broad St." for "the term of two years" after his decease and "to pay the repairs, taxes and all other necessary expenses upon said dwelling house during the said term." Furthermore, his executors were ordered to pay to his daughters "remaining in the said house during the said term the sum of nine thousand dollars per annum in equal and even quarterly payments, the said sum to be charged to the share of income of the estate which may be due and owing to them." In addition, he bequeathed to Zénaïde, Alexine, and Mary all "the furniture, silver plate, library, paintings, wines etc." remaining in his house at the time of his decease, and also his "horses, carriages, Barouches and Vehicles," together with the contents of his stables and greenhouses.

That taken care of, Michel then provided for the partition of the bulk of his estate, which consisted of some $850,000 in stocks, bonds, and real estate. Heading the list of minor legatees were his French relatives, seven of whom received sums ranging from $300 to $600 each. Next came the charitable bequests, $3,600 divided among eight institutions. Special bequests of $250 each were then made to the daughter of his late cook and to his late wife's seamstress. To his clerk, Louis Breschman, Michel left $500, and to each of his seven servants, including his coachman and his gardener, $150.

The remainder of the estate was to be divided equally among the surviving children, "share and share alike," with the provision that should any of them die before Michel, leaving lawful issue, such issue was to take the share that the parent would have taken had he or she been living at the time of Michel's decease. Thus, each of Michel's ten children was to receive roughly $82,300, or about $510,000 in today's money. Of each $82,300 share, however, only $50,000 was to be given to the legatee outright. The remaining $32,300 was to be held by the executors in trust to "pay over to each of said parties respectively . . . the net income of their respective estates for and during the term of their natural lives." These broad bequests were, however, subject to several qualifications based on estimations of the personality and condition in life of each recipient. In the case of the wild and spendthrift Eustache, only $25,000 was to be given him outright and $57,300 was to be held for him in trust. And in the case of the nun, Louise, her entire share of the estate was to be held in trust for the following uses: "to pay her the net income therefrom for the term of her natural life," and upon her death to pay out of her estate $7,500 to be divided equally among the French relatives mentioned at the beginning of the will. "But should my daughter Louise leave the order and return to the world, then I order and direct my Trustees to hold her estate and pay over the same as I have ordered in the case of her other sisters."

Michel evidently feared his hard-earned money might fall into the hands of fortune hunters, so he further ordered that "the incomes arising out of said estates of my daughters shall be paid to each of them for their and each of their sole and separate use... clear from all debts and liabilities whatsoever of any husband or future husband." "And it is my wish and desire," he went on, "and I here solemnly admonish my daughters to retain the monies which I have ordered and directed to be paid to them subject to their own control and would advise them in investing the same always to have and take particular care as to the security of the *principal* sum invested, rather than to any larger interest or income supposed to be derivable therefrom. And on their marriage they can invest the same or such part thereof as they may deem fitting and proper, in a dwelling house and furniture if they so desire, always retaining the title to the same in their own name and subject to their own control."

Michel had loaned his two younger sons money to buy their seats on the New York Stock Exchange. So that these sums would not be charged against them in the settlement and partition of his estate, he excused their debts, ordering, however, that on the death of Louise they would be excluded from any share of her estate.

As for the North Broad Street property, after the term of two years, during which Zénaïde, Alexine, and Mary were to remain living there, the house and land were to be sold and the proceeds divided equally among his surviving children.

And so Michel provided for the economic security of the family he had founded, giving away what had cost him a lifetime of relentless effort to accumulate. The will was signed on November 24, 1873. Two months later his heart condition took a turn for the worse, and by March 1874 he was clearly failing.

Confined by his doctors to his house, Michel watched the last spring of his life flower from his library window. There he would sit, peering quietly at the garden that had occupied so much of his retirement, observing the budding of his peach trees, the first bright leaves sprouting on his grapevines. Doctors would come and go. There were consultations with the family in the hallway. Zénaïde took charge of the patient, assisted by Mary, Alexine, and the servants. Emma and Frank Drexel came to see the old man regularly, along with Thérèse and Jonathan Patterson, and Lizzie and her husband. Even Eustache was around, having come from California as soon as he received word his father's health had begun to fail. On weekends John and Michel would come down from New York with Carrie and John, Jr., and Louise would arrive from Eden Hall. By late May the patient's condition had deteriorated seriously and the doctors ordered him to remain in bed. His children's visits became more frequent. John and Carrie moved to Torresdale for the summer and at Michel's request nine-year-old John, Jr., went to stay at North Broad Street. Zénaïde kept the French relatives informed of Michel's condition in a stream of correspondence that still exists. The French Benevolent Society sent emissaries to visit their ailing president. A parade of visitors came and went from the brownstone mansion.

The Last Visitor finally came on the afternoon of June 9. Philadelphia had just begun the erection of its massive Victorian City Hall, with its thirty-seven-foot-high statue of William Penn.

The United States Centennial was two years away. Michel, eighty-two, had begun his long retreat from Waterloo almost fifty-nine years before.

Family tradition holds that all of Michel's ten children were present at his deathbed. After the last sacraments were administered, Louise stepped forward and placed a silver crucifix in her father's hand, which he held over his massive chest until it suddenly toppled to one side.

The funeral was held in St. Mary's, the old brick church in which Washington and Lafayette and "the armies of the Republic and of France" had celebrated their victory over Cornwallis at Yorktown. It had been the Bouvier parish ever since the family had moved from Front Street. After the ceremony Michel was laid to rest in the adjoining churchyard, in a vault he had reserved for his family. Already buried there were his wife, her parents, brothers, and sister, and the two children she and Michel had lost, Joseph and Josephine.

Not long after Michel's death, several memorials appeared in his honor. One of these was a eulogy written by a close friend, Joseph R. Chandler, under the pseudonym "Senex," subsequently translated into French by Emma Drexel and printed and bound and circulated privately among family and friends. It began with a quotation from Lamartine:

> Ces contemporains de nos âmes,
> Ces mains qu'enchaînait notre main,
> Ces frères, ces amis, ces femmes,
> Nous abandonnent en chemin.

And went on to say, in part, that:

> Mr. Bouvier in dying left for disposition what would, when he was a young man, have been regarded as a palatial fortune. Yet he commenced his career with none of that patrimony which too often is the cause of early death or miserable old age. Mr. Bouvier commenced business with the grander capital of integrity, industry, economy, enterprise and perseverance . . . Rallying under one difficulty after another, he acquired faith in his ability to enter upon undertakings which involved greater risk and demanded augmented knowledge of men and business...

All entering upon a career of business may profit from the example of Mr. Bouvier and even though failing of as complete a success, may gather at least a sufficiency for an honorable old age and for a testimony that virtue, industry and talent may never greatly fail in this country . . . Mr. Bouvier diminished the harassings of business with the undisturbed peace of domestic intercourse, and had a pride in acknowledging that whatever success followed well laid plans of trade, all that succeeded was sweetened if not increased by cordial home participation in its benefits . . . To prove that devotion to and great success in business is not incompatible with the richest domestic enjoyments, I may add that Mr. Bouvier found the opportunity of enjoying the wealth he had acquired in the affectionate devotion of an accomplished wife, and in the loving obedience of his numerous children.

Other memorials included two altars and a street. Louise and Emma installed one of the altars in the chapel at Eden Hall and MC raised the other in St. Patrick's. The one in St. Patrick's would no doubt have amazed the old cabinetmaker had he been given the chance, like Browning's bishop, to see it before he died. On his trip to Europe with Emma, he had admired such altars in the cathedrals of France—monuments dedicated to saints, cardinals, and kings. That one like them would some day be raised to his memory must surely never have crossed his mind. The altar to Michel and Louise Vernou Bouvier in St. Patrick's Cathedral is impressive both in size and in workmanship. Three elaborately carved Gothic spires rise up above a crucifix and niches holding statues of two saints. To the left of the cross stands, in the words of an accompanying plaque, "St. Louis, Crusader and King of France"; to the right, "St. Michel, Archangel, Commander of the armies of God against the powers of evil." The altar rises against a background of stained-glass windows that color its cool white surface with splashes of red, blue, and gold. There are bronze plaques on the chapel walls honoring Michel, his wife, and the donor.

To the Select and Common Councils of Philadelphia is due a more prosaic memorial to Michel, the naming of a street after him. It runs between Seventeenth and Eighteenth and is pronounced by Philadelphians "Bouveer" Street.

Michel's name survives, however, in more than marble, bronze, and sign paint. Five descendants bear his name, and throughout the Rhône Valley, from Valence to Pont-Saint-Esprit, his life is a legend and his name a symbol of *bonne chance*. In the cafés and village squares the old-timers talk of two brothers who went to America, one of whom remained, one who returned to France; one who left each of his ten children "a million dollars," and one who died in a hospital for the poor; one whose great-great-granddaughter became First Lady of the United States, and one whose descendants remained artisans and storekeepers in the villages of the Rhône. Being realists, the Spiripontains and the Valentinois do not ascribe any particular merit to the one or demerit to the other. For two millennia, since the reign of Augustus, the Gallo-Romans of Provence have seen men and families rise and fall on the wheel of fortune. If Napoleon had won at Waterloo . . . If Wellington . . . If the Terror hadn't . . . The old-timers of Pont-Saint-Esprit like to emphasize the if's and but's to inquisitive tourists. "Ce Bouvier," they will say, was very lucky, "un homme qui a eu de la chance."

# PART TWO

## *Birth of an Image*

### THE SECOND AND THIRD
### GENERATIONS

### [1 8 6 9 - 1 9 3 5]

# I

AFTER MICHEL DIED, THE FOCAL POINT OF THE BOUVIER FAMILY shifted from Philadelphia to New York, where John and MC had gone to seek *their* fortunes. In leaving the greene countrie towne for Wall Street, Michel's sons were unconsciously confirming the fact that New York had supplanted Philadelphia as the financial capital of the nation.

Wall Street's gradual conquest of Chestnut Hill had begun in the 1820s when New York banks and brokers successfully financed the construction of the Erie Canal. Soon the financing of other notable ventures, most important of which were the railroads, became concentrated in New York. It wasn't until 1841, however, that Philadelphia's financial preeminence was seriously threatened. In that year President Andrew Jackson refused to recharter the Philadelphia-based Bank of the United States. There followed a technological development that further undermined the financial importance of the haven city: in 1844 the Magnetic Telegraph Company extended a line between Philadelphia and Manhattan Island and suddenly there was no longer any need for two separate securities auctions. It was now only a matter of time before the telegraph would connect Wall Street with all major United States cities and Chestnut Hill would go into a permanent decline. By 1861 Philadelphia had clearly slipped into second place and New York had become, in the words of Oliver Wendell Holmes, "the tip of the tongue that laps up the cream of the commerce of a continent."

It did not take long for the Bouvier brothers to realize what had happened. As soon as circumstances permitted, they headed straight for the top of the bottle. Both had gotten their start in finance through their brother-in-law, Frank Drexel. The Bouvier-Drexel alliance turned out to be one of Michel, Sr.'s most successful speculations. John had begun his financial career with Drexel, Winthrop & Co. in New York, and MC, after serving an apprenticeship with Drexel & Co. in Philadelphia, was transferred, at his own request, to the firm's New York branch. This organization was controlled by Frank's brother, Anthony, who would soon expand his banking empire by joining forces with J. P. Morgan.

After cutting their financial teeth with Drexel, the Bouvier brothers struck out on their own and bought seats on the New York Stock Exchange. The Exchange had been established on May

1, 1869, when Wall Street's two rival securities markets, the Old Board and the Open Board of Brokers, united through what came to be known as the Consolidation Act, a merger that increased the number of memberships by 354 seats, bringing the total to 1,060; provided for a new constitution; created a new governing committee; and, in general, made for a greatly revitalized exchange. A few days after the consolidation, on May 8, John V. Bouvier bought his seat, and then, on June 25, MC followed suit. John set himself up as "John V. Bouvier, Banker and Broker," with offices at 26 Broad Street, and MC founded the brokerage firm of "Bouvier & Wallace," John Wallace having been a colleague of his at Drexel. Later John entered into limited partnership with MC, who soon proved to be something of a boy wonder on Wall Street.

Ostensibly the Bouvier brothers moved to New York to take advantage of the superior business opportunities New York offered. However, there may have been another, unstated, reason: the impenetrability of Philadelphia society. By 1840, Philadelphia's upper class had become a closed corporation, an elite that would not admit anyone whose roots did not extend deep into the eighteenth century—which, of course, had been the era of Philadelphia supremacy. As Nathaniel Burt expressed it: "Let vulgar Washington take over politics, and vulgar New York take over finance . . . let even school-marmish Boston be first in books. Philadelphia would no longer be first in anything, but it would at least be Philadelphian." And being Philadelphian meant, among other things, closing the social doors to anyone whose family had not been prominent in Philadelphia when Philadelphia was first in politics, finance, and books.

The solidarity and exclusiveness of Philadelphia's upper class must have frustrated the Bouviers, and people like them. No matter what one accomplished, no matter what one overcame, admission was denied unless one had the right ancestors. Michel Bouvier had become an eminent craftsman and manufacturer, made a million dollars, erected a magnificent home, contributed generously to charities, raised and educated ten remarkable children. Nevertheless, old Main Line families such as the Biddles and the Ingersolls and the Cadwaladers would not be likely to invite him and his wife to dinner. Sidney Fisher, the distinguished Philadelphia diarist, who married an Ingersoll, expressed the feelings of his class in regard to newcomers when he wrote: "I always feel socially superior to a man who is not a gentleman by birth and I never yet saw one who had risen to a higher position whose mind and character, as well as his manners, did not show the taint of his origins." Correspondingly, a New York woman residing in Philadelphia in 1896 remarked: "Personality counts for less, here, than anywhere else in the United States."

As a result of this emphasis on heredity and tradition as an absolute prerequisite for upper-class status, the tide of newcomers to Philadelphia inevitably flowed to New York, and the haven city became the one Northern metropolis in which native-born Americans remained not only in the majority but in firm control of their city's political and economic life. The Jews, the Irish, and the Italians might succeed in dominating Boston and New York, but they would not get very far in Philadelphia. That had been made abundantly clear as early as May 1844, when the Native American Party—which aimed at preventing further immigration to the United States—burned down St. Augustine's Church, the Bouvier parish at the time, as well as two other Catholic churches, and so demoralized the Irish, whose homes were also burned, that many of them eventually packed up and left.

There was little choice, then, for a newcomer who aspired to the city's highest social stratum. No matter how talented he was, unless he married a Biddle or an Ingersoll or a Cadwalader—and few newcomers ever succeeded in marrying into these families— he had either to settle for less or to leave. In this way Philadelphia society became increasingly one of maintenance whereas New York society became more and more one of attainment. Sidney Fisher expressed the difference between the two societies this way: "The first unpretending, elegant and friendly, containing many persons not rich, but few whose families have not held the same station for many generations, which circumstance has produced an air of refinement, dignity and simplicity of manner, wanting in New York. In New York wealth is the only thing that admits, and it will admit a shoe-black, poverty the only thing that excludes and it would exclude grace, wit and worth."

Thus, in moving to New York, the Bouvier brothers increased not only their chances of making money but also their chances of full social acceptance. Had they remained in Philadelphia, it is unlikely that they would ever have graduated to the Main Line.

When M. C. and J. V. Bouvier arrived on Wall Street, the area was changing rapidly. The old stables, taverns, and coffee houses were being replaced by financial offices, brokerages, and banks. The rival stock auctions were being consolidated. Along South Street, at the tip of Manhattan Island, the loading and unloading of cargo ships was growing increasingly hectic as more and more vessels from all parts of the world crowded the Battery's wharfs. On a typical business day the traffic in the financial district was intense, as hundreds of horse-drawn carriages rattled down Broadway and its narrow tributaries, leaving silk-hatted financiers at their offices.

It was an exciting place to be for an ambitious young man. Like electronics and aerospace in the 1960s, finance in the 1860s and 1870s was a glamour industry that attracted the ablest men in the nation. It was likewise a perilous place. The economic climate after the Civil War was highly unpredictable, speculation was unscrupulous, a few slick operators had much too much power in the markets, and consequently a talented but unwary young man could just as easily be ruined as be enriched.

The activities of the pools were particularly treacherous. A few wealthy traders would get together and bid up a stock, attracting gullible investors to the issue. Then, when the price got high enough to net the pool operators substantial profits, they would sell in concert, leaving their followers high and dry. There were also very wide, unexpected, swings in the market. Four months after the Bouvier brothers became members of the Exchange, Jay Gould's partially successful attempt to corner the gold market precipitated a crash the severity of which was not to be duplicated until 1929. Then, in the early 1870s, the railroad and mining crazes bulled up the market again, only to cause it to crash once more, in September 1873, a collapse which in turn inaugurated five years of bear markets and widespread business recession.

The 1870s also saw the formation of the great trusts and were a time of widespread political corruption. A conspiracy to rob the city of most of its revenue, the Tweed Ring, was exposed in 1872, two years after the Brooklyn Bridge was begun and a year after the population of greater New York reached one million. Meanwhile, magnates like Carnegie and Rockefeller were carving out their industrial kingdoms. In 1875 Carnegie completed his giant steel plant on the Monongahela, the largest in the world at the time. By 1882 Standard Oil had emerged as the first great trust, with John D. Rockefeller in almost complete control of oil refining in America.

During these turbulent times the dominant figures on Wall Street were Cornelius Vanderbilt, Daniel Drew, "Jubilee" Jim Fisk, and Jay Gould, all of whom engaged in practices that would be considered illegal today. Drew, for instance, in his Erie Railroad speculations, was not above printing new shares of the company whenever he needed them to cover his short sales. Fisk and Gould were notorious pool operators whose market machinations earned them fortunes at the expense of hundreds of smaller, unsuspecting investors. And Cornelius Vanderbilt, like Drew, was a master at watering stock.

In order to prosper in these shark-infested waters, a young man had to gain the support and protection of at least one of the bigger fish, and so the Bouvier brothers remained close to their former boss, Anthony J. Drexel.

Anthony Drexel was not a predator, but he had an exceptionally keen financial head and did business with some of the biggest and most voracious sharks on the street. In 1870 he and his brother Frank merged the Drexel firms in Philadelphia, New York, and Paris with J. P. Morgan's firms in New York and London, to form Drexel, Morgan & Co., an organization that in ten years would receive the major share of the Rothschilds' business in America and would obtain control of most of the Vanderbilt interests, becoming, in the words of the *Commercial and Financial Chronicle,* "one of the leading banking houses of the world."

The Bouvier brothers thus came to know J. P. Morgan and received a good deal of business from the new firm, including the management of some of the Vanderbilt accounts. MC would service the accounts, attending to such matters as investment counsel and analysis, while John would execute orders on the Stock Exchange floor. From all indications, it was the successful management of Vanderbilt interests, in collaboration with Drexel, Morgan, that established the Bouvier brothers' reputation on Wall Street.

John and MC were also deeply involved in discharging the responsibilities their father had left them. As co-executors of Michel's estate, along with Frank Drexel and Zénaïde, they were entrusted with liquidating his real-estate holdings in Philadelphia, which consisted of some sixty acres within the corporate limits of the city, in order to satisfy all his bequests. Eventually MC became managing trustee of the estate, shouldering most of the paperwork and making most of the decisions. His seven sisters gave him the responsibility of investing their $50,000 cash bequests; he also took charge of selecting the investments for the money left to them in trust. Michel, Sr., would have approved.

With seats on the New York Stock Exchange, powerful Wall Street connections, and $82,300 apiece in capital, the Bouvier brothers were launched in the New York financial world by 1870s. Starting at the same time, with near-identical advantages, their careers soon diverged. MC had a touch of genius when it came to making money, and before long he was overtaking John in the race for riches. In time he would pile up a fortune that would justify his father's faith in his abilities.

Although competition between John and MC was intense, the brothers remained devoted to each other, enjoying a close, affectionate relationship all their lives. The two were very different, however. John was essentially a family man with simple tastes and moderate ambitions. He lived for his wife and son, his business being only a means to promote his domestic happiness. For MC, however, business was all. A loner, with unusual talents and powerful ambitions, he was determined to make a fortune and was willing to sacrifice most other interests to that goal. While John was at home, enjoying life with his beloved wife and son, MC would still be poring over company reports and new bond issues in his office. John was not very imaginative or venturesome in either his business or his family life. He rarely took a gamble and was not very good at picking winners in securities. MC, on the other hand, was willing occasionally to go out on a limb. He enjoyed taking risks and had his father's ability to recognize a promising investment opportunity when he saw one. John was very American in his tastes and preferences, whereas MC was more European. On a trip to Europe with his wife, his sister Mary, and his son in 1871 John wrote his mother and brother that he did not take to French life at all and was continually homesick for America. The French, in his opinion, were a bunch of self-indulgent time wasters who spent their days idling in the cafés and parks. Mary liked them, but he found them "useless." Anxious to forget his French origins and be as American as possible, he made no effort to visit Pont-Saint-Esprit or look up any of his French relatives, though he had two aunts and several first cousins living in the Midi at the time. MC, however, loved France and made several trips to Pont-Saint-Esprit during his lifetime. Accepting his French background, he collected French paintings and antiques, kept in touch with his French relatives, and even insisted on employing French servants. Physically there were also marked differences between the two brothers: John was dark and slender and plain in both manner and dress; MC was tall and fair, with elegant manners and a taste for stylish clothes.

While their mother and father were alive, the Bouvier brothers would visit the B-Hive in Philadelphia on weekends. A correspondence between MC and his mother has survived from this period. The letters reveal the mother's deep anxiety for her sons' well-being and success, and the father's concern for the perpetuation of his name and his wealth through his sons. Michel, Sr., scrupulously collected interest from John and MC on loans he had made them, and when John decided to join MC's firm he demanded to see "the articles of agreement." On weekends a carriage would meet the Bouvier brothers at the North Philadelphia depot and take them to the family home, where Zenney, Allie, and Moll would be on hand to greet them. Often they would drive out for the day to Emma Drexel's estate in Torresdale. Occasionally Zenney, Allie, and Moll would come to New York, and MC and John would take them to parties and try to get eligible men interested in them. MC's visits to Philadelphia became more frequent after his father's death. As managing trustee of Michel's estate, he not only had to attend to the liquidation of his father's Philadelphia real estate but also had to look after the interests of his three unmarried sisters.

MC did well with the sale of the real estate, and before long he and his co-trustees were able to pay each of the brothers and sisters the $50,000 cash bequests and set up the $32,500 trust funds. MC invested his own $50,000 in common stocks and apparently did extremely well. By 1880, after a little over a decade on Wall Street, he was rich enough, at thirty-three, to buy a four-story, twenty-room brownstone on West Forty-sixth Street, just off Fifth Avenue, in which he installed himself and his three unmarried sisters and in which the four were to reside the rest of their lives. Two years later the B-Hive was sold to La Salle College for $67,500 (roughly $245,000 today), and the proceeds were divided equally among Michel's ten children. It is estimated that at the time of the sale MC was worth over $500,000, and he was only thirty-five. John, however, at thirty-nine, was not nearly as prosperous. His investments had not appreciated as much as his younger brother's and he was still living in the small apartment at 19 West Twenty-fourth Street that he had moved into in 1877. A document that has survived from November 7, 1886, reveals the state his business relationship with MC had come to by that date:

> To M. C. Bouvier:
> In consideration of the advance of fifteen thousand dollars and the generous spirit that actuated the same, I herein agree to confine myself to the Commission business for the period of two years, unless during said term I shall have returned the advance.
>
> John V. Bouvier

As it turned out, John did confine himself to the commission business from then on, becoming what is known on the Street as a "two-dollar broker," or a broker for other brokers, while MC went on to establish his own banking and brokerage firm, "M. C. Bouvier & Co.," destined to become one of the most prosperous and respected smaller houses on Wall Street. It would appear that John had not done very well as an investment advisor and had not been particularly adept at bringing new accounts into the firm, so MC advanced him $15,000 and told him to confine himself to the commission business, in order to get him out of his hair. John's inability to strike it rich on Wall Street was compensated, however, by an idyllic home life. From all accounts, he and Carrie were deeply in love and were absorbed in the bringing up of their only child, John, Jr. Considering the history of the family as a whole, John's role turned out to be as important as MC's. MC might have made the money, but John and Carrie produced the family heir. If it hadn't been for the birth of John, Jr., the Bouvier name would have died out in the second generation.

Although great success eluded him, John managed to earn a comfortable living for his family, and he and Carrie easily won social acceptance in their adopted city. In 1880 the John V. Bouviers were included in the New York "Society List" and they made the first edition of the Social Register, along with MC and his sisters, in 1889. Since MC did not appear in the original "Society List," it may be that John's inclusion was chiefly due to Caroline Ewing, whose family had been socially prominent since Revolutionary times. At any rate, once they had established themselves in New York, the Bouviers finally gained the unqualified acceptance that had been denied them in Philadelphia.

Even though the family was now divided between Philadelphia and New York, the Bouviers in the mid-1880s remained as closely knit as ever, the various branches coming together frequently for large family reunions. The Philadelphia contingent consisted of Louise Bouvier, Dame du Sacré Coeur, the Pattersons, the Dixons, and the Drexels, with the millionaire Drexels as the focal point, while the New York branch was composed of MC, Alexine, Mary, Zénaïde, John, Carrie, and John, Jr., with MC's Forty-sixth Street brownstone as family headquarters. During the summer the entire clan would occasionally gather at Emma Drexel's ninety-acre estate in Torresdale. During the winter there would be reunions at MC's house. Frank Drexel and MC, the two financial wizards of the family, kept close watch over the clan's money and under their guidance the Bouviers' finances prospered. It was a family not unlike the Kennedys of the 1960s: numerous, Catholic, newly rich, ambitious, and united.

The only member of the family who was not in the swim was Eustache. Eustache was a rebel and an adventurer and, so far as he was concerned, his brothers and sisters were pleasant people but a bit dull. Not much is known about Eustache. Since he was the black sheep of a very respectable and status-conscious family, future generations were kept in ignorance of his activities. Consequently, scores of legends materialized about him. It was whispered that he had several illegitimate children, that he had been involved in violent gold-rush brawls, that he was an alcoholic, that he gambled away enormous sums of money. None of these rumors has ever been substantiated. From what little information has trickled down through the years, only a bare outline of his life can be reconstructed. As the first Bouvier to be born in America, Eustache was his immigrant father's first hope for the continuation of his business and his family. Michel had named him after his father and his brother. Eustache pére had three sons himself whom he had named Eustache, all of whom died before reaching their majority, and his daughter had also had a Eustache who died young. Consequently, Michel's son was the only Eustache to survive. Since he died childless and in ill repute, the name died with him: no more Bouviers were to be given a name so accursed.

Eustache Bouvier, born June 4, 1824, had the typical characteristics of a Gemini: he was unpredictable, inconstant, and rebellious. The loss of his mother when he was only two years old accentuated these tendencies, increasing his restlessness and making him a lifelong searcher, never satisfied, always on the move. It was his additional misfortune to be the son of a man who, early in his career, was tyrannical, hard-driving, and ruthless, a father who expected his son to measure up, to follow in his footsteps, continue his business, and perpetuate his name.

Eustache loved clothes, money, and women and hated steady jobs. By the time he was thirty he was known as a flashy dresser, a free spender, and a tireless Don Juan, three avocations his sober, frugal father couldn't accept. Regular hours and routine work were abhorrent to him. He would make his money fast or not at all. Consequently, he was repeatedly engaged in get-rich-quick schemes of one kind or another, risking his father's hard-earned capital in ventures that rarely paid off.

In 1851, at twenty-seven, Eustache rushed to California, along with thousands of other Americans, to try to find gold. He remained there more than twenty years, subsisting, it appears, on checks his father periodically mailed him. Only three references to his California days have survived, but they are sufficient to give us an idea of his fate.

Writing to her French cousin, François Baudichon, in May 1866, Zénaïde gave the following news of her older brother:

> Three weeks ago we received a very interesting letter from our brother Eustache who has been living in California for the past fifteen years. He does not write us very often so we are very happy when we hear from him. He will probably pay us a brief visit this autumn. His nature is too inconstant to remain always at Father's house. We are anxious to see him. He has led a very different life since he became separated from us. Fifteen years makes quite a difference in a man's appearance, and the crude life he has led in the mines has no doubt aged him prematurely.

And in a letter from Louise Vernou to MC, dated September 15, 1870, we find this brief reference to the prodigal son:

> Zennie received a very nice letter from Eustache this morning. As yet he has had no success in business. He talks of going to San Francisco to spend a week or two. I fear he will never make his fortune. It is much easier for him to spend, than make.

Again, on May 2, 1871, she wrote MC:

> Zennie has just received a nice letter from Eustache in California acknowledging the receipt of Father's cheque which I fear will not do much good towards advancing his interests.

Louise turned out to be right. Eustache did not strike gold in California and his father's checks evidently did not advance his interests very much, for he returned to the B-Hive in 1873, a year after his mother's death, broke as usual. This time, however, he stayed for a while. Several letters from young J. V. Bouvier, Jr., to his mother have survived from the years 1873 and 1874 and they repeatedly refer to his erratic uncle: " . . . Uncle Stash came over to night and brought some storeberys with him." "Uncle Stach took Aunt Allie to the depot." "I went to the Simmons and the Slocums with Uncle Stache last night." JVB, Jr., eight at the time, was staying at the B-Hive. Why did the wild, restless Eustache, hitherto always on the move, remain at 1240 North Broad Street during the last year of his father's life? The explanation might have to do with filial duty and affection, but more likely the reason was money. Eustache was forty-nine when his father contracted his final illness in 1874, and he had gotten nowhere financially. It is quite possible that Michel had written him out of his will or left him only a token legacy. Or if he hadn't, perhaps Eustache thought he had. At any rate, Eustache was out of favor with his father, and he had to make amends. And so, toward the end of his father's life, Eustache attempted a reconciliation with Michel, remaining by the old man's side, making himself useful, trying to get back into the family's good graces. The policy worked. On November 24, 1873, Michel wrote his last will and testament, excluding Eustache as an executor but leaving him the same legacy as his other children. And on June 9, 1874, Eustache inherited more money than a lifetime of get-rich-quick schemes had netted him. Michel, however, had shrewdly left most of the money in trust, and so Eustache had to endure the humiliation of receiving his income from those unadventurous younger brothers of his, MC and John, and that dull banker type, Frank Drexel.

Shortly after collecting his cash bequest, Eustache took off again, this time for Australia. What he did in Australia can only be guessed at. All we know is that his religious maiden sisters, Zenney, Allie, and Moll, were always praying for their wild, anticonformist older brother's safety and salvation: their letters during the late seventies refer time and again to his mad efforts to make a fortune Down Under, and how worried they were about him. More than likely, Eustache was looking for gold also in Australia, the nuggets having eluded him in California. And no doubt he went through his $25,000. Throughout the late seventies and early eighties he would occasionally return to Philadelphia and New York, now in splendor, now begging for charity. MC, Zenney, Allie, and Moll in later years remembered him appearing without warning at their New York brownstone, dressed to the teeth, staying a few weeks, taking out chorus girls, buying new clothes, telling his relatives fantastic stories of how he was on the verge of making a colossal fortune on some mining speculation, then asking them if they could spare a few dollars. His sisters could never get over how charming he was, how fun-loving and carefree, though he had led such a "useless," "wasteful" life. As Catholic as they were, they fully expected the hell fires to anticipate the wastrel's death. When he would take off again, however, after one of his brief, storytelling, money-begging visits, they would suddenly find they missed their profligate brother terribly. Then, as they mused over his stories, other stories would be generated and a new cycle of rumors about the Wild One would make the rounds of the nine white sheep in the family, compelling Louise, R.S.C.J., to add a few extra Hail Marys to her daily devotions.

Eustache was fifty-six when his thirty-three-year-old brother, MC, bought his brownstone on Forty-sixth Street. MC by that time was well on his way to becoming a millionaire and Eustache was still trying to make his fortune. He did not give up until he was incapacitated: it took his last illness finally to extinguish his dreams. Returning to New York in 1882, still unmarried, after failing to find gold in Australia, he was stricken with tuberculosis in January 1883 and had to be confined to a room on the third floor of MC's brownstone, where he died three years later, at sixty-two. The funeral of the first American-born Bouvier was held at Old St. Mary's in Philadelphia and was attended by all his brothers and sisters. He was then laid to rest beside his father in the Bouvier vault in the adjoining church yard. After a lifetime of filial rebellion, he had finally returned to the fold.

Eustache was out of step both with his times and with the milieu in which he was brought up. If he hadn't had the typical second-generation American's prejudice against his father's homeland, he would probably have been better off in Southern France, where later generations of Bouviers would occasionally go to play. Certainly the new age of industry and high finance, demanding individualism but also steady application and the perfection of professional skills, was not his. Nor was the inhibiting moralism of the times suited to his hedonistic temperament. Though he searched for gold all his life, the gilded age was not for him. His entire life was a reaction against what his family and his society expected of him. His father's early hours and philosophy of hard work were repugnant to him. So were his dynastic ambitions. His stepmother's withering Catholicism also irritated him. As for those younger brothers of his, their conventional Wall Street success didn't make *him* stand up and applaud. Think of all the fun they missed!

Eustache's name died with him, but his disreputable memory would often be invoked by Bouvier parents as a warning to children who in any way resembled him. And there were several in whom his traits reappeared. Since he died before they were born, the fourth and fifth generations would remember him only by his swarthy portrait at M. C. Bouvier & Co. It hung in one of the "back offices" and was used as a dart board by the clerks and messengers.

# II

WHILE JOHN AND MC WERE SEEKING THEIR FORTUNES ON WALL Street, and Eustache was seeking his in the gold fields of California, their seven sisters remained in Philadelphia. The oldest, Thérèse, wife of Jonathan Patterson, Jr., busied herself with her ménage of seven children. The second oldest, Elizabeth, wife of Joseph E. Dixon, had her family of three girls to look after. Louise had been a Sacred Heart nun for almost two decades. Zénaïde, Alexine, and Mary, still unmarried, lived at 1240 North Broad Street. And Emma, as the wife of Francis Drexel, had commenced a unique chapter of Bouvier family history, a career of singular devotion to charity and the Catholic Church, which would one day result in a missionary movement of national significance.

Of all Michel's children, Emma had the greatest influence on her generation. Her story and that of her children has a strange ring for our worldly, mid-twentieth-century ears. Here was a family of enormous wealth whose members shunned the world of fashion and pleasure to found a private civil-rights movement before the NAACP even existed.

What gave Emma Bouvier and her daughters this singleminded dedication? It would be fashionable today to assign a non-altruistic motive: guilt at having received so much for so little; desire for approval; a feeling of power over the oppressed. Perhaps all these were part of the equation. The ultimate cause, however, was the thorough religious grounding they received during their formative years.

Louise Vernou had given her daughters a severe Catholic upbringing. Their formal education, from the first through the twelfth grades, was received at Sacred Heart schools, first the convent on Walnut Street, then Eden Hall. So thoroughly had Louise instilled the doctrines and practices of Catholicism in her children that, inevitably, religion dominated their lives. Thérèse and Lizzie immersed their families in Church activities. Louise became a nun. Zénaïde, Alexine, and Mary, remaining spinsters and daily communicants throughout their lives, lived as nuns without taking the veil, boasting in their old age that they would die virgins. And Emma and her children would establish convents and Catholic schools for Indians and Negroes all over the United States.

The immense work of charity which Emma Bouvier Drexel and her children undertook was made possible by the immense financial resources of the Drexel family. The founder of the family, Francis Martin Drexel, was born the same year as Michel Bouvier, 1792, in Dornbirn, a small village in the Austrian Tyrol. A painter by profession, he emigrated to America in 1817, settling in Philadelphia, where he opened a studio at 131 South Front Street, and began painting portraits. In his own words, he did "middle well." After a while he married the daughter of a grocery-store owner, Catharine Hookey, by whom he had two sons, Francis and Anthony. Drexel senior, however, became dissatisfied with his earnings in Philadelphia and decided to try his hand at painting in South America. Leaving his family behind, he traveled throughout Ecuador, Peru, Chile, and Argentina from 1826 to 1830 and throughout Mexico from 1835 to 1837, painting landscapes and portraits. Again, he did "middle well" financially, but "middle well" was not well enough for him. And so in 1837, at the age of forty-five, Francis Martin Drexel metamorphosed into a banker . . . and made a fortune. A Gauguin in reverse, he abandoned canvas and palette and opened an exchange brokerage in Louisville, where he began trading in North American currencies. The following year he moved his business to Philadelphia, where he soon engaged in lucrative transactions in foreign money and in the acquisition of foreign gold and silver in redemption of the accumulated notes of interior banks. Taking his two sons into the business, before long he was financially strong enough to open the banking firm of Drexel & Co. and offer monetary aid to the United States government. In 1847 the Drexels helped float loans to cover the cost of the Mexican-American War, and in 1861 they supplied vast amounts of gold to help finance the Union Army. By the time Francis Martin Drexel died in 1863, he had accumulated a fortune of over a million dollars.

His sons, Francis and Anthony, who inherited the business, were to multiply that fortune into one of the largest in America. The conservative Francis and the adventuresome Anthony proved to be perfect counterparts and, together with such future titans of high finance as J. Pierpont Morgan and E. T. Stotesbury, they built a banking empire that became one of the great financial institutions of the Western world.

In 1854, nine years before his father died, Francis A. Drexel married Hannah Langstreth, by whom he had two daughters, Elizabeth and Katharine. Hannah Drexel did not survive the strain of Katharine's birth, dying two weeks later. Two years after her death, Francis married Emma Bouvier, then a young woman of twenty-seven. The Drexels and the Bouviers had a lot in common. Not only were the founders of both clans born in Europe in the same year, but they both came from small villages and families of very modest means; both had been involved in Napoleon's wars, albeit on opposite sides; both had begun careers as artisans; both emigrated to Philadelphia, and both made the transition from artisan to businessman successfully, each amassing a fortune. For some time Michel, Sr., and the elder Drexel had been close friends. A common destiny and a reciprocal admiration bound their two families together.

Emma Bouvier was considered a perfect match for the serious, hardworking, and recently bereaved Francis. A young woman of keen intelligence and high moral standards, she gave promise of being a good stepmother to Drexel's two daughters. A photograph taken of her in the 1860s shows the thoughtful, ascetic face of a woman too sensitive and intelligent ever to be really happy. And in fact Emma's temperament inclined toward melancholy: she had to struggle against unwarranted depression and irritability all her life. She had a high forehead, penetrating eyes, a prominent nose, thin, unsensual lips, and a slightly receding chin. Taking after her Scotch-Irish ancestors rather than the French side of the family, her severe, puritanical appearance commanded more respect than it did compliments.

Emma and Francis went to Europe on their honeymoon and one of the places they visited was Pont-Saint-Esprit. Francis could be stuffy on occasion. After recording in a wedding-trip diary, in which he hardly ever mentioned his bride, his initial embarrassment at the Spiripontain custom of kissing relatives on both cheeks, he wrote:

> After considerable management we retired at 9 o'clock and did not rise until 8 o'clock next morning. It took us long to dress and get ready, grandma having delicately hinted that we should appear in our Sunday-go-to-meeting clothes, and with the privilege that age should always take suggested the kind of dress that Emma should wear. We were

the grand relations and we were to be shown off for the benefit of our own relations and the gratification of the villagers who with open mouths and staring eyes pressed to the doors and windows as we passed with our good friends through the narrow streets.

Describing the surrounding countryside, the fastidious Philadelphia banker noted:

> . . . The productions of the country are nasty smells which dwell continually in the air—black hogs on stilts, mulberry trees, silk worms, lizards, Luzerne wheat rope, soled shoes--men pushing go-carts while playing the fiddle.

The couple spent two days at Pont-Saint-Esprit, wandering through the village, visiting relatives in the countryside, inspecting silk factories in a neighboring town, then decided to continue on their travels. The head of the family of relatives, however, who was probably Etienne Bouchard, second husband of Emma's Aunt Elizabeth, insisted that they stay one day longer:

> and it was a difficult matter to resist his solicitations joined with that of all our good relatives, but we stood our ground firmly to depart at the time we fixed, namely 8:30 next morning . . . Our dinner this evening degenerated from that provided the previous day—no more meat than a roasted fowl stuffed with black olives and trimmed with bacon being provided—(the day before the dinner had consisted of about ten courses many made with sweet oil and but few vegetables)—At 10 o'clock after having repeatedly hinted that we were fatigued, our kind escort left us alone to retire, smoking a bad cigar in our chamber, being the last one out, having previously offered us better apartments, and sent us an eiderdown cover. We arose at 5 1/4 o'clock May 4 and packed up, took a light breakfast, performed the osculatory all around in the Pont-St.-Esprit fashion and stepped into the omnibus escorted to the depot by four of our kind friends.

On returning to America, Mr. and Mrs. Drexel settled in a large brownstone town house at 1503 Walnut Street, in which Emma, true to the tradition established by her mother, installed an oratory where she and her husband and their children were to pray almost every winter evening of their lives. Mr. Drexel was an accomplished organist and he often followed the prayers with a little Bach or Mozart. The Drexel home life was quiet, formal, and exceedingly reserved. Mr. Drexel rose early every morning and went to the bank, where he worked, with no more than an hour off for lunch, until six or seven in the evening. Mrs. Drexel, aided by a retinue of servants, looked after the children and managed a large household that usually included guests at dinner, who were served with an exacting etiquette by liveried butlers and secondmen. In October 1863, Emma gave birth to a daughter, Louise Bouvier Drexel, and a few years later the Drexels bought a ninety-acre farm at Torresdale. The site had been selected because of its nearness to the Sacred Heart convent where Emma's sister Louise was stationed. Emma remodeled the estate's old farmhouse into a mansion with a mansard roof, a covered porch across the entire front, and several new wings. Cottages were built for the servants, and a stable, a carriage house, and a barn were also constructed. The place abounded in old trees—oak, maple, pine, and elm—and there were gardens planted with larkspur, verbena, foxglove, and daisies. The estate was given the name St. Michel, after Michel Bouvier's patron saint. A statue of the saint carved in Caen stone was placed above the front door, and a stained-glass window representing him was installed in a recess at the head of the first flight of stairs. St. Michel remained the Drexels' summer home until Francis died in 1885, at which time it passed to his daughter Elizabeth and her husband, Walter George Smith. After their death, a church was built on the property, named the Shrine of the True Cross, in which almost the entire Drexel family was eventually interred, and the mansion became a mission center for the Sisters of the Blessed Sacrament, an institution founded by Francis's second oldest daughter, Katharine.

At both 1503 Walnut Street and St. Michel, Emma Drexel organized charities in which she gave her children conspicuous roles. Twice weekly, during the fall and winter, the poor gathered in the back yard of her Philadelphia brownstone to receive food, clothing, and financial assistance from "Lady Bountiful," as Emma came to be called, and her daughters Lizzie, Kate, and Louise. In a day when organized social services and professional social workers did not exist, these back-yard charity assemblies attracted a good deal of attention from the public and the press. They were called "The Dorcas," after Dorcas in the Acts of the Apostles, "full of good works and almsdeeds which she did." It is estimated that the Dorcas cost Emma Bouvier over $20,000 a year.

During the summer Emma had her daughters hold a school in the laundry at St. Michel for the children of poor farmers and men who worked around the place. Both the Dorcas and the summer school often were held at the same time as meetings of a very different order at the Drexel homes, meetings between Francis A. Drexel, Anthony J. Drexel, J. Pierpont Morgan, and E. T. Stotesbury, in which deals involving tens of millions were discussed and decided upon. In time, permission was obtained to hold mass at St. Michel, and visitors to the estate would witness the seemingly contradictory spectacle of a meeting of financial titans breaking up so the participants could attend a religious service or listen to Francis play a Bach fugue.

Charitable work, however, did not prevent the Drexels from taking frequent trips abroad. In 1874 Emma and Francis took their three daughters on a grand tour of Europe which included London, Paris, Switzerland, Austria, Italy, the Vatican, and the ritual visit to Pont-Saint-Esprit.

In Rome they had a lively audience with the Pope. The man who arranged the encounter, referred to in Louise's diary as "Monsieur L'Abbé," suggested that they present His Holiness with a new calotte. Accepting the suggestion, they bought a new white silk calotte from a shop on Piazza Minerva and went to the Vatican at the time specified. When Piux IX reached the Drexels, Louise stepped forward and said: "Très saint Pére, voulez-vous accepter cette calotte et me donner la vôtre?" Whereupon the Pope banteringly told the young girl that most likely hers wouldn't fit him and his wouldn't fit her. Then, as he acquiesced to the exchange, Johanna, the Drexels' maid, suddenly lunged forward and threw her arms around the Pope's knees, exclaiming, "Très Pater . . . Holy Father . . . praise God and His Blessed Mother . . . my eyes have seen our dear Lord himself." And the audience was temporarily disrupted as attendants led the poor woman from the room.

On their way back to Paris, the family made a detour to Emma's ancestral home. In a droll letter to her governess, Kate described the visit:

. . . Guess or reckon, Miss Cassidy, where the next morning's sun found the D. family. At the grand, the magnificent, the colossal little inn at PONT ST. ESPRIT! Now don't suppose that the Sun saw us only through the muddy windows of the Hôtel de l'Europe, for he condescended to follow us with his cheerful eye, to the little village church and there shone most brightly through the stained glass windows. You may imagine that dear grandfather was often in our mind during Mass, for this little church in which he used to pray when a mere child reminded us particularly of him.

After Mass, we, accompanied by Miss Louise Barry and some more of our relations (I won't tire you by naming), took a walk around the whole village and saw everything from the bridge under which one may observe the brown "gushing of the arrowy Rhône" to the cemetery where "the rude forefathers of the hamlet sleep." Then we dined at Mrs. Pélagie Barry, and what with talking and eating, for our relation was so hospitable that one was obliged to partake largely of the sumptuous meal, it was quite late in the afternoon when we started to see Mr. & Mrs. Barry (another branch of the family). And a very pretty little house, or farm, they have out in the country! But it was killed we were of kindness, for an ample supper was prepared for us, and though we had scarcely risen from dinner, of course we were expected to do justice to this second repast. Suffice it to say that on that day at least we did not starve. Our kind relations had many an agreeable plan laid out for the morrow but Papa felt anxious to push on to Paris as soon as possible. Mamma managed to excuse our hasty departure in such a delicate manner that I do not think that they took any offence at our starting early next morning.

June found the Drexels back at St. Michel, where they easily took up the summer routine. The school for children of poor farmers was resumed, as were the meetings of the titans of high finance. The horses and flowers were fussed over. Prayers were said every evening in the oratory, and mass was heard there almost every Sunday. Emma, repeatedly referred to by her family in their letters as a housekeeper "sans pareil," often had as many as fifteen house guests at a time to look after and was frequently called upon to produce last-minute dinners for as many as twenty people. True, she had all the servants she needed to help her, but they were often difficult to manage and the strain told on a nervous system that only an iron will and an exacting sense of duty kept from breaking down. In the summer of 1878, two years after the United States Centennial, the family launched a new institution, the *St. Michel Journal,* which would record the daily activities of the household and the estate until its dissolution twelve years later. Among the entries of that summer we find several obituaries, bordered in black ink:

> Died on Friday night of the cholera, a little pig.
> The friends of the family are invited to the funeral.
>
> EPITAPH
> "I came to see the farce of life one day
> Tired of the first act, so went away."

> DIED
> At St. Michel on the afternoon of the 21st inst.
> LENORE.*
>
> EPITAPH
> So soon it is that I am done for,
> I wonder what I was begun for.
> > > > Louise

> \* A pet crow

And so life flowed on for the Drexels. Francis grew steadily richer as the Drexel banks expanded their operations in Europe and North America. The Dorcas at 1503 Walnut Street grew more and more complicated and more and more munificent. The summer school at St. Michel continued. There were trips to the White Mountains in New Hampshire in the fall, followed by meetings of the titans of finance as usual. Francis Drexel continued to play the organ and the family continued to say prayers together in the oratory every evening; exceedingly formal dinners were given with the usual frequency; the traditional Christmas party for the poor of Torresdale continued to be held every year at St. Michel; Madame Louise, R.S.C.J., visited the family regularly. Little by little, the three girls grew up, and Elizabeth and Kate made their debuts. Emma never let up on her family responsibilities, governing two large homes and a large household staff as conscientiously as always; the Drexel fame and fortune multiplied; less affluent relatives clustered around the flame of its success, hoping a spark of it would ignite their unspectacular careers; and then, in 1883, Emma Bouvier Drexel died of cancer at the age of forty-nine. The disease had taken her and her family by surprise. For some time she had been looking thin and tired, but when finally a doctor was summoned, it was too late.

On February 1, a requiem mass was held for her at St. Mary's, after which she was interred in the Bouvier vault in the adjoining churchyard. Later it was learned that in addition to having founded several schools and charitable institutions, Emma Bouvier Drexel had been paying the annual rent of more than 150 families and had distributed, by way of the Dorcas, over $500,000 to the poor during the preceding twenty years.

St. Michel was a far different place that summer. So keenly did Francis and his three daughters miss Emma that they decided to take a trip to Europe in the fall rather than have the same feeling of loss descend on them a second time at 1503 Walnut Street. They sailed early in October and spent seven months traveling through Holland, Germany, Italy, France, and England. It was not long after their return that Francis also passed away.

Francis Drexel left an estate of approximately $16 million (about $120 million in today's currency). Two million were to go to twenty-nine charities he had already given a considerable sum of money to. With the remaining $14 million, his will provided that three equal trust funds be established for his daughters, Elizabeth, Katharine and Louise. The money was left in trust to discourage any potential fortune hunters. Furthermore, it was stipulated that if one daughter died without issue, her share would be divided among the other two, and if all three died without issue, their shares would all go to the twenty-nine charities.

The Drexel girls, then, were left with a considerable inheritance. Each was assured an income of more than $190,000 a year for life, in an era when taxes on unearned income were still negligible. Elizabeth at the time was a tall, slim woman of thirty whose blond hair, blue eyes, and fair complexion proclaimed the Austrian Tyrol from which she was but two generations removed. Kate, at twenty-seven, was shorter, stockier, and darker, with large, almost masculine, features and an energetic temperament. And Louise Bouvier, at twenty-two, was a younger edition of her older sister, tall, trim, blond, and sensitive, the most feminine of the three.

Healthy, attractive, intelligent, and rich, they had the world at their feet. But they were not interested. Not long after their father's death, they began to devote their energies and resources to helping those at the other end of the social spectrum: orphans, Negroes, and Indians. For some time they had been concerned with the plight of the Indians, thousands of whom were suffering from poverty and disease in the Western states. Father O'Connor, who had been pastor of St. Dominic's Church in Holmsburg, where the Drexels occasionally attended mass while at St. Michel, had become Bishop of Omaha and had written to the sisters about the miserable condition of the Indians in his diocese, and the girls had responded with donations for Indian mission schools. On a trip to Europe in 1886, which they took to help overcome their grief over their father's death, Kate Drexel had an audience with Pope Leo XIII during which she pleaded with His Holiness to send more missionaries to the American Indians. She also told him that it had always been her intention to enter a contemplative order of nuns, but if she did, she would be neglecting the Indians, who were in such need of help. What was she to do? Whereupon the Pope suggested that she herself become an Indian missionary. The suggestion was taken to heart.

The trip was also fruitful for Elizabeth. Concerned over the fate of the orphans of three asylums her father had been aiding over the years, she planned to establish an industrial school at Eddington, near Philadelphia, which would help train the orphans when they reached the mandatory age for leaving the asylum. The school was to be named after her father's patron saint, Saint Francis de Sales. Unsure, however, of how to organize the school, Elizabeth made use of her trip to inspect industrial and technical schools and orphan asylums in France and Germany. Upon her return to Philadelphia, she drew up final plans for the institution and in the fall of 1886 laid the cornerstone of the St. Francis de

Sales Industrial School for Orphans, at Eddington. It was the first of more than sixty schools the Drexel sisters would establish.

Louise in the meantime turned her energies to helping Negroes, founding Epiphany College for Negroes in Baltimore in 1888. The following year she married Edward V. Morrell, a wealthy Philadelphia lawyer and future congressman, and brigadier general of the state militia, who enthusiastically joined in her philanthropic enterprises. That same year Kate entered St. Mary's Convent of Mercy in Pittsburgh as a novice, and Elizabeth, not to be outdone, announced her engagement to the lawyer Walter George Smith, who later became president of the American Bar Association.

The sisters were now launched on their respective careers. Edward and Louise Morrell established homes at 1825 South Rittenhouse Square in Philadelphia and at Torresdale, building an estate adjoining St. Michel, which they christened San José. Elizabeth and Walter Smith temporarily set up house at St. Michel, then departed on a six-month wedding trip to Europe. And Kate continued her new life as a postulant of the Sisters of Mercy. Then, in September 1890, tragedy struck St. Michel. Shortly after returning from her wedding trip, Elizabeth Drexel Smith, six months pregnant, entered into premature labor, and before anything could be done to save her, she and her baby were dead. Later, the Sisters of the Blessed Sacrament, the order founded by Kate, interpreted the tragedy as a manifestation of the divine will, since it meant that Elizabeth's share of the trust fund established by her father, which was now worth considerably more, could be devoted to helping underprivileged children.

Katharine did not waste time putting the money to use. On the day that she took her vows as a Sister of Mercy, February 12, 1891, she founded the Congregation of the Sisters of the Blessed Sacrament for Indians and Colored People and as its appointed mother superior set up a temporary convent and novitiate at St. Michel. Soon several destitute Negro children were housed there, and before long the new congregation boasted over a hundred nuns, a new headquarters (called St. Elizabeth's), and a network of schools for Indians and Negroes across the country.

Although the Indians had been their first concern, Mother Katharine and Louise Morrell soon came to focus their attention predominantly on the problems of the Negroes. Both shared an abhorrence for the pattern of racial segregation and denial of equal opportunity that had characterized American society. Their mother had been especially vehement on this issue, regarding racial discrimination as a living denial of the principles on which America was founded, and out of respect for her memory Louise selected the name St. Emma for an industrial and agricultural school for Negro youth which she founded at Rock Castle, Virginia, in 1894. Xavier Academy for Negroes in New Orleans followed, and then Xavier University in the same city, the most important educational institution for Negroes she and Mother Katharine established during their long careers.

Awarded the resounding title Eucharistic Apostle of the Indians and Colored People, Mother Katharine was active not only in religious and philanthropic pursuits but in financial enterprises as well. She had inherited from her father an uncanny ability to make profitable investments, especially in real estate. Often outwitting seasoned realtors, she had a sixth sense about buying the right properties at the right time. Quadrupling her inheritance, she poured the profits into her schools and convents. Taxes absorbed a good deal of her trust's income, however, and so, with Mother Katharine, among others, in mind, Congress in 1921 changed the income-tax laws to make her income, since it was going wholly to charity, tax-free. By now her enterprises ranged all over the country, and she was in continual demand as a speaker at religious and educational institutions. She spoke chiefly about racial discrimination in education and housing. Audiences, curious to see the millionaire nun, were amazed by the vehemence with which she denounced current discriminatory practices.

Her half sister, Louise, was in the meantime supporting St. Francis Industrial School and St. Emma's, and succeeded, after much effort, in finally combining white and colored catechism classes at St. Emma's. During the Depression she maintained a soup kitchen for Negro children at Ninth and Lombard Streets in Philadelphia. In 1930 she built, at St. Michel, the Shrine of the True Cross, a brick church in Romanesque style, containing a crypt that would become the mortuary chapel of the Francis A. Drexel family. Then, in 1936, at Louise's request, Kate made St. Michel the headquarters of her congregation, and a few years later Louise formally presented the church and St. Michel to Mother Katharine and her Sisters of the Blessed Sacrament.

Although she dedicated her life to the poor and the oppressed, and shunned the world of wealth and fashion, Louise Morrell lived on a scale no Bouvier ever equaled until one of her cousins twice removed married the Greek shipping magnate, Aristotle Onassis. In addition to her town house in Philadelphia and her 345-acre San José, she and her husband maintained a house in Newport, a showplace in Bar Harbor called Thirlstane, two yachts, and a 160-acre island off the coast of Maine containing a rustic cottage and a chapel. From eight to twelve servants were in their employ, and they had a private chaplain who said mass for them every morning at eight in whatever residence they happened to be in (there were chapels in both San José and Thirlstane, as well as in Calf Island). Remembering their visits to "Cousin Louise" at San José, twentieth-century Bouviers would recall watching from the bedroom window in the morning as the priest arrived in Louise's Lincoln, accompanied by two altar boys in black cassocks and white lace tunics, carrying chalice, missal, and communion bells. Awe-struck by the magnificence in which she lived, Louise's less affluent cousins had difficulty believing San José was the domain of a relative. The great house, with its dark-wood paneling, stained-glass windows, gothic-arched doorways, religious statuary, and unbelievably high ceilings, looked more like a cathedral than a home.

In 1945 Louise Bouvier Drexel Morrell died, leaving no children, and Mother Katharine became the sole beneficiary of her father's estate. The estate was now worth over $50 million. After her death, people wondered whether Louise had purposely abstained from having children, so that Mother Katharine would eventually receive the entire inheritance for her schools and missions. Since neither of the Drexels who had married left children, and since Mother Katharine would never marry, the entire principal of the trust was destined, after Katharine's death, to go to the twenty-nine charities Francis Drexel had mentioned in his will. These, of course, did not include Mother Katharine's enterprises (which were not in existence at the time of the will). Thus, Mother Katharine was compelled to work harder than ever. She was eighty-seven and she wanted to make available to her congregation as much money as she could before its life blood was taken away. But soon her strength began to give out and, suffering from heart and arterial trouble, she found herself confined to a wheelchair. The direction of her congregation had to be assumed by others, but she continued to follow its activities and make decisions about the allocation of funds. New institutions for Negroes were founded and additions made to Xavier University in New Orleans. During her last years, as her strength slowly ebbed, Mother Katharine poured every penny of her enormous income into her congregation. Meanwhile distinguished visitors from all over the world came to St. Elizabeth's convent to pay their respects. Leaders of the NAACP were frequent callers. The President of Haiti, Elie Lescort, came to present her with his country's "honneur et mérite" medal. In 1953, at ninety-five, she received the Award of Merit, as Philadelphia's most distinguished lady, from the Catholic women of the city. Papal tributes were forthcoming from Pius XII. But her strength, by now, had practically run out. Unable to move from her wheelchair, she would spend hours sitting before the window of her room in the Motherhouse, clutching a little picture of Pius X, which she always had with her. Then her mind began to wander. A visitor would arrive and she would look up and call "Janna, Janna," referring to her childhood nurse, Johanna, who had died many years before. Or she would call out for her mother, as if Emma were in the next room. Then, on the morning of Wednesday, March 2, 1955, at the age of ninety-seven, Mother Katharine contracted pneumonia. She died that afternoon, surrounded by the sisters of the congregation. Five days later, after thousands had paid their respects at the Cathedral of Philadelphia, and after a long funeral procession through Torresdale, past the Shrine of the True Cross, St. Michel, and Eden Hall, she was buried in the crypt of St. Elizabeth's.

The entire Drexel estate was now to be distributed to the twenty-nine charities mentioned in Francis Drexel's will. In her own personal account Katharine had only $25,000 left. It is estimated that she gave over $40 million away during her lifetime. Those $40 million had been transformed into a legacy to the nation's Indians and black people which consisted at the time of her death in a congregation of five hundred nuns in twenty-one states, a university for Negroes in New Orleans, and sixty-one schools and missions for Negroes and Indians throughout the country. In Philadelphia and Torresdale, Katharine Drexel had left four parochial schools for Negroes, a convent, church, and mission center for her congregation at St. Michel, a junior college and boarding school at Cornwells Heights, and the great Motherhouse of the Sisters of the Blessed Sacrament, where the latest novices and postulants of her order are now in training. Katharine Drexel's life work had been both prophetic and exemplary. Ten years after her death, when civil rights had become the chief domestic issue of the day, her efforts in behalf of America's Indians and Negroes were given extraordinary recognition: a cause was opened for her beatification. The American tribunal which studied the cause met once a week, at the Roman Catholic archdiocese headquarters in Philadelphia, from December 1965 to November 1967. It consisted of four judges, a "promoter of the faith," and three notaries, presided over by a monsignor. Witnesses were called before the body to testify to Mother Katharine's sanctity, and records of their testimony were sent to the Vatican, where another tribunal met to examine them and decide whether to carry the cause further toward declaring Katharine Drexel America's third canonized saint. That cause culminated in Rome on November 21, 1988 when Mother Katharine Drexel was officially beatified by Pope John Paul II in St. Peter's. In his eulogy of Mother Katharine the Pope emphasized her lifelong dedication to educating Blacks and Indians, describing her life and work as "the most significant of any Catholic of this century."

One of the incidental functions of convents and monasteries in Europe has been the preservation of the family papers of their founders, abbots, mothers superior, and other benefactors. A thousand years of European social history are recorded in the archives of such great houses as the Abbey of Cluny and the Badia della Trinità at Cava, near Salerno. It would no doubt surprise Michel Bouvier to learn that the major source of information on the early history of the family he founded in America is not in the possession of any member of his family but in the archives of a convent in Cornwells Heights, Pennsylvania, founded by his daughter's stepdaughter. And yet there, at St. Elizabeth's, most of the early Bouvier documents rest. Portraits of Michel Bouvier and Louise Vernou, and a portrait of Emma, hang on the walls of one of the convent's "visiting rooms." A collection of Bouvier letters is kept in the library, along with Emma's diary of her trip to Europe with her father in 1853, her lifetime journal, and the diaries of her daughter Louise. The nuns also keep a silver locket engraved with Michel's and Louise's names, containing intertwined strands of their hair.

# III

---

A VISITOR TO THE BOUVIERS' FORTY-SIXTH STREET BROWNSTONE IN THE 1890s would be plunged into an atmosphere of such aristocratic distinction he would find it hard to believe its occupants were the children of a once penniless immigrant from Southern France who had started out in America working with his hands. The maroon brougham with coachman and footman would be waiting outside in a reserved parking space to the right of the main entrance. The doorbell would be answered by a liveried secondman who would guide the visitor into the main hall, demand his card, then carry it on a little silver tray to the Bouvier the visitor wished to see. While he waited, the caller would straighten his cravat and whisk his sideburns in one of the huge ceiling-to-floor gilt-framed Louis XV mirrors in the hall and admire the great bronze-railed, red-carpeted staircase leading to the three upper stories. If word came back that he would be received, the visitor would be ushered into the drawing room, where he would be greeted by a dazzling collection of paintings, antiques, heirlooms, heraldry. The long, cluttered room, whose walls were hung with red damask, looked out on Forty-sixth Street at one end and led into the library from the other. The décor was a mélange of Victorian and Empire, with red and gold the dominant colors. Red velour portieres with golden tassels separated the rooms. There was scarcely a space on the red walls that was not occupied by a painting, usually in a gilt frame. Other paintings stood on easels, often obstructing those on the walls. Among the works, collected not for their value but for the pleasure they gave their owner, were two Corots, a Schreyer, a Meunier, a Díaz, two Millets, a Rembrandt Peale, and a portrait of Louis Philippe as King of France. A beautifully carved golden eagle, a gift from Joseph Bonaparte, hung from the red damask above the fireplace, not far from the superb Tiffany chandelier at the center of the room. Statues on marble pedestals were everywhere: busts of Napoleon, Greek gods, neo-classic goddesses, copies of several Canovas. As numerous as the statues were the footstools. Literally dozens of them were scattered throughout the room, some in conjunction with Empire fauteuils, others independent entities. And there were almost as many clocks in the room as there were footstools, including another Bonaparte gift, the magnificent white-marble and bronze doré horloge with golden eagle and jet sphinxes that Joseph had left Michel through his administrator, Louis Mailliard.

The drawing room led to the library, where the visitor would notice framed replicas of the recently adopted Bouvier and de Vernou crests on the oak-paneled walls, along with a framed copy of the Bouvier motto, "Sans Peur et Sans Reproche." Among the many books on the shelves, he would observe a fifty-volume *Histoire de France* in magnificent red-leather bindings, and complete sets of Voltaire, Montaigne, and Molière in French. Here there were more paintings and more clocks. There was also a mahogany-veneered secrétaire à abattant made by Michel Bouvier, cabinetmaker, and several objects that were particularly dear to the head of the house, a magnificent pair of Empire vert antique marble urns, with bronze doré lids, on pedestals, and an elaborately inlaid petite armoire. Further on, in the dining room, the visitor would notice two ancestral paintings, portraits of Michel Bouvier and Louise Vernou, done in their last years; a superb gold service displayed on the sideboard; and a statuary group representing the Three Graces, beyond which two high French windows opened onto a garden filled with fountains and more statues. Upstairs were the apartments of the four Bouviers in residence, the servants' quarters, and the family chapel with its white marble altar, potted ferns, and painting of "The Agony in the Garden."

The Bouvier who was to receive the visit would be announced by the butler, and the meeting would usually take place in the library, with another servant in attendance. There were ten servants in all in M. C. Bouvier's employ, most of them French. They were required to speak French with both their masters and the guests unless asked to do otherwise and were trained to observe an exacting etiquette. It would appear to an unknowing visitor, from the high style in which the Bouviers lived, that they had been aristocrats for centuries, a family adorned with years of noble traditions and distinctions. And yet, only seventy years before, its American founder had been "taking down and putting up beds" in the houses of the Philadelphia rich, and his brother's descendants were still artisans in the villages of the Rhône delta.

How Zénaïde, Alexine, and Mary came to live with their bachelor brother in New York and how the four organized their spinster household and transformed their family into descendants of French nobility is one of the more curious chapters of Bouvier family history. After Michel's death in 1874, Zenney, Allie, and Moll had the mansion on North Broad Street all to themselves. As we have seen, their father's will stipulated that they be "permitted" to live there for two years on an annual income of $9,000 after taxes, plus upkeep—what would amount to around $32,000 a year today. As it turned out, they lived there eight years more, and they probably would have stayed there forever if it hadn't been for the perfidy of an Italian prince whom Alexine fell in love with in Paris in the spring of 1881. The trio, bored to death with their spinster existence in the Quaker City and tired of their vast, empty mansion, had gone abroad in 1879 for an extended tour of Europe and the Middle East. They had taken with them their nephew and the family heir, J. V. Bouvier, Jr., whom they called Jack, and planned to be away at least a year. The trip turned out to be a merry one, so full of excitement that the Misses Bouvier's lives were never to be the same again. Finally they were away from Philadelphia and their stifling old maids' existence in the drafty void of the North Broad Street mansion. Paris. London. Vienna. Rome. Romance. Romance had evaded them over the years, and now, as they approached middle age, there was not much time left for it. Zenney, forty-four, had given up hope long ago, but Allie, forty-two, and Mary, thirty-eight, still harbored expectations. And so the Misses Bouvier, with their fifteen-year-old nephew Jack, plunged into the fleshpots of Europe, hungry for adventure and excitement. Now they were in Vienna getting themselves photographed in a noted studio and attending a brilliant ball. Then in Pont-Saint-Esprit. Then Spain. Then Florence, Venice, and Rome, and an audience with the Holy Father. Later Athens and Istanbul. Then Palestine and Syria for a trek through the Holy Land. Then Paris again before returning home.

While they were in Pont-Saint-Esprit, their father's half sister, Pélagie Barry, overwhelmed them with hospitality. The Barrys were fascinated by their Philadelphia nieces. By 1879, considerable differences had developed between the American and French branches of the family. Zenney, Allie, and Moll had never worked a day in their lives and had all the time and money they wanted to travel around the world. Pélagie Barry, on the other hand, had never known anything but work. After her husband, Pierre, died in New York, she and her son, Michel, had returned to Pont-Saint-Esprit and opened a general store, where they worked every day of their lives except Sundays. A diary one of her grandnephews kept gives this picture of his American cousins (all of whom apparently lied about their age), during their eight-day visit:

> ... They are extremely charming ladies but very different types. The eldest, Zénaïde, who is thirty-eight, speaks French very well and is most ingratiating. She replies charmingly to compliments. She is small and far from being pretty. Alexine, at thirty-two, comes next. She is a woman accomplished in every way, a pretty brunette with a very lovely figure, who must have been a beauty at eighteen years of age, sweet and alluring. She understands French very well, but has difficulty speaking it. Lastly there is Mary, a completely original and fantastic type; in her one really recognizes la grande Dame, much more proud than the other two. She seems to feel that no one is worthy of her and that everyone should do her homage. She is very susceptible to flattery. She has a lovely figure but is not as pretty as Alexine.

Several months after their visit to their father's birthplace, the Bouvier sisters went to Palestine and Syria, where they engaged a Lebanese dragoman by the name of Antonio Macklouf to guide them and a friend, Henrietta Graff, on a thirty-five-day tour of the Holy Land. The agreement drawn up between the Misses Bouvier and Antonio Macklouf stipulated, among other things, that the "said Antonio" would provide "three twelve-roped tents, and one kitchen tent ... mules, horses, side saddles for the ladies, servants and a cook ... guides, guards, night-watchmen and all backsheeshes . . . three good meals a day besides tea, coffee, chocolate and fruit ... a change of unsatisfactory riding animals at such places where substitutes can be found ... Palanquins for certain parts of the journey"—all for twenty-five shillings a day.

And so, for thirty-five days, Zénaïde, Alexine, and Mary, and Henrietta Graff, plodded across the desert wastes of Palestine with Macklouf, taking their afternoon tea in palm-choked oases, camping out in their twelve-roped tents, fending off beggars, flies, and marauders, visiting the great temple at Baalbek, the Holy Sepulcher, Nazareth, the Sea of Galilee—fulfilling, at last, one of the countless dreams of adventure that had occupied the idle hours of their spinsterhood en trois at 1240 North Broad Street.

The Bouvier sisters' two-year tour of Europe ended in Paris, and it was there that the beautiful but fading Alexine lost her heart to a nobleman reputedly related to the Italian branch of the Bourbons. Not much is known about the Prince Vallerie or his romance with Alexine. Italian noblemen in the 1880s and 1890s were notorious fortune hunters, and no doubt the Prince sensed there was money somewhere when he met the Bouvier sisters in the spring of 1881. At any rate, a romance budded between Prince Vallerie and Alexine Bouvier which eventually flowered into an engagement. Alexine, Zénaïde, Mary, and Jack returned to America in October 1881 and the formal engagement was evidently solemnized by letter sometime that winter. By July 1882 the wedding date had been set and the invitations had been sent out for what promised to be one of the social highlights of the season, Allie Bouvier's marriage to a Bourbon prince. The Prince was due on July 2 and a representative of the family was sent to the pier to meet him. The subsequent events were reported in the *Philadelphia Record* the following day:

## A PRINCE'S MARRIAGE DEFERRED

Quite a flutter has been caused in the circles of high society by the postponement of the wedding of Miss Allie Bouvier with the Prince Vallerie. The lady is well known and comes from an old Philadelphia family. Her sister is the wife of banker Frank Drexel. As the story goes, while Miss Bouvier was travelling abroad a short time since she met the Prince, who was engaging in his manners, and is said to be of the Italian branch of the Legitimists, his mother being a Bourbon. The Prince and Miss Bouvier met each other frequently, and finally it was decided they should get married. Then the trouble began. The Prince did not desire to get married in France, because of the trouble with the law, but was willing to come to America for the wedding, so it was decided that the ceremony should take place in this city. The fact that the wedding was to occur in this city caused considerable talk in society circles, and the young lady was congratulated upon all hands for her good fortune in having captured a real Prince. The most elaborate preparations were made for the event, and the invitations were prepared. The Prince promised when he left his inamorata in Paris to follow her to the United States as soon as he settled up some small business matters. A relative went to New York, but the Prince failed to arrive on the steamer. Letters and telegrams failed to reach him, and nothing has been learned of the whereabouts of the Bourbon since. The wedding has been consequently postponed until the Prince is found, and Mr. Dickson, a relative of the young lady, has been dispatched to Paris to clear up the mystery, and, if possible, find the Prince. The family and friends of the lady believe that some accident has happened, and until apprised otherwise they will be loth to believe anything else.

Whether the Prince was unable to fulfill his promise to marry Alexine because of "some accident," or because he found out that Allie wasn't as rich as he thought and was, after all, forty-three, or because he, as a member of the nobility, decided the Bouviers of Pont-Saint-Esprit were beneath him, or because he wasn't really a prince and feared exposure, we shall never know. After Prince Vallerie stood up Allie Bouvier on that July 2, 1882, a curtain rang down on the whole affair. No letters or documents have survived to tell us what Joe Dixon found out in Paris. Perhaps Joe challenged the perfidious bastard to a duel. Perhaps the Prince refused to receive him. In any event, Alexine was embarrassed beyond repair. In fact, the entire family was mortified. No such snub had come a Bouvier's way since Waterloo. A Bourbon prince, related to the kings of France. Those beautiful wedding invitations with the Bouvier crest at the top and the Prince's name and titles taking up two full lines. The lavish reception that had been planned at 1240 North Broad Street. The social event of the season—and the scoundrel never showed up. Poor Allie Bouvier. Allie couldn't endure the snickers, the knowing glances, the gossip; she was unable to show her forlorn face in Philadelphia ever again. It was decided that the trio must leave the B-Hive forever. Accordingly, in October of that year the mansion was sold to La Salle College, and Zénaïde, Alexine, and Mary Bouvier moved into their brother's brownstone in New York.

Alexine's mortification was so disabling that not only did she never return to Philadelphia again but she fell into a state of neurotic invalidism that lasted until her death. Future generations remembered her in her third-floor apartment at Forty-sixth Street, sitting in a wheelchair, dressed in a lavender negligee, before the altar she had installed in her room, praying endlessly to the Virgin Mary.

The official family explanation of Alexine's fiasco was that MC had called the marriage off because he thought the Prince Vallerie was really after her money. Future generations of Bouviers would be given still another version; namely, that it had been MC who had been engaged to a French countess, whom he jilted because he learned she was after *his* money.

Not long after the Misses Bouvier's transfer to New York, a struggle for power broke out among the three which saw Mary, the youngest, emerge as head of the household, assuming the role of her brother's "wife"; Zénaïde, the oldest, become the housekeeper, or "châtelaine," as they called her, taking charge of the servants and assuming responsibility for the functioning of the ménage; and the beautiful, rejected Alexine turn into a parasite waited on by all three. Mary took her place at the head of the table at meals and occupied a choice apartment on the second floor, where MC had his quarters, MC taking the front suite overlooking Forty-sixth Street, and Mary taking the back one facing the garden. Zénaïde armed herself with an enormous bundle of keys, kept a pencil and pad in constant readiness in her pocket, and occupied the front apartment on the third floor, while Alexine, defeated not only in love but also within her own family, took the back room on the same floor. As for MC, thirty-five and still unmarried, he resigned himself to a life of faith, love, and obedience to his single sisters, who clearly had him trapped. If they would never have husbands, at least they would have him.

These strange, bachelor Bouviers became, in time, the wonder of the family. Future generations would refer to "Uncle Miche's" as if it were a foreign enclave. The personalities of its inhabitants became a favorite topic of conversation, and rumors of their combined wealth became so outlandish that their net worth was estimated to be on a par with that of the Vanderbilts. Of the three sisters, who came to be referred to variously as the Holy Trinity, the Vestal Virgins, and the Three Graces, Mary had the most brilliant personality. As a teenager she had been dubbed EL

(Elegant Loafer) and had gained a reputation for being very witty and entertaining. Being Michel's youngest daughter, she had been brought up after her father had made his money, whereas Zénaïde had not known wealth as a child. Consequently, Mary never developed the domestic prowess her older sister attained. When Zenney was a child, she had to help with the housework. When Moll was a child, maids took care of all the chores. Wealth and leisure had freed Mary from mundane practicalities and allowed her to lead the life of a grande dame. Stylish and very social, she loved to entertain and be entertained and eventually acquired quite a reputation as a hostess. A militant Catholic, she disdained alcohol and tobacco, and was extremely proud of her virginity. Her Catholicism was uncompassionate and uncompromising. She would not speak to one of her grandnephews, Bud Bouvier, after his divorce, and would be furious with her nieces if they committed the slightest breach of Church etiquette, such as going to communion without gloves on. She was an odd-looking creature, with some excellent features and some very unattractive ones. Tall and slender, her figure was considered near perfect. She had a wasp waist, slim ankles, an ample bosom, and graceful arms. But although her eyes and mouth were pretty, she had huge, cauliflower ears and a large nose. If she received a compliment from a man, it would invariably be for her wit. She loved food but never gained weight. Her nieces remembered her forever eating chocolate mousse and whipped cream. Always dressed to the teeth, she kept herself tightly corseted, wore a solitaire diamond at her throat, a wig with blond puffs and curls, and birds-of-paradise feathers in her hats. Louise, her French maid, used to complain it took three hours for mademoiselle to get dressed. For all her physical peculiarities, Mary was often described as "regal" and "grandiose " MC was proud to have her at his side, at church, receiving guests at home, walking along Fifth Avenue, at parties and public functions.

Zénaïde was a very different type. Practical and down-to-earth, she had been her father's favorite daughter. He had named her after his first loves in America, Sarah Anne Pearson and Zénaïde Bonaparte, her full name being Sarah Anne Zénaïde Bouvier. She had been her mother's busiest helper as a child, and her father's faithful secretary and correspondent as a young woman. After her mother died, she took over as housekeeper at 1240 North Broad Street and ran the household until 1882, when the trio moved to New York. As one of the four executors of her father's estate, she looked after her sisters' financial interests and kept a close watch on their expenditures. She herself hardly spent a cent of her own and was admired for driving a hard bargain with merchants and service personnel. While Mary had aristocratic pretensions and was something of a snob, Zénaïde cultivated no airs. She was the only member of the family who kept up with her French relatives. She also was one of the few who kept up with Eustache, and Eustache usually wrote only to her. It was Zenney who bossed the servants at their house in New York, held the keys, made sure the clocks were wound, ordered the food and coal, kept the accounts, and paid the bills. Physically she was plain, having been cursed with a lantern jaw and horse teeth. She was short, brisk, and mannish and never had any beaus. Such was the rapidity of her father's financial rise that she and Mary, separated in age by only six years, were raised in two economic worlds, belonged, it seemed, to two different classes.

As for Alexine, she had always been regarded as the beauty of the family, the only one of seven daughters considered attractive enough by her parents to merit having her portrait painted. The painting, now in the possession of Mrs. Bouvier Putnam, a grandniece, shows a lovely, sensitive girl with large, trusting eyes, blond hair, and a soft smile, who seems to take after the Scotch-Irish side of the family more than the French. She was the only one of the trio who had boyfriends and she often confided to Mary and Zenney that she planned to make a brilliant marriage. She played very hard to get, however, and soon was in her late thirties and still without a man. A trip to Europe in 1875, when she was thirty-six, failed to produce a suitable contender, and so her romance with Prince Vallerie in Paris six years later seemed to be a veritable gift from the gods. Unfortunately, the affair awakened dreams so exalted that any disappointment was bound to be overwhelming. The Princess Alexine Vallerie. What a beautiful name! She would adorn the courts of Europe. All her Philadelphia girlfriends would be sick with envy. Every once in a while she would be a good samaritan and have Mary and Zenney over to her town house in Paris to relieve their boredom. And if MC and John could be trusted not to make any faux pas, she might have them over too. Allie's pride was, of course, premature. Still, the eventual downfall was great. Unlike Mary, she had not wanted to die a virgin. She had nurtured desires, or at least velleities. Now her sexual starvation would become a lifelong famine, her dreams of aristocratic privilege a torture to recollect. Allie Bouvier's Drexel nieces had found her (before the fall) gay, inquisitive, carefree, a girl who took "a flattering interest in everything." Yet here she was in the mid-1880s, aged forty-nine, bruised by disappointment in love, bruised from her struggle with her sisters for a place in MC's esteem, relegated to a back room in his house, with little to console her but her religion. After that warm July day in 1882 when her prince failed to walk down the gangplank, Allie had withdrawn from society. Illness, real or feigned, was usually her excuse for not showing herself in public. When Emma's daughter, Louise, married Edward Morrell in Torresdale, the entire Bouvier clan was present except Allie, who was described in a letter to Katharine Drexel as "too sick to go (with la grippe they suppose)." It wasn't la grippe, however. Allie had become, without anybody consciously realizing it, a perennial neurotic, always too "sick" to do anything. In her fifties she developed a crippling arthritis which put her in a wheelchair for the rest of her days. Confined to her room, she grew fat in her old age. When a relative would pay a call on her, she would force a smile on her face and hold out a blue hand to be kissed, rarely uttering a word. Her heart had become the morgue of her sentiments.

The ultimate beneficiary, or victim, of Prince Vallerie's rebuke to the Bouviers was MC. He had come to his sisters' rescue and invited them to New York. Now he was stuck with them for life. His sisters would see to it that he stayed single. On the other hand, the arrangement resulted in a domestic situation that allowed him to enjoy the best of two worlds. In his beloved sister Mary he had a woman who headed his household with dignity and taste, always made a good impression on guests, and yet did not make excessive demands on either his finances or his energies. And in Zénaïde he had the perfect housekeeper, someone who relieved him of all practical details connected with the running of the house, including the thorny problem of dealing with the temperamental French servants. Thus MC was free to have all the romance he wanted on the side. As long as his affairs did not gravitate toward marriage.

Future generations remembered life at Fourteen West Forty-sixth Street as ordered, ceremonious, and serene. The Bouviers in residence evidently got along well together, once their roles in the household were defined, and they soon established a routine that would last their entire lives. By 1890 they had ten servants to assist them, nine of whom were French. Each of the sisters had her own personal maid who looked after her needs exclusively. Then there was the couple, Eugene and Louise, a butler-maid combination, and the chef, Louis, whose cuisine earned his patron a reputation of serving some of the best food in New York. Rounding out the staff were two secondmen, a coachman, and a footman, the coachman, Thomas, being the only one on the payroll who was not French. The footman was probably the most superfluous member of the staff. His only function was to open and close the coach door and pull the lap robe over the passengers' knees. Among the formalities observed by the butler, guests would recall that upon being served at table they would be told: "madame est servi."

MC collected clocks and had over forty of them scattered throughout the house, many of them extremely valuable. He was particularly fond of the one that had belonged to Joseph Bonaparte. MC often said that if it hadn't been for Napoleon's brother, the Bouviers might never have risen above the artisan class. It was an obsession of MC's that all his clocks be kept running on time. One of his servants was assigned the task of keeping them wound, a labor that took two hours every afternoon. If they all chimed at once, MC was content, but if one tinkled a minute before the hour or added a note after the others had ceased, the clockwinder would be summoned and asked to explain. Visitors liked to stay to hear the hour struck, especially if it was noon. From all over the house, top floor to bottom, a shower of tinkles and tonks would reverberate, some light and rapid, others deep and measured, followed by a silence, then the inevitable late peal of some delinquent clock MC would immediately have investigated.

Liquor and tobacco were *défendu* at West Forty-sixth Street, although wine was tolerated. Mary once described herself as "tinctured with abolitionism," and Zenney and Allie never smelled a cork in their entire lives unless it came from a bottle of Côte du Rhône. Even MC abstained until the last years of his life, when his doctor recommended that he take a little Scotch and water occasionally.

Religion played a major role in the household. Not only did the Bouviers maintain an oratory in Alexine's bedroom, but Zenney and Mary kept prie-dieux and votive lights in their rooms also. Huge crucifixes on the walls dominated most of the rooms in the upper stories. Relatives coming to call would often notice the hats of prelates on the hall table. Archbishop Lavelle, Pastor of St. Patrick's Cathedral, was a frequent caller. St. Patrick's was the Bouvier parish at the time and the great church was very much a part of the family's daily routine. Mary went to mass there every morning. When Allie was well enough, she would often spend the entire afternoon in the Lady Chapel. And there was never a Sunday when MC and his three sisters were not punctually in their pew for eleven o'clock high mass. The Bouvier altar, raised to the memory of their parents, was a project all four Bouviers devoted themselves to with particular enthusiasm. Pouring $25,000 into the memorial, they conferred endlessly with the architect and the sculptors, often bursting into the latter's studio without notice to see how the work was going. The altar would witness scores of Bouvier baptisms, yet was denied Caroline Kennedy. Permission was asked to baptize her there, but the cathedral's administration would not allow it: under the new dispensation, babies, no matter who, could be baptized only at the font near the entrance to the church.

In 1895 MC bought a summer place at Narragansett, Rhode Island, which he christened Lasata, an Indian name meaning "Place of Peace." The house was a many-gabled Victorian structure with a large porte-cochere and second-story veranda, located about three miles from the ocean, on Central Avenue. One of the reasons MC bought the place was that it was near a Catholic church. Not long after he and his sisters moved in, he had an arbored cinder path laid down from the house to the church, enabling Mary to continue her morning devotions and the crippled Alexine to be easily wheeled to hers. Bouviers recollecting summer visits to Narragansett remembered guest rooms full of pin cushions (Mary liked them as well as MC liked clocks); washing stands with pitchers and basins made of blue and white china; MC's black Lincoln entering the bluestone driveway, sounding its horn, and all five servants appearing under the porte-cochere to greet the arrivals; the entire entourage walking to mass Sunday mornings down the arbored path, with MC and Mary, arm in arm, in the lead, followed by Zénaïde and then Alexine being pushed along in her wheelchair by a servant, the others, nieces and nephews, bringing up the rear, the women wearing ankle-length dresses and ostrich-feather hats, carrying parasols, the men in stiff collars, morning coats, and pepper and salt trousers. MC swam at Narragansett Beach as often as he could, but Zenney, Allie, and Moll never went near the ocean. While their brother was in the water, they would usually be in church.

Once or twice a year MC and his sisters would visit Louise Morrell at San Jose, and pay a call on her half sister, Katharine Drexel, at nearby Cornwells Heights. These were hieratic occasions for Mary, Zénaïde, and Alexine, who regarded Katharine Drexel as a living saint and contributed thousands to her charities. While at San José they would attend daily devotions at St. Elizabeth's and treasure the hours they would be allowed to be in Mother Katharine's presence. The visit would inevitably result in renewed pledges of support for her and Cousin Louise's schools and a renewed feeling of pride in what had become the mainstay of their spinster lives, their faith.

For over fifty years, from 1882 to 1935, MC's household was the focal point of the Bouvier family, the center around which the clan revolved. Since his older brother, John, remained a modest commission broker, he could never afford a home like MC's, or even a summer place. Consequently, major family get-togethers were always held at MC's, and even though he had no children, he was considered head of the family. Once a year, usually around Christmas, there would be a reunion of the entire clan, with MC and Mary presiding with great punctilio and style. With a dozen Pattersons, five Dixons, and four Drexels representing the Philadelphia contingent, and seven Bouviers comprising the New York branch, it made quite a gathering. Liquor would not be served, but Mary would lubricate the party with her wit, firing her usual barrage of quips at everybody and telling stories that would hold the entire assemblage enthralled. At the end, favors would be distributed. The Philadelphia group would then return home in a private rail car, and John and his family would take Louise back to her convent, while the Bouviers of Forty-sixth Street would go back to their clocks and votive altars.

Surrounded by beautiful objects, surfeited with servants, listed in the Social Register, allied, through Emma Drexel's family, to one of the great financial dynasties of America, and possessing all the time and money they needed, the Bouviers of West Forty-

•

sixth Street had arrived, by the tacitly accepted standards of the day, in the American upper class. When they looked back into the family's past, however, and when they met their French cousins on trips abroad, it was only too obvious that they had not come from the French upper class also. In fact, they had not even come from the upper middle class of France. This was disconcerting, in view of the family's growing aristocratic pretensions. So disconcerting, in fact, that the Bouviers were eventually unable to reconcile their social status with their origins: they had to invent an aristocratic past.

Two of the Misses Bouvier, Mary and Alexine, had enough time on their hands to devote themselves to image-making. While MC was working long hours on Wall Street and the indefatigable Zénaïde was governing his household, Mary and Alexine were free to spend their time dreaming and sentimentalizing. Especially Alexine. Alexine had been so crushed by Prince Vallerie's rejection, so abruptly deprived of her dreams of princely love and splendor, that the reality of her situation had become intolerable to her. She had to take refuge in religion and other dreams, and those other dreams, it appears, took the form, in part, of fabricating an aristocratic heritage for herself and her family. It is not known whether Mary had ever been disappointed in love, but it is known that she had queenly airs and was something of a social snob. Between Mary and Alexine, two wealthy, unmarried women in their fifties, with highly susceptible imaginations and plenty of time to indulge their fantasies, a beautiful family lineage was generated that eventually developed into two small volumes of "family history" conferring an exalted ancestry on the Bouviers which was in part fable but which future generations were to accept wholly as fact.

The creation of the Bouviers' aristocratic image was an effort born of wounded pride. Ever since the Bouviers had arrived in America, they had had to struggle against a social establishment dominated by white Anglo-Saxon Protestants. They were white French Catholics, and not too white at that. During his early years in Philadelphia, Michel Bouvier had waged an uphill fight for acceptance and finally attained it in his old age. He attained it, first of all, by marrying a girl whose mother, Elizabeth Lindsay, was reputedly the daughter of a white Anglo-Saxon Protestant; then by proving himself the equal of the white Anglo-Saxon Protestants in business; and last by marrying three of his daughters into Anglo-Saxon families, the Dixons, Pattersons, and Drexels, and having his son, John, marry into an old colonial family, the Ewings. Michel's success was so total, so spectacular, that in one generation he lifted himself from the petite bourgeoisie of Southern France to the top of the American social heap. Most American families who "make it" take several generations to arrive at the top. The Bouviers, thanks to their phenomenal founder and his wife, made it in one. Still, there remained that Southern French, Catholic tinge. People wondered who the Bouviers *really* were. It was left to Mary and Alexine, and one imaginative helper, to find out.

The imaginative helper who finally hammered the Bouviers' aristocratic image into shape was John Vernou Bouvier, Jr., only son of JVB, Sr., and Carrie Ewing, adored nephew of the Bouviers of Forty-sixth Street, and the only member of his generation who could perpetuate the Bouvier name. John, Jr., had gone to Europe with his maiden aunts in 1880 when he was fifteen. He had traveled with them throughout France, visiting his grandfather's birthplace and meeting his French cousins, and no doubt being duly depressed by the humbleness of his origins, and he had also been in Paris at the time of Alexine's romance, where he was correspondingly impressed by the exaltedness of the Prince's origins. Later, when Alexine was rejected by the Prince, he was as offended by the slight as any other member of the family. Did the Prince Vallerie reject Alexine because he found out who the Bouviers of Philadelphia really were? Had the Bourbon sent an emissary to Pont-Saint-Esprit to investigate his future bride's origins? The Bouviers never found out for sure, but they were left with the suspicion that that had been the case. It remained to prove the Prince wrong. Far from being the daughter of proletarians, Alexine Bouvier was the daughter of aristocrats, by God! To establish this, however, took some doing: it was necessary to research the Bouvier past before the family moved to Pont-Saint-Esprit and try to find noble ancestors in Père-Eustache's native city of Grenoble. It was also necessary to explore the ancestry of Louise Vernou, reputedly the daughter of titled nobility. With the help of several cooperative genealogists, the money to pay them, and the fertility of Mary's, Alexine's, and John, Jr.'s imaginations, the Bouviers concocted a pedigree going back a dozen generations and a set of crests and heraldic symbols brilliant enough to impress the most haughty of bluebloods.

The definitive birth of the family's aristocratic image occurred between 1890 and 1898. It was in 1890 that John, Jr., discovered a noble Bouvier family from the province of Dauphiné, the Bouviers de la Fontaine, which he promptly appropriated as his own, adopting both its motto and its coat of arms, and it was in 1898 that Alexine Bouvier wrote a little book called *Our Grandmother's Story* about an episode of family history, already mentioned, which parenthetically awarded a most aristocratic pedigree to the grandmother in question.

Alexine's book was completed in Lourdes and published privately in Philadelphia, under the pseudonym "Jeanne d'-Outre-Mer." The grandmother about whom the book was written was Louise Vernou's mother, Elizabeth Lindsay, who had evidently held her grandchildren spellbound time and again when, on specific occasions, she would tell her story to them. Elizabeth Lindsay, it will be recalled, had suffered greatly as a young woman. At twenty-one she had lost her husband, Francois de Savoie, during an insurrection on Santo Domingo, and had returned to Philadelphia penniless, to find that her entire family had in the meantime been exterminated by yellow fever. Alexine had suffered greatly too, and it was only natural that she, of all her brothers and sisters, would sympathize enough with her grandmother's story to make the effort to preserve it for posterity. Alone, in her sickroom on the third floor of MC's brownstone, surrounded by the symbols of her consolation, she had mused over her misfortune and had found in her grandmother's story a tragedy somewhat similar to hers: Elizabeth Lindsay's French husband had been murdered; Alexine's Italian husband-to-be had . . . What had they told Alexine? Did they tell her that her prince had been killed too, or did they tell her the truth? In any case, she too had been deprived of a husband. In *Our Grandmother's Story* Alexine transferred her own feelings of deprivation to her grandmother. "Often and often," she wrote, "whilst in her hiding place, lying upon her lonely couch, had she dreamed that she was dreaming of the tragedy that so changed her life, and awakened suddenly to find that it was no dream but an appalling truth . . . O bitter awakening! Only those who have dreamed such dreams, and have awakened to realize their pitiless truth, can know what there is of human anguish in a dream that is not a dream, but a woeful reality . . . But time heals deepest wounds, though the scars remain."

Although the main purpose of the narrative is apparently the expression of a tragic story with which she was very much in sympathy, Alexine went out of her way to award her protagonists illustrious ancestors. According to Alexine's account, her grandmother was the daughter of one of Washington's most distinguished officers. And the man she married after the murder of Francois de Savoie, Jean de Vernou, was an "émigré driven from home by the French Revolution."

All this would be unimportant, were it not for the fact that the Bouviers adopted unquestioningly the aristocratic pedigrees of the Bouviers de la Fontaine and the de Vernous de Bonneuil and absorbed them into their flesh and blood. One wonders why they felt so insecure. Just how difficult had their road to social acceptance been? We shall never know precisely, but we can assume it must have been very difficult, for it appears beyond doubt that the Bouviers were under an irresistible compulsion to forge an aristocratic image of themselves that would end the humiliations they had had to endure during their initial struggles to make their way in America. In the end, their efforts were successful. During the twentieth century the only humiliations Bouviers ever received were from each other, as the family scaled heights of social prestige beyond their ancestors' wildest ambitions.

Now that they had discovered an aristocratic lineage for themselves, the Bouviers were free to be French for the first time since they had arrived in America. It was fashionable to cultivate French ways as long as they reflected upper-class life in France. It certainly would not have been fashionable to adopt the customs of their ancestors. Frank Drexel, on his trips to his father-in-law's birthplace with Emma, had been unimpressed by the Spiripontain cuisine— "roasted fowl stuffed with black olives and trimmed with bacon . . . ten courses made with sweet oil"—and the habit his wife's relatives had of smoking bad cigars in their bedrooms before retiring. Michel Bouvier, Sr., not having had a superior culture to that which he acquired in America, always made every effort to be as American as he could be. He changed the spelling of his first name shortly after arriving in Philadelphia, writing Michael Bouvier in his Bible, and kept it that way to the end, signing Michael to his last will and testament. He also referred to his son MC as Michael and, with two exceptions— Alexine and Zénaïde—gave his children names not necessarily associated with France. MC, however, reverted back to Michel, and future generations bearing the name would go to great lengths to see that the name was not spelled Michael. Furthermore, in the twentieth century the Bouviers tended, for the first time, to give French names to their children—Jacqueline, Michelle, Reppelin—and take pride in their French "heritage." A French *mot*, "Sans Peur et Sans Reproche," was adopted as the family motto, and the altar MC raised to his parents' memory in St. Patrick's was done in French Gothic style and was adorned with statues of French saints.

While the Bouviers were creating their new aristocratic image, MC was busy making the money to allow them to live up to it. The Bouviers were fortunate to have a man like MC in charge of finances, for his career on Wall Street was successful from the start. Not only did his shrewd investment strategy soon double and triple his sisters' inheritance, and substantially increase the principal of their trusts, but his own brokerage firm of Bouvier & Wallace made giant strides as well. MC's coolness during the panic of 1878 brought him to the attention of no less a magnate than William Vanderbilt, the commodore's son, who, on the advice of Morgan, Drexel & Co., opened an account with him the following year. With Vanderbilt interests to look after, Bouvier & Wallace soon attracted other heavyweight customers, and, before long, the firm had all the business it could handle. At the same time MC continued to discharge his responsibilities as managing trustee of his father's estate, partitioning Eustache's estate among his brothers and sisters after he died in 1886 and Louise's after her death in 1902. Michel, Sr., had stipulated in his will that $7,500 of Louise's estate be distributed among seven French relatives, but by 1902 only two of those had survived: Clémentine Chabert, daughter of the unfortunate François, and Pélagie Barry. And so on January 24, 1903, two modest French families, one in Pont-Saint-Esprit, the other in Arles, received windfalls from MC's office amounting to $3,556 each.

In 1898 MC dissolved Bouvier & Wallace and formed M. C. Bouvier & Co. in partnership with two former employees, John G. Bishop and Russell Coykendall. The new firm, destined to last until MC's death, did both a banking and a brokerage business. The banking business was particularly lucrative. MC would borrow anywhere from $400,000 to $1,000,000 from the Central

Hanover in the morning, lend the money out to other brokers during the day, and collect it at the close of business, netting two percent interest on the transactions. One year M. C. Bouvier & Co. netted $1,000,000 on interest alone. As a brokerage, the firm had as its biggest single customer Cities Service Co., which speculated heavily in the market after World War I. MC became well known for his ability to acquire control of a company for a customer by buying shares as offered, without bidding. Once he obtained complete control of the Fourth Avenue Railroad for a speculator from Virginia, without forcing the price of the stock up as much as a point. In addition to his banking and brokerage activities, MC also speculated heavily in real estate, buying and selling huge tracts of land in Denver. By 1910 MC had become a millionaire several times over, and his sisters were worth over $400,000 each. Zénaïde left $403,355 when she died: MC had quintupled her inheritance. It was estimated that by the mid-1920s MC's net assets amounted to approximately $7,500,000, or $20 million in 1993 dollars, and Mary was worth almost a million in her own right. On February 16, 1920, MC's eminence in the financial world was solemnized by a feature article about him in the New York *Herald Tribune* which summarized his career on Wall Street and reported his views of the changing stock market.

Shortly before the crash in 1929, MC's seat on the Stock Exchange, for which he had paid $4,500, reached an all-time high of $625,000, or 129 times his original investment. During the twenties he had received rights toward a second seat, which he sold for $125,000 on October 10, 1929, nine days before the market broke. Although the crash hit him hard, MC was able to salvage at least half his fortune: in 1934 his net assets were calculated at $3,500,000, or $24 million today. In the end he left forty-five times the money he had inherited. During the last decade of his career he became Dean of Wall Street brokers, the Exchange's oldest member, with William Fahnstock and John D. Rockefeller his immediate juniors. MC made no bones about his respect for money, and was perhaps overly impressed by the very rich, but he was very generous with the money he made, donating thousands to charities. His favorite causes were those established by his sister Emma, her daughter, Louise Morrell, and Katharine Drexel. It was not unusual for him to send an unsolicited check for $10,000 to St. Emma's Industrial School or surprise the Sisters of the Blessed Sacrament with one for $25,000. And his family charity was almost limitless. He loaned thousands to relatives without ever demanding repayment, repeatedly footed the bills for his nephews' and nieces' education, and was always ready with financial aid in a family crisis. His support of his French relatives was particularly generous. He must have felt their plight keenly, for he gave one of his uncle François's daughters a semi-annual stipend of 1,000 francs and virtually supported two of his sons.

The opposite was the case with brother John. John remained a floor broker all his life, doing a commission business for other brokers, which never earned him more than a modest living, but his lack of financial success was more than compensated for by the wonderful relationship he had with his wife and son. Their grandchildren would remember their love as one of the most inspiring influences in their lives. It was a rare marriage. John had wed Carrie when he was a twenty-one-year-old veteran of the Civil War, without money or exceptional prospects. The first decade of their married life was beset with economic difficulties, yet their love never faltered. Their grandchildren remember them embracing affectionately when they were in their seventies. "Caddie, come over here and hold my hand," "Grampy Jack" would say. And the two would sit arm-in-arm on the sofa like newlyweds.

Their love for each other was matched only by their love for their son. Carrie had lost a daughter (named Caroline) in 1869, shortly after the child's second birthday, and so John, Jr., was all she had. She adored him and he was devoted to her. Later, in his book of family history, he would describe her as "Earth's noblest thing—a woman perfected," "a wondrous creature cleaving to the right and to the good under all change; lovely in youthful comeliness, lovely all her life long in comeliness of heart." To him she was "the holiest thing alive." "To her, with rarest truth, may be applied the words of Wordsworth: '. . . thou shalt show us how divine a thing a woman may be made.' " From all reports, John, Jr.'s eulogies of his mother were well founded. Caroline Ewing Bouvier was an exemplary woman. Unlike her sister-in-law, Mary, she was a forgiving, compassionate Catholic more devoted to Mary Magdalene than to the Virgin. When her grandchild, Bud Bouvier, was divorced, and was spurned by Mary, Carrie took him into her home. She once served as president of the New York Foundling Hospital and throughout her life was a tireless worker for Catholic charities. The most blue-blooded member of the family, she was the least interested in ancestry and never went out of her way to seek genealogical distinctions. Her deep family piety, however, led her to conserve family letters and documents, and it is to her that we owe the presentation of many early Bouvier and Ewing records. On October 22, 1914, she and John celebrated their fiftieth wedding anniversary, attended by the entire family. The invitations and place cards were printed on gold paper. The table was set with golden plates and a golden service. And MC gave the couple $5,000 in gold coins.

John V. Bouvier was, it seems, a man of strong character. Unlike his shrewd, charming, elegant brother, he was plain, direct, and affectionate. He had few pretensions and was devoted to his country. His French heritage, whether real or manufactured, didn't interest him. He was an American and had no need of aristocratic French ancestors. Because he was not much of a businessman, MC treated him somewhat condescendingly, almost as a son, but even so, their relationship remained loyal and affectionate to the end. That John was able to overcome envy of his younger brother's success was one of the triumphs of his character, for the economic disparity between the two toward the end of their lives was staggering. It was Carrie, above all, who kept the brothers close. MC had a particular esteem for his sister-in-law. After she was widowed, he saw her almost every day, and he left her $50,000 in his will.

The chief beneficiary of this serene home life was John, Jr., the favorite of two households. On one side he was fussed over and spoiled by his rich uncle and three maiden aunts, and on the other by his adoring parents. The aunts had taken him to Europe with them for over a year. MC would often travel with him during the summer, taking him out West, or to Canada, and would frequently have him to his home for meals during the winter. His was a strange situation. Here he was, the only child of an unpretentious stockbroker, living in a small midtown apartment three blocks from what was an altogether different world, even though it too was his family: the opulent, celibate ménage of MC, Mary, Zénaïde, and Alexine, with its chapel, ten servants, and forty clocks. To both households he was the hope of the family, the only one who could carry on the Bouvier name, and ultimately the heir to most of its money and all its traditions.

As the new styles of the twentieth century began to take shape, the Bouvier household at Forty-sixth Street slowly acquired the status of an antique. MC and his sisters were uncompromising in their allegiance to the nineteenth century. By the time a fourth generation of Bouviers came into being, the gap between the oldest and the newest generations was unbridgeable. It was after World War I that the contrast became especially violent. Until 1914, New York remained essentially nineteenth-century in taste and outlook. But things changed in the roaring twenties, and so, by the time John, Jr.'s children, born between 1891 and 1905, came of age, MC and his ménage had become a museum piece. MC in his high stiff collar, diamond stick pin, morning coat, gray vest, striped trousers, and gray spats seated in his highbacked, red and gold chair. Mary with her great wig, solitaire diamond choker, corseted waist, and long Victorian gown, seated in her highbacked, red and gold chair. The servants standing in attendance, the butler in a red and black striped jacket, brass buttons, black trousers, and white gloves; the secondmen in green and black striped jackets; the maids in black, with white aprons and white caps. And the callers, the poor nieces and nephews, the rich nieces and nephews, grandnieces and grandnephews, great-grandnieces and great-grandnephews, before the burnished thrones of Aunt Mary and Uncle Miche. Five o'clock. Tea time, and a glockenspiel chorus would float through the old brownstone as forty clocks tolled the hour, and the maids would appear with giant silver kettles and trays of cups, cookies, and cakes. "And tell us about *you*, Michelle," Aunt Mary would intone from her cathedra. "What have *you* been up to lately?" And if Michelle had not been up to anything in particular, or if she said something dull, Mary would respond, "How perfectly silly," and pass on to the next niece. So they were sitting on $8 million between them. Did that mean everyone had to grovel or perform? It is a wonder no one rebelled. But no one did. Aunt Mary and Uncle Miche were sacred. They were the last survivors of the era in which the family had been founded. They had actually known that mythological person, Michel Bouvier of Pont-Saint-Esprit, had listened to his stories about Napoleon's wars, Joseph Bonaparte at Point Breeze, and Eustache père at Yorktown. They remembered the Civil War and Lincoln's assassination. And Mary could tell *Our Grandmother's Story* the way the original grandmother had told it. What a moment it was when the blacks entered her hut and demanded: "Leper come forth!" Or when Elizabeth learned her husband had been murdered. When MC and Mary reminisced about their family and their country, it seemed to their nieces and nephews that history herself had been momentarily incarnated and had descended from her cloud to pass the record on to the future, so grandiose were their recollections, so oracular their pronouncements. "And when President Lincoln was assassinated, the whole city was in mourning. The doors of the houses were draped in black and all businesses were closed. Mother and Father took us all to church and we prayed for the President's soul and the preservation of the Union."

Along with history, the Bouviers of West Forty-sixth Street transmitted to the next generations a sense of style, a heritage of elegance, and a love of beauty unusual in American life in their day. In contrast to typical Anglo-Saxon inattention to dress and surroundings, the Bouviers would always be very conscious of their clothes and ambiance, gaining a reputation for impeccable taste in dress and furnishings. Other legacies, good and bad, complimentary and contradictory, included an almost fanatical devotion to the Catholic Church, a sense of *noblesse oblige* in regard to the poor, a love of money and luxury, an exaggerated insistence on privacy, a bias against marriage, an egocentricity bordering on narcissism, a wonderful sense of the fitness of things, a subdued theatricality, and a somewhat exalted family pride. In time these bequests, imbibed *cum lacte* by the next generations, would be built into the flesh and marrow of the Bouviers, forming a unified family style.

As the twentieth century wore on, Forty-sixth Street between Fifth and Sixth gradually turned commercial and MC was forced to buy the brownstone next to his for protection. Soon huge office buildings were rising up on both sides of the street, dwarfing the Bouvier enclave, and the police hung a NO PARKING sign in front of MC's place that infuriated the old man because he couldn't buy either the sidewalk or the street. The gradual encirclement and isolation of the Bouviers' brownstones was symbolic of what was happening to MC's generation. Before long, there would be no more brownstones or Bouviers on Forty-sixth Street.

Zénaïde was the first to go. MC was deprived of his housekeeper on February 7, 1914, a week after her seventy-ninth birthday. She had been active to the last, both in running the household and in dispensing charity to the poor and sick. The funeral was held at St. Patrick's, then she was taken to the Bouvier vault at Old St. Mary's in Philadelphia. Nine months later Alexine, at seventy-seven, joined her. Alexine had spent the last years of her life entirely immersed in her religion. Unable to walk and quite overweight, she never came down from her third-floor apartment, where she spent her days in endless devotions. The only outsider who ever saw her was the family priest, who would come to her room to say mass and hear her confession. Toward the end she surrendered unconditionally to the world of the New Testament. With her shades drawn, she would sit for hours in semi-darkness, her votive candles flickering, surrounded by the only scenes that were real to her any more: the Agony in the Garden, the Virgin in Prayer, the Crucifixion. When death came, it found her well prepared: in a sense she had long since ceased to live. After the funeral, MC and Mary accompanied her to St. Mary's, where she was laid to rest beside Eustache and Zenney. It was the first time she had returned to Philadelphia since she was shamed into leaving thirty-two years before.

As more office buildings went up on Forty-sixth Street, MC watched more members of his generation disappear. His oldest sister, Thérèse Patterson, died in 1916 at eighty. His brother John died in 1926 at eighty-three, and Carrie died in 1929 at eighty-five. Meanwhile a new generation was coming into being. A great-grandnephew with a familiar name, Michel Bouvier, was born in 1920, and a greatgrandniece, Jacqueline Bouvier, came forth three and a half months before the crash in 1929.

When the Depression set in, MC was eighty-three and Mary was eighty-nine. Now, as they entered their last years, the poor relations—called the "black crows" by the rest of the family— began to circle around MC's brownstones with increasing regularity. They were four in number, widowed daughters of MC's older sisters, Elizabeth Dixon and Thérèse Patterson, and they had practically no money of their own. Their names were Mary Dixon Walsh, Louise Dixon Ewing, Elizabeth Dixon Noël, and Mary Patterson Stuart, and from 1930 on, whenever a Bouvier went to 14 West Forty-sixth Street he would find one or more of them perched in the drawing room. As times got worse, they would turn up for meals more and more frequently. Although the Depression reduced the value of MC's assets considerably, he never cut down on his standard of living, maintaining a large staff of servants, a stable of horses, his two brownstones, and his place at Narragansett to the end. To the crows he was an imperishable dike against the financial distress that was overtaking so much of the country, and their only hope for a comfortable old age. Ultimately their faith and hope in him would be justified.

The "black crows" were not only takers, however. After Mary died on Thanksgiving Day, 1931, a month and a half before her ninety-second birthday, they became MC's greatest consolation, helping to prevent loneliness from embittering his last years.

Mary's death was a terrible blow to MC. A deep, powerful relationship had always bound the two together. For half a century they had lived practically as man and wife, sharing everything life had to offer them. A letter MC wrote to his French cousin, Pierre Solard, in 1931 gives us a hint of the desolation he felt after his beloved sister died:

> December 11, 1931
> My dear Pierre,
> I am enclosing your draft for one thousand francs from my sister's estate and myself.
> Also two drafts in the sum of 250 francs each for your two daughters, Jeanne and Louise.
> You will grieve to hear that my dear sister Mary died on November 23 after a short illness. She was in her ninety-first year. I am the last of my generation and I am in my eighty-fifth year. You may imagine my distress and loneliness.
> With best wishes for a blessed Noel I am, sincerely yours,
> MC Bouvier

Mary Howell Bouvier's funeral at St. Patrick's was attended by an enormous throng. Her family and close friends had followed her from the chapel in Alexine's old room to the cathedral, where before the high altar the Right Reverend Monsignor M. F. Lavelle celebrated the high mass, assisted by the Bishop of Philadelphia and the vice-chancellor of the diocese of New York. Over fifty nuns of the Sacred Heart and Sisters of the Blessed Sacrament took part in the procession as the body entered and left the church. Later, when she joined her ten brothers and sisters in the vault at St. Mary's, the crowd of mourners was so vast the churchyard couldn't contain them.

Her obituary in the *Catholic News* emphasized her contributions to Katharine Drexel's charities:

> Mother Katharine's great enterprise for the Indians and
> Negroes is believed to be unequaled by any other in-
> dividual charitable effort in this country or perhaps the
> world,. . . Miss Mary Bouvier was vitally interested in this
> work.

Of her $469,300 net estate, left to MC for distribution to
sixty-three legatees, $104,300 went to charities, servants, and
employees, with $25,000 going to Mother Katharine's schools for
Negroes; $65,000 was left to various friends and relatives; and the
rest went to the poor relations, the "black crows," each of whom
received roughly $75,000.

With Mary gone, the clause MC had included in his will
making her the chief beneficiary of his estate was automatically
nullified and immediately a long list of heirs stood to inherit his
fortune. MC had drawn up his will with even more care than his
father. Since he put so much stock in money, literally devoting
his life to managing and accumulating it, his will stands as one of
the most convincing testaments to his character we have. The
document was thirteen pages long and there were sixty-eight
legatees. The sum of $261,000, in amounts ranging from $500 to
$50,000, was to go to thirty-one relatives, friends, and former
servants or employees, and $50,000 was to be left to J. V. Bouvier,
Jr., to be distributed among a secondary list of friends and relatives not specifically mentioned in the will. The sum of $150,000,
in six legacies of $25,000 each, was bequeathed to MC's three
brokerage partners and three senior clerks, and $7,000 was left to
the servants in his employ at the time of his death. The charitable
bequests amounted to $145,000, of which $70,000 was to go to
Drexel institutions for Negroes. The four "black crows" were left
$200,000 each, in trust, and JVB, Jr., was left $200,000, plus the
residuary estate, which would amount roughly to $1,000,000 at
the time of his uncle's death. Literally all MC's relatives, including
five distant French cousins he scarcely knew, were mentioned,
and every man and woman who had served faithfully in his
employ, whether in his office or his homes, was remembered.
Like his father before him, MC left very little to chance, providing
his executors with detailed instructions about the sale of his

houses and the liquidating of his business. The faith the document reposed in J. V. Bouvier, Jr., was extraordinary. Not only did MC make his nephew an executor and leave him $1,200,000, but he trusted him with the distribution of $50,000 to a list of people not even included in the will.

With his affairs in order and his conscience at ease in regard to relatives, friends, and employees, MC awaited his end with equanimity, lonely in his empty brownstone but active to the last and essentially at peace with himself. As he approached ninety, relatives and associates were amazed by his stamina and fortitude. It was a rare day when the Dean of Wall Street was not at his office, and his ability to weather the storm and stress of floor trading at his advanced age never failed to astound his fellow brokers.

When death finally claimed him on July 29, 1935, at eighty-eight, MC's brownstones were the last private residences on Forty-sixth Street and he was the last Bouvier of his generation. He was also the last of his family to be interred in Old St. Mary's churchyard. Not long after the burial, his brownstones were emptied and soon became a pile of toppled masonry. Not a trace of them remains.

As his father's most trusted son, MC fulfilled all that was expected of him, confirming once again the sureness of Michel, Sr.'s judgment. His high standards, extraordinary business ability, and unfailing generosity were to make it possible for two more generations of Bouviers to lead lives untroubled by serious economic problems, and his reputation for honor and integrity was to benefit the Bouvier image even more than his nephew's borrowed heraldry.

No mortal could ever be expected fully to live up to the exalted motto JVB, Jr., had appropriated for his family, but MC, if we ignore his cautious love life, came as close as any Bouvier to being "Sans Peur et Sans Reproche."

# $IV$

"THE FUTURE OF THE FAMILY DEPENDS ENTIRELY ON YOU. YOU ARE our only hope." "If it weren't for you, we would become extinct." John Vernou Bouvier, Jr., became accustomed to refrains of this kind at an early age. As soon as he was old enough to understand, he was told in no uncertain terms by his grandfather, his uncles, his aunts, his parents that he was the heir apparent, that if the Bouvier name was to endure after the second generation it would be through him and him alone. It was an ironic situation. Michel had labored hard to establish a family that would carry his name and achievements into the future. Twelve children had sprung from his two marriages and he had made enough money to guarantee each of the ten who survived reasonable financial security. And yet, at the time of his death, only one of his thirteen grandchildren was in a position to perpetuate the name Bouvier. The blame lay in a combination of bad luck and a predilection for celibacy among his sons as well as his daughters. Eustache and MC—like four of their sisters—never married. Joseph Bouvier died at the age of four. And after the birth of her daughter, who died at two, Caroline Bouvier was unable to have any more children. John V. Bouvier, Sr., used to tell his son that not only his life but the life of the whole family had hung in the balance after the Second Battle of Bull Run. If it hadn't been for that old Negro woman who had nursed his wounds, the Bouvier name would have died out in the second generation.

The duties associated with being the only male heir to a family that had to struggle so mightily to establish itself in the New World were taken to heart by the heir apparent. JVB, Jr., would one day tell his children that since the age of eight he had felt the burden of having to live up to tremendous expectations, that both his father and his grandfather had led him to believe that his family had an important destiny awaiting it and that he would be responsible for its realization.

In the last year of his life, Michel, Sr., had summoned his young grandchild to 1240 North Broad Street. The old man knew he was dying and wanted his family's future standard bearer near him as he approached the end. His parents too placed on the eight-year-old a special responsibility. Writing to Philadelphia from the New York Stock Exchange in February 1873, JVB, Sr., told his son: "You are not forgotten by us at any time," and urged him to pay

strict attention to his studies, complimented him on his penman-
ship, and concluded his letter with an extraordinary admonition,
considering the age of the boy: "How is your grandfather. I hope
you look after him well. You must keep in mind that if anything
goes wrong whilst you are in Philadelphia you will be held to be
responsible for it. Your Affectionate Father, J. V. Bouvier."

Young Jack evidently felt the need to assure his parents that he
was measuring up, for that same year he wrote his mother:

> I sed that I wood send you a letter and so I will do all my
> promeses so you can no that I am a good boy Mary [told]
> you then that I am not a good boy but mother I tell you that
> I am a good boy. Your loving son, Jack Bouvier.

As young Jack grew older and his aunts and uncles became
more confirmed in their bachelorhood, as the years passed and it
became certain that John and Caroline would have no more
children, more and more attention was lavished on the boy. MC
and Eustache—when Eustache put in one of his rare appearances—would take him on excursions. Spinsters Zénaïde, Alexine,
and Mary not only took him to Europe but repeatedly entertained
him at Forty-sixth Street. Childless cousin Louise Morrell often
had him down to San José. Nuns Louise Bouvier and Katharine
Drexel fussed over him whenever the occasion permitted. And
his adoring parents, resigned to not having any more children,
dedicated their lives to his upbringing.

One would think the boy would have been so smothered with
affection that he would have been spoiled beyond repair. Surprisingly, however, he grew up a courageous, hardworking young
man who returned the love he received rather than passively let
it soften and corrupt him. A particularly warm and understanding relationship existed between him and his mother. Corresponding with her at the age of eight, he wrote:

> My dear Mother,
> How is yourself and father. Dear Mother I dreamed of you
> the other night. that I was rubbing your Back in Bed. Father
> was looking on.
> Your dear son Jack.

And in another vein, at nine, he wrote her:

Soon I will be in my little bed at home Mother I will speak some poetry for you who formed the little sparrow and gave it wings to fly who shealed him from the arrow when flying in the sky are Father god who rains in heven by whome are all our blessings given your one son Jack Bouvier.

In later years, when he had grown to manhood and established family of his own, he would write her letters such as this:

My adorable Mother:
    'Tis declared that from the same flower the bee extracteth honey and the wasp, gall. Thou art unto the bee, darling Mother; sweetness is secured by you from every source whether in the flora of Nature or in life's human circle, of which to my eye you are over the centre.
    Others' weaknesses, particularly my own, have throughout your wedded years fallen under an indulgent forgiveness, which is but the counterpart of
        "Charity that will rather
        wipe out the score than
        inflame the reckoning."
    Within two years of three score, you have been the matchless Wife and for slightly lesser time the incomparable Mother, while for all time yours is the priceless example of what God undoubtedly designed perfect Wifehood and Motherhood to be.
    A thousand blessings upon your adorable head and a thousand wishes for your unbroken health and happiness.
                      Your devoted Son
                         Jack:
October twenty-sixth.

If his mother both gave him and awakened in him an imperishable love, his father instilled in him a sense of duty and purpose equally beneficial and enduring. He also imbued him with a lasting respect for military valor and exploits of physical and moral courage. JVB, Sr., never tired of narrating his Civil War adventures to his young son, who, after the stories were over, would invariably ask to see his father's wounds, even though he had seen them hundreds of times.

Later on in his life, JVB, Jr., would extol courage as the primary virtue, emphasizing its importance to his children and often quoting Churchill's "Courage is rightly esteemed the first of human qualities, because it is a quality that guarantees all others." In a book of axioms which he had privately printed in 1939 he included one of his own quotations on the subject: "All goes if courage goes."

It took courage to accept with equanimity the pressures his parents and relations placed upon him at so early an age. He could not let them down and he didn't, but for a while the going was not easy. In 1880, when he was fifteen, his health failed him as a result of overwork at the Columbia Grammar School in New York, which he had been attending with distinction since 1877. His subsequent trip to Europe with his aunts was supposed to restore his health and spirits, and evidently it did. Upon his return in the fall of 1881, he prepared for college at De Mille's tutoring academy and passed his entrance examinations for Columbia the following year.

By the time he was ready for college, JVB, Jr., had already lived up to the high standards demanded of him. At the three schools he had attended he proved to be both a top student and an outstanding leader. He was a strong young man, with a compact, muscular physique and large, virile features. His nose, chin, and ears had been a bit too big for his face, as a teenager, but as he filled out, they eventually came into harmonious proportion, giving him an impressive dignity and strength. Those who remembered his grandfather Michel maintained he was the old Frenchman's replica, having inherited not only his rugged looks and physical power but also his passionate temperament.

The year he entered college, 1882, his father had printed on cards a list of recommendations on how JVB, Jr., should employ his time. The advice was evidently taken to heart, or at least respected, for John, Jr., would keep his father's precept cards for the rest of his life, carrying one in his pocket and always keeping one on his desk. The instructions listed were Franklinesque in their plainness and simplicity:

TO J. V. BOUVIER, JR.                    January 1st, 1882

## A FEW PRECEPTS FOR YOUR GUIDANCE.

---

If anything needs attention, give it at once. Every moment is a particle in life, that helps make up the whole. If one of these small atoms of time be improperly employed, so the record is affected accordingly.

Start out on rising in the morning, to commence at one particular labor, and on its completion, continue on with another, thus utilizing time until the day has spent itself.

You will find by so systematizing your daily action, what may seem a burden in an irregular life, will lighten to a pleasure.

The economy of time is of immeasurable value, and brings with it the consciousness of doing your best according to your opportunities.

Have a purpose in everything you plan to do, and if on trial a new departure fails to bring in its profit, discard it then and there.

When meal hours arrive, hold them sacred to eating.

When recreation hour comes around, secure the rest your body needs.

When pleasure hour is on the dial, enjoy yourself always within bounds, and when bed-time calls for sleep, retire without delay, to be fresh again in the morning.

                                        FATHER.

John V. Bouvier, Jr., was the first member of his family to receive a college education and the first Bouvier to have intellectual interests not related to making money. To the joy of his parents, aunts, and uncles, his career at Columbia was a brilliant success. Avid for both scholastic and extracurricular honors, he plunged into his studies and a wide variety of college activities with great determination to succeed and emerged four years later with a collection of triumphs, graduating Phi Beta Kappa, and delivering his class's valedictory address. In addition, he was vice president of his class, a major contributor to and managing editor of the college newspaper, an editor of the college yearbook, a member of the rowing squad, one of his class's leading debaters, and a straight-A student.

Among those who applauded the valedictorian's address that sunny June day of 1886 were John, Sr., and Caroline, Uncle Michel, the ailing Uncle Eustache, and Aunts Zenney, Allie, and Moll. As a reward for his good work at college, MC took his nephew on an extended trip out West that summer, returning in time for the boy to reenter Columbia, this time as a candidate for a Master's Degree in political science. He received this degree in the spring of 1887.

During his postgraduate year, JVB, Jr., was tormented with the decision of decisions: what was he going to do in life? His father and uncle expected him to follow in their footsteps and go to work on Wall Street. MC, in fact, was reserving a place for him in his firm. Nothing would have been easier for the young man than to accept the position. But John, Jr., knew himself well enough to realize that his vocation did not lie in the world of finance. In college he had proven a competent writer and public speaker with a wide range of interests and a highly competitive temperament. Would these capabilities and inclinations be of more value to him on Wall Street or in some other profession? His conflict, in the end, lay between a deep feeling of loyalty to his uncle and father, combined with a consciousness of having been offered a great opportunity, and his own urge for self-realization. Finally, after a long inner struggle, he chose to be loyal to himself. He announced to his family that he intended to become a lawyer and entered Columbia Law School in the fall of that year. That MC and JVB, Sr., accepted his decision with understanding was a tribute to their generosity and open-mindedness. JVB, Jr., was able to begin his law career without feeling that he had let his family down. After passing his New York State bar examinations with flying colors in June 1888, he won a position with the firm of Hoadly, Lauterbach and Johnson, where he remained ten years, the first five as managing clerk and the remaining five in trial work. The latter became his specialty, what would be a lifelong dedication to the courtroom.

From 1888 on, the J. V. Bouviers spent their summers in a white and gray clapboard house at Quogue, on Long Island. Among the summer residents were the William R. Sergeants, who had a beautiful daughter by the name of Maude. When John and Maude first met is uncertain. They were engaged sometime in 1889, the year John got his job with Hoadly, Lauterbach and Johnson, and were married on April 16, 1891. He was twenty-four, she twenty-one. The bride's father was a prosperous wood-pulp merchant and paper manufacturer who had emigrated from Kent, England, at an early age. His wife, the former Edith W. Leaman, was the granddaughter of a wealthy British businessman who once owned all the houses on the north side of Twenty-third Street between Eighth and Ninth Avenues in New York, now known as London Terrace. Maude was an astonishingly beautiful young woman in a family whose members were all exceptionally good-looking. The fourth and fifth generations of Bouviers, also noted for their attractiveness, were to derive their beauty not so much from their Bouvier ancestors as from the Sergeants. JVB, Jr.'s children would be much more handsome than his father, aunts, and uncles.

After their wedding, John and Maude left for Europe and spent a three-and-a-half-month honeymoon touring the continent. The couple returned to New York in the fall, and the following spring Maude gave birth to a son, whom JVB, Jr., named after himself and his father: John Vernou Bouvier III. The boy was born on May 19, 1891, under the same sign as his greatuncle Eustache: Gemini. They would share more than astrological similarities.

The news of JVB III's birth sent waves of joy through the Bouvier family. Zenney, Allie, and Moll almost felt as if they had just had a child of their own. MC, still a bachelor at forty-five, felt much less guilty about his celibacy. Childless Cousin Louise Morrell had a mass of thanksgiving said in her private chapel at San Jose. The Pattersons, Dixons, and Drexels sent emissaries to New York to look over the baby. John, Sr., and Caroline were overcome with gratitude. As for John, Jr., the birth of his first son was an immense fulfillment. His family had counted on him so much to do honor to and to perpetuate the name Bouvier. And here he was, at twenty-six, already a practicing lawyer and the father of a son. The future, now, was limitless. With MC's financial backing, his family's moral support, his own talents, and a charming wife and son, what could prevent him from surpassing the expectations that had weighed on him so heavily as a child?

Now that they had a son to bring up, and hopefully more children to come, the Bouviers decided to move to the country. The move, however, was postponed and postponed, until one day in January 1892, when the cramped living in New York and the baby's crying got especially on his nerves, JVB, Jr., grabbed the paper, went through the real-estate notices, found a house for rent in Nutley, New Jersey, and drove out to see it, in a blizzard, the next day. Not long after, he moved his family into the place. Two years later, with funds borrowed from MC, the Bouviers built their own house in Nutley, which they named Woodcroft and occupied in 1895. It was a large white clapboard house with a huge porch and grounds that included a front lawn, a flower garden, a barn, and a high, all-encompassing hawthorn hedge. The family would live there until 1914, with JVB, Jr., commuting every weekday to his office in New York.

The year 1892 was an important one for JVB, Jr. In addition to moving, he was also admitted to practice before the U.S. District and Circuit Courts and elected to membership in the Union Club—the first of a long series of social distinctions he was to achieve. Shortly after settling in Nutley, he was elected to the town's Board of Education, to become, several years later, in what was regarded as a social breakthrough, the first Catholic president of the Board in Nutley's history.

As hoped for, the Bouvier home was soon blessed with more children. Another son, William Sergeant, eventually to be known as Bud, was born at Nutley on April 28, 1893, and on October 5 of the following year a daughter was born, named Edith Ewing after her two grandmothers, Edith Leaman and Caroline Ewing. John and Maude Bouvier now had three children. Friends and relatives were repeatedly struck by the almost Spanish or Italian beauty of the three remarkably good-looking youngsters, in whom the fine features of the Sergeants and the Ewings were combined with the dark, fiery blood of Provence.

After Edith's birth, years passed and no more children were born to the Bouviers of Nutley, New Jersey. This was intentional: Maude, a Protestant, made sure her brood would not increase. Meanwhile, various convulsions shook the nation. A rebellion in Cuba in 1897 led a year later to the Spanish-American War. On

September 6, 1901, William McKinley was shot by an anarchist and Theodore Roosevelt succeeded to the Presidency. TR's militant patriotism and his policy of speaking softly and carrying a big stick won him the support of people like John V. Bouvier, Jr., normally a Democrat but temporarily a convert to Rooseveltian Republicanism in 1904. For John and Maude, the years following the birth of their last child were dedicated to their family and their professional responsibilities. Things did not always go smoothly. JVB, Jr., was often frustrated by the reptilian slowness of the firm he worked for to recognize and reward genius like his. And both Jack and Edith turned out to be "difficult." They were mischievous, unruly, self-indulgent, and disrespectful of authority. Before long, JVB, Jr., felt a twinge of disillusionment over the family life he had worked so hard to promote. The feeling, however, was dispelled by an event that astonished everyone: nine years after the birth of her last child, Maude "accidentally" became pregnant. Seven months later she was so enormous that she suffered an attack of phlebitis that left her unable to walk. It was decided that if a boy were born, either singly or in company, he would be named Michel. Then, on August 4, 1905, Maude went into labor at her home in Nutley, and the result was twins. The doctor had not suspected it would be a multiple birth and remarked to Maude, after the first daughter was born, that apparently she would have a considerable afterbirth. The first baby was named Maude, and the afterbirth Michelle.

What astonished people as much as the multiple birth and the ten-year interval between children was the totally different appearance of these two latest additions to the Bouvier fold. As the babies grew, it became apparent that they were the opposite of their swarthy, Latin-looking brothers and sister, for, lo and behold, they turned out to be red-headed, fair, and freckled!

JVB, Jr., was forty when the two girls were born, and Maude was thirty-six. The other children were fourteen, twelve, and eleven. The arrival of these two lively redheads into a family that had already established its hierarchies and patterns was a trauma Jack, Bud, and Edith apparently never recovered from. The twins were a bomb that exploded during the most unsettled period of their lives, their adolescence. Immediately little Maude and Michelle received the lion's share of attention. Jack and Bud were even physically displaced. Much to their annoyance, their choice room on the second floor was given to the twins, while they had to move to cramped quarters on the third floor, where the maid and nurse lived. In defense, Jack would take to teasing his twin sisters unmercifully, even leading them to believe they were "found in an ashcan." As for Edith, the belle of the family, now she had twin belles to rival her. Years later, when Edith's marriage had crumbled and she had become a recluse, she would tell people: "Everything was wonderful until the twins came . . . they spoiled it all."

While his family was growing by accident, JVB, Jr.'s law practice was growing according to well-laid plans. Exasperated by the longevity of Hoadly, Lauterbach and Johnson's partners, who had a policy, it seemed, of keeping young talent stifled, he had quit the firm in 1899, at the age of thirty-four, and had founded his own firm, Bouvier & Warren, with offices at 31 Nassau Street. By the time the twins were born, he had a sizable independent practice and had earned a widespread reputation as a forceful advocate in the courtroom. During the years 1905 to 1917 he evidently did very well, for on applying for a commission as a Major Judge Advocate after the United States's entry into World War I, he received a number of extraordinarily flattering references from some of the most prominent members of his profession. Benjamin M. Cardozo, Associate Justice of the United States Supreme Court, wrote:

> Mr. Bouvier is one of the ablest and most brilliant lawyers in the State of New York. He is a man of wide experience, of fine training and of broad culture. I cannot think of anyone more admirably suited for the position he seeks.

And Judge Harlan F. Stone, at one time Dean of Columbia Law School, later Attorney General of the United States, and finally Associate Justice of the Supreme Court, seconded Cardozo's estimate.

> I cannot recall anyone in my professional acquaintance better qualified for the position of Major Judge Advocate... He is an exceptionally skillful trial lawyer and is especially well qualified by his training and long experience for the work of trial counsel.

Needless to say, JVB, Jr., won his commission. Subsequently he spent six months in Washington, as a Major Judge Advocate on the staffs of Brigadier General Samuel Ansell and Major General Enoch Crowder, returning to his practice in New York after being honorably discharged on December 20, 1918. Three days before his discharge, he was admitted to practice before the U.S. Supreme Court. One of the many legacies of JVB, Jr.'s brief, unbelligerent military career was his title. Henceforth he would be known as Major Bouvier and would be called Major until his death.

On returning to New York, Major Bouvier formed a new firm, admitting two Southern friends to partnership, Phelan Beale of Montgomery, Alabama, and Colonel Francis G. Caffey of Kentucky, formerly U.S. District Attorney for the Southern District of New York. The firm, called Bouvier, Caffey and Beale, was instantly successful and JVB, Jr., embarked on the best years of his career, the decade 1918-1928. Colonel Caffey and Phelan Beale were corporate and estate lawyers who never entered a courtroom. Major Bouvier, on the other hand, was strictly a trial lawyer, "a one-celled animal" as Phelan Beale liked to describe him, who gloried in being where the action was. During his courtroom career he handled more than four thousand cases, mostly relating to insurance and securities. Among his many professional associations, he was general counsel for Aetna Life Insurance, The Travelers Insurance Company, Equitable Life, and the Metropolitan Street Railway of New York. His fee was $1,000 a day, or part of a day, and he averaged $100,000 a year or more from his practice during the last ten years of his career. Reputedly one of the finest trial lawyers in a city where forensic competition is unbelievably fierce, Major Bouvier became famous for his flamboyantly persuasive courtroom technique, a technique he occasionally attempted to impart to his fellow "laborers in the vineyard," as he called them, in writings and speeches. One of his most celebrated lessons was given in an address before the New York Bar Association on November 11, 1920. It has since been incorporated in a book edited by Asher L. Cornelius called *Trial Tactics*, under the chapter title "The Trial of a Lawsuit," and presents the clearest expression we have of his very realistic courtroom philosophy.

The fundamental premise of Bouvier's argument is that "juries are preeminently human . . . the jury system the most human of institutions." Therefore, "counsel will try to establish human contact with the jury," will "endeavor to direct appeal especially to the heart and the emotions." For example, there exists among jury members "a prejudice against the possibly enriched defendant and in favor of the palpably poor plaintiff." In fact, "the prejudice against the rich is almost insurmountable." Therefore, counsel for a rich defendant must do everything possible to minimize his client's affluence in the eyes of the jury. It is just as important to do this as to set forth a well reasoned case. In actions involving "breach of contract for employment," if "the jury has a chance the plaintiff will prevail for the purely human reason that 11/12ths of those who sit on a jury are employees themselves with grievances against employers." Therefore, in an action against an employer, great care must be taken by the employer's counsel to indicate how generous and kind, how lovable and paternal the employer is to those who work for him, and to emphasize, if possible, that he himself was once a mistreated employee. Not only juries, but judges too, have human weaknesses and prejudices. It is therefore extremely important for counsel to get close to both judge and jury, to have a "smile in his voice" and an ingratiating manner. So far as dress is concerned, "juries are affected by objective evidences presented by the attorney as those objective evidences may be sartorially expressed." "A cheap coat makes a cheap man, a loud coat makes a loud man, a sporty coat, a sporty man, and a gay waistcoat makes a marked advocate." In conclusion, "intuitiveness plays the controlling part in a jury's deliberations"; what a juror feels is more important than what he thinks. Lawyers, be human. Keep a smile in your voice and never forget the primacy of the human heart.

JVB, Jr.'s human approach to the law reaped him rich rewards, both materially and psychologically. Besides providing him with a $100,000 a year income, his practice won him scores of devoted friends: former clients he had gotten out of trouble, lawyers he had helped early in their careers, poor widows he had provided with free counsel. It was a hard blow to bear when in the late 1920s he developed a deafness in one ear that soon began to mar his effectiveness in the courtroom. By 1928, when he was sixty-four, he had become so hard of hearing that he could no longer try a case in court and was forced to retire from his profession. To help compensate for his feeling of deprivation, his eighty-two-year-old uncle MC took him into his Wall Street firm as a limited partner in 1929. And so JVB, Jr., ended up in the business he had rejected forty-three years before.

JVB, Jr., was so absorbed in his law career that he had almost no time to devote to his five children. He would leave the house at seven in the morning and not return until 7:30 in the evening, or later, and he usually worked on cases at home over the weekend. Thus, Jack, Bud, and Edith grew up almost wholly under the influence of their mother, and the twins' upbringing was dominated by their German nurse. Maude Sergeant Bouvier had a tendency to indulge and protect her children excessively. Especially her sons. All-forgiving, all-compassionate, all-understanding, she was the epitome of the Latin mother, a haven to which her children could flee from the cruel realities of the world and the uncompromising morality of their father. Her pet was Jack, and Jack was the most mischievous child she had. In school he was a prankster who was constantly in trouble with his teachers. At home he was a tease constantly in the hair of his sisters, brother, and sisters' nurse. The twins were among his favorite targets. He would hide their clothes and their dolls and contrive ways to get them into trouble with their nurse. When Edith, who was musical, would sit down to play the piano, he would sit down to play too. The nurse, whose name was Pauline, believed in spirits, and so Jack would appear on the ledge outside her window in the dead of night in a sheet, emitting ghostly sounds. One night he scared her out of her senses by crawling under her bed, waiting there until she slipped in and fell asleep, then poking the mattress with a stick from below. Jack's mischievousness was repeatedly attributed to his "French blood." "It's that naughty French blood coming out in you again," his mother would say, as she promptly forgave him his latest misdeed. Before JVB, Jr., returned from the office, Maude would spread the word: "For heaven's sake don't tell Father what Jack did." Thus, almost all of Jack's misdemeanors would be covered up. Occasionally, however, he would commit some outrage when his father was around and would fall victim to the Major's Olympian wrath. If his mother was very indulgent, his father was correspondingly strict. It was confusing for the boy to be petted and forgiven his trespasses ninety percent of the time, then suddenly be hammered into the ground. One day, after his father had given him a thrashing for teasing the nurse, he was found in the barn by one of his sisters, pricking and squeezing his finger. When asked what he was doing, he replied that he was trying to squeeze all the naughty French blood out of himself.

Edith was indulged too, but in another way. By the time she was ten, she was already a girl of striking beauty and considerable talent. Her large, wide-apart blue eyes; long, almost blond hair; full, naturally red lips, and lively expression gave her a theatrical appearance that exactly suited her talents, for she proved to be a singer and pianist of above average ability. Both her beauty and her talent were so indulged by her mother that she soon did nothing but cultivate the two. If Edith wasn't combing her magnificent hair, making up her face, going over her wardrobe, or buying clothes, she was singing and playing the piano. No housework, no humdrum chores for mother and father. No boring social responsibilities. Just caring for her beauty and her voice. The result was a charming, artistic young woman who made a dazzling impression on everybody but who would have difficulty coping with the harsh problems life would eventually offer her.

Jack and Edith represented two extreme personality types, and the outcome of their lives would not disappoint those who predicted equally extreme destinies for them. Bud occupied more middle ground. He was a strong, affectionate, gentle boy with a love of outdoor life, and a loyal, obedient nature, who was everybody's darling. His parents adored him. Edith loved him. The twins idolized him. And Jack took him over the coals. He would have been the family favorite, had it not been for the twins. But Maude and Michelle were irresistible. With their long red curls, freckled noses, their cheerful voices, their merry ways, they attracted the major share of attention, gradually forcing their brothers and sister to the sidelines while they occupied the center of the family stage. Visitors to the Bouvier home would always fuss over the twins. When the family went to church, the twins would be lionized after mass. Everybody asked the twins to costume parties, because in identical costumes they would make such a hit. Artists would ask to paint their portrait without charge. Yet, for some reason, they were not spoiled by all the attention they received. Perhaps because they were brought up more by their German governess than by their indulgent mother. Pauline was a spartan taskmaster who exacted a strong sense of responsibility from her charges. With Maude getting on in years and only too happy to be relieved of her motherly duties, Pauline came gradually to dominate the family, exerting a particularly powerful influence on the twins. At any rate, apparently from the start, the twins were dutiful and hardworking, pitching in and helping their mother with the household chores, doing everything possible to please both Pauline and their parents. Jack and Edith, of course, regarded them as goody-goodies and would continue to think of them that way as long as they lived. As the years passed, the rift between Jack and Edith and the twins would widen until it eventually became insurmountable. By the time they were all past fifty, there would be no common ground left between them, and when they met, which was rarely, their encounters were so charged with conflicting emotions, so argumentative, that an outsider who might be present would not be able to tell the saints from the sinners.

By 1914, commuting from Nutley had become too exhausting for JVB, Jr., and so the Bouviers decided to move to New York. To make the transition easy, the family took up temporary quarters in a smart "apartment hotel" at 512 Fifth Avenue, the Hotel Renaissance, where they could conveniently order gourmet meals from the restaurant and avail themselves of dozens of servants without having to hire any. The following year they bought an apartment at 247 Fifth Avenue, where they lived for the next ten years.

In time the house in Nutley was sold, and Maude, with funds inherited from her father, bought a house on Appaquogue Road in East Hampton called Wildmoor, where the family spent their summers until 1926, when they bought a much grander place on Further Lane. John and Maude Bouvier loved the Hamptons. From 1914 on, the Bouviers would establish deep roots in East Hampton, involving themselves in the community's affairs and becoming pillars of the summer colony.

One of the incidental reasons for moving to New York was to make it possible for Edith to have a more exciting social life than she had in Nutley. By 1914 Edith had graduated from Miss Porter's School at Farmington, made her debut at Sherry's in New York, and developed into a glamorous young woman of twenty whose beauty and musical talents made her much in demand at parties in New York and Long Island. For a year after the move to New York, she played the field with relish, acquiring an eager following, then fell in love with her father's future law partner, Phelan Beale, who was twenty years her senior. Phelan Beale was a high-powered corporate lawyer with an international clientele, including the eventually infamous Deutschamerikanischer—the German-American Trade League—consisting of 1,100 German firms which had business with the United States. He was born in Montgomery, Alabama, the son of a judge and the grandson of a distinguished Confederate officer who had fought on the side opposite J. V. Bouvier, Sr., at the Second Battle of Bull Run. Phelan had gone to college at Sewanee, became intercollegiate wrestling champion there, took a law degree at Columbia, and stayed to practice his profession in New York. Edith accepted his marriage proposal about the time he was put on the British trade blacklist for his association with German interests, a fact that added considerable publicity to their engagement. To marry Edith, Phelan became a Catholic, then after the wedding in St. Patrick's he never set foot in a Catholic church again.

John and Maude Bouvier decided to spare no effort for their daughter's wedding, sending out hundreds of invitations, planning an elaborate ceremony in the cathedral and a sumptuous reception at the Gotham Hotel. When the great day dawned— January 17, 1917—it was snowing so furiously that the bride's parents were sure no one would show up at the ceremony or the reception. Instead, a throng appeared at St. Patrick's—both invited and uninvited. By the time the bride and her father marched up the long center aisle, after prenuptial prayers at the Bouvier altar, there wasn't a seat to be had and the side aisles were jammed with standees. Edith, theatrical to the end, had seen to it that music would play a conspicuous part in the ceremony, providing personally for a huge choir and a soprano solo which she confessed to her family she would like to have sung herself, if only she could have slipped away from the altar a few minutes. But the twelve-year-old twins stole the show. Following the bridesmaids, they scattered petals and smiles to the immense crowd, to the crowd's immense delight. Later, at the Gotham, they were fussed over as much as the bride and groom at a reception as splendid as the old hotel had ever seen. MC and Mary, John, Sr., and Caroline, John, Jr., and Maude were, of course, delighted. For the Bouviers the day had been a thunderous success. For the newlyweds, who made off to a suite at the Vanderbilt Hotel, and then Nassau, it was a prelude to a long battle involving endless heartaches and suffering.

At the time of Edith's marriage, John Vernou Bouvier, Jr., was fifty-two and a man who had already made his mark in the world. In addition to his professional renown, he had also earned a reputation as a personality with a very specific stamp, a "character" whose style had become famous in a certain layer of New York and Long Island society.

The personality JVB, Jr., developed reflected his particular ancestral background. From his father's side he had inherited certain Mediterranean characteristics, or tendencies, which were often at odds with the Anglo-Saxon and Scotch-Irish qualities he had acquired from his mother. Like a good Latin, he was gregarious, theatrical, extroverted, hot-tempered, self-centered, and emotional. He also had a typically Latin love for stylish clothes, sumptuous surroundings, and beautiful women. And he was as naturally histrionic as an Italian, always behaving, in company, as if he were performing before a large audience. But these traits and preferences did not always mesh with the colder, more puritanical qualities he had derived from the Ewings and the Lindsays, who hadn't a drop of Southern European blood in their veins. Thus his native Latin exuberance and sensuality were often inhibited by a conscience, a sense of duty, a moral and ethical integrity that were distinctly Anglo-Saxon. And his Provençal emotionalism was usually held in check by a dignity many people found offensive. Occasionally, however, his Northern restraints would give way and his Mediterranean soul, his humanity, would reveal itself. Such as when he witnessed the burial of his wife in East Hampton on April 5, 1940. She had died, after a brief bout with pneumonia, two days before. Throughout the funeral at St. Philomena's Church, and on the way to the cemetery, he was the essence of quiet, dignified grief. But then at the graveside, when Maude's casket was lowered into the ground, he broke into a lamentation no one present would ever forget. It was a Sicilian, a Spanish, scene there at St. Philomena's that hazy April afternoon. Old Major Bouvier wailed, he implored, he roared, he beat his breast and shouted to the heavens. For a few minutes the dignified, urbane New York attorney became a Mediterranean peasant howling against the injustice of death.

Physically, Major Bouvier was an impressive figure. He was not tall—only five feet ten but he had a beautifully proportioned body that remained firm and muscular to the end. His enormous head was leonine in the breadth of its planes and in its natural dignity. His clerks, in fact, nicknamed him Leo, without knowing he was born in mid-August. Like most Bouviers, he had a forceful, protruding chin, wide-apart eyes, and a rather heavy, stubby nose. As he grew older, deep vertical creases appeared in his cheeks, and dark half moons under his eyes. A mustache filled the rather large expanse between his nose and his upper lip, the ends of which he eventually waxed into two finely pointed barbs. His bearing was so kingly it inspired instant derision or instant respect. One had the feeling, on meeting him for the first time, that here was a man of powerful convictions who was not to be trifled with.

JVB, Jr., made the most of his virile good looks by paying careful attention to his dress. He preferred a continental cut to his clothes and kept his tailors, Imant and Bell, busy refurbishing his vast wardrobe. His typical winter uniform would include either a dark, double-breasted suit, or morning coat with striped trousers, high stiff collar, gray vest, large knotted gray tie with a pearl stickpin, black homburg, silver-handled cane, and spats. His Phi Beta Kappa key would be prominently displayed on his vest watch chain, and he would invariably carry his Union Club rosette in his buttonhole.

Professionally JVB, Jr., was authoritative, forceful, and strongwilled. His energy and persuasiveness in the courtroom were famous in New York and he was known to hold fixed, dogmatic opinions. A born leader of men, he was patriarchal in his family and imperious with his servants and employees. People were often afraid of JVB, Jr. His combustible temper and detonating glances would cower relatives, employees, and associates, and he had an irritating tendency to trespass on people emotionally. Of his employees he demanded complete, accurate, honest answers, and if he didn't receive them he fired the employee who failed to deliver. Litigation was a way of life with him and he was utterly brazen in family argument or courtroom battle. If he worshipped a god, it was victory. He would win at all cost. His greatest failing was self-deception. He had an uncanny ability to see only what he wanted to see, to eliminate from consideration anything that challenged his image of himself, his family, and his world. Thus he could be surrounded by personal tragedy in his own immediate family and not see it, or feel it, because he did not want to see it or feel it. One of his better qualities was a capacity for genuine friendship. His affections and devotions were deep and lasting, never diffuse or superficial: those whom he befriended knew him to be loyal, steadfast, and trustworthy. His gregarious nature allowed him to draw his friends from an unusually broad spectrum of society. Among his close friends were such diverse personalities as the socialite Lion Gardiner, owner of Gardiner's Island, the humorist Irvin Cobb, two unsuccessful candidates for the Presidency, Al Smith and Charles Evans Hughes, the artists Childe Hassam, Hamilton King, and Albert Herter, and Mayor Bannister of East Hampton.

Although Major Bouvier gave the impression of being very tough, he had a sentimental streak in him which often surprised his family and friends. Once, when his beloved twins cut their long red hair, he burst into tears. Anniversaries of his mother's birth and marriage would elicit unbelievably sugary poems from his pen, and he had a sentimental reverence for his ancestors so extreme that his writings about them were often downright embarrassing.

Perhaps his greatest foible was his love of elegant, sumptuous living. His expensive taste in clothes, furnishings, cars, and homes, the high style of his way of life, was to strain the family finances to the limit and endow his children and grandchildren with preferences and habits so extravagant that only enormous incomes, which were not always forthcoming, could satisfy them.

The first two generations of American Bouviers had rather narrow interests. Michel, Sr., John, Sr., and MC had little on their minds besides making money and caring for their families. JVB, Jr., however, had cultivated interests beyond family and moneymaking. One of these was literature or, rather, writing. He had begun writing at Columbia, where he contributed to the college's literary magazine. Although he never wrote professionally, he was an amateur poet and essayist all his life, turning out a quantity of verse, correspondence, oratory, and miscellany that eventually amounted to a considerable oeuvre. His style was rhetorical, prolix, baroque, lacking genuine literary sensibility but full of literary pretensions. As a reader he was a devotee of Shakespeare, Macaulay, Edgar Wallace, Ngaio Marsh, and anything to do with George Washington and the American Revolution. Among his many writings he turned out a stream of articles and speeches on American history and politics, several essays on the law, a study of Shakespeare's amatory poems, a history of the

Bouvier family, a 379-page *Pocket Agendum* of miscellaneous information, hundreds of poems, 33 volumes of diaries, and an immense correspondence.

His most ambitious editorial effort was his *Pocket Agendum*, a work which affords us considerable insight into the quality of his mind and the nature of his beliefs. The volume, which he had privately printed in 1939, is advertised on the flyleaf as having been "compiled by and for the personal convenience of the author" and is divided into seven sections: "Lexicon (somewhat after the manner of Dr. Samuel Johnson)," "Quotations," "Quotations from the Latin," "Qualities and Personalities," "Axioms (rugged maxims hewn from life)," "Mythology," and "Similes." Among its many uses, Major Bouvier employed the *Agendum* as a handy reference for speech and letter writing and as a reserve of big words and weighty expressions for use in court when he was up against an unsympathetic judge. Apparently the use of long, unusual words and Latin quotations which no one understood would impress a recalcitrant judge with JVB, Jr.'s vast erudition and often win him over to his side. The longest and most interesting section of the *Agendum* is the Lexicon, consisting of a vocabulary of unusual words, a biographical dictionary, a short chronology of world history, and a long series of quotations on every subject imaginable. In the vocabulary we find such impressive words as accipitrine, acidulate, abditive, anamorphosis, abluent, cockatrice, curtilage, docimasy, ithyphallic, nocent, olla, oneiromancy, parasceuastic, supralapsarian, and thrasonical. In the biographical dictionary there are brief identifications of most of the great men of world history, from Aeschylus through Correggio and Pericles to Wycliffe and Zoroaster. And the world chronology is a relatively simple summation of what each century stood for. If we can assume that the quotations JVB, Jr., selected for such important Lexicon topics as "democracy," "education," "marriage," etc., reflect his own views on those subjects, then we can readily reconstruct an outline of his credo by quoting from them. Thus:

> DEMOCRACY: "A pleasant lawless constitution giving equal rights to unequal people" (Plato). "The right of every man to enjoy in accordance with his aptitudes .... The material and spiritual opportunities that nature and science have placed at the disposition of mankind (Walter Page). "The

defect of democracy is its tendency to put mediocrity into power" (Spinoza). "He who seeks equality between unequals seeks an absurdity" [No author given—was it Bouvier?].

HISTORY: "The art of choosing among many lies that one which most resembles the truth" (Rousseau).

MARRIAGE: "In primitive society marriage was a contract, not a sacrament. It was by purchase or exchange. The widower inherited his wife's sisters but not necessarily her property. Actually the man acquired a sole sexual use" [Bouvier?]. "Marriage was defined by Lord Beaconsfield as 'The triumph of hope over experience.' " "It is a biological truth that all rapacious animals including the vulture are monogamous. Not so, however, with humans. Abraham, Mohammed and Charlemagne had more than one wife at the same time. The Abbot elect of St. Augustine at Canterbury in 1171 had 70 children in a single village" [Bouvier?].

REVOLUTION: "Generally: the phenomena of: there is a general increase of wealth, power and intelligence among the repressed classes before a revolution. Only those who have tasted better conditions revolt. Revolutions are not started by classes in the depth of privations" [Bouvier?].

WOMEN: "Original status for nearly ten thousand years was 'a household slave, a social ornament or a sexual convenience' " [Bouvier?]. "Jehova grouped wives and mothers with cattle and real estate" [Bouvier?]. "Schopenhauer and Nietzsche held women as contemptibly inferior. 'When thou goest to a woman remember thy whip,' said Nietzsche." "Man's excuse for seduction: 'Since he has given something not in the woman's possession he had robbed her of nothing'" (The American Scholar). "In wearing of her ring woman should remember that it is a symbol that has been only slightly changed in its locus in quo; since it was originally worn about the neck as a sign of serfdom to her master" [Bouvier?]. "She was a great man whose only fault was being a woman" (Voltaire on his mistress, Marquise de Chalet). "Earth's noblest thing—a woman perfected" (Lowell). "Praise a wife but remain a bachelor" [Bouvier?].

Under "AXIOMS: rugged maxims hewn from life," JVB, Jr., lists, among others:

"Dress is the badge of lost innocence" (Santayana).
No food is so bitter as the bread of dependence and no ascent so painful as the staircase of a patron" [Bouvier?].
"He that wants money wants everything" (Fuller).
"The highest price a man can pay for a thing is to ask for it" (Ray).

One of the funniest and most self-revealing sections is the one entitled "Quotations." In it the Major had the temerity to intersperse his own immortal observations, duly laced with obscure words, among those of such giants as Milton, Shakespeare, Bacon, and Goethe. Thus, we find a typical page containing this mixture:

"He that dies pays all debts" (Shakespeare).
"His conduct was rapidly becoming albescent" (Bouvier).
"Grief is the agony of an instant, its indulgence the blunder of a life" (Disraeli).
"His timidity amounted to a moral diplopia" (Bouvier).
"The theater is to the mind as the bow to the fiddle" (Bacon).
"Christ was not the only avatar" (Bouvier).
"There is nothing humbler than ambition when it is about to climb" [Author not given].
"An idler is a human clotheshorse" (Bouvier).

Under "Qualities and Personalities" JVB, Jr., included a number of statements pertaining to the sex life of famous people, including enough relating to infidelity to give rise to the suspicion that he might have been trying to justify his own occasional lapses:

"Goethe caroused and had numerous affairs with married women."
"Montaigne had a mistress next door to his wife's home."

"Napoleon had innumerable mistresses not only in Paris but in his campaigns, one of his officers was his procurer."

JVB, Jr., composed scores of poems for his children's and grandchildren's birthdays during his lifetime. And his children and grandchildren would reciprocate by writing poems for his birthdays. Here is one his grandchildren—Jacqueline Bouvier, Michelle Scott, Edith Beale, and I—wrote to commemorate his eightieth:

> Here's to Grampy, they call him Jack
> He's the best of all the pack
> At sinking putts without a peer
> And always bringing us joy and cheer.
> > CHORUS—Oh here he comes with fife and drum
> > Always bringing his family fun
> > The Squire of Further Lane, oh!

> Here's to dear old lovable Gramps
> Who dislikes long pajama pants,
> With his scissors you will see
> Cutting them off above the knee.
> > CHORUS

> Here's to Grampy, they call him Jack,
> He's the best of all the pack,
> At bridge he always makes a slam
> And he's East Hampton's favorite man.
> > CHORUS

> Here's to Grampy, what a man!
> He's the head of the Bouvier clan,
> And when he's looking for a pub,
> You'll find him at the Union Club.
> > CHORUS

> Here's to the Major whom you'll find
> Has the greatest legal mind.
> When not engaged in making rhymes
> You'll find him reading the New York Times.
> > CHORUS

Here's to Grampy who likes to Scout
And turn the Electric Light bulbs out.
To those who leave them on is sent
A note that will make them repent.
>CHORUS—Oh, here he comes with fife and
>drum
>Always bringing his family fun,
>The Squire of Further Lane, oh!

Major Bouvier's generation was patriotic in the extreme and Major Bouvier was a typical representative of his generation. His flag-waving was of the same intensity as Theodore Roosevelt's and can justly be termed chauvinistic. One of the ways he expressed his deep love of country was by joining patriotic societies such as the Sons of the American Revolution, the Society of the Cincinnati, and the Military Order of the Loyal Legion of the United States—although, admittedly, membership in these organizations, which was primarily based on lineage, carried social as well as patriotic distinctions he was equally proud of. JVB, Jr., joined the Sons of the Revolution of the State of New York in 1913, became president of the organization in 1929, and was elected General President of the General, or national, Society, comprising the societies of all forty-eight states, in 1931. He derived his claim to membership in the SAR from his mother's ancestors and specifically from her great-grandfather, Lieutenant John Griffith, who had fought in the War for Independence. In his capacity as General President of the General Society, Major Bouvier delivered several important addresses, one of which propelled him momentarily into the national spotlight and was perhaps the culmination of his career as a public speaker. The occasion was the dedication of the George Washington Bridge, spanning the Hudson River between New York and New Jersey. The ceremonies took place at the New York approach to the bridge, on October 24, 1931, before 5,000 invited dignitaries, 300,000 spectators, and a national radio audience. Among the other speakers were the Honorable Charles Francis Adams, then Secretary of the Navy and a direct descendant of two Presidents, one of whom had been Washington's Vice President, and the Honorable Franklin D. Roosevelt, then governor of the State of New York. John Vernou Bouvier, Jr., as General President of the national SAR had been designated "Orator of the Day," and it was with great pride that the Bouviers, from the eighty-four-year-old MC to the twenty-six-year-old twins, watched their standard-bearer deliver the day's principal address, with so many other distinguished speakers on the platform.

The address Major Bouvier delivered was typically his own, rhetorical, flowery, a bit exaggerated. After praising the engineering feat, for the George Washington was then the largest suspension bridge ever built, and evoking the history of the site (the defense of Fort Washington), he came out with the mighty generalization: "He [Washington] is the outstanding figure of all time," and concluded: "As Washington is virtue's spiritual symbol, so the Flag is its concrete emblem. Each stands for patriotism, valor, loyalty, sacrifice and service, the noblest attributes vouchsafed by God to man. Hence let both forever in your thoughts remain one and inseparable."

JVB, Jr., was a great admirer of George Washington and so his membership in the Society of the Cincinnati meant even more to him than his exalted position in the Sons of the Revolution, for Washington had been the first President General of the Cincinnati, holding the office from the organization's founding in 1783 until his death in 1799.

Founded by commissioned officers of the American Army who, with their French allies, had fought in the Revolutionary War, the society was named after Lucius Quinctius Cincinnatus, the fifth-century B.C. general who saved Rome from two invasions, then returned to his farm with no thought of personal reward. Cincinnati, Ohio, in turn, was named after the society. Its original purpose was to help preserve the rights and liberties for which its first members had fought, promote and cherish the union between the states, "render permanent the cordial affection subsisting among the Officers," and extend "beneficence towards those Officers and their families who unfortunately may be under the necessity of receiving it." Pierre Charles L'Enfant, French architect and planner of the city of Washington, designed the society's emblem, and a blue and white ribbon—"symbolic of the association of America and her ally, France"—was created for its members to wear. Thirteen constituent state societies were organized, one in each of the thirteen original states, and a fourteenth was organized in France. All fourteen are still in existence.

Eligibility to membership in the Cincinnati was restricted to officers of the American and allied French Army and Navy who had served during the war, and was made hereditary "to per-petuate the Society and preserve inviolate and immutable the principles stated in the Institution." John V. Bouvier, Jr., derived his membership here too from his mother, this time from her paternal grandfather, Captain James Ewing, who had reputedly been one of Washington's officers.

The Society of the Cincinnati was attacked by many veterans of the Revolution, especially enlisted men, the year after its founding, on the grounds that it created a privileged class and a hereditary peerage, dividing the state into two orders: "Patricians or Nobles on the one side and the Rabble on the other." In France, Mirabeau castigated it as "That nobility of Barbarians."

JVB, Jr., was admitted to that nobility, which fortunately never became what its original detractors feared it would, in 1918, the year he was admitted to practice before the Supreme Court, and soon became deeply involved in the society's activities, which consisted mostly in the formal celebration of national holidays, the support of historical research, and the granting of scholar-ships. Today his twins keep up the family tradition by taking an equally active part in the Daughters of the Cincinnati. Major Bouvier's membership would eventually pass to his son Jack, and Jack would pass his on to his nephew, Michel. Since the Bouviers had eligibility to membership from two "lines," the Ewing and the Griffith, places in the society are now being reserved for two of JVB, Jr.'s great-grandsons, Michel Bouvier IV and John F. Kennedy, Jr.

With his active membership in two patriotic societies and his reputation for being a Revolutionary War buff, JVB, Jr., was much in demand as a speaker on national holidays. Washington's birthday, Lincoln's birthday, the Fourth of July always found him delivering a flag-waving address somewhere. In time, his patriotic speeches became famous. When Hamilton King was commissioned to do a series of murals for the Maidstone Club in East Hampton, which were supposed to caricature the club's members, he portrayed Major Bouvier standing before a vast audience, eating a dictionary.

JVB, Jr.'s patriotism was closely associated with his interest in war. That his maternal ancestors had fought in the American Revolution, his grandfather had fought for Napoleon, and his father had fought in the Civil War was a source of infinite pride to Major Bouvier, matched only by the pride he felt when his younger son, Bud, volunteered at the outbreak of World War I, his cousin, Walter Vernou, became an admiral, and he himself in 1917 became a Major Judge Advocate. How he gloried in his son's subsequent exploits at the front in France and in his own title! How he loved himself in his uniform and saw to it he would be called Major for the rest of his life! If there was a sure way to JVB, Jr.'s heart, it was to praise the military exploits of his ancestors and his son and make a point of calling him Major.

Politically, JVB, Jr., was an independent, inclined toward the Democrats, until Franklin D. Roosevelt, whom he knew, completed his first year in office, at which time he metamorphosed into a permanent Republican, vehemently opposed to the New Deal.

As a Son of the Revolution, JVB, Jr., felt it his duty to be, as he once expressed it, "a factor for conservation." He explained his position in an address he gave before the Pennsylvania SAR in 1932 as General President of the General Society:

> I am derived from those who made this country possible....
> The least I can do is to make my contribution toward the preservation of the institutions my forebears constituted.

That he saw no contradiction between his conservatism and his forebears' revolutionary spirit is a commentary on what a hundred and fifty years can do to a revolution. Be that as it may, Major Bouvier became a defender of the status quo. A rough indication of the vehemence of his reaction to Roosevelt's revolution may be had from the entries he made in his Lexicon, under "New Deal":

> "In their sexless orgies of intellectual delirium they have stressed the necessity for a 'regimented public opinion' which obviously is the antithesis of the individualism that made this country possible, the succubus of the genius of our institutions and the blatant challenger of the principles embodied in the Declaration of Independence."
>
> "The Congress having abjectly surrendered its powers and authority to the Executive Will, there remained only the Supreme Court of the United States as the

Constitution's defender. Obviously this barrier must be assaulted and levelled to further the interests of personal domination and control."

"At the worst the New Deal Administration's socio-economic therapy was alleged to be a 'beneficent dictatorship.' As well speak of an amiable assassination, a chaste seduction or a mule in foal."

As the day approached when he would inherit part of MC's fortune, JVB, Jr., became quite vehement on the subject of the New Deal tax structure. Again from the Lexicon:

Taxes ("New Deal"): There is an astonishing narrowness of the Federal Income Tax structure. The number of persons paying Federal Income Taxes for 1932 was just under 2,000,000, representing only 4% of the total voting population. Less than 10% of the taxpayers paid 87% of the total tax, while less than 3% paid 75% of the total tax. Thus 1/5 of 1% of the voting population pays three-quarters of the income tax. To make the people generally tax conscious, whereby they will be interested in cutting down administrative expenditures, our entire tax structure must be broadened at the base.

Major Bouvier enjoyed historical ironies. One wonders whether he would have had the necessary detachment to appreciate the irony that a son of one of the most rabid New Dealers, by marrying one of JVB, Jr.'s granddaughters, would be responsible for bringing JVB, Jr.'s family more fame than the Bouviers had ever been able to earn by themselves.

JVB, Jr.'s conservatism extended also to his religious life. From his very Catholic forebears he had inherited a venerable religious tradition. One of his aunts was a nun, four others were fanatically Catholic, Katharine Drexel was considered a saint during her lifetime, his parents and grandparents had all been Catholics, and MC remained a pillar of St. Patrick's Cathedral until his death. In spite of this tradition, however, JVB, Jr., learned to think for himself on religious matters and eventually came to reject several of the cornerstone dogmas of his faith. In a letter to Miss Atherton M. Leach of the Pennsylvania Historical Society, in connection with some genealogical research she was doing for him, JVB, Jr., included an aside that gives us a fairly good idea of his position:

> Despite the fact that I am a Catholic, heretically styled "Roman," I cannot bring myself to believe in the doctrine of Original Sin, or of its corollary the Immaculate Conception, or the theological fiction of the Virgin Birth. Perhaps I might, therefore, be called a Socinian and Pelagian, the former specifically denying the doctrine of Original Sin, and the latter denying the Trinity, the personal devil, Original Sin, and Eternal Punishment.
>
> How I can square my beliefs with my attendance at church each Sunday, I shall not occupy your time in explaining, but to my own thought my position is entirely consistent.

How JVB, Jr., did square his beliefs with his attendance at mass every Sunday, we shall never know. The fact remains that he *did* go to church on Sundays and holy days of obligation, he *did* go to confession and to communion, and he did bring his children up to be Catholics. His position, in the end, was to observe the outward forms of his religion, even though he did not fully believe in what they stood for. Catholicism was his heritage. For that reason, primarily, he would conserve it.

It was unfortunate for his children and grandchildren that JVB, Jr., was not as conservative with his money as he was in his politics and religion. The first Bouvier to leave less money than he had inherited, JVB, Jr., lacked the financial acumen of his grandfather and uncle and their interest in moneymaking, yet he was a more extravagant spender than either one of them. Not good at making profitable investments—again, he was the first Bouvier repeatedly to sell for less than he had bought—he was, however, adept at living beyond his means. In the depths of the Depression, on an income of approximately $43,000 a year (before taxes), derived from investments amounting to a little over a million dollars, he maintained two estates in East Hampton, one of which was a showplace, and a deluxe eight-room apartment at 765 Park Avenue, kept up memberships in five expensive clubs, and employed, full time, a male secretary, a gardener, a chauffeur, a cook, and two or three maids. He also gave generously to various charities—more, in fact, than was in his capacity to give.

Large contributions would go to Katharine Drexel's and Louise Morrell's schools for Negroes and Indians, and he would always send a sizable check in the twins' names to the "neediest cases of *The New York Times*." Again, he had a tradition to uphold: MC, Zénaïde, Alexine, and Mary had given tens of thousands to charities in their lifetime and had left tens of thousands to charities in their wills, and JVB, Jr., felt that he had to follow suit. He also gave money freely to his children and loaned fairly large sums to them as well, including a $50,000 loan to his son Jack which was never repaid. He was not, however, so generous to his employees. He would give his faithful secretary, John Ficke, who had been with him for many years, a Christmas bonus of only $50; he paid his personal maid, Esther, only $45 a month; and his gardener, who had a wife and three children, only $200 a month.

Unlike his grandfather, who had left each of his ten children equal legacies, JVB, Jr., played favorites in his will, leaving his five children unequal legacies. As a result of his inability, or unwillingness, to increase his capital through shrewd investing, his extravagance, and the division of his estate among his children, the family's financial fortunes would go into a decline after his death from which they would never again recover.

The Bouviers had traveled a long road from Eustache's shop in Pont-Saint-Esprit. In fact, by the 1920s Pont-Saint-Esprit had all but been eliminated from the family's consciousness and the descendants of the Bouviers who had remained behind had been almost totally forgotten. Looking back over the decades at the by now murky origins of his family in France, Major John Vernou Bouvier, Jr., wealthy New York attorney, member of a dozen exclusive clubs and societies, pillar of East Hampton's summer colony, and member of Society with a capital S, proved incapable of seeing those origins for what they were, and so when he set out to write a book about them in the early 1920s he accomplished a miracle, turning a few loaves of bread and a jug of water into some very big fish and some very choice wine. The incarnation of this miracle—a slim volume of family history entitled *Our Forebears*— was to bolster the family's social image beyond repair and leave an impact on the Bouviers' collective and individual psychologies so pronounced, many of them would never recover from it. For with *Our Forebears* the Bouviers took still another step toward social beatification, suddenly becoming descendants of courtiers to the kings of France.

# $\mathcal{V}$

"A people which takes no pride in the noble achievements of remote ancestors will never achieve anything to be remembered, with pride, by remote descendants" (Lord Macaulay).

"To forget one's ancestors is to be a brook without a source, a tree without a root" (Anonymous).

"They sought their register among those that were reckoned by genealogy, but it was not found; wherefore, were they, as polluted, put from the priesthood" (Nehemiah, Book VII).

WITH THESE JUSTIFICATIONS, JOHN VERNOU BOUVIER, JR., PREFACED the book that was to have such a profound influence on his family. With these justifications, also, JVB, Jr., unconsciously expressed the great change that had taken place in the Bouviers' feelings about their social status: their self-promotion to the upper class. JVB, Jr.'s father and grandfather couldn't have cared less about genealogy. Michel Bouvier, Sr., knew he had come from very humble origins, and JVB, Sr., knew he was the son of a *parvenu*. But JVB, Jr., far enough removed from his grandfather's generation to be able to ignore Michel's original status and his early struggle for social acceptance, was determined to bestow upon his family an aristocratic background.

The promotion John Vernou Bouvier, Jr., gave his ancestors was, above all, an expression of his deep sense of family piety—what amounted, in his case, to a veritable religion of the blood. For JVB, Jr., was utterly devoted to and absorbed in his family. His thirty-three volumes of diaries indicate that he spent most of his waking hours thinking about his children and grandchildren. He wanted them to succeed at all cost, to do honor to the name Bouvier. The more help he could give them in promoting their careers, the more he felt he was fulfilling his duty as a father and grandfather. One of the ways he felt he could help his progeny succeed was to give them as secure a feeling as possible about their social status. It was with this purpose ultimately in mind that he composed his idealized history of the Bouviers.

The first edition of *Our Forebears*—paid for by MC—came out in 1925, when its author was sixty. For thirty years JVB, Jr., had been doing research on his French ancestry. It is curious that a man whose profession demanded the rigorous testing of evidence did not apply the same critical spirit to the practice of genealogy. Evidently his need for a distinguished ancestry was so urgent that it overcame the mental habits cultivated in a lifetime in the legal profession. For, with testimony to the contrary staring him in the face, he still categorically asserted that both the Bouviers and the Vernous were descended from French nobility.

It was an old story. During the Italian Renaissance, another era of self-made men, a family that had obtained some eminence would employ historians and genealogists to discover noble ancestors, so it could be on a social par with the decadent aristocrats it had replaced. Federico Sforza, a Lombard soldier who had risen from the landless peasantry to the Dukedom of Milan, was reported to have employed a squad of researchers to investigate his background; they discovered that he had the blood not of one but of seven imperial dynasties in his veins. Five hundred years later, similar genealogical sleights of hand became fairly common in America, especially in JVB, Jr.'s generation. Coincidentally, one of the most prodigious feats of genealogical abracadabra in America was performed by a member of a family that would one day be associated with the Bouviers: the Auchinclosses. Surpassing JVB, Jr., in both wishful thinking and historical alchemy, the late Charles C. Auchincloss spent a good part of his life working up an elaborate genealogical chart showing how his family had descended from no less than three royal lines, those of England, Scotland, and France, a claim about as reliable as the ancestry once ascribed to Julius Caesar, among whose forebears, it was proved, there were several gods.

In all fairness to J. V. Bouvier, Jr., and Charles C. Auchincloss, it must be admitted that their efforts to promote their families' status were conditioned by the social climate in which they lived. American society in the 1890s and the early twentieth century was still very much under the influence of traditional European concepts of social rank. Although, with great effort, class barriers could be crossed, the categories were much more sharply defined than they are today and the class structure was taken much more seriously. Ancestry was a vital factor. To be accounted a gentleman, one had to have a grandfather, at least, who was a gentleman. To attain the upper class, one had to have more than mere wealth or talent; one needed an illustrious lineage.

To proclaim a distinguished ancestry was the mission of *Our Forebears*. Discovering it and proving it was not always easy, however. JVB, Jr., had distinguished colonial American ancestors, thanks to his mother. As we have seen, both her great-grandfather, John Griffith, and her grandfather, James Ewing, were wealthy Maryland plantation owners who had been officers in the American Revolution. The French ancestors, however, were another matter. It would take considerable imagination and ingenuity to ennoble the Bouviers and the Vernous.

JVB, Jr., began his account of the Bouviers by citing some passages from a volume entitled *Armorial de Dauphiné*, containing "Les Armoiries figurées de toutes les familles nobles et notables de cette province," in which he had found, and appropriated as his own, a noble Bouvier family described as "an ancient house of Fontaine, near Grenoble." Among numerous irrelevant items, he stated that a "François Bouvier was a counsellor in Parliament in 1553," that "Dauphiné Bouvier intermarried with one François Reynaud of Grenoble, a celebrated lawyer in Parliament about 1620," who "was ennobled in 1609." But he did not make the slightest effort to link these illustrious Bouviers convincingly to his own family. The reader was simply led to assume they were bona fide ancestors. A description of the Bouvier arms followed: "d'azur au lion d'or; au chef de même chargé de trois huchets de gueules." This was the coat of arms of the noble Bouvier family mentioned in the *Armorial* and had nothing to do with JVB, Jr.'s Bouviers, who, it will be recalled, did not originate in Dauphiné but in Savoy and had not been important enough to have a coat of arms.

After the quotations from the *Armorial,* and the description of the coat of arms, JVB, Jr., came up with his first flesh-and-blood ancestors, Georges Bouvier (1705-1754) and François Bouvier (1773), grandfather and father of Eustache. He does not say anything about Georges or François, but we are to assume—since "it may be observed that the given name François has, since the day of François Bouvier, Counsellor in Parliament in the year 1553, been borne by some Bouvier in the generations succeeding"—that there was a connection between the two François Bouviers.

In fact, there was none. François Bouvier was definitely JVB's great-great-grandfather, but he was far from being related to the nobility and to "Counsellors in Parliament." He was, instead, one of the petite bourgeoisie of Grenoble, a *marchand quincaillier* who kept a small hardware shop specializing in kitchen utensils. He and his wife, the former Benoît Repelin, were members of the parish of Saint-Laurent, and the records of their children's births are still in existence in the church's archives. These records indicate the modest class to which the François Bouviers belonged, for they give the names and professions of all the children's godparents. It was a class of industrious, honorable, but humble artisans. At the baptism of their son, Claude, on April 9, 1755, for instance, the godfather was Claude Aquette, "domestic servant to Monsieur de Pinar, Counsellor in parliament," and the godmother was Reine Doulene, wife of "Claude Arnaud, farmer to Monsieur Dumolin." Other godparents of Bouvier children included a draper, a tailor, and a glover. The section of Grenoble in which these modest, hardworking people lived was one of the poorest in the city, a maze of narrow alleys and low, tile-roofed buildings quite removed from the better residential areas of the town. Most of its inhabitants were glovers. It was a section noted for its social discontent, full of real and potential revolutionaries. During the French Revolution the inhabitants of Saint-Laurent-de-Grenoble were conspicuous in the storming of the local bastille. And in 1815 Napoleon received the most tumultuous welcome after his return from Elba from residents of this section, the welcome that was to spur him on to Waterloo. And yet, JVB, Jr., true to his noble-ancestors obsession, always told his children and grandchildren that their ancestors were noble émigrés fleeing from persecution by the leaders of the French Revolution.

One of the most blatant distortions in *Our Forebears* lies in the renaming of Eustache père. Throughout the book JVB, Jr., refers to him as André-Eustache, yet the name André does not appear in his baptismal record or his marriage record or his death certificate. Where did JVB, Jr., find the name André, and why did he confer it on his great-grandfather? More than likely, he plucked the name out of the *Armorial de Dauphiné,* which lists an André Bouvier as one of the noble Bouviers of the province. And he awarded it to his ancestor both to ennoble him and to distinguish him from his profligate grandson of the same name.

Eustache Bouvier and Thérèse Mercier had thirteen children, six of whom died in infancy, but in *Our Forebears* JVB, Jr., mentioned only one of them, his grandfather, Michel. He thus eliminated succeeding generations of the French side of the family from his book, for if he had included Michel's brothers and sisters, he would have had to mention their descendants, and it would be immediately obvious to the reader from their names and occupations that they were not nobility. JVB, Jr., was perfectly aware that these descendants existed: he occasionally gave them financial assistance. And yet none of his children or grandchildren was ever told of these French relatives, and his book on the family ignored them completely. In the unusually long entry under "poor relations" in the *Pocket Agendum*, JVB, Jr., gave away his attitude toward his modest French cousins.

> A poor relation referred to by Chas. Lamb as:
> "An odious approximation."
> "The most irrelevant thing in nature."
> "Agathocles Pot."
> "The hail in the harvest."
> "The ounce of sour in the pound of sweet."
> "An amiable futility."
> "A rebuke to your rising."
> "A blot on your scutcheon."
> "A mote in your eye."
> "A Mordecai (Esther's cousin who saved the Jews from extermination) at your gate."
> "A Lazarus at your door."
> "A sentient futility" (Bouvier).
> "A domestic exiguity" (Bouvier).

The irony was that several of his contemporary French relations were far from poor. The descendants of Elizabeth Bouvier, Michel's sister, were, in fact, almost as prosperous as he was. But they were not titled nobility.

Another revealing omission in *Our Forebears* concerns the early life of the founding father. JVB, Jr., made much of Michel Bouvier's later business activities, his career as a manufacturer of veneers, an importer of marble and mahogany, and a real-estate operator. But he never breathed a word about his early days as a cabinetmaker.

He therefore also omitted mention of the true nature of his grandfather's association with Joseph Bonaparte. According to *Our Forebears*, the relationship was purely social: Michel and

Joseph were good friends who occasionally visited each other's homes.

What is sad, and a revealing commentary on the social prejudices of his times, is that JVB, Jr., was unable to appreciate his grandfather Michel's true nobility: by working his way up from nothing in the face of great odds, Michel had proved himself more of an aristocrat, in the original, Greek sense of the word, than any Bouvier before or since. Equally sad was his inability to appreciate that a family of lower-middle-class status in Europe could rise to the upper class in America, and that this was something to be proud of. The Bouviers' saga was not by any means an isolated case among distinguished American families. The Du Ponts had also come from the petite bourgeoisie of France; the Rockefellers had come from a class of small farmers; the first Vanderbilt emigrated to America as an indentured servant; and the first Ford arrived in the New World in 1848 a poverty-stricken victim of the Irish potato famine.

The promotion John Vernou Bouvier, Jr., gave the Bouviers in *Our Forebears* was nothing, however, compared to what he did for the Vernous. If he inferred that the Bouviers might have noble ancestors, he openly stated that the Vernous were of the aristocracy, that several of them had served at court.

The lineage he turned up for Louise Vernou's ancestors went back so far and was so distinguished that it took up more space in *Our Forebears* than any other pedigree. It began with an elevated preamble:

> The family of Vernou is one of the most illustrious and ancient of the Province of Poitou . . . it has been in existence since the year 1086 and has had many high honors and dignities conferred upon it. It contracted alliances with the most powerful families of the nobility of France, and was confirmed in its nobility of ancient extraction by two royal decrees of August 23, 1667 and May 29, 1719, respectively.
>
> Arms: D'azur au croissant d'argent Couronne: de Marquis-Supports: deux Griffons-Devise-"Intacta Veneno" "This device was given to de Vernou, Baron de Chancelee, Comte de Malzeard, Marquis de Bonneuil, by King Louis XIV, who nominated him a Chevalier of his Orders by reason of his resistance to Prince Marillac at the epoch of the internal troubles in France, wherein de Vernou by his

example and his influence maintained the fidelity of the nobility of Poitou to the King."

It was Marie-César-Antoine de Vernou that John Vernou Bouvier, Jr., claimed was the father of John Vernou. According to JVB, Jr., who got his information from the Archives de la Noblesse et du Còllege Héraldique du France, an organization which once specialized in compiling pedigrees for descendants of noble French families, but which no longer exists, Marie-César-Antoine had, among others, a son by the name of Jean who emigrated to America sometime during the decade following the French Revolution. Surprisingly, a Jean-Marie-Maximilen Vernou did exist about the time of John Vernou, but they were two different persons. Jean-Marie-Maximilen Vernou de Bonneuil was born in Guadeloupe in 1776, the son of the noble François-Henri Vernou and Marie-Adelaide Gaalon de Barzay, and, with the exception of a brief period in America, spent most of his life in Guadeloupe. John Vernou, on the other hand, emigrated to Philadelphia around 1797, was naturalized in 1808, and remained in Philadelphia until his death.

The question is whether one of the distinguished Vernou de Bonneuil family, no matter how temporarily impoverished, would have allowed his daughter to marry someone of such modest social status as Michel Bouvier, in spite of Michel's potential as a breadwinner. In rigidly stratified France, the Bouviers and the de Vernous would have been poles apart. If John Vernou was Jean de Vernou, he was forced out of France by the revolution the Bouviers had helped ferment. And Michel Bouvier was, in turn, forced out of France by the restoration of people like the de Vernous.

After exalting his ancestors, JVB, Jr., devoted the remaining sections of his book to a presentation of the living generations of his family: his children, grandchildren, and himself. With characteristic obliviousness to anything that might tarnish the family image, he reported the births and marriages of his children but not their divorces. By the 1940 edition of *Our Forebears*, four of his five children had been divorced and eight of his ten grandchildren were separated from one of their parents. There was a great deal of bickering between the divided couples. But to read *Our Forebears*, one would imagine the Bouvier nest to be perennially joyous and united.

It was typical of JVB, Jr., to ignore the shortcomings of his family, whether they were ancestors, children, or himself. The picture he presented of himself was so glorious one would think he had never known a failure in his entire life. After telling us that he had been vice president of his class, an honors man, Phi Beta Kappa, winner of the Chanler Senior Historical Essay prize, and valedictorian of his class at Columbia, after informing us of all the exclusive clubs and patriotic associations he belonged to, and the offices he had held in them, he enumerated his many professional, military, social, and literary achievements, capping them with the eulogies he had received from eminent members of the bar.

Other complimentary remarks from noted legal personalities were interspersed among these "flattering credentials," as he called them, to complete JVB, Jr.'s tribute to himself. The book then announced the news that his son John Vernou Bouvier III was "duly elected a member of the Maryland Society of the Cincinnati, Feb. 22, 1940; a contemporary membership of father and son, which, if not definitely unique, may, nevertheless, be regarded as unusual." And concluded: "Thus have we reached the emergent year 1947 with the honorable record unimpaired and no 'blot upon the scutcheon.' It may well be said in humble thanksgiving that 'we have kept the Faith.' "

JVB, Jr., did research on his forebears to the end of his life. When he was eighty-one, he sent this revealing letter to a French government employee in Nice who had claimed he was a relative:

May 24, 1946

My dear Mr. Bouvier:

. . . The gist, as I gather, of your communication is to invite my interest in a research of the Bouvier family descent. This, I may inform you, I made as early as 1880, and caused to be printed for my grandchildren the results of my investigations in 1925, 1930, and 1940. I am herewith enclosing a condensed excerpt from the latest printing.

What I expended in time, in labor and, incidentally in money, is at the present not a comforting reflection, but I did secure that which is, in my judgment, relevant and authentic and for our mutual benefit perhaps it might be expedient to check my statements of facts and conclusions based thereon.

Specifically, however, I should wish to ascertain:
1) The name of the *father* of Georges Bouvier
2) The dates of his birth and death
3) The name of his wife
4) The dates of her birth and death
Naturally I should be extremely gratified if in your research you could provide me with:
1) The name of Georges Bouvier's *grandfather*
2) The dates of his birth and death
3) The name of his wife
This data will permit me the more readily to bridge the limbo between 1620 and 1698, a period of nearly two score years, but not, I should imagine, too formidable a task.

Should you be successful in the particular researches above indicated, my requirements will have been fulfilled and I should be extremely gratified to compensate you adequately for your labors.

Perhaps you may regard it as a little pretentious to claim the stemming from a family once so notable as the "ancient House of Fontaine near Grenoble." This does not spell pride, but merely intelligent satisfaction. Internally we have in this country, as well as abroad, instances of the rise, the fall and the resurgence of families from the social and other angles, and all the internal evidences that I have in my possession, but have not for obvious purposes set forth here, justifies my claim of descent.

Trusting for your successful investigations, I am

Sincerely yours,<br>J. V. Bouvier

Jr.
To: Marcel Bouvier, Esq., Nice, France

JVB, Jr., had absolutely no "internal evidence" to justify his claim of descent from the ancient house of Fontaine near Grenoble, but his self-deception was so pronounced that he had probably convinced himself that he had. Because it was his nature to believe only what he wanted to believe, no matter how it squared with objective truth, it can be said that Major Bouvier was not actually lying when he ascribed an illustrious lineage to his French forebears. In all likelihood he really believed the Bouviers and the Vernous were descended from the nobility and would have been surprised, rather than chagrined, if someone had disputed his claim. It would have been inconceivable for him that the residents of 1240 North Broad Street, St. Michel, San José, 14 West Forty-sixth Street, and Lasata could have stemmed from Montagnard charcoal burners and woodcutters.

In the preface to *Our Forebears*, JVB, Jr., stated that he intended "to arouse no unbecoming pride of birth, but rather to excite a worthy spirit of emulation." Unfortunately, the book itself often contradicted this purpose. *Our Forebears* did arouse "an unbecoming pride of birth" in many Bouviers, instilling in them a sense of unshakable social superiority. Had the true story of the family been told, JVB, Jr.'s averred intention might have been more easily realized. At least his progeny would not have assumed that the Bouviers had been on the top of the social heap since the beginning of time. The rags-to-riches career of the first Michel would have instructed them that their family's social and financial success had been won at the cost of a lifetime of sacrifice and hard work. Surprisingly, however, the book did have some beneficial effects. The social confidence it helped build was to be of inestimable value to those members of the family who had particularly demanding social obligations.

JVB, Jr., produced four editions of *Our Forebears* between 1925 and 1947. Each time he brought out a new edition, he solemnly presented a fresh copy to each of his children, grandchildren, and in-laws. The presentations usually took place at important family gatherings—at Thanksgiving, Christmas, Easter—and were accompanied by flowery patriotic speeches, mostly about the glorious Bouvier military record. Prospective in-laws, much to their surprise, and often to their annoyance, were also presented with copies, just so they would know what kind of family they were marrying into. And JVB, Jr., also saw to it that copies were sent to the New York Public Library, the Library of Congress, the New York Historical Society, the library of Columbia University, and the Pennsylvania Historical Association, thus assuring his fables widespread circulation.

If John F. Kennedy had not been elected President, Bouviers today would still be sunning themselves in the glow of *Our Forebears*. The book would never have come under critical scrutiny, and its myths would never have been exploded. But when the Kennedys came into the White House, *Our Forebears* suddenly was much in demand. Journalists requesting information on the new First Lady and her family were presented with copies of her grandfather's book. Its erroneous information was incorporated into thousands of newspaper and magazine articles, and Jacqueline Bouvier Kennedy's noble pedigrees were given general currency. Eventually, of course, someone was bound to check, and that someone was Francis J. Dallett, former director of Philadelphia's Athenaeum and a scholar of considerable reputation, who wrote an article for *Antiques* on Michel Bouvier's furniture. Dallett did not openly criticize JVB, Jr.'s book but limited himself to saying in the bibliography that *Our Forebears* was "so full of errors that it should be checked against other sources." The bibliography, however, did not come to the attention of the press or the general public, and so the Bouvier myths continued to propagate themselves over the land.

In spite of the vanities, misplaced values, self-deceptions, and social insecurities *Our Forebears* reveals in the soul of its author, the overall mitigating fact remains that JVB, Jr., wrote it primarily out of love for his children and grandchildren. If he had had no posterity, it is unlikely that he would have put pen to paper in the first place. As he saw it, he was doing his family a considerable service in setting forth what he conceived to be their history. It was with an enormous feeling of pride and affection and fulfillment, then, that he dedicated his book: "To my grandchildren and to those who may later add to their joyous company."

In the flyleaf of each grandchild's copy, JVB, Jr., wrote a brief dedicatory poem. The one he wrote in mine was typical of the others and faithfully expresses the purpose he hoped his book would fulfill:

> Jack, my lad, just con these pages
> And profit by your forebears' lives.
> While your interest still rages
> You may become extremely wise.

With his ancestors' lives duly recorded, an aristocratic image of his family successfully promulgated, and a large brood of children and grandchildren begotten to do honor to the name of Bouvier, JVB, Jr., as the sole male Bouvier of his generation, felt he had done his duty as a grandson, son, father, and grandfather. It remained for his posterity, and those who would later add to their joyous company, to justify his hopes, to realize in the future what he had been compelled to invent in the past.

# PART THREE

---

## *Tail of the Comet*

---

### THE FOURTH GENERATION

### [1914-1948]

# I

ON JUNE 28, 1914, JOHN VERNOU BOUVIER, JR., DID NOT BOTHER TO enter in his diary the news that the Archduke Francis Ferdinand, heir to the Austrian throne, had been shot by a Bosnian schoolboy in Sarajevo. Since it was his habit to record in his journal what he considered to be significant world events, often emphasizing them with several asterisks, it can be assumed that he omitted mention of the assassination because he did not consider it particularly important.

And yet, before long, that seemingly insignificant event had kindled a blaze that would devour dynasties, bring American soldiers to fight in Europe for the first time in history, and profoundly modify a way of life and a system of values that had lasted, relatively unchanged, since Waterloo. During the holocaust that saw the nineteenth century die, a generation of Americans was forged whose members would repudiate many of the ideals and values of their parents, indulging, after the slaughter, in previously unheard-of excesses, only to suffer grievously from the consequences of those excesses in the Depression that followed. It was a turbulent, unbalancing period that took an immense toll of life and sanity, and very few Americans survived unscathed.

The Bouviers were among the families that suffered more than most from the convulsions of the era. The lives of JVB, Jr.'s five children were to mirror the enthusiasms and the successes, the failures and tragedies, of their generation. In Jack and Bud and their wives, and Edith and the twins, Fitzgerald and Hemingway would have recognized their beautiful and their damned.

In 1915, a year after leaving Nutley, when Jack was twenty-one and the twins ten, the JVBs, Jr., moved from the Hotel Renaissance to a luxurious duplex on the sixth and seventh floors of 247 Fifth Avenue. The apartment contained a large living room, a dining room, a library, three bedrooms, three baths, an upstairs and a downstairs hall, kitchen, pantry, and two servant's rooms with baths. It became the winter headquarters of the new generation. To keep the place up, the Bouviers employed two live-in servants, a cook and a maid, and maintained a full-time seamstress and German governess for the twins. With MC and Mary at 14 West Forty-sixth Street and John, Sr., and Caroline at 987 Madison Avenue, the family, eleven strong, was firmly ensconced in Manhattan. To the Bouviers, Philadelphia now seemed almost as remote as Pont-Saint-Esprit.

By the spring of 1917, JVB, Jr.'s older children were pretty much on their own. Edith had recently married and was living with her husband in the same building on Madison Avenue—now the Hotel Carlisle—in which John, Sr., and Caroline had their apartment, and Jack and Bud were in the Army. The twins stayed with their parents while they attended school at the Sacred Heart Convent, 533 Madison Avenue, an institution at which their grandaunt Louise had once taught French and which is now the Women's Exchange.

While at 987 Madison, Edith and Phelan Beale had two children, Edith and Phelan, born in 1917 and 1920, respectively. They were JVB, Jr.'s first grandchildren and JVB, Sr.'s first great-grandchildren and were, of course, doted on by the entire family. By the time Phelan, Jr., was born, Phelan, Sr., was a law partner of his wife's father, counsel for the Wall Street firm Jack would soon be associated with, and an international corporate lawyer of considerable reputation and income. To manifest his success and provide more space for his growing family, he bought a sumptuous three-bedroom apartment at 405 Park Avenue and moved Edith, the children, the nurse, and the maid into it in 1920. An extravagant $50,000 having been spent in decorating the place, the Beales' huge, apple-green living room was one of the first in New York to have the new stippled walls that were to become so fashionable in the mid-twenties. Before long, the apartment became a favorite place for Bouvier get-togethers, with Edith and Phelan proudly presiding at Thanksgiving and Christmas galas attended by the entire clan.

While Phelan Beale was on a business trip to Berlin after the war, he bought his wife a magnificent Benz limousine and presented it to her, along with a chauffeur, on his return. A year later Edith gave him his third child, a son whom they named Bouvier Beale.

With a wealthy, successful husband, a magnificent Park Avenue apartment, a Benz limousine, three healthy children, two servants, and a chauffeur, Edith was doing pretty well for herself by 1923. Released by her servants from having to bother with household chores, and indulged by an adoring husband and an overattentive mother, she could devote herself to the two activities she had always been most interested in, the cultivation of her appearance and her voice.

The twins were very different. If Edith was theatrical, self-indulgent, and impractical, Maude and Michelle, who had been raised by a spartan German Fräulein, were domestic, dutiful, and full of common sense. If Edith left her household chores to her servants, the twins helped the servants keep up their parents' ménage. Since they were so obedient and trustworthy, it was only natural that they became their parents' favorites. As they grew into their teens, becoming prettier and prettier every day, the JVBs, Jr., became immensely proud of Maude and Michelle, sparing no expense to dress and educate them and launch them in New York society.

After attending Sacred Heart until they were fourteen, the two redheads were sent to Miss Spence's at 30 West Fifty-fifth Street, where they completed their freshman and sophomore years of high school with flying colors. As a reward for their good grades and good behavior, they were given a Model T flivver on their sixteenth birthday and a summer trip with their parents to France and Switzerland. For two months, during July and August 1923, the Bouviers toured the land of their forefathers, concentrating on areas those forefathers never knew, Paris and the resorts of the Côte d'Azur. They did not visit Pont-Saint-Esprit, as previous generations had done, and as MC had done seven years before, even though they had several distant relatives living in the Rhône village at the time, including JVB, Sr.'s second cousin, Michel Barry, son of Michel, Sr.'s half sister, Pélagie, who had died, unnoticed by the Bouviers of New York, in March 1922 at the age of ninety-one. Why JVB, Jr., spared his wife and twin daughters a visit to his grandfather's birthplace is anybody's guess. The town was not very far from the golf courses and casinos of Cannes and Juan-les-Pins that occupied three weeks of the Bouviers' trip. Since he was preparing the first edition of *Our Forebears* at the time, one would think Major Bouvier would have wanted to show his wife and daughters the village they would soon read about in his book. But, then, the true purpose of *Our Forebears* was not the mere narration of family history.

After the trip to Europe, the twins entered boarding school. The question of where to send them had constituted a sharp point of contention between the J. V. Bouviers, Jr., for months before the final decision was made. Major Bouvier wanted to separate Maude and Michelle, for he feared they would become too emotionally dependent on each other if they remained in the same school for two more years. Mother Maude, however, felt Michelle would languish if removed from her twin and insisted on keeping them together. In the end, mother won and they were both sent to Miss Porter's in Farmington, Connecticut, a school to which Edith's and Jack's daughters would also be sent one day. Miss Porter's was very much a finishing school when the Bouvier twins entered. Considerable emphasis was placed on imparting the social graces and household civilities. Its students were taught how to dance, set a table, arrange flowers, and walk into a room. A course in the minor arts enlightened the girls on how to distinguish English King silverware patterns from American King patterns and recognize Sèvres, Capodimonte, Limoges, and Royal Doulton chinaware at sight.

During the Christmas and Easter holidays Maude and Michelle were able to put their Farmington training to good use at dozens of dances, benefit teas, and dinners in New York. Always turning up in identical dresses and hairdos, they would dazzle the boys at the Junior Holidays and the Junior Assemblies with their beauty and poise and soon were two of the most celebrated pre-debutantes in the city. Every Sunday afternoon they were in town they would serve tea at their parents' apartment to five or ten swains. In 1923 Michelle led the Yale prom and a year later, on December 20, 1924, the Titian-haired Bouvier twins made their debut at Sherry's, described by *The New York Times* as "one of the most interesting social events of the early season." Maude wore a shell-pink dress embroidered with pearls and Michelle wore a shell-pink dress embroidered with pearls. The orchestra, under the direction of the society pianist and conductor Miss Burns, played such current hit tunes as "I'm Just Wild About Harry," "Margie," "Kitten on the Keys," and "I Left My Love at Avalon," and Tom Gates, a cousin from the Ewing side of the family, who would one day become Eisenhower's Secretary of Defense, brought flowers from Battles in Philadelphia, whose pins, the twins were astonished to find, were made of pure gold.

Once out of school and into society, the twins came into great demand at parties in New York and Long Island and their photographs, always in identical clothes, began to appear regularly in the Sunday rotogravures. Although they were both red-headed, fair-skinned, and freckled, they were far from identical in personality and appearance. Maude was physically and emotionally stronger than Michelle, with larger features, a heavier figure, and a more independent nature. Michelle's face was more delicate and refined than Maude's, and her temperament less even. Maude could stand alone, but Michelle depended on Maude. Because they were both beautiful, in different ways, yet had the same color skin, hair, and eyes, artists vied to paint their portrait—Albert Herter, father of the future Secretary of State, winning the unorganized competition by offering to paint it for nothing, provided he could take the canvas on an extended exhibition tour.

As might be expected, Major Bouvier, clubman par excellence, lost no time in getting his twin daughters into all the exclusive clubs and organizations they were eligible for, and so, not long after they made their debut, Maude and Michelle found themselves in the Junior League, the Colony Club, the DAR, the Colonial Dames, and the Daughters of the Cincinnati, a roster glorious enough to intimidate the most exacting of snobs.

And so the twins were launched. As they approached their respective marriages in a world of seemingly endless dances, benefit committee teas, "charity cabarets," and wedding parties, feted by New York society, pursued by photographers, and worshipped by their parents, they became something of a cult in the family, a double deity against whose sacred status their brothers and sister would compete in vain. Eventually they would unintentionally monopolize their mother's and father's affections almost entirely, and Edith, Jack, and Bud would find themselves almost strangers in their parents' hearts and home.

It would take time, however, for the twins to overtake Jack and Bud. Until the mid-twenties the Bouvier brothers held privileged places in their parents' esteem—in spite of their erratic careers—and were particularly beloved by their mother. What they lacked in scholastic ability, they made up for in charm. Both brothers were unusually handsome and most adept at winning people to their sides. Jack, destined to become the father of the future First Lady, was the oldest by two years, had a rougher nature than Bud and more rugged looks to match it. His broad face, wide-apart blue eyes, and decisive chin were reminiscent of the powerful features of the first Michel. Combined with this strength, however, was a sensuousness derived from an extremely dark complexion and unusually full lips, characteristics which had not been noticeable in the family before. Bud's features were not unlike Jack's; they were just softer and more refined. His nature was gentler too, less egotistical and aggressive. If Jack was mischievous, Bud was restless. If Jack was cynical and irreverent, and very much a realist, Bud was believing and idealistic, something of a romantic. Since Jack was endowed with a powerful, assertive ego and Bud was somewhat on the sensitive side, Bud had a hard time keeping up with his older brother. In fights Jack usually gained the upper hand. Jack, however, was not as good an athlete as his younger brother. Bud was an outdoorsman who loved hiking and excelled at swimming and riding. The only sport Jack ever practiced seriously was courting girls.

Both brothers' scholastic careers were desultory. After attending the Morristown School in New Jersey, Jack was enrolled in Exeter, but poor marks and a penchant for playing cards eventually led to his withdrawal. To get him into college, he was sent to Princeton Prep, then to Harstrom's tutoring academy, in which schools he finally buckled down to work sufficiently to win admission to Yale, entering the Sheffield Scientific School in the class of 1914. At Yale, Jack halfheartedly pursued the Select Course in Science and Literature and had a relatively undistinguished career, making no mark in athletics, studies, or extracurricular activities and changing roommates every year. The class of 1914 yearbook stated, among other things, that he "took his senior year in doses," and in fact he took four years to go through what was then a three-year college. Since JVB, Jr., had such a brilliant college career, both from an academic and from an extracurricular standpoint, JVB III's performance was something of a disappointment to his father. Socially, however, Jack took advantage of his years at college to make contacts that would benefit him considerably in the future. If he had a career at Yale, it was preeminently a social one. He wore stylish clothes, gave gay parties, and could always be relied on to produce a beautiful date for a friend. His fraternity, "Book and Snake," became the focal point of his college life and he would go out of his way to cultivate campus heroes of other colleges, like the Olympian Hobey Baker of Princeton, whom Jack invited several times to Nutley to meet his parents, Edith, and the twins. When he finally graduated in 1914, the only laurel he carried away was a reputation for being debonair and social, a young man who knew all the right people—the most eligible bachelors and the most beautiful girls. Since he eventually became a Wall Street customer's man, that reputation would do him no harm.

Much to his father's dismay, Bud's school and college career was even more erratic than Jack's. Like Jack, he had gone to Morristown and Exeter, but it was necessary for him to attend a special preparatory school—the Irving School in New York—to be admitted to college. In 1911 he entered his father's alma mater, Columbia, with the class of 1915. He made the freshman rowing squad and received average grades in his studies, and then quit Columbia the following year to enter Yale. Under a compulsion, it seemed, to compete with his older brother, he enrolled in the same school as Jack, the Sheffield Scientific, and soon became active in university athletics, particularly boxing and polo, two sports in which Jack had no competence. Elected to the St. Elmo Society, he formed deeper friendships than Jack but never acquired anything like his brother's stable of "important" acquaintances. Yale's social life at the time revolved around weekend drinking parties and it was through these affairs that Bud picked up a dependence on alcohol that was to plague him the rest of his life.

Three weeks after Bud completed his junior year at Yale, the insignificant event occurred at Sarajevo, and before long, German armies were invading Luxembourg, Belgium, and France. Early the following year the Germans sank the British liner *Lusitania*, with a loss of 114 American lives. On January 27, 1916, President Wilson, reacting to increasingly anti-German sentiment in the country, made a speech in New York foreseeing the need of U.S. military and industrial preparedness. Throughout 1916 the conflict intensified as the world saw tanks, flame throwers, and poison gas being used in warfare for the first time in history. With 1917 came the renewal of unrestricted submarine warfare by the Germans, resulting in the sinking of the *Algonquin* and three other American ships in March. As American indignation mounted, Congress declared war on the Central Powers, and on August 6 President Wilson approved the declaration, in order "to make the world safe for democracy."

The reactions of the Bouvier brothers to the war were as divergent as their personalities. The patriotic fervor that spread so rapidly among the youth of the country, as the Germans committed outrage after outrage against American neutrality, never reached Jack but filled the more impressionable Bud with feelings of moral indignation and dreams of military glory.

After graduating from Yale in 1914, Jack had gotten a job through his brother-in-law, Phelan Beale, as a customer's man for the Wall Street brokerage firm of Henry Hentz & Co., rejecting an offer from MC to start in his firm as a clerk, on the ostensible grounds that he did not want to expose his uncle to accusations of nepotism. One of Hentz's partners was Hartwig N. Baruch, Bernard Baruch's brother. Jack made such a favorable impression on Hartwig Baruch that before long he became the Hentz partners' fair-haired boy. Young Bouvier was good with figures, had a quick mind and a winning manner, and took a genuine interest in the market. Furthermore, he had many wealthy acquaintances with money to invest in stocks. By the time America became involved in the world war, Jack was doing very well at Henry Hentz & Co. and was most reluctant to give up his job to enter military service, much to the disappointment of his chauvinistic father. Jack's unwillingness to volunteer was interpreted by JVB, Jr., as evidence of a lack of patriotism and caused the first of several major rifts between father and son. There was nothing Jack could do about the Selective Service Act, however, and so, to avoid being drafted, he finally enlisted in the Navy as a seaman. To a man who placed as much emphasis on clothes and rank as Jack did, the awkward uniform and lowly status were humiliating, and so he soon set about trying to pull some strings. Eventually Hartwig Baruch— who had important connections in Washington—came to the rescue with a miraculous transfer to the Aviation and Signal Corps of the Army, in which Jack was commissioned second lieutenant in August 1917. Subsequently he was stationed at Scott Field, St. Louis, Missouri, where he met, became engaged to and then disengaged from a girl named Nancy Bates. Their rupture was the first of many broken engagements Jack was to collect. He never went overseas.

For Bud Bouvier it was a very different story. Bud had been deeply influenced by his father's patriotism. As a boy, his susceptible imagination had been fed on stories of his great-grandfather's service under Napoleon and his grandfather's valorous deeds during the Civil War. He had been permitted to view JVB, Sr.'s chest wound many times and had listened as often to the old veteran's account of the Second Battle of Bull Run. Furthermore, he had taken his French heritage— ignored by his brother—very much to heart. The violation of French territory by the German armies had affronted all Americans, in view of the fact that the soldiers of Rochambeau and Lafayette had helped bring America into being, and Bud Bouvier, highly conscious of his French descent, was quick to feel sympathy for the French cause. This, combined with the fact that his career at Yale did not, by the end of his junior year, promise him exceptional distinctions, led him to withdraw from college to join a volunteer unit training in Canada. A little less than a year later, when the Germans renewed and intensified unrestricted submarine warfare against Atlantic shipping, Bud left Canada and joined the Citizens' Training Corps at Madison Barracks, New York, an American volunteer unit organized several months before the United States declared war. Subsequently, on August 15, 1917, two months after the arrival of the first division of American Expeditionary Forces in France, W. Sergeant Bouvier accepted a commission as captain, Infantry, Officers' Reserve Corps, and entered active duty on the same date at Camp Dix, New Jersey. A year later he was in the thick of the fighting in France.

# II

BEFORE BEING ASSIGNED A COMPANY, CAPTAIN BOUVIER WAS GIVEN a week's furlough, which he chose to spend at Wildmoor, his parents' summer home at East Hampton. The Bouvier place—a modest, tree-shaded clapboard and shingle house with a widow's walk around the second floor—stood on a lonely stretch of flat-lands in the Appaquogue district, not far from the Atlantic. From its widow's walk a sweeping view could be had of potato fields and salt marshes, with the dunes, a few isolated houses, and the ocean in the distance. Besides his proud parents, the twins and Jack welcomed Bud at Wildmoor when he arrived, Jack also being on leave from the service.

For American soldiers during that August 1917 a week's leave was a godsend: perhaps the last significant interval of freedom they would enjoy before being sent overseas. Freedom, of course, meant girls, and Jack and Bud wasted no time in getting into action.

Not far from Wildmoor, in a house on the dunes which could be seen from the Bouviers' widow's walk, there lived a stunning, hazel eyed blonde of twenty-four, Emma Louise Stone. She was the daughter of the widowed Madeline Masters Stone, who had remarried a Mr. Nils Grön, and a niece of Edgar Lee Masters. Masters, a lawyer turned poet, had rocked the literary world in 1915 with his *succès de scandale, Spoon River Anthology*, in which he depicted his sister somewhat unflatteringly as the globetrot-ting Hortense Robbins, a portrait that displeased her so much she became estranged from her brother for life.

Madeline Grön had brought up her daughter Emmy Lou in Europe, where, in the words of Edgar Lee Masters, her name

> . . . used to be in the papers daily
> As having dined somewhere,
> Or traveled somewhere,
> Or rented a house in Paris . . .

And where she

> . . . entertained the nobility
> . . . was forever eating or traveling,
> . . . or taking the cure at Baden-Baden.

Being a niece of the renowned Edgar Lee Masters and having traveled extensively in Europe during her girlhood added an exotic dimension to the considerable native fascination of Emmy Lou Stone, and Jack Bouvier was quick to feel the vibrations radiating from her house on the dunes. He saw a good deal of her that summer, dating her every weekend he was able to get off duty. Late in July he asked her to marry him and was refused. Jack had so many girls on the string, however, that a refusal from one did not unduly distress him, and so, when Bud appeared on the scene a few weeks later, he generously introduced them, wishing his brother better luck. The first meeting between Bud and Emmy Lou took place Wednesday morning, August 22. By 5:00 P.M. Saturday, August 25, they were married.

The three-day interval had witnessed a tempest of love against the radiant backdrop of East Hampton in August which had Bud's and Emmy Lou's families alternately entranced and aghast. Long walks along the beach, with the surf booming and frothing at their feet— and with Emmy's mother or governess trailing discreetly along. Resting on the sand, hand in hand, looking out over the waves toward what would soon be the next theater of their love—with Emmy's mother or governess waiting on a nearby dune. Riding horseback wherever their whims took them, past East Hampton's bright green lawns, groves of orange beach plums, potato fields, windmills, saltbox mansions, golf courses, honeysuckle fences, and clumps of blue hydrangeas. Bud looking virile and confident in his uniform, all belted and booted; Emmy looking lovelier than ever in a long blue dress with a purple scarf and a plumed hat. A game of golf, another walk on the beach, tea at the Maidstone, then evening would fall, the fog would roll in over the dunes, and Bud would take Emmy back to her mother's and he would stay for supper and they would dance to the Victrola afterwards. And the second day, while they were riding horseback along the beach, he asked her and she said "Yes!"

When Bud told his father on Friday that he was going to marry Emma Louise Stone the next day, JVB, Jr., realized that sustained opposition was futile: his initial outburst was met with a defiance that secretly warmed his heart. Bud was so in love he would rather die than give up Emmy, and since he would soon be in the trenches, he might never have another chance to marry her. Still, Bud's impulsiveness and insubordination prompted his parents to forego the wedding. No, they would not attend. But sleep brought compassion and forgiveness, and the next day Mr. and Mrs. John V. Bouvier, Jr., decided to go to their son's wedding after all. Accordingly, around ten o'clock the Bouviers got into the family Oldsmobile and drove to New York. Bud and Emmy Lou and Mrs. Grön had driven in the day before, in Emmy's Chalmers, to get the marriage license and make the arrangements at St. Patrick's.

There had been no time to send out invitations, but Emmy and Bud spread the word to their friends by telephone Friday that the wedding would take place at the cathedral the following afternoon at 4:30. Few people were expected, but a mob turned up. Bud and Jack's Yale friends were there in force. Almost all of Emmy Lou's East Hampton following showed up, and even a generous representation of JVB, Jr.'s friends put in an appearance. The ceremony took place in the rectory, since Emmy Lou was a Protestant and the Church at that time forbade the celebration of mixed marriages in the cathedral itself. Bud wore his uniform, and Emmy Lou a khaki dress to match. Afterwards the couple knelt to pray at the Bouvier altar, then the entire assembly left for Sherry's, where Mrs. Grön had hastily organized a reception. A one-day honeymoon occupied Sunday. Then, on Monday, August 27, Captain Bouvier reported back to Camp Dix, settling Mrs. Bouvier in the Pig and Whistle Inn in nearby Pemberton, New Jersey.

There followed eight months of intensive training for battle, during which Bud Bouvier was finally given a unit to command, the 23rd Company, 6th Training Battalion, 153rd Depot Brigade of the 78th Division, an outfit he led with distinction until May 26, 1918, when he was transferred to Company C, 303rd Ammunition Train, of the same division, a unit destined for immediate duty overseas.

Bud Bouvier had had difficulty finding himself in school and college, but in military life he finally came into his own. The erratic scholar became a disciplined, capable officer who won the lasting respect of his men. By the time his division was ready to go overseas, Bud had erased the reputation he had earned for being unreliable and inconstant and had regained the esteem of his family. While he was at Camp Dix the twins knitted socks for him, his father enrolled him in the Sons of the Revolution, his grandfather visited him and told him for the hundredth time about the Second Battle of Bull Run, MC and Aunt Mary sent him checks, and the two women in his life, his mother and his wife, prayed the war would end before he was sent overseas. Their prayers were denied. In April, Bud learned that his division was due to depart for France late in May, and the Kaiser had given no indication by then of retiring to his farm.

May 1918 was a desolate month for tens of thousands of American families as mothers and wives from coast to coast watched their husbands and sons board troop trains for Philadelphia, New York, and Boston and a fate in the trenches of eastern France they dared not contemplate. The surge of pride and sorrow the Bouviers shared with countless Americans rose to a climax for them on May 27, when the 78th Division left Camp Dix for Philadelphia. On arriving in the city of his forefathers, Bud telephoned his parents to tell them that before boarding the troop ship for Halifax he was going to St. Mary's churchyard to pay his respects to his forefathers' graves and say a prayer for victory in the church in which Lafayette and Washington had given thanks for their victory in 1781. Then, suddenly, he was gone.

On May 28 his father wrote a brief entry in his diary:

> Dear Bud (God Bless and Preserve Him) sailed from Philadelphia for "Over There" at dawn.

"Lafayette, we are here!"

The doughboys' battle cry was coined by one of General Pershing's aides, Captain C. E. Stanton, who shouted it to a wildly cheering crowd at a wreath-laying ceremony before the tomb of le Grand Marquis on July 4, 1917. For the susceptible imagination of Bud Bouvier, the slogan was doubly significant. He had been brought up to believe that his great-great-grandfather Eustache had come from France with Lafayette to fight for American independence in 1780. Now, 138 years later, he had come from America to fight for the life of France.

By the time the 78th Division arrived in Brest on June 8, eleven American divisions were already in France; thirty-two more would follow. The doughboys had entered the conflict at a dark moment for the Entente. The Allied offensive of 1917 had been disabled by the temporary breakdown of French fighting power and severely undermined by the collapse of Russia and the terrible humiliation of the Italians at Caporetto the same year. Millions of French, British, Russian, and Italian soldiers had lost their lives in four years of inconclusive battles during which the Germans had firmly established themselves in French territory and the French had been unable to force them to withdraw.

General Ludendorff, Supreme Commander of the Kaiser's forces, had driven three great German wedges into the western front, but none were deep enough to cut a vital highway or railway, and he had been unable to fill in the spaces between the three thrusts. This strategic failure had left the Germans with an indented front whose teeth invited flanking and pincer attacks by the Allies. The task of the Americans was to starch the limp French and British units that had been fighting on the front for over four years, in an all-out effort to erase the German penetrations.

The doughboys' first opportunity to show their mettle came in June 1918, when the 2nd and 3rd Divisions halted a German offensive trying to cross the Marne at Château-Thierry on what was supposed to be a drive for Paris. The Americans' valiant "stand on the Marne" was a great tonic for French and British morale and sent a wave of confidence surging through Pershing's inexperienced army. If they could halt the Heinies on the Marne, they could hurl them back in the Argonne.

Since the 78th Division had only just arrived, Bud Bouvier did not participate in the Marne engagement. Before being sent into action, the 78th had to undergo three more months of training in trench warfare, and so its 15,000 men, commanded by Major General James H. McRae, were dispatched from Brest to Mencon, near Vannes, a town not far from the coast of Brittany, where the American Expeditionary Forces had established a camp at which front-line battle conditions were simulated over terrain not unlike that which they would eventually encounter at Saint-Mihiel and the Meuse-Argonne.

The 78th Division called itself the "White Lightnings" and was composed, for the most part, of drafted farmboys from the mountains of western New Jersey and upstate New York. The division's insignia was a shoulder patch depicting a white lightning flash on a bright red field. Its brother division, the one it was destined to relieve in the furious battle of the Argonne, was the 77th, a melting-pot outfit made up of draftees from Brooklyn, Manhattan, and the Bronx, who called themselves the "Metropolitans" and were called by others the "Bowery Backwoodsmen." Bud Bouvier commanded the 303rd Ammunition Train, 153rd Infantry of the Lightning Division and as such was in charge of four platoons, or 250 men. The task of his company in combat was to keep the front-line forces supplied with ammunition and provide secondary fire power when called upon.

By the end of August, the White Lightnings were pronounced ready for combat and rushed to the front. Marshal Foch, Supreme Allied Commander, had assigned "Black Jack" Pershing to help eliminate one of the three great German wedges into France, the Saint-Mihiel salient, and Pershing, in turn ordered the 78th, as part of the First Army, into the fray. This was to be the first action of the Americans as an independent army.

The battle of the Saint-Mihiel salient began in earnest on September 12. That morning Bud Bouvier had his first glimpse of the new warfare that had so profoundly shocked the civilized world. Mudfilled trenches with bullets whistling overhead. Barbed-wire barricades. Gas-shell bombardments. Mortar barrages. Bayonet charges. Aerial attacks. Flame throwers. Tank assaults.

Among the soldiers who charged forward along with Captain Bouvier and 700,000 other men that September 12 were Captain Harry S. Truman, Colonel George Catlett Marshall, Colonel George S. Patton, Jr., and Brigadier General Douglas MacArthur. In one furious engagement, Patton led a tank charge during which his leading tank was disabled. Instead of playing possum, he leapt out of his tank and descended on the German attackers with pistols blazing, killing several of them before he was wounded and carried away.

Captain Bouvier's role in the battle was not nearly as spectacular. Remaining in reserve with his untried division, he followed the advance midst bursting shells and clouds of poison gas, supplying relay teams to the front lines with ammunition. He did not, therefore, participate in the exultation of the 1st and 26th Divisions when they met on September 14 at Hattonchâtel, closing the Saint-Mihiel salient. But he was able to savor some of the joy of victory in the chase that followed, as the doughboys drove the retreating Germans back in shocked disorder toward Metz.

If the stand on the Marne had been a tonic to French and British morale, the elimination of the Saint-Mihiel salient was an even greater boost for the Allies, giving the Entente its first real hope of victory in four years of fighting. After the battle, Hindenburg was compelled to announce to his people: "We have suffered a severe defeat."

Following the victory at Saint-Mihiel, Marshal Foch ordered the American forces to attack another German wedge, the Meuse-Argonne, a vast salient jutting out between Ypres and Verdun, guarding Sedan.

The Argonne forest, along and through which the Americans were to advance, was a ten-mile-long tangle of near-jungle growth, rocky slopes, deep, water-filled ravines, canyons of old trenches, and granite boulders, its terrain shell-holed like the moon. Much of the forest had been burned, its trees now blackened spikes stabbing at the sky. Between this horrendous landscape and the Meuse stretched a wasteland of broken bridges, roofless farmhouses, blasted roads, fallen trees, ditched trucks, and caissons.

The battle opened early the morning of September 26 with a roar of four thousand guns in the darkness, followed by a glare of bursting shells. Then 250,000 doughboys started moving forward between the Argonne and the Meuse. Among them was the 78th Division.

The spectacle Bud Bouvier saw the morning of September 26 was too titanic to be frightening. Later, when he returned home, still suffering from the gassing he sustained, he told his father that he had thought he was witnessing the end of the world and that the gruesome pageant had given him a weird exhilaration. Miles and miles of infantrymen approaching the battle sector in the night, singing "Mademoiselle from Armentières" and "Over There," passing through deserted villages most of whose houses had had their roofs blown off. Endless supply trains—trucks, pack animals, horse-drawn covered wagons—inching forward through the mud. Artillery trains consisting of thousands of 8-inch howitzers being pulled along by horse-drawn caissons, many of which became hopelessly sloughed in washed-out embankments. And then the equally endless lines of ragged peasant refugees coming the other way, with all their possessions on their shoulders, telling the doughboys, in a nearly incomprehensible patois, that there was no hope, that an inferno awaited them ahead. And all the while the deafening roar of cannon, the bursting of shells, the incessant crackling of machine guns and rifles.

The battle conditions were the worst imaginable. There were tangles of barbed wire everywhere. The Germans used toxic shells that spread mustard gas and the deadly Conta. The trenches were filled with water and mud and dead bodies. There were no miracle drugs to relieve the wounded, no sulfa or antibiotics. The food was abominable. The doughboys called the corned-beef rations "barn rat," and the year-old hard-boiled eggs, "hen grenades." Lice infested the doughboys' uniforms: "seam squirrels," they called them. There were no more than a couple of hours of sleep at a time, and when a doughboy slept, he slept in mud.

By October 1, Colonel Marshall had moved about one million men over rough terrain between the Meuse and the Argonne. By October 12, the doughboys had pressed six miles into the German positions. It was during the final phase of the battle—between October 15 and the armistice on November 11—that Alvin York, a backwoods corporal from Tennessee, enjoyed his famous turkey shoot in the Valley of the Aire and Bud Bouvier's division finally got into front-line action.

The objective on the extreme left of the Meuse-Argonne sector was to seize the citadel of Grandpré, high on a hill east of the confluence of the Aire and the Aisne. The key to Grandpré was the village of Saint-Jurin, and the 77th Bowery Backwoodsmen, veterans of front-line action at Saint-Mihiel, were ordered to assault it from both flanks on October 12. After bitter fighting, led by Major General Robert Alexander, Saint-Jurin fell on October 13 and the victorious 77th was then ordered to the rear for rest, to be replaced by the 78th White Lightnings, who were given the job of capturing Grandpré. Bud Bouvier would soon receive his baptism of fire.

Meanwhile, back in New York, Emmy Lou was pulling every string to get to France and be near her beloved Bud. He had written fervent love letters to her during the summer while he was at Mençon and she was visiting his family in East Hampton, letters the twins had stolen an excited look at and told everybody about. Then, when the 78th went into action, the letters suddenly stopped coming. Emmy could not bear the silence: she *had* to get overseas.

By the time the Saint-Mihiel drive began, Emmy's father-in-law had won his commission as a Major Judge Advocate and was hobnobbing daily with several generals in Washington, and so it was to him that she turned for help. Major Bouvier, exalted by that time with patriotic fervor, was quick to answer the call: he persuaded a certain General Marsh to get her onto an army transport and provide her with the necessary papers to enter the base camps behind the lines of France. And so, while her husband was grappling with the Germans in the Argonne, Emmy Lou was counting the days before the transport would take her to his side.

After relieving the Bowery Backwoodsmen, the White Lightnings took aim on the fortified village of Talma, the one obstacle remaining between them and Grandpré.

Grandpré looked ominous to the White Lightnings as they approached it through the Valley of the Aire on the morning of October 26. The old medieval hilltop town, with many of its ancient walls and battlements still intact, had been converted into a massive fortress by the Germans. When its artillery opened fire on the 78th, the smoke puffs came from all over the place: from the walls, houses, goat sheds, public buildings; even the church seemed to be firing. Part of the town was perched above steep granite cliffs, part above rocky slopes used for goat pasture.

Major General James H. McRae had decided to storm Grandpré with everything he had, sending inexperienced troops up the granite hill along with his regulars. After executing a series of feints from various directions to divert German fire from the approach he had chosen for his main assault, he sent his New York and New Jersey mountain goats up the slopes in an all-out attack on Grandpré's right side. Soon Germans and doughboys were wrestling hand to hand on the town's tiled roofs and Captain Bouvier was moving his ammunition train into a cover from which he could supply his comrades with the grenades and Mills bombs they needed to knock out the German field pieces.

For two days the fighting raged, with the whole of Grandpré smoking from battle. The 78th's finest hour came toward the end of the second day of fighting. After having eliminated most of the German emplacements on the side of the town on which they had made their initial approach, the 78th made a concerted attack on the remaining German positions, and by nightfall Grandpré was theirs.

The 78th's last assignment before being relieved was to capture the village of Boult-aux-Bois, to the right of the Bois de Bourgogne. On November 2 the Lightnings began their assault, an oblique across the Aisne's twin courses. Boult-aux-Bois was bris-

tling with German field pieces and they met the oncoming doughboys with a hail of shells, many of which contained poison gas.
Although nearly crazed by lack of food and sleep, the Jersey and
upstate farmboys pushed on through the barrage, their ranks
thinning as they advanced, and eventually seized Boult-aux-Bois
on November 3. During the final phase of the battle a toxic shell
exploded near Bud Bouvier, felling him and killing several of his
pack animals. For several hours he lay retching on the field, with
only gassed mules for company. Intent on the assault, his comrades had stormed past him with only one thought on their
minds: blast the Heinie bastards out of Boult-aux-Bois. As he lay
in the mud, his nerves shattered by the gas, Bud had one consoling thought: the story he was going to tell his grandfather.

Bud Bouvier, badly gassed, was removed by stretcher from the
combat area during the last week of the war. As he was being
carried back, he was joined by thousands of other doughboys,
shrouded in blood-stained white sheets, who were little more
than sieves of wounds, and he passed scores of decapitated
bodies and corpses whose unraveled leggings revealed the loss
of their legs. Among the wounded being evacuated were long
lines of soldiers with bandaged eyes who had to plod through the
mud with their hands on one another's shoulders, the blind
leading the blind. Everywhere there were dead pack animals,
wrecked trucks, abandoned tanks, and caissons sunk in the mire.
To Bud Bouvier the lines of dead and wounded seemed longer
than those of the replacements he passed, and when he and the
other wounded of his division finally reached the temporary
army hospital at Dugny, near Verdun, he was not surprised to
find there was no more room in the building. Thousands upon
thousands of stretchers surrounded the hospital, and there were
not enough attendants to treat even the critically wounded before
it was too late. By the middle of November there would be 190,000
Americans in hospitals throughout France.

Bud Bouvier remained at Dugny, undergoing treatment for
gassing, until mid-December, when he was sent to the Officers'
Convalescent Camp at Saint-Aignan, in Touraine, a place which
also served as a depot for casual officers and enlisted men awaiting repatriation. Saint-Aignan is a charming village located on the
river Cher, a tributary of the Loire, but since it had been used as
a replacement center while the fighting was going on, and living
conditions there at the time were abominable, the doughboys had

dubbed it St. Agony. Not long after Bud was sent there, his wife, worried sick over the gassing he had suffered, finally managed to get passage to France and by mid-January was on her way to his side.

At St. Agony, Bud Bouvier was given further treatment—and also a good deal of liberty. While he was there he managed to enjoy a revel in Paris, during which he somehow lost all his identification and official documents, and a trip to Pont-Saint-Esprit. Bouvier relatives in the Rhône Valley today, descendants of Eustache's marriage to Louise Perboz, recall their mother's story of a haggard American officer appearing in Pont-Saint-Esprit a month or so after the Armistice, who said his name was Bouvier and that his great-grandfather was from the village. He was in uniform, so the story goes, and said he had been badly gassed in the Meuse-Argonne. Before returning to camp, he asked to see Eustache Bouvier's grave.

Soon after that, Emmy Lou arrived on the Continent. Posing as Bud's sister, for it was strictly against Army regulations for wives to visit their soldier husbands in France, she succeeded in coaxing a pass from the AEF in Paris to visit the Casual Officers' Camp at Saint Aignan, and, in great excitement, took the first train she could for Touraine.

When she arrived at Saint-Aignan, Emmy Lou found herself surrounded by hordes of servicemen who hadn't seen an American girl in months. St. Agony was overflowing with dough-boys awaiting repatriation, and when Emmy Lou told the first one she met that she had come to see her brother at the camp and wanted to know how she could find him, she started a sort of stampede and soon had an escort that seemed as large as a regiment. Doughboys fought to be at the side of this exquisite blonde from New York, so refined and soft-spoken, so brave and trusting, who had traveled over three thousand miles to see her gassed brother. They kissed her. They hugged her. They carried her aloft. They gave her the names and telephone numbers of their sweethearts and wives in the States, urging her to tell them they were well and would be coming home soon. They sang. They marched. They shouted at their buddies to join the fun. By the time Emmy reached camp, her escort numbered in the hundreds and an audience had been unintentionally formed for the drama that followed at the gate.

Had she written her brother she was coming? Yes, but the letter obviously got lost: she had heard nothing from him since. Did she have a pass? Yes. Who issued it? AEF in Paris. Let me see it.... A few seconds of puzzled scrutiny, then: "Wait here, miss, and we'll see if he's in."

Emmy waiting at the gate to the camp. The sentry sending a doughboy in for Captain Bouvier. To tell him his sister was here ... Bud, startled by the news, wondering if it really was Edith: it surely couldn't be one of the twins. But why would Edith ... ? Where's Phelan? Maybe it wasn't ... But the twins were too young ... Running out of the barracks ... Heading for the gate. What is all the fuss? Who's that? Edie! Is it you?

... Emmy!

As Bowery Backwoodsmen and White Lightnings marveled at the affection between brother and sister, Bud and Emmy Lou embraced, then walked off, arm in arm, to pick up Emmy's bags at the station.

Capt. and "Miss" Bouvier were together at Saint-Aignan for a little over a month before Bud's division was shipped home early in March. Since regulations forbade military personnel to live away from the camp, Emmy Lou stayed at an inn in town and Bud remained at the officers' barracks. Being the only American woman in the area, Emmy Lou was feted from reveille till taps. The inn was filled with top brass directing repatriation, and the streets and shops of Saint-Aignan were filled with soldiers waiting to go home. When she wasn't with her "brother," she was fending off doughboys and generals by the droves. On weekends the couple would flee St. Agony and its inmates for the château country to the north and feast their eyes on the Renaissance splendor of Chenonceaux, Azay-le-Rideau, and the Clos-Lucé at Amboise. And there, midst all that past magnificence, they would talk about the future, their future: where they would live, what Bud was going to do, the children they would raise.

Toward the end of February that future, so much thought of and discussed, suddenly drew near, with Bud's transfer to Cherbourg and his subsequent embarkation, along with three thousand other soldiers, on a Navy troop transport bound for New York. The ship sailed on March 3, with Emmy Lou the only woman on board. Major Bouvier and General Marsh had done well. Although Bud had to stay with his division, Emmy had been assigned an officer's stateroom all to herself and was allowed to see her "brother" on deck twice a day.

On arriving in the United States on March 11, exactly four months after the Armistice, Bud was immediately sent to Camp Dix, where he was to be mustered out of the service, and Emmy went to wait for him at his parents' apartment in New York. Eight days later Captain W. Sergeant Bouvier was honorably discharged from the United States Army. In his record it was noted that as a company commander he had never had to hold so much as a summary court-martial, and as a result of his service in France he had been awarded the World War I Victory Medal, with battle clasps for Saint-Mihiel and the Meuse-Argonne.

Bud had decided to go to work as soon after his discharge as possible. Since he was without funds of his own, he and Emmy Lou had to settle temporarily at Major Bouvier's Park Avenue duplex, not the best arrangement to start married life anew, since Mother Maude had a tendency to spoil her children and criticize their spouses, but, of course, it saved the W. Sergeant Bouviers a lot of money. While Bud was looking for a job, he and Emmy eased back into the social whirl of New York and Long Island which the war had interrupted two years before.

The America to which Bud and Emmy Lou returned that spring of 1919 was heaving with unrest. It was a time of strikes, Red scares, race riots, and unsettling economic fluctuations, marked by an open rebellion against puritan morals. The war had discredited many of the old ideals. Victorian gentility and hypocrisy were on the way out, and a rowdy but honest vulgarity was coming into fashion, along with a frank new fascination with sex.

On returning to New York, Emmy Lou found that skirts were still long—no more than six inches from the ground; hair was still long; and it was still fashionable to have a figure tall, flat, and slightly slouching. By 1921 a female rebellion against overly modest clothes saw the first short, tight bathing suits come into fashion and the first significant hike in skirts. A correspondingly new trend in men's fashions was also underway: shaped jackets, wide lapels, high shirt collars, sideburns, pencil-thin mustaches, slicked-down hair—the Rudolph Valentino look—a style admirably suited to the Latin-lover appearance of Bud Bouvier.

March and April 1919 were wonderful months for the W. Sergeant Bouviers. Bud was a handsome young war hero, doted on by his proud parents and lionized by the girls, and Emmy Lou, considered a heroine in her own right, never looked lovelier. The couple were so popular that their entire existence seemed to be taken up with parties. Post-deb affairs at the Ritz and the Plaza. Dinner dances on the North Shore. Wedding receptions. Charity balls. The only dampener in their lives was their lack of money. Emmy refused to accept charity from her husband's parents, beyond temporary room and board, and yet her husband's Army severance pay was running out. To remedy the situation, Bud managed to land a sales job in the insurance-brokerage firm of Schiff and Terhune. It was not what he really wanted to do, but it was at least something until a better position came along.

Soon, however, Bud became bored with insurance. Like his granduncle Eustache, steady, routine work had never appealed to him. He had rebelled against it at school. He had rebelled against it at college. He would do something more exciting with his time than write insurance contracts, something that would give him the sort of pride and exhilaration his military service had given him. Insurance! He couldn't be less interested. Even the stock market was more exciting than that: Jack was having a great time on Wall Street.

Bud fretted at his desk at Schiff and Terhune, in a room filled with other desks and other fretters, feeling more and more stifled every day. In retrospect, the Army seemed a paradise. Was his life from now on to be nothing more than an appendage to those two tumultuous years? There was so much excitement and adventure to be had in the world, so many frontiers to be conquered, and here he was, having to peddle insurance in New York.

What Bud really wanted was what his granduncle Eustache had wanted, an adventurous outdoors job that would enable him to get rich quick. Mineral prospecting or the oil business. Shopping around among his old Yale and Army buddies, he eventually gravitated toward a small oil concern operating in the Southwest—the Morton Oil Company—from which he wrested a job as a field assistant.

The oil industry was still in its infancy when Bud Bouvier became interested in it. In 1919 the vast petroleum resources of Texas and Oklahoma had scarcely been tapped. It was, therefore, with high hopes for quick riches that Bud Bouvier left his job with Schiff and Terhune not long after he had begun it and headed, with his wife, for the oil fields at Cisco, Texas.

Cisco, Texas, in the summer of 1919 was a hot, dusty oil town of 7,000 inhabitants which had only just emerged from the disorder and violence of the Wild West. It had none of the civilized amenities Bud and Emmy Lou were accustomed to, and no charm or natural beauty to compensate for their lack. Besides oil and gas, the town was also devoted to mules and peanuts, both of which were raised in the vicinity. Although Bud, as an Army veteran, had known worse, Emmy Lou found it the dirtiest, meanest, most degrading town she had ever been in. The little house she and Bud occupied was a flimsy clapboard box, situated, among dozens of others the same size and shape, on a dirt street that led to a desert of oil rigs and gas lines. The smell of gas was always in the air, the smell of oil was always on her husband, the heat was unbearable, it never rained, and in those days there was no such thing as air-conditioning.

In the middle of the blazing, dust-bitten summer, Emmy Lou Bouvier discovered that she was pregnant, and Bud had to go back to New York on business for Morton Oil. He remained East five weeks, weekending at his parents' home in East Hampton, then returned to Cisco. When he rejoined Emmy, he was informed that he might have had business in New York but he had no business leaving his pregnant wife alone for five weeks in a one-horse Texas inferno while he galavanted around East Hampton: she was not going to stay in the place much longer. She simply couldn't take the heat, the dust, the flies, the smells, especially in her condition. Accordingly, in the fall of 1919, Bud moved his wife back to New York, settling her in the Hotel Seville, and contented himself with a life divided between Cisco and New York. Meanwhile, the entire Bouvier family held its breath in expectation of a male heir.

The dawning of the year 1920 brought renewed determination to Bud to strike it rich, an attack of double pneumonia to his wife, and unbounded joy to his dynastically-minded family. When Emmy Lou became sick, during the last stages of pregnancy that cold New York January, her doctors feared she would lose the child. Her case of pneumonia was particularly virulent, and as the child's birth approached, it got worse and worse. It was, therefore, with tremendous relief and joyous thanksgiving that the Bouviers learned, on January 29, that Emmy Lou had, in her own words, "coughed up" a perfectly normal, though premature, five and one half pound baby boy at the Hotel Seville and was pronounced out of danger herself shortly thereafter. Bud had no trouble finding a name for his son. Eight months earlier he and Emmy Lou had agreed he would be called Michel.

With a son and family heir to bring up, Bud Bouvier found his problems magnified. In a family like the Bouviers, which had mounted such a drive for acceptance in American society, the responsibilities associated with having a son, enough normally to age a man five years, were particularly burdensome. Since Jack was still unmarried and gave little indication of ever seeing an engagement through to its conventional consequences, the Bouviers now looked upon Bud, Emmy Lou, and Michel to carry the family into the future. Bud responded to these expectations by buckling down to his job with renewed vigor, while at the same time keeping an alert eye open for whatever new opportunities might come by.

In due time he became a field superintendent for Morton Oil, in which capacity he had charge of several oil rigs, and was at last earning a decent salary. But the money he was making was not nearly enough to satisfy his ambition or provide the sort of standard of living for his family his father had provided for him. In addition, he had to live away from his wife and son most of the time, since Emmy did not regard Cisco, Texas, as habitable, much less a place in which to raise a child, and therefore remained in New York.

Several opportunities eventually presented themselves, however, and Bud was able to take advantage of one of them. During a summer visit to East Hampton, a friend by the name of Juan Trippe tried to interest him in investing in a commercial airline. Trippe, an imaginative young man who had already started an embryonic airline in Florida, was dreaming of operating a fleet of planes between major cities. Since Bud had no capital to invest in the venture, he asked his father and MC to lend him the necessary funds. They refused on the grounds that Trippe's idea was far too risky and harebrained to merit serious consideration. In the words of JVB, Jr.: "Aviation has no future." The airline Juan Trippe went on to found, with other investors' money, became Pan American.

That JVB, Jr., and MC were unwilling to risk their capital in a field as new and promising as aviation was a commentary on what had happened to Bouvier enterprise and imagination since the family had made its money and established its position in

New York and Long Island society. The ossification of initiative and foresight that JVB, Jr., and even MC, displayed from 1920 on was in glaring contrast to the venturesomeness the first Bouvier showed to the end of his life. Michel, Sr., would have probably given the airline a whirl.

Although he missed out on an opportunity to get in on the ground floor of aviation, Bud did seize a chance to get in on the ground floor of an oil company. While on a business trip to New York, he joined a syndicate of promoters headed by William Crapo Durant, the automobile manufacturer and legendary stock manipulator, which was speculating in oil leases in Texas and Oklahoma, and promptly left his job with Morton Oil. To join the syndicate, Bud had to put up some money, and so, once again, he approached his family for funds. This time MC came across with a loan. The old stockbroker had no doubts about the future of oil.

The syndicate Bud invested in and joined became the Independent Oil and Gas Company, and Bud eventually became one of its vice presidents. With actual field experience behind him, Bud was now in a much better position to judge oil properties than when he had first started out in the business, and it wasn't long after he helped found Independent Oil and Gas that he struck it rich. Several of the unexploited properties his company had bought for practically nothing became active oil producers, and by 1925 they had made Bud Bouvier, at thirty-two, a fortune, on paper, of over a million dollars.

*Michel Bouvier (1792-1874), founder of the Bouvier family in America*

*Louise Vernou Bouvier (1811-1872)*

*M.C. Bouvier (1847-1935)*          *Zénaïde Bouvier (1835-1914)*

*Alexine Bouvier (1837-1914)*          *Mary Bouvier (1841-1931)*

*Staff of General Marsena R. Patrick, Provost Marshall of the Army of the Potomac, in 1863. General Patrick is at center. His aide-de-camp, Lt. John V. Bouvier, is second from left*

*Katharine Drexel as Mother Superior of the Sisters of the Blessed Sacrament for Indians and Colored People*

*Emma Bouvier Drexel (1833-1883)*

*John Vernou Bouvier, Jr.*
*(1865-1948), as Major Judge*
*Advocate, World War I*

*John Vernou Bouvier, Jr., and*
*his twin daughters, Maude*
*and Michelle*

*Lieutenant John Vernou Bouvier III (1891-1957)*

*Captain W. Sergeant (Bud) Bouvier (1893-1929)*

*Mr. and Mrs. John V. Bouvier, Jr., and their grandchildren at "Lasata."*
*Jacqueline Bouvier is lower far right, John H. Davis is second from right*

*Jacqueline Bouvier, age five, with her dog Scotty, East Hampton, August,*
*1934*

*John Vernou Bouvier III and daughter Jackie at a South Hampton horse show, 1934*

*Mr. and Mrs. John Vernou Bouvier III, East Hampton, 1936*

*Jacqueline Bouvier and her stepfather, Hugh D. Auchincloss, arriving at Saint Mary's Church in Newport, Rhode Island for her wedding to Senator John F. Kennedy, September 12, 1953. The bride's mother is to the left*

***President and Mrs. John F. Kennedy***

# III

WHILE BUD BOUVIER WAS MAKING HIS FORTUNE IN TEXAS, HIS brother was making his on Wall Street. Jack Bouvier had been honorably discharged from the Signal Corps in the spring of 1919 and after a long summer vacation in East Hampton had rejoined the brokerage firm he had started out with before the war, Henry Hentz & Co.

Jack was fortunate to have two powerful allies at Hentz ready to further his career whenever they could: his brother-in-law and attorney for the firm, Phelan Beale and Hartwig N. Baruch. On October 16, 1919, Baruch, reacting to insistence from Phelan Beale, bought Jack a seat on the exchange, and J. V. Bouvier III's career as one of the most colorful operators on Wall Street was launched. With funds for trading supplied him by his Aunt Mary, who adored him, he would soon be making money hand over fist.

In the fall of 1920 Jack rented an elegant apartment at 375 Park Avenue where he began throwing parties that were to become famous among the young socialites of New York during the roaring twenties. At these lively affairs Jack liked to mix wealthy and social people with those from the other side of the tracks: graduates of Miss Porter's and graduates of the Ziegfeld Follies, Long Island playboys and boys from the Bronx who had worked their way up on the Stock Exchange from clerks to members. Jack was always very conscious of who had money and who hadn't, but he wasn't a snob. Generally speaking, he liked the have-nots better than the haves, but in his business he had to pay more attention to the latter to survive. His professional need to associate with the wealthy was also reflected in his love life. Jack dated "seriously" only girls with money and position, but he had innumerable brief affairs with "other" girls on the side. Occasionally one of his serious girls would lure him into an engagement. Eleanor Carroll Daingerfield Carter was one of them. Jack became formally engaged to Eleanor, described in *The New York Times* announcement as being "of the prominent Carter family of Virginia and Maryland," on April 7, 1920. She was young, beautiful, rich and had superb connections. Her first cousin was the wife of Lord Acheson of Great Britain. But Jack seemed destined never to take formal vows. A few weeks before the wedding was to take place, it was called off, and he resumed playing the field. A year later Eleanor Carroll Daingerfield Carter married Morgan La

Montagne, a young socialite who was later indicted for selling liquor illegally to the Racquet Club.

Jack's dashing good looks and ruthless but winning ways with the girls soon won him a reputation as one of the most devastating Don Juans in New York society. A man with a great sense of style, an innate flair, he made the most of his good looks by paying inordinate attention to his clothes. Almost everything he wore he had made to order. His tailor, Bell, gave his suits a Continental cut, emphasizing the chest with wide lapels, indenting the waist, and flattening the hips. Tripler made his shirts with high collars and long sleeves, for Jack liked to shoot plenty of collar and cuff, and Tripler also made his ties, which he preferred paisley, wide, and long.

Jack Bouvier's ancestry was just as British as it was French, yet his Provençal blood prevailed, giving him a dark complexion that he made even darker by exposing himself regularly to a sun lamp. So dark did he become that his fellow stockbrokers dubbed him "Black Jack," after Black Jack Pershing, a nickname that remained with him all his life, along with many others he earned, such as "the Sheik" and "the Black Prince."

Jack's personality, too, was more Mediterranean than Anglo-Saxon. Like most Mediterranean men, he was highly susceptible to the fascination of beautiful women and big money, but soon tired of a woman, and spent money faster than he earned it. Unconventional, and lacking in the middle-class virtues, Jack Bouvier had the narcissistic vanity of a Roman and the theatrical flamboyance of a Neapolitan. Unlike many of his classmates at school and college, he was essentially a loner who was reluctant to share the spotlight with others. In company he was more theatrical than social, preferring to make a dazzling impression on people rather than expend a great deal of effort to get to know them. As a man of distinctly erotic temperament, male company bored him: he much preferred the society of women. Since he was so Mediterranean in appearance and personality, and yet came from a family of wealth and long-standing social position, Jack Bouvier was a rather unique being in New York society: a member of the upper class who was more Latin than Anglo-Saxon. The ranks of the Social Register at the time were almost entirely filled with people of British, Scotch, Dutch, or German ancestry, and if there were French members included, chances were that their ancestors had come from northern France, not the Midi. In a sense, Jack and Bud Bouvier were the closest things to Italians in society.

Keeping up a social position in New York requires more money than in most places, and Jack Bouvier addressed himself with energy and determination to the task of making the requisite amount. After serving as a floor broker at Henry Hentz & Co. for three years, he left the firm to become a specialist—that is, a brokers' broker, who keeps up a market in a few selected stocks. Among the stocks he eventually came to specialize in at Post N. 11 were Kennecott Copper, Texas Gulf Sulphur, Kress Department Stores, Colorado Fuel and Power, Baldwin Locomotive, and Holland Furnace.

The task of a specialist is to buy and sell certain stocks for other brokers and maintain an orderly market in the stocks he deals in. To do this, he maintains a "book" in which he keeps a record of all orders to buy and sell. Thus, his "book" in Texas Gulf Sulphur may contain hundreds of advance orders to buy or sell the stock, at varying prices, which he must execute when the shares reach the prices specified. In addition, he must handle spot transactions with no advance notice. At times, when a stock is being heavily traded, the number of transactions to be executed when the shares reach a certain price is staggering. The job calls for a quick, arithmetical mind, very steady nerves, an excellent sense of timing, and a willingness to risk one's own capital to maintain an orderly market. Time and again a specialist is called upon to purchase, for his own account, shares in one of the stocks he specializes in, in order to provide buyers when no buyers are available. Jack Bouvier possessed these abilities to an unusual degree. By the late 1920s he was regarded as one of the ablest specialists on the Exchange and had made a fortune of $750,000 while being recognized as such.

Thus, by the time Jack was thirty-five and Bud thirty-three, the two were already wealthy men—at least on paper. Their financial futures seemed boundless and it would have been a rare Wall Street seer who would have thought otherwise.

However, a perceptive observer watching the Bouvier brothers together could have foretold trouble for one of them. Emotionally Jack held the upper hand over Bud and never let him forget it. He maintained his position of supremacy not merely because he was his father's older son but primarily because he was more aggressive and unscrupulous than his brother and thus was usually one up on him. Bud, however, was much more talented than Jack, having many more strings to his bow. He was a superb horseman, whereas Jack could hardly ride. He was an expert golfer and bridge player and consistently beat Jack in both games. He could draw well and sing even better: his rendition of "I Pagliacci" was famous at parties in New York and Long Island. Bud did everything easily and gracefully whereas Jack had to work long and hard to achieve results. Being sensitive, however, Bud was vulnerable to barbs from Jack, and Jack never spared anyone a barb who left himself open for one. In company, Jack was a thorn in his brother's side. Since he was more aggressive socially, he would often outdo Bud in cultivating important people and kid him in front of people Bud wanted to impress.

The rivalry between the Bouvier brothers had few adverse effects on Jack, but it took a toll on Bud. It was humiliating to Bud to be made to feel inferior by someone he considered less talented than himself. There was one way, however, Bud could hold his own with Jack—through drinking. Liquor brought confidence to Bud and made him less vulnerable to Jack's barbs. Liquor momentarily allowed Bud to feel equal to Jack, even to get the best of him occasionally. Bud had drunk heavily at Yale, then had cut down his intake considerably while in the Army. But once back home with his family, he began again. And gradually he drank more and more, until one day, at an indeterminate date, he found himself with a problem he had not even recognized until he was incapable of solving it.

Meanwhile the United States too was manufacturing problems it would have grave difficulties coping with. A revolution in manners and morals was sweeping the nation. The young, disillusioned with their elders, were beginning to run wild. As Scott Fitzgerald put it: "Here was a new generation . . . grown up to find all gods dead, all wars fought, all faiths in men shaken." It remained to raise up new gods in the temples, more accessible ones, like the pagan deities of ancient Greece and Rome.

By the mid-twenties many new forces were at work in the country, changing the lives of Americans. Among the most powerful were Prohibition, which gave rise to the bootlegger, the speakeasy, the cocktail party, and alcoholism; and the automobile, which not only changed the face of the nation but also soon rivaled the bedroom as the most favored locus of sexual frolic. Other sticks of social dynamite were the movies and the tabloid press, both of which contributed to the revolution in women's status and values.

If the old values and duties were dead, there was no end of new evasions to take their place: the radio, the hip flask, jazz, mahjongg, the Charleston, mass sports, the movies, infidelity, divorce. A movie advertisement of the times summarized the New Jerusalem as a heaven of "brilliant men, beautiful jazz babies, champagne baths, midnight revels and petting parties in the purple dawn."

Along with the new permissiveness and the new evasions came an economic prosperity unparalleled in the nation's history. Spearheaded by the ever multiplying automobile, whose myriad-pronged thrust left hundreds of filling stations, hot-dog stands, billboards, and suburbs in its wake, industry gradually became the ultimate authority and salesmanship and advertising the ultimate spiritual influences in American life. As if to proclaim the new industrial triumph and permanently enshrine it, great new cathedrals of business, the skyscrapers, rose up out of America's cities, and Wall Street became the new Vatican toward which all hearts looked for salvation.

America's puritan heritage, however, was not to be expunged overnight. The new freedom, the new social innovations, proved vulnerable to an old, ingrained sense of guilt. It was not easy for Americans to be hedonistic and self-indulgent. Married couples' experiments with infidelity often boomeranged: adultery was not as innocent or inconsequential as they had thought. Irresponsible pleasure seeking, economic extravagance, the frenzied pursuit of financial success, all these were attended by culpabilities that could easily turn satisfaction into blame. It was no wonder that the bootlegger and the speakeasy thrived. A lot of alcohol was required to dissolve Americans' guilt.

Among the Bouviers, Edith felt the contagion of the times even more intensely than Jack and Bud. In the early twenties she and Phelan Beale had bought a house in East Hampton, not far from the JVBs, Jr.'s place on Appaquogue Road, called Gray Gardens, and it was there that Edith began taking to the bohemian ways that were to drive her husband and father nearly out of their minds. The house was ideally suited to Edith's unconventional personality. Its former owner, a noted horticulturalist by the name of Robert Hill, had created a lush, walled-in garden to one side of the house which contributed, along with the high box hedges that surrounded it, the dense foliage of the trees that shaded it, and the mantle of ivy that draped it, to give the place an offbeat aura of mystery and theatricality not unlike the character of its new owner.

By 1925 Edith's children, Edith, Phelan, and Bouvier, were seven, five, and three respectively; Phelan, Sr., was increasingly prosperous; and Edith herself was still liberated from ordinary household chores by a retinue of servants which included a conscientious and understanding nurse called Molly. Edith used her free time to cultivate interests and ideas no one in her family could appreciate or comprehend. She played the piano and sang to a husband who would have preferred that she have the faucets in the bathroom fixed, his laundry done on time, and his tuxedo cleaned and pressed for the evening. She invited people to the house—painters, writers, theatrical types—who seemed phonies and time wasters to her husband. She dressed in an arty way that would inevitably draw snickers from the stuffy people who invited her to cocktail parties and dinner dances on the Island. And in matters religious and philosophical she became an outlandish freethinker, renouncing the religion in which she had been baptized and indulging in speculations and opinions her lawyer husband and lawyer father regarded as utterly beyond the pale.

The divided life Bud Bouvier was leading in the mid-twenties made him particularly vulnerable to the temptations the new permissiveness generated. Living between New York and Texas in the winter and East Hampton and Texas in the summer gave him little stability, and his family life suffered accordingly. An interval in New York promoting oil properties, during which he would try his best to be a good husband and father; then he would be off again to Cisco, Texas, or Okmulgee, Oklahoma, for a few weeks or a few months. In Cisco there wasn't much to do after work in the winter but drink, or take out a girl in Fort Worth a hundred miles away. Oklahoma in all seasons was just as monotonous. If they could have been together summers, the winters would have been more tolerable to the W. Sergeant Bouviers, but, as it was, summer brought little relief to their divided existence: if anything, Bud and Emmy Lou had to endure even longer separations. When he came East on business in July and August, Bud was able to join Emmy Lou and little Michel in East Hampton only on weekends. The rest of the time he would stay at his apartment in New York alone. Those summer evenings in New York during the roaring twenties were not without their enticements. Jack, for instance, knew plenty of girls he was only too happy to introduce to his married brother, and he had good connections at the speakeasies too. As for weekends in East Hampton, they were not too different from evenings in New York. East Hampton was discovering the cocktail party at the time, and Emmy Lou, tired of being alone all week, was understandably eager to sample the new invention with her husband. There was no relief from alcohol during Prohibition.

And so Bud's life unfolded in an irregular cycle of long, hot days on the oil fields, wild nights in Fort Worth, hurried trips back East, brief family reunions in New York, night trains to Texas, prospecting trips to Oklahoma, financial conferences on Wall Street, partying weekends in East Hampton, gay summer evenings in Manhattan, trains back to Texas. It was an active and often adventurous life, and he was doing very well in the oil business, but after a while the disquieting realization began to intrude into his thoughts that although he was making a lot of money he was losing his wife and his health in the process.

It was in the spring of 1925, around his thirty-second birthday, that this realization was confirmed with unexpected intensity by his wife. Upon his return to New York on business after a long absence, Emmy Lou noted his worn-out, jaundiced appearance and informed him that if he didn't settle permanently in one place, and cut down on his drinking, she would sue for divorce. Arguments to the effect that the sort of life he was leading was necessary to the making of his fortune were to no avail. After Emmy's ultimatum, Bud was anguished by a choice he had never expected to have to make. What came as the greatest shock of all was the realization that he really didn't have a choice. As much as he loved his wife, he could not give up the life he had been leading for four years. And so his only hope to keep Emmy lay in the possibility that she might not want to keep her promise.

That hope was dashed in the summer of 1925, when, after another spurt of traveling and drinking, he returned to East Hampton to be told by Emmy Lou that she was suing for divorce. She had every reason to do so. How could she bring up little Michel serenely and confidently with a husband who was rarely at home, who would disappear for weeks without letting anybody know where he was, whose financial support was irregular and unpredictable, and who, when he *was* home, repeatedly drank himself into a stupor?

There followed a month or so of futile wrangling. Then it happened. Bud Bouvier lost his wife and child and was ordered by the court to provide support for them at the rate of $800 a month. The fortune he had made while still in his early thirties now had cost him the two people he loved most in the world. He was left with a million on paper and a void only alcohol could fill.

To make matters worse, his family's reaction was, generally speaking, one of harsh disapproval. Aunt Mary let it be known that Bud was no longer welcome at 14 West Forty-sixth Street. Divorce was against the teachings of the Church, an outrage against God and his Sacraments. This was the first time such a scandalous thing had happened to the American Bouviers since Michel, Sr., had established the family a hundred years ago. There had been dozens of marriages, and they had all held together. And what would Mother Louise, R.S.C.J., have said, were she still alive, she who had dedicated her entire life to her Church and God?

Major Bouvier's and MC's disapproval was not based on religious convictions but on dynastic considerations: the family was losing little Michel. The Bouviers' lone male heir now belonged almost exclusively to Emmy Lou. And he bore the name of the founder of the family! And chances were, there would be no more males born to the Bouviers: Bud, worn out at thirty-two, would probably never remarry, and Jack seemed to be taking after MC as he entered his thirty-fifth year of bachelorhood. It was a calamity, this divorce, a blot on the Bouvier image and a blow to the family's future, and JVB, Jr., and MC let the prodigal know it.

Life, however, was not entirely without sympathy and understanding. Bud still had his mother and grandmother to comfort him, and Edith and the twins also showed compassion for his plight. Maude Sergeant sided vehemently with her son, taking up his cause against Aunt Mary, MC, her husband, and Emmy Lou. And Caroline Ewing was her usual saintly self. If Bud was no longer welcome at 14 West Forty-sixth Street, he would always be welcome at 987 Madison Avenue. And there, in fact, he would stay from now on when he was in New York.

To forget his troubles, Bud turned to the two things that had cost him his marriage: his business and his escape, moneymaking and drinking. About the time of his divorce, *The New York Times* reported in its financial section that W. Sergeant Bouvier had purchased a substantial block of the stock of the Kay Copper Corporation. Shortly after the transaction, he went to inspect the company's new mine at Canyon, Arizona. The next five months saw him out West most of the time, busily investigating and promoting mineral, oil, and gas properties in Arizona, Texas, and Oklahoma. While he was on the job, he was able to put his troubles aside, but in the evening they would be back. There was only one way he could relieve his distress on those long, lonely Western nights, and that was at the saloon. And so, before long, Bud Bouvier's life became a contest between the two rivals which had caused his misfortune and which were now helping him to forget it.

It was in the year 1926 that the conflict was finally resolved, to give way to an even deadlier struggle. In that year Bud retired from business and devoted himself to his business's long-standing rival. He returned permanently to the East in the spring of 1926, where his existence now degenerated into a new contest, one between the bottle and his life.

There were bright spots, however, to the Bouvier picture in the roaring twenties. Although Bud's cloud always hung, dark and heavy, in the sky, shafts of light repeatedly broke through to ignite the family scenes in the foreground. One of the brightest was Michelle's wedding.

The Bouvier twins had been leading charmed lives since their double debut at Sherry's in 1924. While Bud's tragedy was unfolding, they were enjoying a round of parties and dates that only their marriages would halt. Since they were very beautiful, and nearly identical, they continued to be among the most sought-after decorations in Manhattan. One institution of the times, which has since disappeared, claimed them again and again: the charity cabaret. These musical shows, performed by young socialites for various New York charities, invariably featured the Bouvier twins in a costumed singing and dancing act that would always bring down the house and always bring a fresh crop of suitors to 521 Park Avenue.

Although Michelle's beaux were many and varied, only one was persistent enough to win an enduring place in her affections. He was Henry Clarkson Scott, son of Mr. and Mrs. Samuel Scott of St. Louis, and one of the great college athletes of his day. Voted the best all-around athlete at St. Paul's, he had gone on to earn eleven major Y's at Yale, playing fullback on the football squad, left wing on the hockey team, and pitcher on the baseball team. In 1924 his forty-six-yard field goal against Princeton won Yale the game and the Big Three title. A short, stocky young man, as red-headed and freckled as Michelle, he was immensely popular with his classmates, making the best secret society at Yale, Skull and Bones, and was one of the heroes of the twins' generation. The girls at Miss Spence's and Miss Porter's went wild over Scotty, the triple threat, whose roommate, Winslow Lovejoy, was no less than the captain of the Yale football team.

Michelle first met Henry Scott in the spring of 1922, when he was a freshman at Yale and she was a sixteen-year-old schoolgirl at Miss Spence's in New York. There followed a four-year romance, punctuated by several family-imposed moratoria, during which the plucky Scotty never abandoned his quarry. With the same tenacity he had displayed as a fullback, he steadfastly pursued his prey through a field containing many more players than he had ever fought at Yale. By January 1926 he had, in the words of Major Bouvier, finally "kicked his way into Michelle's heart." The couple was formally engaged on February 1 and married five months later.

During her engagement Michelle was plagued with doubts about marrying Scotty, because of her attachment to her twin. All her life she had never been able to endure separation from Maude. Now she would be separated from her forever. Although she loved Scotty, for he was sincere and goodhearted and generous, she dimly realized that she was already wed, in a sense, to her twin, and so it was with mixed feelings that she prepared for the day that would unite her to the man she loved and take her from the sister she adored.

That day, July 6, dawned with a splendor and radiance she would never forget. It was a day of days, the best that East Hampton could offer, with brilliant sunshine, powder-puff clouds, and a soft ocean breeze. The ceremony was scheduled for 1:30 P.M. in the formal Italian garden of Lasata, the sumptuous new estate Major and Mrs. Bouvier had bought on Further Lane the year before. The garden was a sunken, rectangular tract blazing with color and bounded by tall box hedges and mossy brick walks. A low brick terrace with steps led from the back of the house to the flower beds and a small, hedge-enclosed lawn. At the far end of the lawn stood a gurgling Italian fountain and two bird-spattered statues of shepherds. For the wedding a flower-decked altar had been erected on the terrace and seats for two hundred guests had been set up on the garden lawn.

When her great moment came, Michelle, wearing a gown of cream lace and trailing a tulle veil from a gold coronet wound with orange blossoms, entered the garden, by the fountain, and marched up the mossy brick walk, on her father's arm, past beds of dazzling zinnias, larkspur, and Madonna lilies, to join the bridal party at the altar. Maude, who was maid of honor, was standing nearby, holding a bouquet of yellow flowers, and as her twin passed, she threw one of the blossoms at her feet. Edith, the matron of honor, was in mauve satin, and young Edith, the flower girl, was a miniature replica of her mother. Among the ushers were the groom's brother and best man, Lytton Scott, John Vernou Bouvier III, W. Sergeant Bouvier, and Winslow Lovejoy. After the ceremony, lunch for four hundred guests was served on the front lawn, with four generations of Bouviers, from the octogenarian Mary to six-year-old Michel, among them. Then, when it was all over, Michelle changed clothes and said goodbye to her twin.

Confetti, rice, shouts, hugs, kisses, and she and Scotty were off in an open car, bound for their honeymoon at Château Frontenac. As they drove down the crackling, bluestone driveway, Michelle could not conceal her tears.

Once in French Canada, her feeling of loss and homesickness faded, but then she received a clipping of the wedding from her twin, and there was a picture of the bridal party attached to it, showing her beloved Maudie looking like an angel. At the sight of her, Michelle burst into tears, and the tears wouldn't subside, she missed her twin so much. She missed her so much, in fact, she felt she couldn't stay away from her any longer, so she made Scotty drive her back to New York. The couple returned to the Bouvier apartment at 521 Park, which was unoccupied, since the JVB, Jr.'s were in East Hampton; and Maudie drove in to see her other half. Shortly thereafter, in the fall, the Henry C. Scotts settled in a small apartment of their own at 105 West Fifty-fifth

Street, and Jack Bouvier gave his newest brother-in-law a job on Wall Street. It was an ideal situation: Jack and Scotty were together, and Michelle was only two blocks from her twin.

Michelle's wedding must have had a disquieting effect on Bud, for JVB, Jr.'s July 1926 diary entries state that during the days immediately following it he was "in very bad shape," "drinking heavily" and falling into spells of prolonged ill humor. August brought little improvement to his condition, and Major Bouvier was compelled to confide to his diary that his son seemed worn out and exhausted all month long. Early in September, JVB, Jr., extracted a written promise from Bud that he would go permanently on the wagon, then sailed for a three-week vacation at Aix-les-Bains in Savoy, not far from Champlaurent, the village where the Bouviers had originated. While in France, the Major received a letter from Jack saying that Bud had resumed drinking.

On returning to New York in October, JVB, Jr., found his son in worse shape than when he left, and decided to put him under the care of a physician. A month and a half of intensive cures at Crichton Hall in Harmon, New York, and White Sulphur Springs, West Virginia, followed. Then Bud, hoping he was finally restored, went to Oklahoma to try to regain control of his business affairs. He had been forced, because of ill health, to resign his position as vice president of the Independent Oil and Gas Company several months before and had been living on his dwindling capital ever since.

What happened to him during that last attempt to pick up the threads of his business life, we don't know. He had intended to remain out West until the spring but was back in New York within a month, having accomplished nothing in the interval. From now on he would be unable to get interested in anything, even his own recovery. Becoming the slave of forces within himself he could no longer control, he would now be compelled to witness the terrifying nightmare of his own gradual disintegration.

For Bud Bouvier, 1927 was an interminable succession of lost weekends, resolutions to abstain, relapses, night sweats, nurses, sedatives, and crises of despair. Losing confidence in himself, he yearned for a permanent amnesia, a way to extinguish the consciousness of his personal bankruptcy. The easiest way was through the very agent that was causing his destruction. And so, no sooner would he resolve to give up drinking, and succeed in abstaining for a day or two, than he would set in again to conquer the feeling of emptiness that would overwhelm him.

To aggravate his problem, several speculative ventures he had invested in had not panned out and the value of his shares in the Independent Oil and Gas Company had begun to decline. By the middle of 1927 his financial worth, on paper, was less than half what it had been at the height of his fortunes in 1924. Unemployed, and therefore without income, he was having to sell his remaining investments to meet his living expenses, his enormous doctors' bills, and his alimony payments to Emmy Lou. On May 24, 1927, *The New York Times* carried an article informing its readers that W. Sergeant Bouvier had been sued for back alimony for his wife and son. In August of that year another *Times* article stated that Bouvier had appealed to his wife to waive the $800 a month alimony payments in favor of allowing him simply to pay her rent and the support of her child.

With W. Sergeant Bouvier's financial and matrimonial disasters being aired all over town by the *Times*, the Bouvier family became increasingly annoyed with their prodigal son. It had taken a lot of sacrifice and hard work and talent and love to build the Bouvier image to the point where whatever the family did in New York attracted the attention of the press, and here was the father of the present family heir bringing down the structure. Had Michel Bouvier of Pont-Saint-Esprit labored like a Hercules for fifty-nine years, only to have the family he had established come to this? MC and Aunt Mary were most displeased. And Major Bouvier was clearly at a loss for what to do. His youngest son, his beloved Bud, had become a torment to himself and his family, a burned-out wreck at thirty-four.

With 1928 came further financial reversals for Bud Bouvier, a court order requiring him to make good on all his back alimony payments, more doctors' bills, and a general worsening of his condition. Living between the Yale Club and several dehumidifying clinics in and around New York, he gave friends the impression of being shell-shocked. Those who remembered him as a handsome young infantry captain of incredible charm, warmth, and grace blamed his deterioration on the gassing he had received during the war, and gradually this interpretation of his misfortune became the prevailing one, the official explanation offered by his family and friends.

If Jack had been doing badly in the meantime, Bud's fate would have appeared bleak but not as desolate as it seemed. But Jack was doing magnificently. A resounding success on Wall Street, making $75,000 a year by the time he was thirty-five, and one of the most dashing men about New York, he was even showing—joy to his parents—an inclination to get married and settle down.

Fingers were crossed, however, in the winter of 1928 when the James T. Lees of New York and East Hampton announced the engagement of their daughter, Janet, to John Vernou Bouvier III. Jack had known Janet for a long time but had only taken serious notice of her the summer before. She was originally a friend of the twins, and for several years Jack had paid little attention to her: the twins, fourteen years younger than he was, and their friends were not exactly in his league. But then, suddenly, Maude and Michelle came of age and their friends did also, and Jack found himself falling in love with Janet. When the couple told their friends that they were going to get married, their friends were politely incredulous. Jack Bouvier was having too good a time as one of New York's most eligible bachelors to get married, and his two broken engagements were well known. Poor Janet was sure to become another Nancy Bates or Eleanor Carroll Daingerfield Carter.

Janet Lee, however, was made of different stuff. The daughter of a modest New York family of Irish descent that had risen from obscurity to riches in one generation, she was not about to let a man of such impeccable social and financial credentials as Jack Bouvier slip away from her. For, to Janet, the Bouviers possessed the precise attributes her own family lacked. The Lees were *nouveaux*, whereas the Bouviers had had money and position for several generations. The Lees lacked style, whereas the Bouviers were among the most elegant, and fashion-conscious, families of New York.

Not that Janet Lee had any reason to be ashamed of her family. Her father, in fact, was one of the most remarkable self-made men of his generation. James Thomas Lee was born in New York in 1877, the son of Dr. James Lee and Mary Norton, children, in turn, of humble Irish immigrants. After working his way through City College and Columbia, where he earned a B.S., an M.A., and a law degree, he practiced law in Manhattan until 1916, speculated successfully in real estate, became a vice president of the Chase National Bank, then joined the New York Central Savings Bank, eventually becoming president and Chairman of the Board and making a multimillion dollar fortune in the process. In 1903 he married Margaret A. Merritt, daughter of another Irish family, who bore him three children: Marion, Winifred, and Janet.

Jack and Janet were as attractive a couple as East Hampton had ever seen, and as their wedding day approached, they drew a great deal of attention from both the local and the New York press. Jack at thirty-seven had a smouldering Levantine handsomeness, the wild, rakish look of a Barbary pirate, and Janet had a vivacious beauty distinguished by large, lively eyes and a unique, slightly one-sided smile. Would she accomplish the reputedly impossible feat of finally leading the Sheik to the altar?

Fingers were not uncrossed until the last moment, that is, until the morning of Saturday, July 7, 1928, when John Vernou Bouvier III and Janet Norton Lee were married in St. Philomena's Catholic church at East Hampton. Among the bridesmaids were the twins, who actually did keep their fingers crossed until their brother brushed past the yellow snapdragons that decorated the altar rail. They also kept them crossed for their older brother, for Bud was best man. To their immense relief, W. Sergeant Bouvier performed his duties ably, though he had not been well in recent days. Marion Lee, who had in the meantime married John J. Ryan, Jr., was the matron of honor, and Winifred Lee the maid of honor. Among the ushers were Henry Scott, Phelan Beale, and John E. Davis, Maude's fiancé. After the ceremony a reception for five hundred guests was held in the hedge-enclosed garden of Avery Place on Lily Pond Lane, the Lee home that summer. During the reception Meyer Davis played the latest hits and Jack had an explosive argument with his father-in-law, the first of many to come. Later the newlyweds drove to the Savoy-Plaza in New York, where they spent their wedding night, then sailed the next day for Europe on the Aquitania. How had little Janet done it, everybody wondered. So many other girls had tried and failed. Those who wondered underestimated the woman who would one day prove herself to be a person of indomitable courage and fortitude, the mother of the most celebrated woman in the world.

After his brother's wedding, Bud went from bad to worse. Major Bouvier's diaries indicate that his youngest son was in "very bad shape" before the wedding and in even worse shape after it. In mid-July the JVBs, Jr., debated whether or not to "throw him out of the house." When in August Jack and Janet returned from their honeymoon and found him the way he was, they agreed with Major Bouvier "not to speak to him." There remained, however, one more family task for Bud to perform which necessitated his presence at Lasata and his being on speaking terms with his closest kin, and that was to be an usher at his other sister's wedding.

The second wedding at Lasata was held on Labor Day, September 3, 1928, and would have been a near twin of the first had it not been for the foul weather. The same altar on the low brick terrace; the same seating arrangement on the garden lawn; and the same itinerary for the bride: entering by the fountain, then taking her father's arm and marching up the mossy brick walk. The same Bouviers would be there and almost the same guests. But the day brought a veritable monsoon, one of those autumnal downpours that every year puts an end to the East Hampton season. And so the ceremony had to be held inside, in the living room, with its great oaken beams and its portrait of the twins over the fireplace. When Maudie awakened that morning and saw the pelting rain, she was momentarily heartbroken, remembering the superb day in July when Michelle was married, but later she told her twin, who dressed her and combed her long red hair, that if it were God's will she would accept it.

It was Jack who introduced Maude to John E. Davis. The two men were stockbrokers, with seats on the Exchange, and had been brushing elbows daily on the floor for several years. At first the straight-laced Maude was suspicious of him. She assumed that since John was a close friend of Jack's he was as wild and rakish as he was. Sensing he was vulnerable to guilt by association, John bent over backwards to promote a sedate image of himself and eventually won Maude's confidence. Actually the couple had a good deal in common. John Davis's father had come to New York from Philadelphia at about the same time that J. V. and M. C. Bouvier had migrated from the haven city, and they had all joined the New York Stock Exchange at about the same time. Long before Maude and John met each other, their grandfathers had been friends, and MC had been a frequent caller at Davis, Sr.'s old brick house at 24 North Washington Square.

It was crowded and stuffy in the living room of Lasata that afternoon of September 3 when Maude and John made their vows. Maude remembers that just as she said "I do" the sun streamed through the great French windows, and Jack nodded his head and pointed with his thumb, like a hitchhiker, to the terrace. The bridal party and the guests got the signal, for as soon as the ceremony was over, the whole entourage headed outdoors.

Once outside, the bridal party assembled on the garden lawn for photographs, and the orchestra, hastily transferred to one side of the terrace, began playing a Charleston. Immediately brides-maids and ushers started bobbing up and down to the beat. Michelle, who was matron of honor, and who, like her attendants, wore a fall dress of tangerine tulle, started her bridesmaids high-kicking like Rockettes. And Jack Bouvier did the same with his ushers. Standing out among the group as the most dashing man present, deeply tanned, as usual, and shooting an enormous quantity of blazing white collar over his cutaway lapels, Jack led the dancing on the lawn with his usual style and bravado. He was proud of what he had done for his twin sisters. He had given Michelle's husband a job and Maudie a husband. As he led the dancing at Lasata that now rainy, now sunny September after-noon, he looked like a man on top of the world, which he was. With money, looks, a stunning wife, and a position as heir to a family whose rise had yet to be checked, Jack Bouvier in Septem-ber 1928 was one of the anointed. There was nothing in sight that even hinted at the reverses to come.

Except the condition of his brother. Bud had the same quality as litmus paper: he registered. Although he was not aware of it, his deterioration was to foreshadow a general deterioration in his family's life. Bud Bouvier looked the opposite of his ebullient, cocksure brother that September afternoon. The motion pictures of him taken at the wedding by Hartwig Baruch show a man gaunt and lifeless, one who was merely going through the mo-tions expected of him, without interest or zest: when Jack began dancing, Bud turned and walked away. That night he did not return to Lasata and when he was carried back the next day by a girl friend he was in pitiful condition. Major Bouvier, in an outburst of parental impatience, was moved to describe his favorite son in his diary as "a contemptible parasite and a dirty nuisance."

There remained only one solution to Bud's problem: to commit him to a sanatorium. Which was done in October. While at Dr. Wadsworth's, near South Norwalk, Connecticut, Bud pulled himself together sufficiently to make an effort to overcome his demon. He also returned to his religion. During his stay at the clinic he visited a Jesuit retreat house on Keyser Island, off the Connecticut coast, called Manresa Institute, where he came under the influence of a priest who blamed his illness on the fact that he had drifted away from the Church. Bud had, in fact, not practiced his faith for some time. Like countless others of his generation, he no longer saw any meaning in institutional religion and had veered toward a wholly secular outlook on life, based on a worship of material success. When that faith failed him, he had nothing to take its place.

Major Bouvier and his wife were gratified by their son's progress at the sanatorium. At last the most distressing problem in their lives was getting the daily attention it had needed for so long. It was doubly painful therefore when Bud would have a relapse. The most serious setbacks would inevitably occur at family gatherings and family milestones. He had a very bad one the day his grandmother, Caroline Bouvier, was buried, January 20, 1929. And another on April 13, when his son, Michel, aged nine, made his First Communion. After both ceremonies, which he attended along with his estranged wife and most of his family, he lost control of himself before returning to the sanatorium.

Bud Bouvier's six-month commitment at Wadsworth's was up at the end of April and he was released forthwith, having spent a small fortune on his cure. He went to the Yale Club to live and soon suffered a serious relapse that left him in the same condition as before. His will to recover, though, was not completely daunted by his setbacks. He longed to recapture his health, to establish himself in business again, win back the respect of his family, and be a good influence on his young son. It was these longings that prompted him to make one more effort to defeat the monster that was destroying his life.

If he could only get away to some beautiful place with his son, some far-off place where he would not be pestered by his family or reminded of his failures. If he could only spend six months, or a year, in some quiet, sunny place where the air was clear and there were lakes and streams and mountains and plenty of space, and horses he and Michie could ride together. Then maybe he could come to grips with this thing inside him, and conquer it once and for all, and return East the man he once was.

During his travels out West in the early twenties Bud had found such a place. It was in Southern California, in the Santa Ynez Valley, and it was called Los Olivos.

There nature had been bountiful beyond belief. A sun-drenched valley whose golden fields were studded with solitary stands of oak. A slow, sinuous river, teaming with trout. Grass-covered hills. The distant San Rafael Mountains, blue as the sky, from whose crests one could see the Pacific. Great forests of oak, sycamore, and pine. Lakes and waterfalls. Old Spanish missions.

The place was full of fascinating Indian and Spanish names, names one would never encounter back East, names that would hold no unpleasant associations. Las Padres National Forest. Nojoqui Falls. Figueroa Mountain. Lake Cachuma. And there were magnificent horse and cattle ranches whose cowboys were called *vaqueros*. And even quaint little Danish settlements, like Solvang, with windmills and many-gabled, Tudor-like houses. It was almost a foreign country. Yes, there he might succeed in reclaiming himself. There, in those far-off, unfamiliar spaces, he might come to life again.

And so, on July 3, 1929, Bud Bouvier left New York for the state in which his granduncle Eustache had spent twenty fruitless years searching for gold. He took his small son with him and he told his parents he was not coming back until he was well.

When they arrived at Los Olivos, Bud and Michie put up at an old stagecoach inn called Mattei's Tavern, now a historic landmark of California, for it was founded by pioneers almost one hundred years ago. Although it had comfortable accom-modations and was run by pleasant people, it was not the best place for Bud to be, for among its major attractions was a bar, which looked as if it had been transplanted whole from a Western movie and which was the chief evening rendezvous for the residents of the inn and the town.

Bud and Michie had a great time together during their first few weeks in Los Olivos. Bud had been engaged by a Captain Mc-Kittrick to train polo ponies at his ranch in the Santa Ynez Valley and he would bring his son to training sessions and take long rides with him through the valley and the Los Padres Forest. They went to see the falls at Nojoqui and rode up to the old, sun-dried Santa Ynez Mission. And they fished together in Lake Cachuma. The weather was marvelous, warm and dry, with hardly ever a cloud in the sky, and the crisp mountain air was invigorating. Just to keep one's eyes open was to be healed. Everywhere Bud looked, he was greeted by unparalleled splendor. Mount Figueroa, towering over the valley, changing colors constantly, blue in the morning, gray at noon, coral at dusk. The great oaks shadowing the river. Sunsets that would set the whole valley on fire. Bud was soon convinced he had made a wise decision. To be in Los Olivos that summer was to receive a benediction.

It is not known whether Bud's family wrote him while he was in California, but if they did, two news items must certainly have been imparted to him: the birth of a six-and-a-half-pound daughter to Michelle and Henry Scott on July 8, whom they named Michelle; and the birth of an eight-pound daughter to Jack and Janet on July 28, who was named Jacqueline, after her father.

As for Bud's child, the privilege of having him expired in early August and the boy had to be sent home. Having Michie with him during his struggle for rehabilitation had meant everything to Bud, and so it was with a terrible feeling of loss that he took the ten-year-old boy to the train for the long journey to his mother.

What happened to Bud in Los Olivos after his son left can barely be surmised, for the only testimonies to the story that have survived are a report from a doctor and a memory of Emmy Lou's. Up to the time of his son's departure Bud had been doing very well. But once Michie was gone, he was reminded all too forcefully of the losses he had sustained. Michie did not belong to him; he belonged to Emmy Lou and he had lost Emmy forever. Now, when he rode out onto the honey-colored plains of Los Olivos, he could not respond to the mountains and the oaks and the river the way he had when Michie was with him. The immense open spaces that had exhilarated him so in recent weeks had lost their power. The beauty was still there, but the radiance and the magic had vanished.

Early in September, after a serious relapse, Bud placed himself under the care of a physician. He must have been terribly discouraged by his failure to abstain, yet he still had the will to recover. But he had been under the care of physicians many times before. What good was a doctor when the patient had lost not only his health but his wife, his son, his job, his money, and his self-respect? A three-day "cure"? . . . New resolutions to abstain . . . A brief period of self-denial. Then . . .

The evening of October 7 he returned to Mattei's Tavern from a day of riding in the valley. After dinner he went to the bar. Sometime during the evening he telephoned Emmy Lou and asked her if she would take him back if he stopped drinking and she said she would. The reprieve demanded a resolution which he had the will to make but no longer the strength to keep. For early the next morning he had to be carried to his room. The doctor arrived shortly thereafter, but he could do nothing to save him. For Bud there would be no more reprieves.

# *IV*

BUD'S DEATH FULFILLED THE DIREST PREDICTIONS THAT HAD BEEN made about him by his family and touched off an agony of blame and guilt that would last for years. Who was at fault? What could have been done to save him? For Major Bouvier the tragedy represented the first great failure of his career. For his wife it marked the end of her best years: from October 8, 1929, on, Maude's mouth would gradually droop into an expression of permanent grief, her eyes would dim, and the few more joys remaining to her would always be chilled by one ever present memory. As for the carefree Jack, he would now turn against himself in recurring fits of self-incrimination which he could relieve by occasionally doing favors for little Michel. Only Edith and the twins escaped the burden of guilt, for they had remained sympathetic to Bud during his decline, defending him against the moralism of his father and the impatience of his brother.

After he received the telegram from police headquarters at Los Olivos notifying him of his son's death, Major Bouvier sent Jack to claim the body and bring it back to New York. Jack returned on October 14, accompanied by Charles Mattei, owner of the inn where Bud had died, and the body was taken, at Jack's insistence, to Jack's apartment. The following morning, at ten o'clock, a funeral mass was said in the chapel of the Helpers of the Holy Souls on East Eighty-sixth Street, an institution supported, in part, by MC and Aunt Mary. Then W. Sergeant Bouvier was interred in the Gate of Heaven Cemetery, beside one of the few people who always stood by him, his grandmother Caroline. Emmy Lou and little Michel were among the mourners at the graveside. Maude, still in a state of collapse, was unable to attend.

Six days later a panic on Wall Street dealt the Bouviers, along with millions of other investors, another blow. And eight days after that, the basis of the Bouviers' prosperity and confidence was shaken by the gigantic 16,410,030-share sell-off that inaugurated the Great Depression.

The crash found every male adult in the family involved with Wall Street. MC, at eighty-two, was close to being the senior member of the Exchange. JVB, Jr., sixty-four, was a special partner in MC's firm, and JVB III, at thirty-eight, was a specialist on the floor. Furthermore, JVB, Jr.'s three sons-in-law were active on the

Street, and almost all the family's wealth was tied up in securities traded on the New York Stock Exchange.

Immediately before the collapse, the entire clan was at the peak of its financial fortunes. Seats on the Exchange—and there were three of them in the family—were selling at their all-time high of $625,000. Jack had sold his rights for a second seat on March 19 for $121,000, and MC had sold his on October 10 for $125,000. That summer M. C. Bouvier & Co. had opened a branch office in East Hampton, with JVB, Jr., in charge, and the volume of business among the resort's summer residents had been enormous. By September 3, the pinnacle of the Big Bull Market, the worth of the Bouviers' respective stock holdings was at its highest. General Electric, in which MC held a 2,000-share position, was 396 1/4. Auburn Motors, one of Jack's major holdings, was selling at 395. And U.S. Steel, in which the JVBs, Jr., had a substantial commitment, was selling at 261 3/4. Since it was possible in those balmy days to purchase stocks by putting up only ten percent of their cost price, and the public was only too eager to buy stocks on that basis, MC, who did an enormous business in lending money to brokers and investors, was reaping huge profits as he made time loans of a day's duration, totaling as much as $800,000 per day, at eight-percent interest. And since the volume of business on the Exchange was so vast, Jack, as a specialist, was harvesting a crop of commissions at Post N. 11 sufficient to give him, when combined with his profits from trading, an annual income in excess of $100,000. The Bouviers, along with several thousand other stockbrokers, were clearly at the right place at the right time. American commercial optimism, eternally bullish, had made the New York Stock Exchange the sweetest hive the world had ever known. The wonderful thing about it for the stockbroker was that there was a prescribed limit to the number of bees but no apparent limit to the honey. "Radio is going to 1000." "Motors will hit 800." "Seats are going to 1,000,000." "Be a bull on America." "Never sell America short." People were buying prices, not values, but that did not matter. No one wanted to miss out on the Big Bull Market.

There were a few investors, to be sure, who, before the inevitable reckoning, had sensed things were out of hand and had accordingly pulled out of the market. William Crapo Durant, the big-time speculator with whom Bud Bouvier had once been associated, was one of them: he got out in May. J. P. Kennedy was another: he deserted it by degrees during the summer. And M. C. Bouvier was another. He had maintained a cash reserve of $1,600,000 during the speculative surge and had unloaded almost all the common stocks in his portfolio before September, with the exception of his General Electric and a few hundred railroad shares, converting most of his holdings into gold, cash, or municipal, corporate, and U.S. Liberty bonds. Furthermore, he had the sense to sell his rights to a second seat for the top dollar only nine days before the first panic in prices. As for JVB III, he had grown bearish during the summer also and had emulated his granduncle by converting many of his holdings to cash. His father, however, still a novice on Wall Street, held on to his investments until they nearly halved in value.

Major Bouvier's diary for October 1929 presents a reasonably accurate outline of the crash and how it affected his family. During the second week of the month his entries were entirely taken up with the death of his son, whom he buried on October 15. There followed three days of convalescence with Jack and Janet in East Hampton, during which the three debated the causes of Bud's tragedy. Then Bud disappeared from his pages entirely, to be replaced by:

> Sat., Oct. 19. Violent decline in prices.
> Mon., Oct. 21. At office. Almost panic in prices.
> Tues., Oct. 22. Recovery we expected came in early hours, then sold off.

On Wednesday, October 23, JVB, Jr., made no entry. It was a six-million-share avalanche of liquidation, with the tape running 104 minutes late, an 18.74 point loss in the *New York Times* composite average, and losses of 77 points in Auburn Motors and 96 points in Adams Express.

> Thurs., Oct. 24.* *Black Thursday* . . . Greatest decline in history of Exchange. Panic. No bids on some stocks such as ITT and PAK. 12,880,000 shares traded. All records broken. Called Jack.
> Fri., Oct. 25. Market Held. Steel opening at 207, closing at 204 1/2. [The Bankers Pool had temporarily buoyed prices.]

> Sat., Oct. 26. Slight advance. Sold 150 shares of C at 103 1/2
> . . . Jack and Janet and little Michel with me at East
> Hampton.
> Mon., Oct. 28. Market worse than Thursday. Steel down 17
> 1/2 points. General Electric down 47 1/2. Westinghouse
> down 34 1/2.
> Tues., Oct. 29. ***Blackest Panic Day of All* . . . Record
> 16,410,000 shares traded. Enormous volume. Richman
> sacrifices 50,000 share lots no bid at last price. No bids. . .
> no bids . . . Jack spent the night with me.

On this day, which was to be the worst in the history of the
New York Stock Exchange, huge blocks of stock were tossed onto
the market for what they could bring. With no buying support at
any level in some stocks, floor brokers found themselves at the
close with pockets full of unexecuted orders to sell. Specialists
like Jack Bouvier, whose function it was to provide buying support when there was none, faced the possibility of near ruin if they
fulfilled their function to the letter of the law. As a result, the close
of the Exchange found specialists' wastepaper baskets as full of
unexecuted sell orders as the commission brokers' pockets. After
the drifts of papers were swept away from the floor, analysts
estimated that if all orders received that day had been executed,
it would not have been a 16,410,000-share sell-off but a 20,000,000-
share liquidation that would have driven prices even lower than
they fell. As it turned out, Auburn Motors sunk another 60 points,
Allied Chemical was down 35, Electric Auto Lite down 45,
General Electric down 28, and ATT also down 28. Across the
nation the hopes of thousands of investors had been shattered in
a matter of hours. Not only millionaires but retired seamstresses
and schoolteachers had lost most of their lifetime savings, and
within the financial community itself the mood had become one
of near-total demoralization and exhaustion.

Although there were a few flickers during the next few days
that optimists called rallies, the general trend continued
downward. On November 6 JVB, Jr., recorded in his diary:
"Market opened with severe decline. Steel went to a new low at
166. Exchange closed at 1:00 P.M. Jack's $100,000 profits swept
away." And on November 13, the day on which the lowest prices
for 1929 were reached, JVB, Jr., recorded: "No bids in many
stocks." By then the *New York Times* index had fallen 249 points

from its September 3 high, and $30 billion worth of securities' value had been lost.

How did the Bouviers react to this catastrophe? MC took it in stride. The old broker, who would soon be Dean of Wall Street, had seen panics before—in 1873, in 1907, in 1917—and had survived them. Although his assets had been worth around $7,500,000 on paper at the height of his fortunes, he came out of the crash with $3,800,000 solidly intact, enough to guarantee him an income, before taxes, of at least $150,000 a year. In addition to getting himself out of most of his common stocks before the crash, he had also pulled his sister Mary out of most of hers, so that, when she died, in November 1931, four days before Black Friday, she still had over $500,000 to her credit. From all accounts, MC was maddeningly cool on October 29, 1929. While mobs of angry investors were storming Wall Street, and commission brokers and specialists were going into frenzies on the floor of the Exchange, and speculators were committing suicide from coast to coast, he remained in his office at 20 Broad Street congratulating himself on his $1,600,000 cash reserve, his lack of indebtedness, and the quality of his municipal, corporate, and U.S. Liberty bonds.

JVB, Jr., was much less serene. Having been a lawyer all his life and having lived off that profession until recently, he was new to the market and inexperienced in its arcane ways. The first substantial sum of money he ever invested was his mother's inheritance of $250,000, which he received only nine months before the crash. He did not withdraw it from the market before October 29, and it is estimated that it was at least halved in value by the great collapse. Furthermore, he had given up his career in law, because of deafness, in 1928 and had become a limited partner in his uncle's firm, so his financial future was directly linked to the fortunes of the stock market. Under the original partnership agreement he was supposed to receive ten percent of the firm's profits, with a guaranteed annual minimum of $15,000. After the crash, MC negotiated a new agreement with him, still awarding him ten percent of the profits but cutting his guaranteed minimum to $10,000. With his capital diminished, his law practice ended, and M. C. Bouvier & Co.'s profits taking a plunge, JVB, Jr.'s future in the fall of 1929 was far from reassuring. His only hope for a secure, affluent old age was his uncle. Whether MC realized it or not, his last will and testament had become, by

December 1929, the last and only hope for the financial future of his family. With a stroke of the pen he could have decimated the entire clan.

Curiously, JVB III actually made money in October 1929, only to lose his profits in November. Sensing the market was on the verge of collapse, Jack began selling short the stocks he specialized in, a few weeks before October 19. Then, after the October 29 debacle, he covered himself at what he assumed were the lowest prices his stocks would reach. A few days after the 16,410,000-share sell-off, his clerk, Paul Maricondo, reported that his boss had made a $100,000 profit in short sales off the crash. The gain, however, was not long-lasting, for, contrary to his expectations, stock prices plummeted even lower in November, so that by the sixth of the month Jack's profits had all been swept away.

When 1930 dawned and no significant market improvement had manifested itself, Jack had to face up to the fact that his chances of becoming a rich man were considerably diminished. Even though he had converted some of his securities to cash before the sell-off, he ended up taking a substantial beating from the crash.

Jack's losses on the stock market, coupled with a decrease in his commission income due to reduced trading volume, made him vulnerable to a series of humiliations from which he never fully recovered. He was forced to seek financial help from his family but was able to get only $25,000 from MC and was therefore obliged to ask aid from his father-in-law, James T. Lee, with whom he had never been on very good terms. Lee, a self-made realtor and banker who had vowed he would make a million dollars before he turned thirty, and had, agreed to come to Jack's aid on condition that he cut down his scale of living, give up several club memberships, and, in general, toe his father-in-law's line. The terms were galling for a man of Jack's pride and vanity, but Jack had little choice. Lee eventually made good his promises by allowing Jack, Janet, and Jacqueline to live, rent free, in a luxury apartment building he owned and managed at 740 Park Avenue. Thus, in the space of a little over a year, Jack Bouvier tumbled from independence to beholdenness, and the future of limitless enrichment he had looked forward to so confidently during the twenties suddenly evaporated.

By December 1929 the bear market was already forty days old, and the Bouviers were learning to live with it. JVB, Jr.'s diary for the month reflected the accommodation: it was more concerned with family matters than the state of the economy. On December 1 the subject of Bud flared up at a family lunch, with Jack accusing his father of being partially responsible for the tragedy; at which JVB, Jr., abruptly left the table and returned to his apartment. Three days later he was elected president of the Sons of the American Revolution of the State of New York, and on Sunday, December 22, his granddaughter, Jacqueline, was christened at St. Ignatius Loyola in New York, with the entire family present. Little Michel aged ten at the time, was godfather, taking the place of Bud. After the ceremony Jack and Janet held a reception in their apartment at 935 Park Avenue which allowed the JVBs, Jr., and MC and Mary and Edith and the twins to coo over the five-month-old baby and tell her proud father how much she looked like him.

The year 1930 brought predictions from financial analysts of an "inevitable upturn" on the stock market, but as mid-point in the year was reached, the opposite proved to be the case. On June 18, prices on the Exchange hit a new low, and government statistics revealed that one out of every four American factory workers had lost his job.

It was during 1930 that Jack decided to donate, at considerable expense, a memorial altar in memory of his brother Bud to the Manresa Institute on Keyser Island, the Jesuit house where Bud had gone to seek spiritual solace during the last year of his life. Plans were well advanced by October 8, the first anniversary of Bud's death, when the entire family, including Emmy Lou, attended a mass in his memory at the Helpers of the Holy Souls, on East Eighty-sixth Street. By April 27, 1931, the altar had been completed and had been installed in the chapel at Manresa. The following day the Bouviers gathered in the chapel for a dedicatory mass, celebrated by Father Conway, the priest who had counseled Bud before his departure for Los Olivos. The donation of the altar, everyone agreed, was a magnificent gesture by Jack, who, oppressed with feelings of guilt, had suffered from his brother's death more than anyone in the family except his mother. Of pure white marble, and adorned with sculptured Gothic traceries and mosaic inlays, the altar bore the inscription at its base: "In Loving Memory of Captain W. Sergeant Bouvier." Eventually, after thirty-four years of peregrination, it turned up by accident in a chapel only five miles from where Captain Bouvier's sister Maude lived in Connecticut.

Bud's tragedy was never far from the thoughts of the Bouviers, and so, when on June 12, 1931, Major Bouvier went to Denver for the Triennial Convention of the General Society of the Sons of the American Revolution, he took advantage of the trip to visit Los Olivos. The meeting in Denver was a triumphant occasion for JVB, Jr., for during it he was unanimously elected General President of the nationwide society and in that capacity addressed a crowd of several thousand, including the governor of Colorado, on Flag Day, June 14, in front of the Colorado State Capitol. Immediately after his SAR victory, he left for the scene of what had been his worst defeat.

Arriving at Los Olivos on June 16, he put up at Mattei's Tavern, where he found consolatory telegrams from his closest friend, Harry Holden, and his wife. During his stay he visited the room in which his son had died and discussed the circumstances of his last hours with one Julia Goodager, a maid, and Gus Berg, a waiter. Was he trying to find a way of exculpating himself? No doubt everyone at Mattei's Tavern reassured him that he was not to blame. Since it was his nature to disbelieve what he did not want to believe, it may well be that the purpose of his trip to the Santa Ynez Valley was to gather testimony that would refute Jack's interpretation of one of the causes of the tragedy. Then again, as a lawyer, he may simply have wanted to investigate the circumstances of his son's death to quell whatever doubts he might have had about them. Or, as a bereaved father, he may have gone to Los Olivos to mourn at the place where one of his fondest hopes had been shattered. In any case, he was at Mattei's three days, talking to people who had known his son and making occasional excursions into the surrounding countryside. Then, apparently satisfied with his mission, he returned home.

That summer found almost the entire Bouvier family in East Hampton. Edith and her three children were at Gray Gardens. The JVBs, Jr., were at Lasata with the twins and their children. And Jack and Janet, with Jacqueline and little Michel, were in a rented cottage on Egypt Lane.

At twelve years, Michel Bouvier III was a robust, energetic boy with the same broad face and widely spaced features as the original Michel. Attending St. Bernard's School in New York during the winter, he spent his summers, until his mother's remarriage, with Jack in East Hampton.

Since Bud's death, Jack had assumed the role of father to Michel, helping to support the boy and giving him the male guidance a child so urgently needs at twelve. Emmy Lou had, in the meantime, become an interior decorator in New York, to contribute to her son's maintenance. As the only male member of his generation bearing the name Bouvier, "Miche" was very precious to his family, so precious, in fact, that Major Bouvier was moved to offer Emmy Lou, at a session in the Hotel Roosevelt, $33,000 if she would let the boy stay most of the year with him. She refused. A year after the offer, she solved the problem of what to do with her life by marrying Lieutenant Carlisle Allan, a career Army officer who had been an aide to General Pershing, had edited the general's memoirs, and bore a close resemblance to her former husband.

On July 28, 1931, Michel's cousin and godchild, Jacqueline, made her debut in the society columns as she celebrated her second birthday and attended a dog show with her parents. She was already a small edition of Jack, with the same wide-apart eyes, snub nose, and complexion. Another Bouvier birthday fell on August 4—the twins' twenty-sixth—and was celebrated at Lasata with every member of the family present except MC and Mary, who were at their home in Narragansett. Although the times were bleak, the Bouviers did not find it necessary to tighten their belts unduly. Jack still maintained a stable of jumpers, and the John Vernou Bouviers, Jr., continued to live sumptuously at Lasata, assisted by a full-time gardener, a chauffeur, a cook, and two maids. As the Depression continued, and incomes dropped precipitously, the family would prove incapable of cutting down its standard of living, preferring to delve into capital rather than forego the luxuries it had been accustomed to. Thus the Depression would doubly erode the Bouviers' finances, diminishing both their income and their capital, and paving the way for the day when its proud members, used to being considered among the indomitably rich, would suddenly realize that, financially speaking, they had fallen back into the middle class.

It was especially difficult for the Bouviers to adjust to the new economic climate because, being optimistic and having behind them sixty-five years of experience in the stock market, they always considered prosperity was just around the comer. The "inevitable upswing" would occur next spring, next summer, next fall. That hope would be only temporarily dashed by a day like November 27, 1931, known to Stock Exchange history as Black Friday, when again prices dropped to record lows. Such abysses were "good times to buy" for "the higher prices ahead."

It is hard to see what hopes the Bouviers could have sustained in 1932. During this, the cruelest year of all, the streets of New York became crowded with beggars, panhandlers, and vagrants; shantytowns mushroomed in the suburbs; and reports became more and more frequent in every community of certain hitherto wealthy gentlemen who were now selling apples on the sidewalk or driving taxicabs or living in bowery flophouses. It was a time of profound disillusionment for all Americans. With 15 million unemployed, the American Dream was crumbling and there was nothing to take its p]ace. It was no wonder, then, that Franklin D. Roosevelt won the Presidential election by promising a way out. On election day of that year JVB, Jr., recorded in his diary that he and Maude had gone to East Hampton to cast their vote for "the only man who can get us out of this mess."

Roosevelt did help. He brought a new surge of optimism, the exhilaration of bold, imaginative leadership, to the American people, and that spiritual tonic was enough to buoy sagging hopes across the nation. The day before his inauguration a daughter was born to Jack and Janet whom the couple named Caroline Lee, after her paternal great-grandmother, Caroline Ewing, and her maternal grandfather, James T. Lee. Two days after that inconspicuous birth, the nation took a new lease on life. Roosevelt's measures were decisive, drastic, and deserved. A banking moratorium. The Stock Exchange closed for ten days. An embargo on gold. A $3,300,000,000 relief bill. The CCC. The Tennessee Valley experiment. A proposal to repeal Prohibition. And skirts dropped to within nine inches of the ground.

By midsummer something faintly resembling a rally was underway on the New York Stock Exchange, the liquor stocks Jack Bouvier had bought in anticipation of the repeal of Prohibition were beginning to soar, and Jack was able to celebrate his fifth wedding anniversary in style. Three weeks later his father-in-law gave a huge birthday luncheon party for his four-year-old granddaughter Jacqueline, at which JVB, Jr., read some appropriate verses. The following day, Sunday, July 30, Caroline Lee Bouvier was christened at St. Philomena's Church in East Hampton, and Jack and Janet gave a garden party at their place for two hundred guests. To crown the summer, clearly the best the family had enjoyed since 1928, Jack picked up a first prize at the East Hampton Horse Show on August 19 with his chestnut hunter, Danseuse.

But the Depression, in spite of all Roosevelt's daring innovations, would not go away. On September 21, 1933, a steep decline in prices on the Exchange melted the entire advance FDR's first hundred days had generated.

Still, Thanksgiving of 1933 found Major Bouvier unhypocritical about the holiday. In a speech before the entire family, assembled around the inevitable turkey, he, in the words of his diary, gave thanks that they were "able to conjugate the verbs 'to be' and 'to love.'"

In the mid-thirties Jack Bouvier experienced little difficulty conjugating the verb "to be," but the other verb, never easy for anyone to inflect, was getting harder and harder to handle. It was not easy to love in a climate of economic uncertainty, especially when one's personal finances were so closely tied to a shaky securities market. By the middle of 1933 Jack had made a $2 million profit off his speculations in liquor stocks. He had deposited his prize in the Chase Manhattan Bank, vowing to his friends and associates that he was going to leave it there until he died. The money, however, proved too great a temptation for his gambling instincts, and so, soon after it was deposited, he withdrew it and hurled it on the market, investing aggressively in Auburn Motors. According to his clerk, it wasn't long before the great decline of September 1933 had evaporated all but a tiny fraction of the $2 million, leaving him a net worth, as of January 1934, of $195,211.94. During the miserable year that followed, things got even worse. In 1934 he earned a mere $4,683.75 in dividends and $2,188.44 in commissions and suffered a trading loss of $43,000. His living expenses, however, had not diminished. In 1934 he spent $38,894.81 for maintenance of a duplex on Park Avenue, a cottage in East Hampton, a wife and two daughters, two servants and a chauffeur, and a stable of seven hunters. Consequently, by January 1935 his net worth had plummeted to another new low of $106,444.94, not very much for a specialist on the New York Stock Exchange.

Jack, and most of his colleagues on Wall Street, blamed their 1934 misfortunes on the Securities Exchange Commission which Roosevelt had instituted that year, an agency designed to regulate the activities of the nation's securities markets. Chosen to head the SEC was a man who knew all the angles because he had played them himself, Joseph P. Kennedy. One of Kennedy's first measures was a ruling that specialists like Jack Bouvier could not buy the stocks they specialized in "on the way up" but only "on the way down." Previously a specialist could buy stock in one of the issues he specialized in when he noticed unusual interest in the stock on the part of the investing public. Watching the stock go from 39 1/2 to 40 between 10:30 and 11:00, literally under his nose, he could buy it at 40 1/4 at 11:15 and sell it for 41 3/4, or more, at 2:00 P.M. Furthermore, if he took a big enough position in the stock, he could attract more attention to the issue and thereby help it go even higher than it normally would have, had he not bought as much of the stock. The opportunities for quick, painless profits for the specialist under this dispensation were almost limitless. Kennedy put an end to the racket, however, by requiring that a specialist be allowed to purchase his own stocks only on the downswing, or at a lower price than that of the preceding sale. It may be assumed that Jack—in view of his $43,000 trading loss in 1934—bought too many stocks "on the way down" that stayed down. Needless to say, Jack, and several hundred other brokers, acquired a thoroughgoing distaste for Roosevelt, the New Deal, the SEC, and Joseph P. Kennedy. The day was not far off when Wall Streeters would make a point of going regularly to the Trans-Lux to hiss "that man." As for J. P. Kennedy, here was an operator who had drawn all the honey he could from the hive when no holds were barred and was now stopping the very practices from which he had earned his fortune. In 1934 Jack's tan would momentarily fade at the mere mention of Kennedy's name.

In 1935, however, something happened that salvaged both JVB III's and JVB, Jr.'s finances at their darkest hour: the death on July 29 of M. C. Bouvier at his summer home in Narragansett. With that event, $3,227,997.44 was suddenly released for distribution to a long list of needy heirs and governments. The United States and New York State took $592,318.64. Charities received $145,000. Thus, $2,490,678.80 remained to satisfy MC's personal bequests. Of that sum, John V. Bouvier, Jr., collected approximately $1,300,000, and John V. Bouvier III, $5,000. John V. Bouvier III had no cause for resentment however, since in addition to his token $5,000 he acquired all of MC's business as well. For on September 30, 1935, the new stock brokerage firm of

Bouvier, Bishop & Co. was formed, advertising itself on its stationery as "successors to M. C. Bouvier & Co." and listing as its partners John V. Bouvier III, John V. Bouvier, Jr., and John G. Bishop, Mr. Bishop having been a partner of MC's for many years.

Acquiring the customers, good will, and prestige of M. C. Bouvier & Co. gave Jack's finances a new lease on life. In 1935 he managed to earn $31,444.20 from commissions and $3,442.11 from trading, in contrast to the $2,188.44 in commissions and the $43,000 trading loss of the preceding year. His living expenses, however, climbed another thousand dollars, to $39,692.25, so his net worth at the end of the year did not show any noticeable improvement. Nevertheless, with MC's business now his own, his future did seem considerably brighter.

For JVB, Jr., aged seventy at the time of MC's death, the future was already here. Not long after he came into possession of his $1,300,000 and assumed the mantle of family patriarch, he moved from his four-room apartment at 935 Park to a much larger, more lavish place at 765 Park, and took his beloved twins on an extended trip to the Pacific Coast to visit his cousin, Rear Admiral Walter Vernou.

As luck would have it, though, just as Jack's financial future began to improve, his marriage began to disintegrate. Not that it had prospered very much in the recent lean years. The year 1934 had been a disillusioning one for Jack, and the reverses he had had to endure inevitably affected his relationship with Janet. It was during the last few months of 1935 and the first eight months of 1936, however, that things between Jack and Janet took a decided turn for the worse, compelling them to try a six-month separation. The agreement became effective October 1 and specified that during the trial separation Mrs. Bouvier would retain custody of the two children but Mr. Bouvier would have the right to visit them "at all reasonable times and places" and on "Saturday afternoons and Sunday mornings as he may wish." As for finances, the final accord stipulated that Mr. Bouvier would pay all bills and debts contracted by Mrs. Bouvier prior to October 1 and that during the period of agreement Mr. Bouvier would pay $1,050 a month for support and maintenance of Mrs. Bouvier and the children. In addition, he would take care of all medical and dental bills and the children's education.

And so Janet, Jacqueline, and Lee remained in Mr. Lee's luxurious duplex at 740 Park Avenue—later they moved to One

Gracie Square—while Jack had to take up residence in one room at the Westbury Hotel. To further aggravate Jack's situation, the Estate of M. C. Bouvier, deceased, began pressing for payment of the $25,000 loan MC had made him in 1930, and the federal government began pressing him for some $16,045.64 in back taxes. This in addition to a $23,000 income-tax claim against him which was pending disposition in court at the time. Although he had had a good year on the Exchange in 1936, earning $48,876.75, it was calculated by the accountant who prepared the figures on which his separation agreement was based that if all real and contingent liabilities were to be settled by the end of the year, John V. Bouvier III's net worth would sink to $56,509.36.

After the six-month separation agreement expired at the end of March 1937, Jack and Janet made another attempt to live together, without success. The reunion lasted until the end of August and was followed by what became a permanent separation.

Friends and family were not surprised at the way things had turned out. Jack and Janet were so different that they had, in a sense, always lived apart. While Janet was extremely conservative in her tastes and friends, Jack was theatrical, swashbuckling, and adventurous, a man who cared little for conventional respectability. As the daughter of a self-made man whose family had only recently acquired a position in New York society, Janet needed more of a sense of security than Jack. Actually Jack, like many other Bouviers, did not possess a vocation for marriage. Lacking the bourgeois virtues of fidelity, thrift, prudence, and temperance, he was never able to make the transition from devastating man-about-town to devoted, monogamous husband.

Probably the severest penalty Jack had to pay for the ruin of his marriage was not so much total separation from Janet as partial separation from his daughters, whom he loved more than anything in the world. And his daughters, in turn, were the ones who suffered most from the break-up.

Jack's love for Jacqueline and Lee was a kind more common in Latin countries than in America and reflected the predominantly Latin tinge in his make-up. In Rome and Marseilles and Madrid it is not unusual to see fathers and daughters promenading the boulevards arm-in-arm like lovers. Or sitting in sidewalk cafés and restaurants taking as animatedly and intensely as if they were *fidanzati*. Without any overt expression of sexuality, the relationship clearly has a special tone to it, a warmth, and even a passion, usually lacking in northern, especially Protestant, countries. To see Jack Bouvier with his daughters when they had grown into their teens was to behold an astonishingly handsome and debonair gentleman, who looked more like a Middle Eastern monarch than an American stockbroker, accompanied by two exquisitely beautiful girl friends. Whether it was an appearance at the Maidstone Club in East Hampton, or at a chic French restaurant in Manhattan, or in the gallery of the New York Stock Exchange, Jack, Jackie, and Lee inevitably turned heads and drew applause.

After his separation from Janet, Jack came to regard the times he spent with his daughters as the supreme moments of his life, his reason for being alive. He grew to dislike the Lees intensely and so felt compelled to compete for his daughters' affections to make sure they would not prefer their mother and the Lees to himself and the Bouviers. As a result, he developed a tendency to indulge Jacqueline and Lee, giving in to their every wish, denying them nothing they asked for. Although times were bleak and he was spending more than he earned, Jack nevertheless maintained three hunters for his girls, permitted them charge accounts at Bloomingdale's, and gave them regular, if meager, monthly allowances. When he had his daughters to himself, at one of the times specified in the separation agreement, he would always do something they especially enjoyed, like taking them to the Bronx Zoo, or riding with them in Central Park, or bringing them to the New York Stock Exchange. And since he was determined to have them turn their backs on the Lees, he would expose them frequently to their Bouvier grandparents and aunts, who, in turn, would indulge them as much as he would.

Jack, in his rivalry with Janet for his daughters' affections, had two advantages that he used knowingly and deftly. The first was money. He held the purse strings and unlaced them or knotted them to the extent to which his daughters paid attention to him or didn't. The second was personality. Living with their mother was colorless and dull compared to living with Jack. Being with their father was a "treat." Staying with their mother was humdrum. Because going to their father's was always such an exciting experience, Jack influenced his daughters profoundly during the most receptive time of their lives, transmitting certain qualities to them that they would one day project to the entire world.

One of these was a sense of style. Jack Bouvier not only paid very careful attention to his own wardrobe but he insisted that the women in his life be equally well dressed. If a woman, whether she was his daughter or a date, had a hat or shoes on he didn't like, he would tell her so, being very specific about what displeased him. On the other hand, he would go out of his way to compliment a woman on her *mise*, noticing everything about her, no matter how seemingly inconsequential, from the way her shoes matched her handbag, or her bracelets complimented her earrings, to the new way she was doing her hair. To receive a compliment from Jack on the way one dressed was a great tonic to one's morale, and Jacqueline and Lee made sure the compliments would be forthcoming. What their father liked, they wore.

What Jack liked in the way of clothes would be termed good New York taste, with a touch of the flamboyant, a pinch of the theatrical. He would wear a dark blue serge suit, tailor made, not unlike that worn by scores of other New York stockbrokers, but the collar of his white shirt would be half an inch higher than anyone else's, his shirt cuffs half an inch longer, and his tan, even in January, would make it seem as if he had just flown in from the Bahamas. And his daughters would appear at parties in dresses not unlike those of hundreds of other New York debutantes, but there would be something about the way they did their hair, or combined their accessories, that would make them stand out from the crowd.

Another quality Jack transmitted to his daughters was an appreciation of what makes women desirable. As a great lover, Jack had considerable experience in the subject. He knew the qualities that made women desirable to him and attempted to inculcate them in Jacqueline and Lee. One quality he always admired in women was unapproachableness. The more a woman refused his advances, the more he was attracted to her. Then, when she finally gave in, he would lose interest in her and move on to someone else. Thus, he would admonish his daughters time and again never to throw themselves at anybody, to be always reticent with men and play hard-to-get.

Jack was individualistic in everything he did—the antithesis of the organization man. He disliked working with other people, unless they were several steps below his social and economic class; hated sitting on committees, unless he were chairman, which he rarely was; and if he was near a spotlight he liked it to be focused exclusively on himself. If he had not been given aristocratic pretensions as a child, he might have made a great movie actor. As it was, he was constantly confused with Clark Gable and would occasionally be mobbed in a subway station or outside a restaurant by people asking for his autograph because they thought he was the actor. This elusive individualism was another trait Jack managed to communicate to his daughters. During their summers together in East Hampton, Jack and his daughters would spend most of their time apart from the other Bouviers at the resort—and there were usually at least ten others around—putting in rare, and therefore highly valued, appearances. While their cousins and aunts and uncles and grandparents lived and played and argued together at Lasata, Jack and Jacqueline and Lee went about their own business, seemingly ignoring the rest of the clan. But let there be a special event, like a birthday party at Lasata, and Jack, Jacqueline, and Lee would most decidedly show up. "Isn't it wonderful Jack and his kids are here," someone would say, not paying particular attention to the fact that the rest of the family would be present. Playing hard-to-get was rewarding. It made one more valuable, much more appreciated.

Although the separation of their parents accentuated the influence of the Bouvier ethos on Jacqueline's and Lee's characters, endowing them with qualities that would one day be of great value to them, its effect on their personalities was typical of what usually happens to children of separated parents everywhere. Inevitably each parent tends to outdo the other in the eyes of the child as he competes for the love of that child. And the child becomes correspondingly confused. In the case of Jacqueline and Lee, Berthe Kimmerle, their governess from August 1937 to December 1938, had this to say at the final divorce proceedings:

> . . . They were very sorry weeping little girls when Mr. Bouvier's custody would come to an end and they were compelled to return to their mother who was staying with her father, Mr. Lee, in East Hampton.

Admittedly, governesses tend to side with the man of the house.

Jack's and Janet's competition for the affection of their children extended also to their respective families. Thus, when Jacqueline and Lee were with their mother they were influenced against the Bouviers, and when they were with their father they were influenced against the Lees. Such a contentious family situation inevitably breeds feelings of insecurity as the child wonders to which family he really belongs and by which family he is really loved. And these feelings inevitably generate a need on the part of the child to prove his worth at all cost. After their parents' separation, it became increasingly apparent to the Bouviers that Jacqueline and Lee, as they grew into womanhood, had fallen under a compulsion not only to prove their worth but to make up, in some way, for the failure of their parents' marriage.

# $\mathcal{V}$

JACK'S MARRIAGE WAS NOT THE ONLY BOUVIER UNION TO CRUMBLE in the thirties and Jacqueline and Lee were not the only Bouvier children to suffer from a broken home. Divorce had not only become more accepted in America but had become almost epidemic during the Depression, and the Bouviers absorbed the contagion in spite of their Catholicism. In 1934 Phelan Beale left Edith, to divorce her in 1946; and in 1938 Michelle and Henry Scott's marriage terminated at Reno. Two years later Jack and Janet's union came to a definitive end, Janet having sued Jack for divorce in 1939 and having obtained her freedom in Reno in July 1940.

Among those who suffered from the Bouvier's lack of vocation for marriage was one of the few members of the clan who enjoyed a successful union, JVB, Jr. For it was upon him that the burden of supporting his divorced children largely fell. Since Edith received only child support from Phelan and had no way of earning her own living, Major Bouvier had to contribute $3,500 a year to her upkeep. Michelle did not receive much of a settlement from Henry Scott either and was unable to earn her own living, so JVB, Jr., also supported her and helped educate her children. Moreover, Jack, who had to make substantial alimony payments to Janet, often out of his principal, was badly in need of money to bolster the capital he was required to maintain as a specialist and had to ask his father for loans totaling $50,000—which he probably had little intention of ever paying back. And there was also little Michel to educate. Thus, no sooner did Major Bouvier inherit his fortune from MC than he had practically the whole family demanding a share of it from him. The responsibility of financing his family, however, was not unduly burdensome, since his family by that time had literally become his life.

The John V. Bouviers, Jr., were due to celebrate their fiftieth wedding anniversary on April 16, 1940. A little over two weeks before the great day, for which a huge party had been planned, Maude Sergeant Bouvier fell ill with bronchial pneumonia and had to be placed in an oxygen tent. Four days later she died.

Since she was an Episcopalian, and Catholics in those pre-ecumenical days were not supposed to attend religious services in Protestant churches, the funeral was held at JVB, Jr.'s apartment at 765 Park, with the rites taking place in the living room and the choir and organ located in the library. Before the service, Maude was laid out in her bedroom, and her four surviving children and ten grandchildren were summoned to pay their last respects, filing into her room and kissing her as she lay in state. At the service a eulogy, written by her husband, was read by the officiating clergyman:

> Infinitely good; pure and animate as a mountain stream, natural lover of the beautiful; courageous, loyal, sympathetic, elevated in thought, quick in intelligence, rich, yet modest in her unchallenged possession of all the Virtues.
>
> A Wife, loving, tender and uplifting; a Mother, devoted, sacrificing and beloved; a Friend, sure, firm and unchanging.
>
> Such a one did God create as an example of His power, that the world might see and hence rejoice in the timeless beauty of her person, the gentle strength of her nature, and the undimmed glory of her character. Thus did He make her as fitting to serve Him, and Him she served according to His purpose. Then God touched her and she slept.

After the service the entire family accompanied her, in a private rail car, to East Hampton, where she was interred in St. Philomena's Catholic Cemetery, beside her beloved Bud, whose remains had recently been transferred from the Gate of Heaven.

Maude Sergeant Bouvier had been an adored wife and mother. If she had had a fault, it was being too indulgent a mother, too forgiving and understanding with her children. In being so indulgent she failed to build a genuine conscience in her older children, what today would be called a super-ego. And so Jack and Edith, especially, had grown up feeling they were perfect, not needing a sense of accomplishment, or rectitude, to feel worthy. Every morning of her life Mother Maude called Edith on the phone, heard her problems, and offered consolations. And Jack always knew that if he was in trouble, or had a serious problem, she would give him a surfeit of sympathy and help. Maude had been particularly close to her first three children, whereas the twins had always been the darlings of their father. And so, when she died, Jack and Edith suddenly felt terribly alone, deprived of the person who had been their closest ally.

To fill the void in JVB, Jr.'s life created by his wife's passing, Michelle moved into 765 Park with her father and became his "chatelaine." And since her twin was never very far away, the two began slowly to dominate JVB, Jr.'s household. Not only in New York but also in East Hampton, for now Lasata was without a mistress. It remained for Maude and Michelle to take over the estate in the summer of 1940, relieving their father of the management of the house and grounds. Thus the twins came to hold sway not only over their father's households but also over his affections, his mind, his entire being.

As might be expected, Jack and Edith were to suffer most from the new distribution of power in the family. Both were divorced, whereas at least one twin was still married; both were a drain on JVB, Jr.'s finances, without giving him any satisfactions in return; both were leading unconventional lives that JVB, Jr., did not approve of. Although Jack managed to hold his own, the situation was too much for Edith. No longer could she ask for a check on Monday and receive it, special delivery, the next day. After Phelan left her in 1934, Edith began her gradual retreat from the world. Now, after her mother's death in 1940, she would withdraw from society almost entirely, seeing no one but her children, a few delivery boys, and her cats.

As their parents' marriages were disintegrating, a new generation of Bouviers was growing up. By 1941 Edith's children were attractive young people who had already distinguished themselves in various ways. Young Edith, "little Edie," the oldest at twenty-four, had graduated from Miss Porter's and was one of the reigning beauties of East Hampton. A tall, blue-eyed blonde with a superb figure, she was known in the resort as "Body Beautiful Beale" and was the envy of her girl cousins for her vast following of boy friends. Phelan, Jr., at twenty-one, was a sophomore at Columbia, having achieved an outstanding academic record at the Westminster School. And Bouvier Beale, known to the family as Buddy, was doing very well at Yale. Michelle's children, Scotty and Shella, were much younger than Edith's and much more involved in Bouvier family activities. By 1941 Shella, twelve, had become Major Bouvier's closest grandchild since she and her mother had moved into his homes in New York and East Hampton and would live in them until he died. Red-headed, freckled, and physically very strong, the Scott children did not resemble the Bouviers as much as they did their father's family, and, like their father, were athletically inclined. It was Scotty's distinction to become the great mischief maker of the clan in East Hampton, repeatedly exciting the admiration of his other cousins, and the rage of his elders, with such daring acts of deviltry as swooping down from the rafters on a rope at a Maidstone dinner dance and landing on a table of old dowagers. Maude's two children were somewhat more subdued. Young Maude, six, was the baby of the family, and I, aged twelve, was already a quiet observer of the family scene. Finally there was Jack's brood, Michel, Jacqueline, and Lee—Michel by that time having become the tallest and strongest of JVB, Jr.'s five male grandchildren, a strapping twenty-one-year-old junior at the University of Arizona who held his younger cousins in awe because he drove fast cars and went out on double dates with Jack. His younger cousin, Jacqueline, who was practically his sister since they had lived together, off and on, for years as children, was twelve and had already proved to be an equestrienne of considerable talent, having picked up blue ribbons at the East Hampton horse show every summer since she was five. The image of her father, she was a strongly built, highstrung young girl with a charming manner that beguiled all her adult relatives, especially her grandfather Bouvier, who rejoiced in the fact that in addition to beauty and manners she also exhibited genuine intelligence. At twelve she attended Miss Chapin's in New York at Jack's expense, spending the summer in East Hampton. Her sister, Lee, eight in 1941, was, along with the younger Maude, one of the babies of the family, a roly-poly little girl whom her cousins called Little Leekins.

The year 1940 was a watershed year for the Bouviers. With Maude Sergeant's death and Jack Bouvier's divorce, the family had to withstand two serious dislocations in the first half of the year, and the personalities of those who were most involved in them were bound to be deeply affected.

The person in the worst immediate plight was Janet Bouvier. After she returned from Reno, she found herself in the typically awkward position of a divorcee in her mid-thirties who has neither sufficient moral support nor money to bring up her children as she would like. It was not easy for Janet to live alone on Manhattan's expensive East Side, raise two daughters, and maintain what she conceived to be a lofty social position on $1,050 a month. Furthermore, she had to endure the humiliation of being politely cold-shouldered by her former husband's family and friends. Janet had been on very good terms with the twins and had been a favorite of Major Bouvier's, but since the twins and Major Bouvier wanted to demonstrate their loyalty to Jack, they tended to avoid Janet after the divorce. To make matters worse, many of Jack's friends tended to do the same thing. And so eventually Janet found herself alienated not only from her husband but from his family and friends as well.

For Jack, on the other hand, things were not nearly so bad. His divorce, in fact, enabled him to return to the life that suited him most, his pre-marital existence as dashing man about town. In the winter of 1941, about six months after Janet returned from Reno, Jack left the room in the Hotel Westbury where he had been staying for some time and settled in a cozy apartment at 125 East Seventy-fourth Street. It was on the fourth floor, facing a sunless airshaft, and consisted of a living room, dining alcove, two bedrooms, a bath, and a maid's room. It would be his headquarters until he died.

With no legal attachments to cramp his style and with his own apartment to guarantee his privacy, with the stock market beginning to pick up, and with his good looks and health intact at forty-nine, Jack was able to resume his former career as *homme du monde* and ladykiller with impunity. From now on, he would dedicate himself to the only activity that ever really gripped him: courting women.

It is a commonplace that, after the trials and errors of youth, people usually end up doing what they do best, and there appears to be little doubt that what Jack did best was court women. Unlike many of his contemporaries of Anglo-Saxon parentage, but like many Latins, Jack took an inordinate interest in women, delighting in winning their affections. For him an attractive woman was a challenge he could not resist. Once a girl aroused his interest, he would go after her with singleminded determination. In a culture where elaborate gallantries in courtship were not generally practiced, Jack's attentive, Italianate wooing was a wonderful experience for the women he pursued. He would send his new inamorata flowers every day. He would praise her beauty and her taste continually. He would never fail to take her to the most chic restaurant or nightclub in town and make sure the maître d' and waiters made a tremendous fuss over her. To these chivalries should be added the fact that Jack was, from all accounts, a lover without peer. Though he rarely remained with the same girl for more than a few months, preferring the brief encounter to a deep emotional involvement, women, even some of those he discarded, adored him. On visiting his apartment, his nephews, including myself, would always be amazed and envious at the number of phone calls he would receive from women in the course of an hour—all of them, judging from Jack's amused reactions, seemingly pleading for his company.

One of the secrets of Jack's phenomenal success with women was his ability to tell instantly who among a collection of girls at a party would be most likely to fall for him. Upon his arrival at a cocktail party or a dinner, he would quickly assess every woman present, then select, in a matter of minutes, the one he instinctively knew would respond most enthusiastically to his attentions. If the party was a place-card, sit-down affair, he would not hesitate to tell his hostess that he would prefer to be seated next to the girl he had chosen, even if it meant the complete rearrangement of the seating. Since Jack's strategies were known in the circle he frequented, a woman who found herself seated at his right at a dinner party would know she had not necessarily been put there by the hostess but had probably been honored by no less than the Black Prince himself. Few women, thus complimented, could resist their glorifier.

Another of Jack's more successful tactics in dealing with women was his policy of freely and frankly talking about them to each other. He would not hesitate, for example, to boast to a girl friend that he and a fashion-model friend had recently been voted the most attractive couple at a ball and that another girl, who was about to sail for Europe, was temporarily moving into his apartment. No member of his harem was ever given the illusion that she was his one and only. Being one of Jack's girls meant being in a highly competitive situation. If a girl didn't measure up, she knew there were others waiting to take her place.

Jack's success with women, however, was by no means entirely due to his skill as a tactician. His striking appearance was an important factor. When *Gone with the Wind* was published in 1936, people immediately identified Rhett Butler as an ante-bellum Jack Bouvier, and when the film of the book came out in 1939, it seemed as if Jack had made his screen debut. His dark, virile looks had come into vogue, and women naturally responded to them.

Also, in a drab, rather bland, age, Jack's elegant clothes, princely bearing, and dramatic style set him apart from other men. In addition, he had impeccable social credentials and was reputed to have money. A member of the Racquet Club in New York, Knollwood, Turf and Field, and the Maidstone on Long Island, listed in both the Social Register and "the 400," and a member, also, of the Sons of the American Revolution and the Society of the Cincinnati, Jack had the special advantage of being on top of the social heap. That he never quite had the money to match his status is immaterial: he always managed to look like a millionaire.

If Jack Bouvier had been a Roman or a Parisian, the sort of life he led after his divorce would have been fully accepted by his social peers. The separated man in his late forties in Italy or France who has fathered two children and who now dedicates his remaining years to the delicious art of courting women is a familiar and much appreciated member of society in the capitals of Europe. But in puritanical Northeastern United States such a man as Jack Bouvier inevitably falls victim to moral censure. In America a mature man is supposed to dedicate himself singlemindedly to his job and his family, certainly not the conquest of women. And so the Black Orchid, as Jack was often called, became a favorite subject of gossip in the Hamptons and Manhattan's East Sixties and Seventies, a name that would inevitably elicit wry smiles and knowing glances from the prudes.

To be sure, Jack's Epicurean life was a departure from the traditional Bouvier pattern. With the possible exception of Eustache *fils*, the Bouviers of Philadelphia and New York had been anything but hedonists. The men, from the first indomitable Michel to JVB, Jr., had all been hardworking, God-fearing, strivers who habitually scrimped on pleasure and piled on the work. And the Bouvier women had been, for the most part, a race of virginate, self-sacrificing ascetics. Jack was clearly the first frank pleasure-seeker of the clan.

It would be unfair, however, to say that after his divorce Jack dedicated himself exclusively to pleasing women, for he had two other powerful interests: the stock market and his daughters.

As a stockbroker Jack had suffered considerably during the thirties. The Depression had sabotaged many of the assumptions upon which he based his original decision to go into the securities business. It had shown that ambition and hard work did not automatically bring success, that you could invest in solid

American blue chips and they would not automatically appreciate, that the American economy was not automatically assured of uninterrupted growth, and that stockbrokers' advice, so revered in the twenties, could appear utterly ridiculous when confronted with certain economic conditions.

Although Roosevelt's innovations had fostered a few rallies on the market, by 1937 it was clear that, for all their originality, they were unable to stimulate the American economy sufficiently to produce anything remotely resembling the bullish spirit of the twenties. Quite the opposite, in fact, for in October 1937 the bear returned, driving prices to new lows, and the following year the market turned as stagnant as the Great Okeechobee Swamp with stockbrokers having to witness the conviction of the president of the New York Stock Exchange, Richard Whitney, for misappropriation of trust funds, and his subsequent consignment to Sing Sing. And, as if that were not enough, there were days like March 2, when only 410,000 shares were traded, compared with 3,450,000 on the same day a year before, and June 3, when only 190,000 shares changed hands, the lowest in thirty years.

Throughout the bearish thirties, however, Jack Bouvier never lost his interest, or faith, in the Stock Exchange. The market, bull or bear, exhilarated him. He enjoyed the excitement of the trading floor and remained confident, even in the leanest years, that stock prices would eventually recover. In the end, it took World War II to justify Jack's faith. The war-production effort proved to be the ultimate solution to the chronic unemployment and economic stagnation that had plagued the nation for thirteen years. After June 1942, both stock prices and trading volume on the Exchange began to rise.

Jack Bouvier's income was wholly dependent on the volume of trading in his assigned stocks: the greater the volume, the more the commissions, the higher his income. Small volume, in fact, was a double curse because, as a specialist, Jack was obligated to buy shares of his stocks from a seller when there was no buyer available. Thus, some of his biggest losses during the thirties were sustained during low-volume markets when he was forced to take large positions in stocks for which there were no buyers. Correspondingly, some of his biggest gains in the forties were made when he was clever enough to take a strong position in one of his stocks before a buying surge.

Specializing was only one half of Jack's professional life; trading for his own account was the other. Jack was not an investor but a speculator. His "investment" philosophy was, more or less, to hell with dividends, go for short-term capital gains, what would be called rapid "growth" in today's market. To make these gains, Jack would not bother to read company reports, or Standard and Poor's sheets, but would simply listen to what the smartest men on the Street were saying about the stocks he was interested in. Then he would "watch the ticker" to note the way those stocks' prices were moving and, when he was convinced the time was ripe, would plunge in and make a commitment, selling when the stock had reached the price objective he had established for it.

We may picture him on the floor of the New York Stock Exchange on a typical business day. He is standing at Post N. 11, dressed, as usual, in a beautifully tailored black or very dark blue suit and is wearing one of his high-collared, starched, white shirts to show off his tan. His silk tie, of paisley design, and matching handkerchief, are in perfect taste, and he may well have his Cincinnati rosette in his buttonhole. Above him, on a sort of marquee attached to his post, are displayed the names of the stocks he specializes in. Inside the oval-shaped post his very able clerk—Paul Maricondo—is frantically taking down orders, messengers are scurrying in and out, and the stock reporter, whose duty it is to transmit transactions to the ticker, is recording the price changes in Jack's stocks. Above and beyond the post, on the great North Wall of the Exchange, looms the vast Annunciator Board whose flapping numbers call the commission brokers to their telephones to receive customers' orders. On one side of the board hangs the American flag and on the other the flag of the State of New York. The atmosphere on the trading floor is tumultuous. Commission brokers are racing around with slips of paper in their hands. Messengers are racing around with slips of paper in their hands. Telephone clerks are jotting down orders and ringing up brokers' numbers via the Annunciator. Reporters are desperately trying to keep up with the transactions. Specialists are barking out quotations on their stocks.

"Hey, Bouvier, how's Kennecott?"

"Three eighths and a half."

"Jack, how's Texas Gulf?"

"Eighth and a fourth."

Everybody knows everybody; the Exchange is a vast gentlemen's club. When business slows down, the brokers joke with one another: the horseplay relieves the tension.

At a lull in the trading, several brokers gather around Jack's post. One of them hangs a mirror on the sign where the price of Texas Gulf Sulphur is quoted, and the others break into a chant:

> "Mirror, mirror on the wall,
> Who is the fairest of us all?
> Black Jack. Black Jack. Black Jack."

A scowl from Jack and a flurry of orders in Holland Furnace scatter the crowd.

At noon Jack leaves the floor for a bite to eat at the Stock Exchange Luncheon Club, located in the same building. The club's dining room is a large, conservatively appointed, red-carpeted room, forbidden to ladies, whose pale green walls are broken up by a series of dark-brown wooden columns and pilasters, between two of which, at the far end of the room, stares an enormous black-faced clock. In all probability Jack Bouvier had breakfasted there earlier, having had nothing but a cup of coffee before he arrived downtown, a cup of coffee which his former partner, John Carrere, asserts he used to drink in his apartment-building elevator, handing the empty cup to the elevator operator when he landed on the main floor.

At lunch Jack would usually eat alone. When he did eat with someone, it would be with his male secretary, to whom he would dictate a few letters, one of which would invariably be to his daughters. He liked broiled meat, especially lamb chops, enjoyed chatting with the waiters, and was very demanding about the temperature of his coffee and beer. The headwaiter at the Luncheon Club, who used to serve him as a waiter in the forties and fifties, remembered Jack seated at his usual side table pouring his beer back and forth between two glasses in protest over its temperature, while he talked on and on about his daughters, often to the exasperation of the waiter, who would normally have several other customers clamoring for his services. Then, promptly at a quarter to one, he would jump up from the table, leaving a generous tip, to return to the trading floor.

Because of his cocksure manner, his elegance and éclat, Jack Bouvier had many admirers, both open and secret, on the floor of the Exchange. One of them was the stock reporter at Post N. 11, Mr. Arthur Plante, in 1966 still a familiar and well-liked figure on the trading floor after forty years of uninterrupted service to the Exchange. It was Mr. Plante's responsibility to report the price changes in Jack's stocks and transmit them to the ticker tape. Thus, from 1928 to 1955 he spent most of his time between 10 A.M. and 3 P.M. standing in front of Jack Bouvier, alternately observing the man and his stocks.

Mr. Plante recalled in 1967 that Jack Bouvier was one of the most original members of the Exchange in his day, a man in a class of his own. He observed that Jack was twenty years ahead of his time in dress in that he was the only man on the floor in the thirties who wore cuffless trousers, and one of the first to wear double-vented shaped jackets whose sleeve cuffs could be unbuttoned and rolled back.

As an illustration of Jack's self-love, Plante recalled a weekend trip he once made with him to the Swordfish Club at Bridgehampton, during which he was amused to find, on entering Jack's room, that the Black Prince had hung no less than six photographs of himself on the wall.

To nourish his self-love, Plante observed, Jack needed the tonic of winning as often as possible, whether the contest was political, a stock trade, or a bet. Particularly a bet. According to Plante, Jack, at a lull in trading, would go out of his way to "look for a good-sized wager." Thus, he would always be at odds with someone over the outcome of a football game, the World Series, national and local elections, a prizefight. Since money meant so much to him, it could almost be said that Jack could take no real interest in an issue or a struggle unless he had a financial stake in its outcome.

Vanity invites ridicule and Plante readily admitted that Jack's narcissism left him wide open to frequent kidding and harassment by other members of the Exchange. His sun-lamp tan would expose him to jokes about his ancestry and earn him nicknames he was not particularly proud of. And his susceptibility to the opposite sex would result in brokers coming to his post and handing him slips of paper ordering him to sell a hundred shares of Peggy, or Alice, or Amanda, or whoever his latest was, at 3 1/8. His tormentors' biggest field day would occur the Monday morning after Yale had been beaten by Harvard or Princeton. Having placed a number of sizable bets on Yale, Jack would be greeted at his post by a swarm of new creditors and Harvard and Princeton graduates who had made a point of arriving on the floor several minutes before they knew he would, so they could serenade him with the victory song of the college that had won the game.

Jack's ego was strong enough, however to take the kidding in stride. All his former associates agree he thrived on the conviviality of the Exchange as much as he did on the exhilaration of trading. The New York Stock Exchange was his world and as such claimed from him an allegiance as strong as his loyalty to his city or his state or his nation. As much as he enjoyed the Stock Exchange, however, Jack's work as a specialist broker never became an end in itself but remained a means to provide him with enough money to impress his girl friends and support and indulge his daughters.

Jack's love for his daughters was undoubtedly the first thing in his life, his steadiest and purest devotion. That his divorce enforced partial separation from them only intensified his feelings. Now, when he would see Jacqueline and Lee, there was no limit to what he would do for them. Proud of their beauty, he would see to it that they wore the smartest clothes within his means to buy. Proud, too, of Jacqueline's accomplishments as an equestrienne, he maintained Danseuse for her all winter at Durland's on West Sixty-sixth Street, so she could ride whenever she wanted in Central Park.

Since Janet, after the divorce, continued to live in New York in the winter and East Hampton in the summer, Jack took advantage of her proximity to involve his daughters in Bouvier family life as much as possible. During the winter, that life revolved around Major Bouvier's apartment at 765 Park, where every Thanksgiving, Christmas, New Year's, and Easter he, as patriarch, would hold a family luncheon that would bring out the entire clan, while in the summer the reunions would take place at Lasata.

It was at Lasata, principally, that the Bouvier ethos was most concentrated. There, on vast, green lawns, in sunken gardens, in the old ivy-covered house, amid the inebriating aroma of August flowers and Atlantic breezes, the family cult received its most fervent devotion. Jack would make sure his daughters were regularly among the celebrants.

EAST HAMPTON. THE MAIDSTONE. LASATA. FOR THE BOUVIERS DUR-
ing the thirties and forties these three names symbolized the
richest delights their family could offer them. Although Major
Bouvier's winter gatherings at 765 Park were sparsely attended
in the mid-forties, his summer reunions at Lasata, the last the
family would enjoy for many years, continued to bring forth the
entire clan until he and Lasata were gone.

Major Bouvier did not own Lasata until his wife died. Maude
Sergeant had bought the estate in 1925 with money she had
inherited from her father, after having spent ten years at the more
modest Wildmoor on Appaquogue Road, a place that came to be
known as the Little House after she moved her family into Lasata.
When JVB, Jr., inherited his fortune from MC in 1935, he bought
the Little House from his wife, and when his wife died in 1940,
he bought Lasata from his children, who had inherited it from
her.

When the Bouviers first came to East Hampton in 1915, the
town, or rather the village, as residents like to call it, was considered a "simple" resort, in contrast to the more opulent and
"dressy" Newport and Southampton. "Summer people" had
been coming since the end of the Civil War, but they had not
disturbed the quiet dignity of the area. Its old elms and windmills,
its seventeenth-century saltbox houses, village greens, and town
ponds had been preserved. And what "improvements" had been
made since the early days were generally in good taste. From its
very beginning as a resort, East Hampton and its satellite villages
of Amagansett, Springs, and Threemile Harbor had attracted
artists. Old residents remember their "umbrellas stuck up all over
town," and farmers perennially lamented the painters were so
"underfoot" they couldn't get "into their cowyards." When the
Bouviers arrived, the reigning artist was Childe Hassam, who
lived in a seventeenth-century house on Egypt Lane, and when
they left, it was Jackson Pollock. Among the many charms of East
Hampton was the uncontrived quaintness of the town's street
and place names, some of which dated from the 1600s: Toilsome
Lane, Pantigo Road, Huntting Lane, Two Holes of Water Road.
Among its residents' more picturesque memories: Enrico Caruso,
who had married an East Hamptonite, Dorothy Benjamin, and
had rented Albert Herter's house in Wainscott, taking a boat out

on Georgica Pond and singing so mightily from that vast stage that the wild swans would take flight and rings of ripples would spiral toward the shore. As a resort, however, East Hampton had as its chief attraction the Maidstone, with its beach club, two golf courses, and lawn tennis club. Life for the summer people revolved around the club. As the saying went: "if you weren't in the Maidstone, you were out of it."

During their treasured summers in East Hampton, the Bouviers divided their time between the Maidstone and Lasata. Lasata began on Further Lane, not far from the ocean, with a long post-and-rail fence smothered with honeysuckle and swarming with bees. The bluestone driveway opened from the lane, passed the fence, curved through a vast, well-groomed lawn under an arbor of young maples, then swept by the main entrance of the ivied stucco house, skirted the garage and gardener's shed, and eventually became a dirt road leading past the cornfield to Jack's stables and riding ring, where it finally terminated in a "back entrance" on Middle Lane. To the Bouviers the twelve elaborately cultivated acres these roads traversed were a preserve of mystery and excitement, a source of unfailing joy and surprise.

There was an itinerary through the estate that had become an unconscious ritual for the Bouvier grandchildren when they arrived for the first time in July. First they would run across the south lawn to the tennis court, a red-clay court whose high backstops were matted with trumpet vines. The red and yellow trumpets would be plucked; an old tennis ball would be found and thrown into infinity; the one-ton roller would be rolled along a base line and it would be fun to have its momentum pull you along. From the tennis court the route would lead to the rose path: wild roses whose single pink petals vanished by July into hard orange pods that resembled unripe tomatoes, which the grandchildren would use as ammunition against squirrels, rabbits, and each other. Down the rose path, past the orchard with its harvest of peaches, plums and pears. Then into the cornfield, a forest of stalks, tassels, and raspy leaves in which you could get lost, or have the distinction of finding the biggest ear. The heavy smell of mowed grass was always in the air those July days. It blended with the sea breeze, saturated with salt and kelp, and the flowers' exhalations, to produce a rich banquet for the senses. The sounds were sporadic against the rumble of the ocean: gull cries, the owlish hoots of doves, an occasional overhead whir of a flight of wild swans—a car horn.

A car horn would announce the arrival of another load of Bouviers, perhaps Jack and his two daughters, or Edith and her children. When the entire tribe of grandchildren was present, its leader would always be Miche, known as Big Boy Michel to his younger cousins, since he was the tallest and strongest of them all. If Jacqueline were along, she would invariably be wearing her riding habit, in preparation for a workout in the ring with her adored Danseuse. In boots, jodhpurs, tweed jacket, derby, with whip in hand, she would stick close to her father, shying away from the boisterous activities of her cousins.

The cousins would take time out to greet the new arrivals, then resume their rounds of the estate. One of the favorite spots to go to would be the Grove of the Three Graces. These three naked attributes of Venus, sculpted from chaste white marble, stood, hands entwined above their heads, in a cool grove of trees near the sunless solarium at the southern end of the house. Pulchritude, Voluptuousness, and Chastity were not known to the Bouviers by their rightful names but were called Mary, Alexine, and Zénaïde, after JVB, Jr.'s spinster aunts. The one pagan touch in an otherwise cloistral Christian home, the Three Graces had stood in the dining room of MC's New York brownstone for over fifty years. After admiring the Graces' bottoms and pasting the ritual three maple fig leaves in their proper places, Miche and his cohorts would storm into the Italian garden at the back of the house, Lasata's chief glory, the winner of a score of horticultural prizes. Here a neat geometrical pattern of box hedges and brick walks guarded the beds of perennials, leading from the back terrace and the sundial to the fountain and the two baroque shepherds. A high hawthorn hedge on either side and a clump of manicured yews at one end emphasized the garden's sunken appearance, for the beds were actually on a level with the cellar. A tangle of yellow roses wreathed the fountain, which was so mossy and water-smoothed it looked as if it had been lifted from some Renaissance cardinal's *giardino del piacere*. The two leaden statues of French shepherds that flanked it were favorite targets of Lasata's most merciless vandals, its grandchildren and its birds. Situated on pedestals beneath ilexes and lindens, they were repeatedly bombed by robins, sparrows, and jays, so that their heads had turned prematurely white. And what fair game they were for BB and .22 riflemen! The Bouvier grandchildren had donated pupils to the eyes of both statues: where there had once been solid blank ovals of bird spattered gray lead, there were now surprised stares through which, on close inspection, insects could be seen coming and going.

From the elegant Italian garden the band of Bouvier cousins would race up the brick steps near one of the shepherds, past the great hawthorn hedge, and enter the "cutting garden," with its annuals, sunflowers, limas, and baby tomatoes. In preparation for the baby tomatoes, the children would have filled their shirt pockets with a mixture of sugar and salt, a pinch of which they would pop into their mouths before devouring the tomatoes whole. The tomato vines were directly opposite the grape arbor, which, in turn, led to the riding ring, past cornfields and mint beds. Looking down the long arbor, you could often see Jackie's Danseuse grazing in a perfect bull's-eye at the other end, or spy Paul, the gardener, coming up the path with a pail of fresh baby limas and a basket full of corn. To one side of the cutting garden stood Paul's shed, and it was there the Bouvier children would usually go next, to inspect the gardener's tools and see if there were any swallows' nests in the rafters. Then from the shed they would run to the garage to look over the "limousine," hoping that Adam, the chauffeur, would be making some of his luscious peach ice cream and they could lick the dasher.

From the garage the driveway led to the front of the house, shaded by two giant elms. If the whole family were present, there would be six or seven cars parked under those elms, three of which were particular favorites with the children: Jack's black Mercury convertible, his father's red Nash convertible, and the all-metal blue Dodge estate wagon. The two convertibles had rumble seats, which for some reason gave the kids a great thrill to sit in, even when the cars were parked. And the estate wagon was almost a room in itself: the whole crowd could fit inside it.

The inspection of cars would end the inspection of the estate and signal the imminence of lunch. The Bouvier young would then dash up the front steps, past the great urns of blue hydrangeas guarding the main entrance, and would burst into the house to join their parents on the back terrace overlooking the Italian garden.

If the full complement of adults was present, it included Jack, Edith, the twins, Maude's husband, and Major Bouvier. It was

Jack's task to make the drinks. His daiquiris, made with two varieties of rum, were justly celebrated, and the tomato juice he concocted for the children was spiked with lime, lemon, and clam juice, celery salt, and the sauces Worcestershire, Tabasco, and soy. Esther, the maid, would pass the results of his bartending around on silver trays, along with the little watercress sandwiches that were a great favorite with the family.

Ten grandchildren were hard to contain on Lasata's intimate brick terrace, and so, in spite of Jack's rich potions, several of them would inevitably spill into the sunken garden among the delphinium, the beds of marigolds and zinnias, the dahlias and snapdragons, and take to racing up and down the washed brick pathways, swinging around the sundial, and throwing crumbs of watercress sandwiches to the fountain's goldfish, while their parents stayed on the terrace, doing homage to Jack's drinks.

As usual, Jack would be dressed in a manner all his own. For a family reunion, on, let us say, a July or August Sunday, he would combine a wide-lapeled double-breasted beige gabardine suit, with its cuffless trousers rolled up slightly to reveal no socks on his deeply tanned ankles, with black evening pumps. With his anthracite complexion, dark glasses, high-parted black hair, and pencil-thin black mustache, Jack contrasted sharply in appearance with his fair, red-headed twin sisters, leading one to doubt the three were born of the same parents.

There was no doubt, however, that Edith was his sister. Big Edie's complexion was not as dark as her brother's, but it was darker than most people's, dark enough to give her the air of a gypsy when combined, as it usually was, with hair askew and long drop earrings. If Edith was a great favorite with the young because she was just as irrepressible as they were, she paid for her popularity by being distrusted by the Bouvier adults and considered a subversive influence to be barely endured at family festivals.

Edith cultivated a talent that was the delight of her nieces and nephews: her voice. An accomplished mezzo-soprano, she drew enthusiastic applause from the young for her singing, and at best a reluctant toleration from the adults. Aware of the power of her popularity with the children, and ever happy to be on stage, Edith would go straight to the living-room piano on entering the house. No sooner would she sit down and sound a few mighty chords, a signal that could be heard all over the estate, than her audience would assemble.

On a typical summer Sunday, that audience would be composed of all ten grandchildren: Miche, Jacqueline, Lee; Michelle's two children, Shella and Scotty; Maude's two; and Big Edie's own brood, Little Edie, Buddy, and Phelan, who were usually not as enthusiastic about their mother's singing as their cousins. "Oh, *Mother, must* you?" Little Edie would cry. Whereupon Edith, who definitely had to, would break into what had become her standard opener: "Because God Made You Mine (I'll Cherish Thee)..."

The living room in which Big Edie would perform was dominated by Albert Herter's portrait of the twins, above the fireplace. There they were, those two "white sheep" in a Latin family, with their Titian hair and pale peach skin, against a background of Herter blue. The twins' mother had carried that shade of turquoise out from the painting onto the ceiling between the oaken beams so that the portrait seemed to give out rays of its own. Albert Herter had painted a portrait of Edith too, and ever since it had been hung in the dining room she had had a predilection for the painter's trademark color, wearing Herter blue whenever she got the chance, usually combining it with a pink scarf and "fatal apple" lipstick.

"...Because God made you mine, I'll cherish thee ... eee ..." Aunt Edie's voice would ring through Lasata, setting the chandeliers tinkling and the dogs barking. It was a voice of tremendous power that never failed to move its listeners. Aunt Edith's figure was a caricature of an opera star's: enormous bosom, heavy arms, large legs. And she put every ounce of her imposing body into her singing. By the time she launched into "Indian Love Call," she would have her young listeners transfixed. Jacqueline might be staring dreamily out of the huge French casement windows in back of the piano; Miche might have sat down at the desk his great-great-grandfather and namesake had made over a hundred years before and struck an uncharacteristically thoughtful pose. While the others might be gazing aimlessly around the room, overwhelmed by the force of their aunt's voice. That room was, like Major Bouvier's bedroom in New York, almost a museum of the Bouvier past. Besides containing a sample of the first Michel's furniture and many pieces from Uncle Michel's brownstone, it also had a gallery of Bouvier military portraits, which was particularly admired by the children, boasting JVB,

Sr., in his Civil War uniform; JVB, Jr., as a Major Judge Advocate; JVB III as a Signal Corps officer; and Bud Bouvier as a captain in the Lightning Division—four Latin gentlemen dressed as American soldiers.

"Indian Love Call" would usually be followed by "Smoke Gets in Your Eyes" or "Stardust." But by the third or fourth song the adults on the terrace would have had enough, and one of them, usually Jack, would come into the living room to break up the performance. He would roar that Edith's throat needed one of his daiquiris badly, set the drink down on the piano, and start rounding up the kids, meaning his daughters, whom he would take by the hand and attempt to lead out of the room. The children would protest, breaking into applause and shouts of "encore," "bis," "sing 'Begin the Beguine,' Aunt Edie," "more, more," "what about 'Un Bel Di'?" At this point the twins would march in, insisting that the children greet their grandfather on the terrace: he had just come down from his upstairs study. A melee would ensue which would find Edith shouting at her brother and twin sisters, they shouting back, and the ten grandchildren adding to the turmoil by siding mostly with Edith: only her own children would go along with Jack. Finally Jack would take his two daughters away, Edith's children would drift out, and Michelle would close the keyboard and force Edith to settle for alcohol instead of applause.

"Grampy" Bouvier would then receive his grandchildren on the terrace with quiet delight. Looking up from the pile of newspapers on his lap, he would allow himself to be kissed by his admiring progeny, each of whom was careful to avoid the barbs of his waxed mustache as they conferred their kisses on a safe space near his left ear. Like his son, Major Bouvier was a stylish dresser. His customary summer Sunday uniform was a high stiff collar, brown tweed jacket, white linen trousers, black socks, and white shoes. After his wife died, he always wore a mourning band on his left sleeve and a black tie. After the ceremonial kissing, during which he would mutter a few wry comments to each grandchild—"Michel, if you get any fatter, you won't make the crew next year." "Jackie, I'm convinced you're going to marry a jockey"—he would turn his hearing aid down and lapse back to reading the Sunday papers, seemingly oblivious to the world around him until the maid came to announce lunch.

Sunday luncheons at Lasata were ritual occasions for the Bouviers. Major Bouvier assumed the role of High Priest, with his twin daughters serving as acolytes, and the others either as hecklers or as worshippers. The only other occasions to equal them during the summer were birthdays, several of which fell in July and August: Shella's on July 8, Jacqueline's on July 28, the twins' on August 4, Major Bouvier's on August 12.

Michelle, who had been keeping house for her father since her divorce, was responsible for the menu and décor for these festivals, ably assisted by her twin sister. While everyone waited behind his chair for Grandfather to be seated, the table would be duly observed and appreciated. In a dining room whose predominant color was a dull mustard yellow, the heavy Jacobean oak refectory table would usually bear a medley of yellow shades on its rough brown surface: a ginger lace tablecloth, amber Venetian glassware, tall brass candlesticks, a centerpiece of topaz dahlias, and perhaps the Royal Doulton service of blue and gold. "It's simply gorgeous, Michelle," her twin would say, and as the maid pushed Major Bouvier's chair in, everyone would sit down.

The sixteen relatives who would then start in on their tomatoes stuffed with crabmeat would not be the only ones in the room. There were several permanent residents also, ancestors whose presence would be generally ignored by all but the reigning paterfamilias, who would occasionally propose a toast to their memory. On one wall hung the tenebrous portrait of the first Michel. Painted late in his life, it portrayed an unpretentious businessman resting from a life's labor of establishing a family of ten children and a successful business in the New World. His wife, Louise Vernou, was next to him, expressing an altogether different attitude: in the turn of her head and the set of her mouth was a pride and hauteur completely lacking in her earthy husband. Opposite Michel and Louise was a painting JVB, Jr., always insisted was the family benefactor, Joseph Bonaparte, resplendent in gold epaulettes and a sapphire-blue uniform gleaming with medals. In reality it was a portrait of Louis Philippe.

A typical Sunday or birthday lunch might start with stuffed tomatoes or jellied madrilene and go on to roast Long Island duckling with apple sauce, Lasata baby limas, and corn on the cob. The steaming duck would have everybody ravenous. "Save me the Pope's nose!" a grandchild would shout. "Give me plenty of that fatty skin," another would call. As was his custom, Grampy Bouvier would put his ear of corn in his water glass to cool, and his grandchildren, in spite of their parents' admonitions, would follow suit. After the ear had cooled, Major Bouvier would pop an entire butterball into his mouth, then attack the corn. Again the children would follow suit. The feast would end with vanilla ice cream with chocolate sauce, then demitasse would be served on the terrace.

During the meal the "conversation" would be desultory and argumentative. Jack Bouvier had the typically Latin habit of complimenting his children to their faces and defending them vigorously against what he would interpret to be slights from the other children. "Doesn't Jackie look terrific?" he would say, glancing at his father and his sisters for confirmation. "Girl's taken all prizes in her class this year, the whole lot of them . . . and she's the prettiest thing in the ring to boot." Or: "Jackie's got every boy at the club after her and the kid's only twelve . . . What are we going to do with her when she's twenty?" Edith and the twins were accustomed to these tributes to Jacqueline and did not usually rise to them; and Grandfather, if he heard them, would acknowledge their appropriateness with a smile. They were not received with delight by the other grandchildren, however, and usually provoked gibes or jokes at Jackie's expense. Realizing that cousins at that age were natural enemies, and enjoying the spectacle of their rivalry, Jack would remain unruffled by his nieces' and nephews' competitive protests and would often attempt to stir things up even more by flattering Lee: "Lee's going to be a real glamour girl some day . . . Will you look at those eyes . . . and those sexy lips of hers?" That Jackie and Lee thrived on their father's compliments was obvious to all: they received continuous transfusions of self-esteem from him. "Vitamin P," as one of her cousins called it, the cure-all pill of Praise.

They also received protection. Jack defended his children as energetically as he complimented them. If one of her cousins had bothered Jackie during the day, or even during the past week, the misdemeanor would be rehashed at lunch. The mischievous Scotty might have exploded a snapper in her face at a birthday party. Or thrown sand at her on the beach. He would pay for the offense over his duckling. A barrage of abuse would descend upon him that would leave the boy numb with dismay and his mother and her twin seething with rage. The snapper could have blinded Jackie for life, ruined her beauty, put an end to her riding career, killed her even . . . from blood poisoning. Sand throwing was just as bad. By God, if there was any more molesting of his daughter he would put an end to it, all right; he would give the offender a thrashing he would never forget . . . Whereupon the whole table would take sides and only the arrival of another course would calm the disputants.

If Jack would try to direct the table's attention to his daughters, Edith would invariably try to direct it to herself. She would often seize upon Albert Herter's twenty-year-old portrait of her as an excuse. "You know," she would declaim in her histrionic voice, "that blue dress in the painting is the same one I have on now: *that's* how poor *I* am." Whereupon Jack would comment that if she'd been cleverer she would have extracted some alimony out of her ex-husband instead of letting him go scot free. To which Edith would respond with a hymn about how *generous* she was, how at least no one could ever accuse her of being a gold digger. At which point the twins, in their traditional role as peacemakers, would intervene with gestures and grimaces meant to discourage the "conversation" for the usual reason: "the children's sake."

Grandfather Bouvier would remain aloof from these discussions by simply turning his hearing aid down and concentrating on his own occupations. One of these was trying out new golf grips with his dessert spoon. This had been a between-courses pastime for him for five or six years. A fairly good golfer, who could easily manage nine holes at the age of seventy-six, he had a scientific interest in grips and whenever he had a spare moment would try new ones out. Whether his "club" was a spoon or a coat hanger made little difference: Grampy was usually gripping some pole.

If the occasion were a birthday celebration, however, he would forsake trying out golfing grips for going over his birthday speech poem. Birthdays at Lasata were major productions. The biggest one of the summer was the twins', usually attended by the entire clan. Since Major Bouvier loved his twins so much, he would not only write them generous checks but would spend considerable time in his study composing a commemorative poem.

Yellow and green go with red hair, and so these were the colors the twins would invariably wear on their double birthday. Likewise, the cake would have yellow and green icing and the table favors would be wrapped in yellow and green crepe paper.

When the huge cake would come in, it would be Edith's opportunity to dominate the proceedings unopposed and she would make the most of it. Rising to her full height, and swelling to her full width, she would lead the table in a triumphant rendition of the Birthday Song: "Happy birthday to you" (and she would look at Maude), "happy birthday to you" (and she would look at Michelle), "happy birth . . . day, dear twinn . . . nnies . . . happy birthday to yooou . . ." (And she would carry the last "you" out to the proportions of an aria finale, her voice soaring over the others and lasting long after theirs had petered out. )

The twins would then simultaneously blow out all the candles but two. Next, with both hands on the knife, they would cut the cake and give the first piece to their father. It was then that Major Bouvier would slip them the two checks he had written that morning, for which generosity he would receive a double hug.

With the ice cream and cake served, and presents distributed, Major Bouvier would signal for the champagne, which Jack would have just uncorked in the pantry, and it would be promptly poured. It would then be time for Grandfather to perform . . . Rising slowly, he would peer out over the table, adopting the stance and attitude of one about to deliver a speech of national significance, and keep a teasing silence before launching into his address.

Maude and Michelle, in the matching gold-bead chokers and gold-button earrings they always wore on their birthday, would hold their red heads up, to hear their father say:

> Children, grandchildren . . . I am not at a loss to express the thoughts and feelings which swell within me on this auspicious occasion for our proud and distinguished family . . . They come as naturally as the rain from heaven. God blessed me and your late mother and grandmother with one of the supreme gifts of life, a double birth, and I deemed it a supernal honor to accept that gift as a humble servant accepts a favor from his master. Born on this fourth day of August, thirty-six years ago, under the sign of the Lion, you, Maude, and you, Michelle, have never failed in your duties toward your Creator. Not have you need to thank him for his mercy. In a sense you have thanked him already by merely being what you are . . .

Twin daughters of Leo
We salute you with brio.
    May your days be long
    And your worries short.
May you keep as strong
As a crusader's fort.
    May your hair stay red
    And your sons well fed.
May your husbands' weal
Be your constant zeal.
    May your minds enlarge
    And your souls recharge.
May your hearts' desires
Be what *God* requires.
God Bless You.

The applause (and snickers) which would follow would be terminated by the necessity of offering a toast to the birthday girls, which Jack would propose with a remark like "Here's to their royal lionesses."

Then the grandchildren would begin picking apart their grandfather's speech and poem . . . "What in the heck does 'supernal' mean anyway?" "What about 'brio'?" "Oh, it's just a word that rhymes with 'Leo'; that's why he put it in." "No, you see it on musical scores, it means . . ." "My English teacher told us obscure words are never as effective as simple ones." "Oh, Grampy just likes to show off . . . 'supernal'!" "Another thing, his meter fell apart with 'crusaders' . . . Did you notice how it sounded kinda queer?" "Yeah, and 'recharge' wasn't good either. It made out their souls' batteries were dead."

"Will you children please *stop* it," Maude would finally interject. "Your grandfather's poem was simply marvelous." Whereupon Edith, siding with the children as usual, would laugh: "Oh, Maudie *always* says the right thing . . . never does, or says, a thing wrong . . . She's a *supreme* gift from God . . . a *supernal* gift . . . Aren't you, Maudie dear?"

If the twins' mother had been present, she would have chirped her favorite refrain for such moments: "Birds in their nests agree, and it is a sorry sight to see them peck and fight." Actually, the Bouvier birds never agreed on anything, but it was not such a sorry sight to see them peck and fight. Their contentiousness was, in a way, a tonic that averted the deadlier sins of dullness and hypocrisy.

Major Bouvier, however, did not particularly like the squabbling that would follow his poetry and prose, of which he was unreasonably proud, and would usually put an end to it by proposing another toast.

> I think it is extremely fitting that on this felicitous occasion we offer thanks not only to our Lord, who made us, but to our illustrious forebears, who were, in a sense, His agents. To my right hang the portraits of my grandparents, Michel and Louise Vernou Bouvier: your *great*-grandparents, Maude and Michelle; your *great-great*-grandparents, grandchildren. It was largely because of their upright lives, indomitable courage and countless sacrifices that we are enjoying the abundance and peace of Lasata on this, the twins' birthday. I therefore propose a toast to their sacred memory.

And amid vehement clinking of glasses the birthday luncheon would end.

It was on occasions like this that Major Bouvier would break out a fresh edition of *Our Forebears* and present inscribed copies to his family. The presentations would often take place in his upstairs study, a sort of covered porch overlooking the front lawn. This small room was adorned with testaments of JVB, Jr.'s supposed lineage and actual achievements, which never failed to make a deep impression on the young. Over his large, rolltop desk hung framed color prints of the Bouvier and de Vernou crests and his Society of the Cincinnati insignia. On the wall to the left of the desk hung his father's Civil War commission and his own World War I commission as Major Judge Advocate. Opposite them were his three Columbia degrees, his B.A., his M.A. in Political Science, and his LL.B. from the School of Law, together with his framed certificate of membership in Phi Beta Kappa.

Lunch ended, each grandchild would go up to the study to receive his copy. Grandfather Bouvier would exchange a few words with each one, then present the volume, encouraging the child to read it. It is doubtful that any of the grandchildren who received a new edition of *Our Forebears* on these occasions bothered to read it right away. It was a book one would poke into off and on at odd moments. It did its work slowly, gradually instilling a somewhat exaggerated pride of family in its readers. At any rate, after the presentations, *Our Forebears* would be quickly forgotten. Plans would have been made for the afternoon which did not include ancestors. Jackie would be off to put Danseuse through her paces. Her father would have a date in New York. The others would head for the Maidstone, to swim or play tennis or golf.

The Maidstone Club was the other focal point of the Bouviers' summer activities. It consisted, as it still does today, of three separate playgrounds, the Beach Club, the Golf Club, and the Tennis Club. The Beach Club was a rambling affair composed of a long row of cabanas facing the ocean, divided roughly at midpoint by an open space, where there was a cafeteria, a bar, and a swimming pool. The wide, umbrella-sprinkled beach was prized for its clean white sand and bracing surf. Beyond the club area, on the dunes toward Georgica Pond, loomed the houses of several titans of Big Business, such as the many-gabled, gray-shingled home, with vaneless windmill attached, of Juan Trippe of Pan American. In the other direction, toward Amagansett, there was only an immense stretch of sand, surf, and sky.

The Bouviers owned a cabana at the Maidstone with three dressing rooms, two open-air showers, and a porch, for which they had paid $8,000 in 1926. Jack, Miche, and the boys had one room; the women had the other two. The cabana was a bleached greeny blue; its plumbing fixtures were coated with green salt; there were foot de-sanders on the porch; the ashtrays were huge clamshells; and inflated mattresses bulged out of every corner.

To get to the beach, or the pool, from the Bouviers' cabana, one had to march down a long boardwalk past all the other cabanas and their owners. "Good morning, Dr. Boots." "How are you, Mrs. Pagel?" "Hi, Mr. Lee," the Bouvier young would chirp as they sauntered down what they came to call the "midway." In those days the Bouvier who attracted the most attention from the other cabana owners at the Maidstone was Little Edie. A curvaceous blonde in her mid-twenties, she would walk down the boardwalk in a tight, elastic, one-piece bathing suit and actually succeed in distracting the tycoons from their Wall Street Journals. Each cabana owner had an idiosyncrasy that created his identity for the Bouvier kids. For example, one of the Maidstone's many millionaire widows, who would sit in her bathing suit on a scorching day reading the newspaper with gloves on so the ink wouldn't rub off on her fingers, was known simply as "Fingers."

One of the greatest characters in the club was the woman who took care of the ladies' dressing room and handed out towels, "Beach Mary." A wiry, red-headed Irishwoman with a "brogue you could chin on" and a "grin that was better than gin," she was a good friend of the Bouviers and was particularly devoted to Jack and Jacqueline. Jack Bouvier used to tan himself for hours on the deck in front of the men's locker room and Beach Mary would wait on him while he did. Passersby would marvel at the amount of sun Jack could soak up. There he would sit, all morning, or all afternoon, stretched out in his deck chair facing the glare with a huge pair of sunglasses on, immobile, the suntan oil glistening on his dark, silvery skin, a newspaper opened at the stock quotations tucked under one of his legs. Every once in a while Mary would bring him a drink, or hand him a towel, or deliver a telephone message. Or Jacqueline would run up from the beach to tell him something. But these interruptions wouldn't distract him from his goal, which was to absorb all the sun he could possibly absorb that day. His lips would move, an arm would raise to grasp a towel, but he would remain in the same position, staring at the sun as if his life depended on it, as if during those two months of July and August he had to make up for having to settle for a sunlamp the rest of the year, in contrast to his ancestors in Provence, who had had the real thing all year around.

If the Bouviers were not at the beach, they would be playing tennis or golf, usually golf. The Maidstone had two courses: the eighteen-hole championship course and the nine-hole "little course." Grandfather Bouvier, in his mid-seventies, played the little course and insisted that the other members of his family play it too. Thus, a typical July or August afternoon might find Major Bouvier with son Jack and daughter Maude and one of Michelle's suitors, trudging around nine holes, with a couple of grandchildren caddying—all for Major Bouvier's sake, since the others would much prefer to have played the bigger course. But Grandfather Bouvier held the power, both psychologically and materially, and anyone who opposed him, as his older daughter Edith did, would surely suffer for it. The natural authority he exuded did not admit of compromise or opposition. One did what Grampy wanted. And then there was also the fact that he was sitting on a modest fortune and had a tendency to play favorites. Who among his not-too-wealthy children would run the risk of disinheritance?

Major Bouvier also liked to win, or at least he did not like to lose too badly. And therefore his children would feel somewhat cramped when they played with him. They would hit good drives and fairway shots, but they usually were compelled to do poorly around the greens. If they were on in two and Major Bouvier was on in four, they had to three- or four-putt the green. So ardently did Major Bouvier like to win that he would frequently resort to sleight of hand to avoid defeat. One of his favorite gambits was to follow a putt toward the hole, then pick up the ball just as it was about to miss the cup, pretending that it was going in. Or, when he had lost a ball in the rough or the woods, he would use the old hole-in-the-pocket ploy and slide a new ball down his leg, which he would stumble over, calling "Found!"

So here they are, the Bouviers out playing golf on an August afternoon. The turf is parched, but the greens are green and the bunkers full of freshly raked sand. The rooftops of East Hampton's summer estates rise up on all sides above neatly clipped hedges and groves of spruce and pine. The ocean thunders in the distance. The air smells of brine and mowed grass. Major Bouvier is trudging along, with his usual determination, wearing a pair of light-gray flannels and a long-sleeved white shirt with stiff collar, tie, and stickpin, under a vest or sleeveless sweater. His daughter Maude walks beside him, with the same determination, the same willful movements as her father, her red hair glinting in the sun, her eyes fixed on her ball ahead. And Jack follows, not nearly as interested in the game as his father and sister, his lackadaisical movements betraying annoyance at having to spend the afternoon this way. Unless Jackie were along, caddying or ball-hawking, in which case he would be giving everything he had to his game.

The third ring of the Maidstone paradise was the Tennis Club, famed for its magnificent grass courts. Spongy and cool underfoot, they were the favorite playground of Michelle's children, Scotty and Shella, whose red heads could be seen bobbing up and down in a game of doubles most any summer afternoon. In

August an important women's tournament was held at the club that would bring out the entire Bouvier clan. For a week, all you would hear at Lasata or the cabana were the godlike names Alice Marble and Sarah Palfrey Fabyan, and the names of their mixed-doubles partners, Gardnar Mulloy and Billy Talbert. The boys would all fall in love with Miss Fabyan, who had fantastic legs and a shy, sensitive look that belied her aggressive game. After the matches the young would play ping-pong in the clubhouse and their parents would have a drink at the bar. There would be dances every once in a while, and a ball after the tournament finals. When all was quiet and the last players had left the courts, the rabbits would come out, and instead of tennis balls, you would see cottontails bouncing around the green turf.

The Bouviers also belonged to the Riding Club and the Devon Yacht Club on Gardiners Bay at the other side of the Island. The swimming was tamer at Devon: there were scarcely any waves, and you could walk out on sand bars for miles. If you sailed, there were races for all classes from June to September. Major Bouvier and the twins would go to Devon for the club's exquisite cuisine, presided over, as it still is, by Henri, who speaks French and cooks French but comes from Torino. Or they would go have tea and cinnamon toast on the club's terrace around five, when the boats were coming in, along with a powerful smell from the fish factory down the coast. Fishing was another sport the Bouviers indulged in at Devon. You could land big porgies and fat blowfish from the dock. And further down the bay, the crabbing was unequaled. All you had to do was throw your hand line out and haul them in. A hundred crabs was a normal catch. But Devon's dances were its main attraction. Held every Saturday night, they stole the show from the Maidstone's bigger, more formal parties. The sailing crowd was younger and wilder than the golf and tennis people, and the yacht clubhouse was small enough to produce the intimate confusion of a bote. They packed them in under the rustic wooden rafters at Devon Saturday nights, and the Bouviers were usually there in force, As at the Maidstone by day, the queen of the Bouvier young at Devon those Saturday nights was Little Edie. The envy of her younger cousins, she was going out with J. P. Kennedy, Jr. You couldn't dance with her for more than twenty seconds at a time. To Jackie and Shella, who were just beginning to go out with boys, she was IT.

And so, between Lasata and the Maidstone, the Bouviers lived their golden summers, never thinking that their way of life would ever end. The delights of East Hampton were perennial. Neither Depression nor war could dampen them. The Bouvier grandchildren, especially, could not imagine a day when there would be no more parties at Lasata, when they could not hold a "blast" in the room where Grandfather would be reading Macaulay, with his hearing aid turned down, oblivious to the fun and racket around him. They could not imagine that the day would come when there would be no more races on the front lawn, no more mushroom picking under the lindens, no more rainy-day games of "go fish" and "slapjack" in the solarium, no more blue hydrangeas, beach plums, baby limas, and Lasata corn . . . Big Boy Michel tearing down the driveway in Jack's black Mercury. Jackie in jodhpurs, with her Bouvier de Flandre wagging its bushy tail. Little Edie parading a new boy friend at the beach. Big Edie shattering the stillness with a tearjerking rendition of "Vissi d'arte." The Italian garden with its shepherds, fountain, and sundial, and inebriating aroma of roses and mowed grass. These were as recurrent and eternal as the seasons.

Their optimism was not unfounded. Somehow Lasata, the Maidstone, and East Hampton withstood the Depression and survived the war. While bread lines were forming in New York and Chicago and banks were failing across the country, while millions were out of work and former investors were reduced to driving cabs, the Bouviers' summers at Lasata remained unchanged. How did Major Bouvier manage it financially, with stock prices so low and their dividends even lower? He managed it by sacrificing the future to the present, by selling several hundred thousand dollars' worth of stock and putting the money into annuities which gave him a guaranteed high return while he lived but which would expire at his death. Those golden summers, enjoyed in the midst of worldwide economic despair, were paid for by those who loved them the most, his heirs.

# VII

JACK'S EFFORTS TO SUBJECT HIS CHILDREN TO THE INFLUENCE OF HIS lively family, and involve them in his family's activities, during what was the most impressionable time of their lives, were highly successful as long as Janet remained unmarried. While Janet was at loose ends, enduring the bitter purgatory of lonely divorcée abandoned to the fates, Jacqueline and Lee identified much more with their father's family than with their mother's, adoring their grandfather Bouvier and enjoying his colorful family reunions to the fullest. But Janet was not about to remain at loose ends forever. It was not a very pleasant situation for a divorcée to have to contend with New York society while she was being shunned by a family as well known in that society as the Bouviers. She should marry again, preferably a man from a family at least equal to that of her first husband. Luckily such a one was forthcoming. His name was Hugh D. Auchincloss, a divorcée, twice over, himself, a stockbroker too, and a man of greater wealth than the Bouviers, and equally formidable social credentials: she couldn't possibly have fallen in love with a more appropriate man.

The Auchincloss family had originated in Scotland and had acquired wealth and prestige in America through a succession of "brilliant" marriages. The primary American ancestor of Janet's new husband was born at Paisley, Scotland, in 1780, son of a modest family of storekeepers, and was himself called Hugh Auchincloss. Emigrating to America at twenty-three, without much to his credit in the way of money or prospects, he arrived in New York on November 23, 1803, entered the dry-goods business, married Anne Stuart of Philadelphia in 1806, fathered thirteen children, had a successful business career, becoming president of the American Dry Goods Association, and died in 1855. It was left to one of his sons, John Auchincloss, to confer some social distinction on the clan by marrying Elizabeth Buck, a descendant of two of the oldest colonial families of New England, the Winthrops and the Saltonstalls. John and Elizabeth Auchincloss, in turn, had nine children, the last of whom, Hugh Dudley, a dry-goods merchant who eventually became involved in oil and mining, emulated his father's matrimonial achievement by making an equally impressive marriage himself, with Emma Brewster Jennings, daughter of Oliver B. Jennings, one of the founders, along with John D. Rockefeller, of Standard Oil. It was from this union that Janet's new husband was born, and it was from the Jennings side of the family that he inherited most of his fortune.

Hugh D. Auchincloss grew up a young man of robust physique and solid Presbyterian virtues, to graduate from Yale in 1920, attend King's College, Cambridge, from 1920 to 1921, and take his law degree from Columbia in 1924. Entering the securities business, he eventually became a general partner of the Washington-based brokerage firm of Auchincloss, Parker and Redpath, in which concern he had invested a significant share of his inheritance. His marriage to Janet Lee Bouvier in 1942 was his third. His first wife had been Maria Chrapovitsky, daughter of a Russian naval officer; his second was Nina Gore Vidal, daughter of the blind senator from Oklahoma, T. B. Gore. The first Mrs. Auchincloss had borne him a son, Hugh Dudley, Jr.; and the second a daughter, Nina Gore, and another son, Thomas Gore. Both marriages had ended in divorce.

The vast fortune which Hugh Dudley and Emma Jennings Auchincloss left their son Hugh allowed him to live on a scale only the very rich can afford. Thus, when Janet Bouvier married him, she found herself suddenly lifted into an economic paradise several circles above anything she had ever known as a Bouvier. The mistress, now, of two magnificent estates, Merrywood in McLean, Virginia, and Hammersmith Farm in Newport, and the mistress, also, of nearly unlimited financial resources, she could finally lead the sort of life she had hoped she would lead when she married John Vernou Bouvier III fourteen years before.

"Hughdie" Auchincloss was the polar opposite of Jack. A tall, large-framed, ruddy-faced gentleman, he possessed the physique of a Scots Guard and the corresponding virtues of stability, industry, and thrift. Jack Bouvier and his colorful family had been much too potent a brew for a woman of Janet's temperament and tastes. Now, at last, she had a man and a family who could give her the financial security and emotional stability she needed.

Jack's reaction to the marriage, which took place in June 1942, though predictably cynical, was not ungraced by a sense of humor. Shortly after the ceremony in Newport, he started a saying on the floor of the Exchange which became a part of Wall Street folklore: "Take a loss with Auchincloss."

As it turned out, Jack took a major loss with Auchincloss, for with Hughdie's marriage to Janet, Jack's daughters acquired a stepfather and new homes which inevitably drew them away from him. Now Jacqueline and Lee would spend part of the winter at Merrywood and part of the summer at Hammersmith farm, and to get them to New York and East Hampton, Jack had to use every trick of persuasion he knew. For Jacqueline and Lee, in turn, their mother's remarriage gave them a third family connection to contend with, still another problem of identification. Torn already between the Lees and the Bouviers, they were now claimed by the Auchinclosses as well.

It was with great sadness and a feeling of deprivation that Jack had to attend Thanksgiving luncheon at Major Bouvier's in November 1942 without his beloved daughters. At the luncheon, during which many poems were read, the twins could not help noting the deflated state of their normally ebullient brother's morale. Jack Bouvier, however, was too proud and devoted a father to lose his daughters to the Auchinclosses entirely. Although he could not have them with him for the rest of 1942, he had them down to East Hampton the summer of 1943, when, on the occasion of the twins' birthday, they were welcomed at another tumultuous reunion at Lasata with every member of the family present save those who were in military service.

In succeeding years Jack became more and more demanding of his daughters' time as he sensed that Janet and Hughdie Auchincloss were gaining a firmer hold on their allegiances. Since he continued to support them, paying for their education, giving them monthly allowances, keeping horses for them, and maintaining charge accounts for them at Bloomingdale's and Saks, he felt he had every right—for he was, after all, their father—to be as insistent as he was. And since the staid Auchinclosses were, in Jack's opinion, a much duller family than the Bouviers, lacking the Bouviers' originality and style, he was reasonably confident that he could keep his daughters from identifying wholly with his rivals. Besides, Jack knew that Jacqueline and Lee were made of different stuff from the Auchinclosses, that temperamentally they were about as Presbyterian Scotch as Spanish gypsies.

While Jack was vying with the Auchinclosses for his daughters' attentions, other Bouviers were experiencing the first repercussions of their nation's struggle with the Axis powers. By the time Janet, Jacqueline, and Lee had taken up residence at Hammersmith Farm in the summer of 1942, Phelan Beale, Jr., and Michel Bouvier were both Army officers about to go overseas, and Bouvier Beale was an Air Force technician destined for combat in Burma. With three Bouviers in uniform, Major Bouvier was, of course, extremely proud. During the war years his speeches at his depleted family gatherings would glorify his grandchildren's military exploits in the Far East and exult in the fact that members of his family had fought as officers in all their country's major wars since, and including, the Revolution.

Following in Bud Bouvier's footsteps, all three Bouvier soldiers of the fifth generation married before going overseas. Michel met his bride, Agnes Mitchell, while attending Columbia; and Phelan, Jr., met and married his bride, Rosella Ramsey of Tulsa, while training in Oklahoma. Both girls were from modest families and both weddings were held with the utmost simplicity. It remained for Bouvier Beale and his bride, Katharine Jones, daughter of a distinguished New York attorney, to stage a more fashionable affair, reminiscent of the Bouvier weddings of old, in New York.

The Beale-Jones wedding took place at St. James on December 12, 1942, before almost the entire Bouvier family and a large gathering of friends. The ceremony was scheduled for four o'clock, and by that hour Major Bouvier, Jack, Michel, the twins, an assortment of Bouvier children, and the Jones family had been settled in their pews for some time awaiting the arrival of one of the most important guests, Edith. Twenty-five minutes later, after the wedding was half over and the family had given her up for lost, Big Edith finally showed up, dressed, as usual, like an opera star, and acting as if nothing were amiss as she strode up the center aisle of the vast, silent church to take her rightful place in the first seat of the front pew.

The incident was taken lightly by nearly everyone, including the bride and groom, but not by Major Bouvier. Furious over what he considered an inexcusable breach of good form, he changed his will, by codicil, two days later, reducing Edith's share of his estate and leaving what remained to her in trust, with her children as trustees.

The drastic measure represented the culmination of a father-daughter désaccord which had always existed but which had become accentuated since Maude Sergeant's death. Edith had never toed her father's line. Her personality was so radically different from his, nothing could bring the two together. Major Bouvier accepted unquestioningly the society he was born into and conformed as fully as any of his peers to its prejudices and conventions. Edith, on the other hand, never gave a damn for social conventions of any sort, preferring to live her life according to an absolutely private creed. She rejected the religion in which she was raised, to adopt another of which she was the sole adherent. Utterly spurning the class system her father took so seriously, scoffing at all the clubs and associations he cared so much about, and refusing to have her name included in the Social Register, she chose what few friends she had from all levels of society. Misunderstood by everyone in her family, with the possible exceptions of her daughter and Jack, she delighted in accentuating the misunderstanding by continually challenging her father's and her sisters' opinions, prejudices, and habits to their faces. To Edith, the entire Bouvier "thing" was an idiotic fraud. All her father and twin sisters ever thought about was what other people thought about them and their family. As for herself, she didn't give a hoot in hell what other people thought of her, and as for the Bouviers, who could care less what people thought of them?! The result of this attitude was an estrangement from her flesh and blood so total that by the mid-forties she could do nothing but withdraw from them and their world entirely.

Edith was not alone, however, in her attitude toward her father and the Bouvier ethos he had spent his life trying to promote. For Jack, too, the Bouvier cult was a tyranny against which his libertine spirit had continually rebelled. As a child he had had the glorious Bouvier history drummed into his ears by his father. Eustache père and James Ewing fighting for American independence. The first Michel battling his way to wealth and influence in Philadelphia. John Vernou Bouvier, Sr., fighting gloriously as general Patrick's aide in the Civil War. MC making a huge success on Wall Street. Bud fighting heroically in the Meuse-Argonne. And he, John Vernou Bouvier, Jr., Phi Beta Kappa, valedictorian, noted New York lawyer, and General President of the General Society of the Sons of the American Revolution, carrying on the Great Tradition . . . But what about John Vernou Bouvier III? What was he doing to bear the banner triumphantly into the future? Precious little, in John Vernou Bouvier, Jr.'s opinion. True, he had made big money at one time, but where was it now? True, he had fathered two beautiful daughters, but where were they now? True, he had cut a dashing figure in New York society, but at fifty, wasn't he getting on a bit to keep repeating the same act? Was he, at bottom, nothing more than a playboy? What in the devil was he going to achieve in the next twenty years?

Major Bouvier's reservations about Jack had been simmering for a long time. Aside from his disappointment over Jack's accomplishments, a fundamental personality conflict had divided father and son since they were first able to communicate with each other. Major Bouvier had done brilliantly in school and college and had maintained a lasting interest in history, literature, political science, and the law: Jack had done poorly in school and college and cultivated few intellectual interests after graduation. Major Bouvier was an accomplished orator: Jack never made a speech in his life. Major Bouvier was an American patriot who gloried in his country's military achievements, worshipped its great political leaders, and played an important role in several distinguished patriotic associations: Jack cared little for politics, less for the military, and belonged to the Sons of the American Revolution and the Society of the Cincinnati only because his father forced him to join. Major Bouvier may have been a liberal spender, but he was a conservative investor: Jack was a gambler to the last. Major Bouvier could never appreciate his son's best qualities. Jack considered his father's best qualities hopelessly passé. In their general attitudes toward life, the father was reverent, the son irreverent; the father a believer, the son a cynic; the father a romantic, the son a realist.

This basic antagonism, however, did not explode into open war until 1943. On Saturday, April 24 of that year, a violent argument broke out between father and son which led Major Bouvier to write in his diary: "I told him definitely everything was off between us." Two days later JVB, Jr., gave force to that remark by executing a new last will and testament which eliminated Jack's inheritance entirely.

Major Bouvier had not written a new will since he had received *his* considerable inheritance from MC in 1935. After 1943, however, he would change his will as often as Edith or Jack pleased or displeased him. Using his recently acquired fortune as a means to bend his children to his wishes, he would repeatedly offer them the bleak alternative of agreeing with him and doing as he wished or facing a poverty-stricken old age. Since neither Jack nor Edith nor Michelle had made any financial provisions for their retirement, their situation was next to desperate. And so there erupted in the Bouvier family, in the mid-forties, an undeclared war between four children and their father over a sum of money which, though by no means immense, had, nevertheless, taken three generations to accumulate and which represented, for three of them at least, their only hope for future economic survival.

It took the slow, sultry months of July and August of 1943 in East Hampton to create the circumstances leading to Major Bouvier's next change of will. During that golden summer the prodigal son returned to Lasata to do his father's bidding. Losing to him, purposely, at golf, and exhibiting his charming daughters to him at the twins' birthday party, Jack succeeded, by September 2, in getting himself reinstated in the Document. The autumn, however, brought harsh winds, a faltering market, and another furious argument between John Vernou Bouvier, Jr., and John Vernou Bouvier III. What the argument was about, John Vernou Bouvier, Jr.'s diary does not tell. All it tells is that on December 14, 1943, John Vernou Bouvier, Jr., executed a new last will and testament, removing John Vernou Bouvier III from its list of legatees.

Christmas brought peace but little good will. On Christmas Day, 1943, no Bouvier family reunion was held at 765 Park Avenue, and JVB, Jr., recorded in his diary that such a breach of family tradition had not occurred in his memory. Jack was . . . where was Jack? Big and Little Edith were in seclusion in East Hampton. Jacqueline and Lee were with their mother at Merrywood. Phelan Beale, Michel Bouvier, and Bouvier Beale were at war. Maude and her family kept to themselves. Only Michelle and her children remained to share the lonely patriarch's turkey.

Whether Major Bouvier realized it or not, by Christmas of 1943 the family he had devoted his life to promoting was in a state of disintegration. The permissiveness of the twenties had weakened what he would have called its "moral fiber." The Depression had eroded its finances. Divorce had shattered its unity and undermined its spirit. JVB, Jr.'s oldest son and erstwhile heir no longer had a family he could call his own. His youngest son had died, under tragic circumstances, eleven years before. Edith lived in a world apart. Michel, upon whom weighed the responsibility of sustaining the Bouvier name and prestige in the future, belonged more to his mother and stepfather than to the Bouviers. Michelle, divorced now for five years, was still at loose ends.

For the first time in the family's history, the Bouvier image was undeniably in distress. JVB, Jr., had grown up amid memories of his unconquerable, self-made grandfather, whose ten children had remained united to the end, and of his brilliant, bountiful Aunt Emma Drexel. His millionaire Uncle Miche had been Dean of Wall Street, and his mother and Aunt Mary had been among the most honored ladies in New York society. In his own generation, Emma's daughter, Louise Morrell, had been the wife of a distinguished congressman and one of the great philanthropists of Philadelphia, and her stepdaughter, Katharine Drexel, had been a national figure in Catholic charities. Among the men of his generation, Walter Vernou, a cousin, had risen to the rank of vice admiral in the United States Navy. As for himself, he, John Vernou Bouvier, Jr., had certainly kept the image polished to the best of his ability. When, as a noted New York attorney and president of the Sons of the American Revolution, he had dedicated the George Washington Bridge before the governor of the State of New York and a nationwide radio audience, the name Bouvier was heard, under the most honorable circumstances, from coast to coast. But what of the children he had produced? What had *they* accomplished that even approximated the high standards set by their forebears? In Major Bouvier's opinion, only the twins had kept the Bouvier image bright in their own generation, but they, of course, did not bear the name Bouvier. In order to maintain some hope in his family's future, then, JVB, Jr., was forced to look to the next generation. It was essentially an expression of his ambitions for them that he chose to dedicate his last edition of *Our Forebears* not to his children but to his ten grandchildren, and to "those who may later add to their joyous company."

# VIII

Jan. 6, 1944. No smoking entire A.M., temperature 97, pulse 58. Feeling weak and miserable all day. Weight 190. Eggnog produced gastritis. Gave up coffee and alcohol.

Nov. 20, 1944. Experiments: 1st time in a year no bi-sodal in A.M., 4 glasses of water instead. Shaved with lanoline, quick and soft. Used Squibb's ointment 1st time on excema. Witch hazel for scalp with Yardley's cream.

Dec. 20, 1944. Bad night. Feeling nervous and mentally blank. Saw Dr. Glazebrook. Blood pressure 138 over 80 !!! No albumin in specimen. Found acidity. No drinks.

BY THE MID-1940S MAJOR BOUVIER'S DIARY HAD BECOME LITTLE MORE than a record of his failing health. During the twenties and thirties he had occasionally recorded his weight and blood pressure, but these clinical observations rarely took precedence over events like a recent Supreme Court decision, a meeting of the Society of the Cincinnati, or a visit from the twins. After 1944, however, the state of JVB, Jr.'s health not only became the first news he would record but would usually be sufficiently detailed to constitute the entire entry.

Along with his deteriorating health, Major Bouvier also suffered a further deterioration in his relations with his two older children. During his prime he had been able to exercise an authority over them which was not wholly related to money. A blend of paternal love and sheer mental and emotional strength, this power was sufficient to enforce at least a minimum respect from Jack and Edith. Now, however, as his vigor ebbed, the only hold he could maintain on his two black sheep was his last will and testament. As a bond between father and children, it proved a poor substitute for affection.

Although his older children gave him little comfort, Major Bouvier was not without some consolations during his declining years. His favorite authors, Shakespeare and Macaulay, offered him philosophical solace; his British lady friend, Mabel Ferguson, did her best to prolong the second youth she had provided him with shortly before his seventy-seventh birthday; Esther, his faithful Swedish maid, pampered him; and on September 4, 1944, the Phelan Beales, Jr., delighted him by producing his first great-grandchild, a little girl with a familiar name: Michelle.

His chief source of comfort, however, was unquestionably the twins. They had always been his favorites. Now, as his strength drained away and his dependence on others increased, they became the most indispensable people in his life. Michelle became his nurse, companion, confidante, servant, secretary, and factotum, a person upon whom he came to rely for almost all the amenities his remaining years still had to offer him. As for Maude, she fulfilled an even deeper need. Like most fathers of his generation, JVB, Jr., had made the mistake of expecting his children to be at least approximate replicas of himself. It was acutely disappointing for him, therefore, to discover that neither of his sons could claim that honor, nor could Edith or Michelle. It remained for Maude, then, to fill the bill. Which she did admirably. Possessing her father's physical strength, will power, optimism, determination, reverence for tradition, and intense family pride, she gave him the flattering satisfaction of knowing that at least one of his five children emulated him while he lived and would carry on like him after he died.

As might be expected, Major Bouvier's open predilection for the twins only aggravated his deteriorating relationship with Jack and Edith, who reacted to his partiality by becoming more and more antagonistic toward him and his favorites, a policy certainly not guaranteed to win them a significant place in his will. Granted, the four siblings had never gotten along very well together: still, up to the time their father began using his will to keep them in line, they had at least observed the formalities of brotherly and sisterly affection and occasionally made efforts to be civil to one another. And at family reunions they would often succeed in appearing affectionately united. Now, however, with their father playing last-will-and-testament poker with their lives—in contrast to the first Michel's testamentary policy of "share and share alike"—they could no longer disguise their feelings. From now on, it was Jack and Edith against the twins, with Edith playing an ineffectual role, and the twins, out of self-defense, against Jack and Edith.

In April 1946, Jack's side was bolstered by Michelle's marriage to Harrington Putnam, a successful insurance executive in charge of the American Foreign Insurance Corporation's operations in

Rio de Janeiro. After the wedding, Mr. Putnam whisked his bride off to Brazil, and Major Bouvier was abruptly deprived of his mainstay at the time he needed her most and Maude was robbed of her closest ally. A void had unexpectedly opened up in Major Bouvier's life, and Jack was quick to fill it. Sensing his great opportunity had finally arrived, he initiated a campaign of reconciliation with his father that turned out to be his last and most successful speculation.

Not long after Michelle's departure for Rio, Major Bouvier's health took a further turn for the worse: he developed cancer of the prostate, bladder trouble, and suffered a breakdown of the nerves in his legs. The remainder of 1946 saw little improvement in his condition, and by 1947 he was clearly failing. His diary for that year documents the prolonged torments of a dying man. For page after page he records nothing but his relentless distress.

His will to live, however, was not daunted by his miseries. His doctors had not told him he had cancer and so he was able to hope for eventual recovery. In an effort to regain his health, he took Maude to Hobe Sound in February for a month in the Florida sun. While they were there, staying at the Jupiter Island Club, Maude allowed her father to beat her at golf—an invigorating tonic. The game was the last he ever played.

For in the summer of 1947 Major Bouvier had to undergo a prostate operation and could not play his favorite sport. Confined to his bedroom at Lasata for most of the summer, he was unable to celebrate the twins' birthday, but felt well enough to preside over his own birthday, his eighty-second, on August 14, on which occasion, according to his diary, he addressed "a few remarks" to his grandchildren. By that time attendance at his family gatherings had been considerably diminished. Michelle and her children were in Rio, and Michel and the Beale boys were with their own families. But Maude and her children were there, as were the two Ediths and Jack, Jacqueline, and Lee, Jack having made sure that his children would be on hand to convince his father that he still held their affection.

After celebrating his birthday, however, Major Bouvier suffered another decline. His diary entries for the last two weeks of August show a man struggling with despair: "Am lacking in hopefulness." "Feel spiritless and dull." "Orientation bad—could not think of 'Montauk.' " "Very despondent." "Discouraged beyond belief with my condition."

It was while JVB, Jr., was in this state of mind that Jack Bouvier made his move to be reinstated in his father's favor. He was wholly justified in taking advantage of his father's weakened condition, for it was manifestly unfair of JVB, Jr., to have cut him off. On Friday, August 29, Maude and her children returned to their home in Connecticut, leaving Major Bouvier alone at Lasata. The next day Jack arrived from New York to spend the weekend with his father. Amid arguments, apologies, promises, and pardons, a reconciliation was somehow effected, for the day after Jack returned to New York, JVB, Jr.'s secretary, John Ficke, arrived at Lasata, and the next day JVB, Jr., made this entry in his diary:

> Poor night. Feel vacant mentally with poor orientation. Physically extremely weak in legs, same hands. Stomach nervous. Garden 11:45. Basked 1/2 hour. Left garden 1:45. Walked 1/2 mile. Executed Last Will and Testament. Given to Johnny for deposit in vault.

The document Mr. Ficke brought back to New York the following morning was the last will and testament Major Bouvier wrote. To protect his position in the document, Jack saw to it that his reconciliation with his father would be enduring. Taking advantage of Michelle's absence in Rio, he spent every weekend at Lasata until his father returned to the city. And once JVB, Jr., was settled in New York for the winter, Jack became a constant caller, making sure his father saw him much more often than he saw his sisters, nephews, and nieces.

Jack had done well to effect a reconciliation when he did, for by December 1947 Major Bouvier had gone into a steep decline. On December 7 JVB, Jr., stated in his diary: "Lost all hope for improvement . . . walked in desperation 1/2 mile." And on Saturday, December 20, he reported that he felt "utterly miserable" and "incapable of the slightest exertion."

Still he would not give up his fight and go to bed. His body may have been disintegrating, but his will to survive was as strong as ever. With cancer spreading throughout his system, his hearing almost gone, his eyesight failing, his digestion ruined, with rheumatism in his arms and legs and neuralgic pains in his head and chest, he still got up early every morning, shaved, dressed, and took a walk. One of his grandsons, Bouvier Beale, remembers him during this dismal period sitting in the library beneath Sully's portrait of Robert Ewing, dressed to the teeth, reading Macaulay. Every once in a while he would suddenly put down his book, clutch his side and roar "Oh, goddamn it," "oh, god," then resume reading. To those who asked him how he felt, he would simply mutter: "Rotten."

On December 24 his diary indicates that he was "feeling profoundly depressed" and could not go to midnight mass. The next day he was unable to hold the traditional Christmas luncheon, even though Michelle had returned from Rio. When she arrived, on Christmas morning, "looking well and charming," her dying father greeted her at the door, saying: "I've waited all winter for this."

Michelle had performed many services for her father during his lifetime. Now she was to do him the final service of brightening, as much as possible, the last days of his life. For on Wednesday, December 31, 1947, Major Bouvier retired to his bedroom for good.

During the next two weeks Michelle remained in constant attendance on her father while doctors, nurses, and relatives came and went. Lying beneath the magnificent golden eagle Joseph Bonaparte had given the first Bouvier, and surrounded by mementos of his family's past, John Vernou Bouvier, Jr., struggled manfully against the fate he now knew was as close to him as his beloved Michelle. Too miserable to contemplate the successes and failures of his life, to draw up anything like a balance sheet of his sins and benefactions, to *think* about anything, he could only fight until he was beaten.

On January 14, when his final agony began, Maude and Jack arrived, the priest and his acolyte came with viaticum and censer, and Michelle held his hand. She held it throughout the night, until 3:00 A.M. the next day, when, exhausted, she was forced to retire. An hour later, with the incense still lingering in the room and the golden eagle glowing above the bed, the Bouviers lost their patriarch.

The funeral in St. Patrick's and the death notices in the papers would have pleased the man they honored. John Vernou Bouvier, Jr.'s was the leading obituary in both *The New York Times* and the *Herald Tribune* on January 17. And the ceremony in the cathedral was characterized by a dignified theatricality that was typically Bouvier. It was held in the Lady Chapel, not far from the Bouvier altar. Jack had organized an order of march to follow the casket based on seniority, and so, as the organ played a processional, the large gathering of mourners in the chapel saw the entire Bouvier family, with Jack in the lead, following their patriarch up the center aisle. After the rites, the family accompanied the remains to St. Philomena's Cemetery in East Hampton, where JVB, Jr., was laid to rest beside his father, mother, wife, and son Bud.

Jack's having put himself at the head of the funeral procession was the first hint his sisters, nephews, and nieces had that he had been reinstated in his father's will. But what were the contents of that will? And what was the value of JVB, Jr.'s estate? It was known to all that he had inherited well over a million from MC in 1935. But how well had he invested the funds and to what extent had his opulent style of life dissipated the profits? Taking all factors into consideration, it was conservatively estimated that he had left at least a million, probably more.

It was with great astonishment, therefore, that the Bouviers learned that Major Bouvier's gross estate amounted to no more than $824,000. Where in the name of Bonaparte had the money gone? Between 1935 and 1948, without gambling, about $400,000 in capital had vanished!

Thus, John V. Bouvier, Jr., whose wealth had been entirely inherited, left less money than Michel, Sr., who had started from scratch. In view of their expectations, the news was hard on Major Bouvier's heirs: $824,000 divided among four children, ten grandchildren, and other miscellaneous legatees would leave no one with a fortune except the government.

In contrast to his self-made grandfather, John V. Bouvier, Jr., had also written a very unequal will. Michel had bequeathed his ten children equal shares of his estate, even though two of the children, Eustache and Louise, had consistently defied him. Major Bouvier, on the other hand, had little mercy for people who defied him, especially those who never retrenched. Thanks to his last-ditch efforts to make up for his lifelong defiance of his father, Jack received a bequest of $100,000 free of taxes, and had a $50,000 loan excused. But Edith, who had stubbornly refused to give in to her father on anything, received only $65,000, in trust; and Michel, who by all rights should have received a fifth of the estate, especially in view of the tragic circumstances of his father's death, got only $28,000. Equal legacies, however, went to the other nine grandchildren, each receiving $3,000. Among his servants and employees, his secretary, John Ficke, received $25,000; his maid, Esther Lindstrom, received $1,500; and his gardener, Paul Yuska, $300. Other miscellaneous bequests, including charities, amounted to $9,000. The United States government took $210,000; New York State, $15,000; the lawyers, $15,000; and the twins, as residuary legatees, divided the $237,000 that remained after all the bequests and taxes were paid and the stocks, bonds, and real estate sold.

During the settlement of the estate Jack expressed no interest whatsoever in receiving any of his late father's books, furnishings, family portraits, and papers. Wholly lacking in reverence for his family's past, all Jack wanted from the estate was cold cash. Consequently, almost all the Bouvier portraits, heirlooms, and papers went to the twins.

A clear indication of where JVB, Jr.'s heart ultimately lay may be had from two special bequests. One was the portrait of his revered maternal grandfather, Robert Ewing, by Sully, to Michelle. The other was what he referred to in the will as "the family heirloom," which he left to Maude. The latter had been his most precious possession, a magnificent silver pitcher given to Michel Bouvier and Louise Vernou by their ten children, inscribed "A nos chers parents" and signed Eustache, Thérèse, Elizabeth, Louise, Emma, Zénaïde, Alexine, Mary, John, Michel.

After the Bouviers lost their chief, Jack made an ill-fated attempt to assume the leadership of his family, offering paternal advice to his nieces and nephews, helping Edith manage on her all but subsistence income, and generally doing his utmost to make his presence felt. But his effort was doomed to failure from the start. He was the legitimate heir to his family's name and traditions, but he was temperamentally unable to play the role of patriarch. Inconstant and self-indulgent, he lacked the solidity, impartiality, and affability needed to hold the respect and devotion of his sisters, nieces, and nephews. Furthermore, he continued to lead a bachelor existence, dating girls as eagerly as the younger members of the clan. How could a man become the leader of a large family if he had no wife or country home, if his children lived apart from him, if he had little regard for his family's traditions, had only modest financial resources, and was essentially a loner? He couldn't. There was, in the end, only one life he knew how to lead and that was the life he had adopted thirty-four years before as a young man fresh out of Yale.

As a result of Jack's inability to draw his relatives to him, the Bouvier family continued dispersing after JVB, Jr., died. Soon Bouviers would be scattered from Oklahoma to Naples, and for the first time since its founding nearly a century and a half before, there would be no focal point around which the entire clan could gather.

If Lasata had remained in the family, things might have been different: there were few Bouviers who wouldn't go out of their way to spend a few weeks in their summer paradise. But Lasata soon became a white elephant, consuming inordinate sums in taxes and upkeep. And there was no one in the family who could take it over after Major Bouvier died. Jack was not wealthy enough to run it; Edith wasn't either; Michelle was with her husband in Rio; and Maude had her own place in Connecticut. Lasata had to be sold.

At the time the property was put on the market, however, times were sour and there were few people who could afford the expense and trouble of keeping up an estate as elaborate as Lasata: the Italian garden alone, not to mention the tennis court, orchard, cornfields, stables, riding ring, cutting garden, and lawns, required a full-time employee. Consequently, it took over two years to sell it. The intrepid buyer was a wealthy businessman from Washington and Palm Beach by the name of Page Hufty and the price he paid was one fifth of what the estate would bring today.

It would have been dramatic if the Bouviers had held one last reunion at Lasata before turning it over to Mr. Hufty, but as it happened, the closing of the estate went unnoticed by most of the family. It took place on a damp April day in 1950, when Maude and I drove down to East Hampton to empty the house and consign it to the new owner's agent.

Lasata never looked more beautiful that day. The spring lawns were a light pea green flecked with dandelions, the honeysuckle on the post and rail fence was just beginning to attract its summer colony of bees, and the lindens were so delicate they looked like green clouds floating over the lawns. Two years without a master, however, had thickened the cloak of ivy that draped the house, so that many of the windows could not be seen, and much of the surrounding shrubbery had reached the upper floor. But the Italian garden was relatively unchanged. Sunk deeper now, it seemed, between its great hawthorn hedges, because those hedges had grown taller, its colors were paler than usual, but its box-enclosed flower beds were still immaculately geometrical, birds still perched on and spattered the French shepherds, and the fountain still wore its shag of wet moss.

It was not until the moving vans arrived that my mother and I felt the full pain of what we all were losing. Although much of the furniture would remain in the family—the vans were to take what was to be saved to the Little House three miles away—it was disheartening to see the interior of the house being dismantled.

It had been decided that whatever was left behind would become the property of the new owner or would be destroyed by the gardener. Distressed that something valuable might be discarded or abandoned, I scoured the house for things to salvage and found that Jack, a few weeks before, had tagged many objects he considered candidates for the rubbish heap. Among them were many of his father's books, most of the old family photographs, and several crates of family papers stored in the attic. I asked the gardener if he knew why my uncle wanted these destroyed and I was informed that Jack thought they weren't "worth anything" and had in fact given orders a year ago, through John Ficke, that many cartons of family papers and pictures be burned, orders that had partially been carried out.

Startled to learn this, I returned to the attic to see what had been destroyed and what had been saved. Among the items already gone were the letters the unfortunate Eustache had written his parents from the gold mines of California and Australia, letters that I had pored over as a child; in addition, many old photographs of the first generation of Bouviers and many documents relating to the business affairs of the first Michel. Tagged for oblivion also were the crate containing Louise Vernou's letters to her son during the Civil War, and MC's correspondence. It wasn't long before I had all the remaining letters and photographs packed away in my mother's station wagon.

Tables, desks, sofas, chairs, vases, Albert Herter's portrait of the twins, beds, screens, chandeliers, candelabra, Herter's portrait of Edith, the portraits of Michel Bouvier and Louise Vernou, terrace furniture, chaise lounges, bridge tables, bridge lamps, golf clubs, dressing tables, bureaus, mirrors, the portrait of Louis Philippe, lamps, sideboards, footstools, bronzes, chinaware, bookcases, more tables, desks, sofas, chairs . . . By late afternoon the procession of Bouvier belongings through the front door was over and the house was almost empty.

It was time to go, but before leaving, my mother and I took a last walk around the estate. The sun was low in the Western sky and there were long, blue shadows on the lawns. The rabbits were just beginning to come out, their cottontails bouncing over the green turf. Walking past the Grove of the Three Graces to the Italian garden, now wholly in shadow, we stood for a few minutes on the brick terrace, listening to the fountain and savoring the garden's incomparable bouquet. My mother and her twin had had their wedding parties in that garden. Her mother and father had spent the best summers of their lives caring for it. Her children and nieces and nephews had grown up in it. She remembered Jacqueline marching down its brick path in her jodhpurs on her way to the riding ring, Michel and Scotty shooting BB's at the French shepherds, Shella doing cartwheels by the sundial, and Bud standing on the lawn singing "Pagliacci" to the zinnias shortly before he left for Los Olivos . . . But Maude was too strong, too stoical, to break down. Just when I thought she was going to burst into tears, she turned and asked me if I had put the papers, books, and portraits in the car. I told her I had and she strode off toward the front driveway. Soon the crackle of tires on bluestone gave way to the rumble of the ocean, and Lasata, for the Bouviers, was relegated to memory.

The death of John V. Bouvier, Jr., and the sale of Lasata spelled the end of an era for the Bouviers, the passing of a gracious and economically secure way of life that few members of the family would ever know again. Major Bouvier and his East Hampton estate had represented unity and prosperity for a family whose rise from obscurity had gone unchecked for almost a hundred and fifty years. When he and his home went, without replacements, the Bouvier family in a sense died. Now there was no vital center to the clan, no common meeting place, no generally accepted source of authority: each Bouvier was on his own and there was nothing on the family's horizon to prevent it from sinking into the obscurity out of which it had so laboriously climbed.

# PART FOUR

## *New Beginnings*

### THE FIFTH GENERATION

### [1948-1993]

# I

JOHN VERNOU BOUVIER, JR.'S GRANDCHILDREN, TO WHOM HE HAD dedicated *Our Forebears*, realized soon after his death that one of the book's implied messages: "Follow in the footsteps of your ancestors," bore little relevance to the particular situation in which they found themselves. The family's wealth was divided and diminished, its prestige on the wane; no longer could Bouviers count on family influence or inheritance to help them get started in life. Disillusioned with their elders, and having come to the tacit conclusion that their grandfather's book had so far bred little but complacency, snobbishness, and slavery to narrow social standards, the Bouviers of the fifth generation were prompted to break away from the family pattern and be the authors of their own lives.

As soon as he got a chance, Michel Bouvier, the presumptive family heir, escaped the Bouvier milieu by taking a job in South America and remaining there, with only one interruption, for ten years. Before this break with family tradition, he was educated at St. Paul's, Columbia, and the University of Arizona, dividing his vacations and summers between whatever post his Army officer stepfather, Carlisle Allan, happened to be stationed at and the Bouvier residences in New York and East Hampton. Although Michel was raised by Emmy Lou and Carlisle, Jack Bouvier continued to pay for his clothing and education until he became self-supporting. While at Columbia, Miche suffered an attack of rheumatic fever which forced him to transfer to the University of Arizona. After World War II broke out, however, he followed the example of his father by leaving college and volunteering for the Army, eventually becoming a second lieutenant in General Patton's 2nd Armored Division. A year later, in 1943, he got into a motorcycle accident while on maneuvers in Tennessee, injuring his knee so badly that he was given a medical discharge. There followed a brief stint with OSS in Washington as a maps and reports officer. Then, unexpectedly, he was given a chance to work in South America. Through his stepfather he met the international business impresario and president of the Ecuadorian Corporation, E. Hope Norton, who offered him a job as assistant to the company's executive vice president in Guayaquil. Jumping at the opportunity, he left for Ecuador in September 1944.

Meanwhile his marriage, like so many wartime unions, had ended in divorce.

When Michel arrived in Guayaquil, he had no money, or connections, outside his job and his boss, to fall back on. Much in the same position as the first Michel, alone and impecunious in a foreign country, he had to swim or sink. As it was, the job he was given forced him to swim in very dangerous waters. The Ecuadorian Corporation at the time operated a brewery, a dairy farm, a cement factory, a cattle ranch, a rice hacienda, a sugar refinery, and a candy factory. Michel was put in charge of the rice hacienda. One of his duties was to reclaim land occupied by squatters. Frequently, when attempting to fulfill this assignment, he was met by bands of armed men who told him if he didn't leave the squatters alone he would be shot. Getting the squatters off the plantation, then, required Michel to wage intermittent guerrilla warfare against them and their partisans. Eventually he succeeded in driving them off the plantation.

Life was crude and wild at the rice hacienda, but Guayaquil offered a few civilized distractions in the evening to compensate for the barbarism by day. The foreign colony met regularly at one another's homes and Michel found himself much in demand at their parties. He was a tall, large-framed man of twenty-five at the time, whose broad features, powerful physique, and mustache made him look something like the young Hemingway. It was in the role of handsome extra man at foreign-colony functions that he met the girl who would one day be the mother of the sixth generation of Bouviers. She was the daughter of Harold Fothergill, the manager of the Bank of London's branch in Guayaquil and the senior member of the British colony in the city. The Ecuadorian Corporation did business through the Bank of London and it was on business there that Michel met Mr. Fothergill, was invited to one of the banker's parties, and was introduced to his daughter Catherine. By January 1946 Cathy and Miche were married. She was nineteen. He was twenty-six.

Living and working in Guayaquil, and being married to a British girl who had been born in Ecuador, Michel could not have been further removed from the milieu in which he had been brought up. As for New York and East Hampton society, the Sons of the American Revolution, the Society of the Cincinnati, the Social Register, and all the other clubs and societies the Bouvier family had been associated with, he was only too glad to be liberated from them.

However, as often occurs with exiles, a time came when Michel began to feel sheepish about forsaking his country. It was about three years after he first arrived in South America. Suddenly becoming restless, because he felt he was letting all his most valuable American contacts go by the board, he decided to make an attempt at repatriation, leaving his job with the Ecuadorian Corporation and returning to New York.

There followed two dismal years in New York and Washington that convinced him that Ecuador was, for him at least, a paradise, and that the Bouviers had little to offer him in comparison to the rice hacienda in Guayaquil. Accepting a job with Jack on Wall Street, with the idea that he might permanently adopt the business his family had made its living from for seventy-seven years, he found the work so much more uncongenial than chasing squatters off rice paddies that he quit only a few months after his first day at the office. Admittedly, Jack had not given him a very stimulating assignment. What Michel had to do was keep Jack's books and figure out what his financial position was after each day of trading. But, boring as it was, he would have learned the specialist's job in the process and then perhaps Jack and Major Bouvier could have financed him a seat on the Exchange, if he had toed their line, and he could have become a specialist himself. But Wall Street was just not Michel's meat. He loathed dealing exclusively with numbers all day found nothing stimulating about the securities business, and didn't give a damn whether four Bouviers before him had worked on Wall Street or not. Accordingly, he went hunting for another position and came up with a job as a ramp agent for American Overseas Airlines at La Guardia Airport, a job that paid him so little, Cathy had to take a position with Venezuelan Airlines to help make ends meet.

What a comedown from his position with the Ecuadorian Corporation! Living in a cramped apartment in New York on practically a subsistence income, with little financial help from either the Bouviers or the Allans, and having to work at a routine airlines job, whereas in Ecuador he had lived in a lovely house, with servants, had been almost his own boss, and Cathy had not had to work. It wasn't long before Miche and Cathy became exasperated by the situation, and Miche decided to go job hunting again.

This time he landed something better, something which promised to take him back to South America: a job in Washington with Peruvian International Airways. It was while they were living in Washington and Michel was working for Peruvian that the Michel Bouviers had their first child, a son whom Miche named after himself. Ironically, the dynastically-minded John Vernou Bouvier, Jr., never learned of the birth of a sixth-generation male heir, for Michel Bouvier IV was born eight months after the old patriarch died. He had been conceived, however, while JVB, Jr., was alive and was therefore entitled to a legacy of $3,000 from JVB, Jr.'s estate under a special provision for great-grandchildren born or conceived before his death.

Joining Peruvian International Airways eventually led Michel to Panagra and Panagra finally brought him and his wife and son back to Guayaquil in January 1949, with Michel as senior representative for the airline in Ecuador. Soon after his return, Michel became one of the top Americans in the Guayaquil hierarchy, as his responsibilities expanded to include supervision of international flights and airport maintenance in Peru, Colombia, and Bolivia, as well as Ecuador. Settling in a large house staffed with two servants, Michel and Cathy couldn't have been more delighted. Their two years in New York and Washington had been a nightmare of boring jobs and financial distress. They had taught Michel one thing, however, for which he was deeply grateful, and that was that the world of his fathers had little to offer him. The Bouvier family, as a historical continuity of shared interests, aspirations, and traditions, had ended with JVB, Jr., or at best lingered on, in a sort of antiquarian way, with the twins. *His* Bouvier family, however, the one he, Michel Bouvier III, would establish, would be something quite different, a new beginning, like the family of the first Michel.

So powerful was the family feeling Major Bouvier generated that all his grandchildren tended to identify with his family rather than the families their parents married into, considering themselves Bouviers first, and Beales, Scotts, Lees, and Davises second. But it was precisely because his influence had been so tyrannical that JVB, Jr.'s grandchildren were anxious to escape it. Thus, Miche was not alone among Major Bouvier's grandsons in his rebellion against the family ethos. Phelan Beale, Jr., after serving with distinction as an Army officer in the Pacific campaign, settled in Tulsa, Oklahoma, where he became an administrative official in the state government. Rarely returning East, he has become an Oklahoman in speech, manner, and outlook. A more radical departure from the Bouvier pattern could not be imagined. Following the example of his cousins Michel and Phelan, Michelle's son, Henry Scott, also succeeded in divorcing himself from the Bouvier environment. After graduating from Yale and marrying Elizabeth Winslow, he eventually moved West, settling in Scottsdale, Arizona. Without any financial assistance from his parents, and, like his other cousins, without any prospect of inheriting a fortune, he had to succeed on his own and did as a businessman in the paper and wood-pulp industry. The youngest Bouvier grandson was myself and mine proved to be the most prolonged exile of all from the family scene. After graduating from Princeton and spending two years as a Naval officer with the Sixth Fleet in the Mediterranean, I was awarded a Fulbright Scholarship for study in Naples, which led to an extended stay in Italy. Eventually I found myself teaching Italian history and literature while running an intercollegiate center for Italian studies, which, coincidentally, was located in a palace associated with Joseph Bonaparte when he was King of Naples. Rarely regretting my absence from the Bouvier scene, I reveled in a sense of liberation from the family.

The only grandson of JVB, Jr.'s who followed somewhat in the Major's footsteps was Phelan's younger brother, Bouvier Beale, known to the family as Buddy. Graduating from Columbia Law School in 1947, much to the gratification of his lawyer father and grandfather, he eventually established his own law firm in New York, Walker, Beale, Wainwright and Wolf, joined one of his grandfather's clubs, Piping Rock, and settled on the North Shore of Long Island, where he raised three sons.

Four of Major Bouvier's five grandsons, then, by the mid-1950s had scattered to such unlikely places as Guayaquil, Tulsa, Naples, and Scottsdale, whereas the four generations of Bouvier males before them, with the sole exception of Eustache, had not strayed from Philadelphia and New York.

JVB, Jr.'s five granddaughters, however, with one exception, were not nearly as anxious as the men to remove themselves from the area where they were brought up. Yet, all the same, two of the four who remained in the New York area still succeeded in departing radically from the family pattern. Thus, the beautiful

Little Edie, who never left her reclusive mother in East Hampton, remaining her nurse and helper until Edith Sr.'s death in 1977, imitated her mother's rebellion against bourgeois conformity by cultivating a bohemian style of life that baffled her Bouvier relatives. And Little Maudie, in her own way, also broke with family tradition. Refusing to have an elaborate coming-out party and declining to join her mother's clubs, she embarked, after taking degrees at Smith and N.Y.U. and spending a year as a social worker, on what has been for her a most rewarding career as a teacher and reading therapist at the Brearley School in New York. Michelle's daughter, Shella, however, managed to fit herself into the traditional Bouvier pattern by having a large coming-out party, marrying a Wall Street investment banker, buying a house in exurbia, remaining in the Social Register, raising a family of four sons, and joining the Daughters of the Cincinnati.

One Bouvier granddaughter made a sharp break with the milieu in which she was raised by settling permanently in London. When Lee Bouvier married Michael Canfield in the spring of 1953, after a year at Sarah Lawrence, a term studying art history in Italy, and a brief period working for the fashion editor of *Harper's Bazaar*, she had no intention of residing permanently in England, but circumstances eventually conspired to keep her there. Her young husband, son of the publisher Cass Canfield, had been appointed to the staff of Winthrop Aldrich, the American ambassador to Great Britain, and that appointment was responsible for bringing her to England initially. It wasn't until after the annulment of her first marriage, however, and her marriage to the Polish nobleman and exile Stanislaus Radziwill in 1959 that she became a confirmed Londoner. Finally fulfilling Alexine Bouvier's frustrated desire to marry a certified aristocrat, seventy-eight years after Prince Vallerie's snub, Lee became the first Bouvier to bear a title and the fourth Bouvier daughter, after Emma Drexel, Louise Morrell, and Jacqueline, to enter the ranks of the very rich.

Her older sister, Jacqueline, was more conservative, for until she married the Greek shipowner, Aristotle Onassis, she did not forsake the milieu in which she had been brought up or depart radically from the traditions of her class.

Growing up in the sheltered world of fashionable Eastern resorts and exclusive schools, Jacqueline accepted the life that fate offered her and did all the things that were expected of her. Like her twin aunts, she went to Miss Porter's, where she earned high grades both in conduct and in academic studies, and spent the summers in Newport and East Hampton riding, playing tennis, swimming, and going out with the sons of socially prominent families. Like Maude and Michelle, she attended the ritual round of debutante parties in Newport, New York, and Long Island and appeared almost as often as they had as debutantes in the rotogravures. At Vassar she again earned high marks, and she attended the equally ritualistic football weekends at Yale, Harvard, and Princeton.

Her outward conformity to the conventions of her class, however, belied a fiercely independent inner life which she shared with few people and which would one day be partly responsible for her enormous success. From an early age Jackie had displayed an originality, a perspicacity, that set her apart from most of her other cousins. She wrote creditable verse. She painted. She was an exceptionally gifted equestrienne. She often said things that were wise beyond her years. In addition, she possessed a mysterious authority, even as a teenager, that would compel people to do her bidding. Once, at the Maidstone, she asked her cousins the name of a song she was humming, and those cousins spent the entire day trying to find out . . . for Jackie. And she always had the courage to be herself, no matter what the reaction to her autonomous behavior was.

Jackie's personality, most Bouviers agree, was powerfully affected by the disintegration of her parents' marriage. It was during the years between Jack and Janet's separation and divorce that the Bouviers first noticed Jacqueline's tendency to withdraw frequently into a private world of her own. Before that unsettling time of her youth, she had been much more outgoing, much less shy and aloof. After it, her withdrawn, distant manner would often give her Bouvier relatives the impression that she was trying to avoid them, or snub them, when in reality she was putting up a defense to hide her feelings of shame over what she perhaps felt had been a personal humiliation. This aloofness, this tendency to erect formidable barriers to protect her innermost feelings, had a reverse side, however, which was most confusing to other people, whether relatives or not. And that was a histrionic inclination, an apparent urge to be seen by an audience and admired, which was as pronounced, in a way, as her shyness and reserve. On an intimate basis, talking, say, with just one person, she would often appear very restrained, even ill-at-ease, yet before a large gathering, at a debutante party, or a horse show, she would be the radiant, outgoing belle of the ball.

It was not merely a journalistic contrivance, then, that Jacqueline was nominated by the society columnist Cholly Knickerbocker "Debutante of the Year" in 1947. At the dinner dance the Auchinclosses and the Grosvenors gave for her and her friend Rose Grosvenor at Newport's Clambake Club that summer, she was radiant. Her Bouvier cousins were amazed to see their shy, sensitive Jackie, who had always been so difficult to talk to privately, dazzling the guests. It was this watertight, interior suffisance, coupled with a need for attention, and corresponding love of being in the center of the stage, which puzzled her relatives so and which in time would alternately charm and perplex the entire world.

Ten Bouvier grandchildren. Ten radically different destinies. Few bonds between them but the determination of each to be the architect of his own existence. Fragmented as a family, but united in attitude. With none of the cohesiveness that characterized the first three generations, yet without the contentiousness of the fourth, the fifth generation, in going their own separate ways, would give the family a new birth.

# II

JACQUELINE AND LEE BOUVIER'S EMANCIPATION FROM THE IN-fluence of the Bouvier family took the initial form of a steadily increasing identification with the Auchinclosses. For most of the Bouviers, this slow shifting of allegiance from their family to Hughdie's went unnoticed and therefore unregretted, but for Jack it was a source of unending affliction, a purgatory that embittered the last years of his life.

Jacqueline and Lee, however, were not to blame for their father's unhappiness. It was Jack's misfortune that he simply could not offer his daughters the advantages Hughdie was able to offer them. Besides, since it is customary for children of divorced parents to live with their mother, it was only natural that Jackie and Lee tended to identify with the family their mother married into.

Janet and Hughdie naturally took pains to cement Jacqueline and Lee to the Auchinclosses. They immersed them in Auchincloss family activities. They brought them to Auchincloss family reunions. In 1945 they presented them with a half sister, Janet, and in 1947 with a half brother, James Lee. Already there were other children from Hughdie's two previous marriages: Hugh, Jr., known as "Yusha," and Nina and Thomas. So Jacqueline and Lee were not wanting for companionship in their stepfather's homes. Nor were they wanting in luxurious surroundings: Merrywood was an enormous place boasting a swimming pool, stables, and forty-six acres of Virginia woods and fields; and Hammersmith Farm in Newport, with its magnificent hilltop view of Narragansett Bay, was equally grandiose. Jack Bouvier was at a distinct disadvantage: although he had much in common with his daughters, physically and temperamentally, and all three shared a fundamentally aesthetic response to life, he could not provide them with the companionship of people their own age, and all he owned in the way of real estate was a sunless four-room apartment on East Seventy-fourth Street.

Nevertheless, what limited resources he had at his command he made available to his daughters.

In the fall of 1947 Jacqueline entered Vassar at Jack's expense. Jack was delighted she was there because Poughkeepsie was much nearer New York than McLean, Virginia. She would easily be able to make it to his apartment on weekends, whereas Merrywood would be beyond her reach. And, of course, he could get to Vassar much more easily than Janet and Hughdie.

For a month or two, things worked out more or less in Jack's favor. He would visit Jackie at Vassar and she would have the glory of showing him off in the Main Dining Room, enjoying the way the girls would gawk at him as if he were a movie star. And she would use his apartment when she went to New York for a date or a dance. But after a while the situation deteriorated. During the winter of 1948 Jack would repeatedly charge his eldest daughter with coming to his apartment only when it suited her convenience, pointing out that she would arrive breathlessly a half hour before her date or her dance, then depart as soon as she got up the next morning. And he would often complain to his sisters that she took advantage of him, that she would write or phone only when she needed her allowance, which at that time was fifty dollars a month.

Jack simply couldn't reconcile himself to the whims and needs of a pretty teenager who was just beginning to go out with boys. Neither could Jack reconcile himself to the fact that Jacqueline and Lee were also Janet's children. Janet had been a good mother to her daughters, though, so far as Jack was concerned, her only aim in life was to take his daughters away from him. Thus, when Janet would schedule dental appointments for Jacqueline in Washington (which Jack would subsequently be asked to pay for), Jack would immediately interpret the action as a way of getting Jackie to come to Virginia and he would angrily counterattack by insisting she have her teeth fixed in Manhattan: he would not pay for any more treatments in Washington, D.C. And so it would go in countless other matters. Whatever Janet did for her daughters would always be construed by Jack as a ploy to take them away from him.

So far as summer vacations were concerned, after Major Bouvier died and Lasata was sold, Jack had very few cards to play to entice his daughters to East Hampton. He could not afford more than a small rented cottage some distance from the ocean. A far cry from Lasata, with its stables, riding ring, tennis court, sweeping lawns, and gardens. A far cry from Hammersmith Farm. There was only one sure way Jack could get Jacqueline to come to East Hampton, and that was to keep her horses there for the summer and not allow them to be taken to Newport. She would certainly come to see Danseuse.

The strategy did not always work. In 1948 Jacqueline took her father by surprise, announcing that she was going to spend July and August in Europe. Jack immediately concluded she had been influenced to take the trip by her mother, and therefore opposed the junket. In spite of his protests, however, the trip was made, at his expense, and Jacqueline had her first experience with the land of her forebears. Touring France, Switzerland, and Britain with three friends—Julia Bissell and Helen and Judy Bowdin—she became especially enamored of France and determined to return. And so Jack, of course, missed out on having her with him in East Hampton.

He also missed out on having her with him as often as he would have liked after her return to Vassar. In the fall of 1949 he often complained to his brother-in-law, with whom he shared an office, that Jackie was going to Merrywood much too often and that probably the only way he could get her to see him was by withholding her allowance. He rarely withheld his daughters' allowances, however. No matter how much he felt they neglected him, no matter how often they chose Merrywood over his apartment, he was generous to them to the end. In addition to their monthly stipends, and the charge accounts he maintained for them, he paid for their education, and gave them special checks on holidays and birthdays.

He also offered abundant advice on how to act with men. Make the boys come to you, he would counsel them. Never go after them and show them that you like them; that is fatal. Also, bear in mind that most men are rats. For this reason take every suitor with a grain of salt, play the field, and try not to become too involved with any one man.

In a different vein, he would also advise them not to neglect their Aunt Edith. After Edith's house was partially destroyed by fire in 1949, he would repeatedly urge both his sisters and his daughters to extend her their help and sympathy, telling them how much Edith, who led such a deprived existence, would appreciate hearing from them.

Although Jack was usually critical of Jacqueline's conduct toward him during her college years, and his counsel tended to be negative, there were occasions on which he would compliment her and offer constructive advice about her future. When she won admission to the Smith Group's Junior Year in France program, he beamed with pride at the honor, and when she told him that she had decided not to return to Vassar after her year in France but to become a photographer's model in New York instead, he gently discouraged the plan and advised her to stay at Vassar, offering her a secretarial job in his brokerage office at $50 a week if she would come live with him after she graduated.

Graduation was two years away, however; now the important thing for Jacqueline was her year of study in France. As a concession to Jack, since, after all, as he frequently pointed out, he was paying for the Smith Group program, Jacqueline spent the last two weeks of July with him in East Hampton, then sailed for her year abroad in late August. The Smith program called for her to spend September and October studying French intensively at the University of Grenoble, and the rest of the academic year taking courses in French literature and history at the Sorbonne in Paris. She was the second Bouvier daughter who would spend a year studying in the country of her forefathers, having been preceded, ninety-seven years before, by her great- grandaunt Louise.

Once Jacqueline was in France, Jack's relations with her improved considerably. Now, at least, she was not in a position to choose Merrywood over East Seventy-fourth Street.

Jack's long-distance honeymoon with his eldest daughter reached its most affectionate stage when she was in Paris. After she left Grenoble and took up residence in the French capital at the Countess de Renty's apartment at 78 avenue Mozart, Jack confessed to the twins that his love for Jackie had never been greater, that in fact he was thinking of flying over and seeing his best girl—though in the end he didn't do it, perhaps out of fear of breaking the spell.

Jacqueline thrived in Paris. She got along very well with her countess landlady, a courageous woman whose family had fallen from a position of wealth and influence, and whose husband had died in a German concentration camp, and she also enjoyed her classes at the Sorbonne. In Paris she clearly had the best of two worlds: the spirited student life of the boulevard Saint-Michel and the more elegant *monde* of American Francophiles and international exiles who congregated at the Ritz. The two milieus allowed Jacqueline to be herself in a way she was never able to be at Vassar. Paris, in fact, spoiled Vassar for Jackie. By the middle of her year abroad she was determined not to return to Poughkeepsie.

The spring went by as auspiciously as the fall and winter, so far as relations between father and daughter were concerned. It was clear that having Jacqueline in France was much better than having her at Poughkeepsie. No battles with Janet and Hughdie. No choices between 125 East Seventy-fourth Street and Merrywood. No visitation periods without visits.

Jack's relations with his younger daughter, Lee, were, generally speaking, not nearly as volatile as his relations with Jacqueline. Lee was a frailer, more feminine, more dependent person than the tomboyish Jackie, so Jack at least had the satisfaction of having her come to him for advice and cry on his shoulder more often than his older daughter. Still, he could become just as annoyed with Lee as with Jackie when he felt she was taking advantage of him, frequently complaining to his brother-in-law and his sisters that although he was happy to give Lee an allowance she seemed to write or telephone only when she was broke and would never visit him unless she needed money. To which his sisters would inevitably reply: "What do you expect from a pretty girl in her teens? That she would come to see you to sew buttons on your shirts or listen to your complaints about your slipped disc?"

Lee frequently needled her father about his way of handling money and women. Jack always assumed that her criticism originated with her mother and so would make comebacks that somehow reflected on Janet. To Lee's gibes about his girl friends, who more often than not did not come from socially prominent families, he would reply that he would much rather have the girl in question than what he would refer to as "those old bags in Newport who are supposed to be at the top of society."

Picking on Jack's girl friends, and kidding him about his love life, past and present, was a favorite diversion for Jacqueline also. Wherever Jacqueline went—Newport, East Hampton, Washington, Palm Beach—she inevitably met women who had once been taken out by her father, and would demand to be told once more why he courted so many women. To which Jack, in perfect sincerity, would reply that in the first place the women she ran into should have felt complimented that he had honored them by taking them out, and second, she, Jackie, should be proud her father made such a devastating impression on them.

If Jack's relations with Jackie improved with distance, the opposite was the case in his relations with Lee. As a rule, Jack got along much better with Lee when he was with her. After Jackie left for France in August 1949, Lee spent two weeks with Jack in a rented cottage in East Hampton and both father and daughter had a wonderful time. And in the fall Jack went to Farmington to see Lee act in the play *You Can't Take It with You,* spending a gay weekend with her and returning to New York to tell the twins that he was so impressed by Lee's acting talent he was thinking seriously of launching her on a stage career.

During the summer of 1950, however, relations with both daughters took a sudden turn for the worse. In the spring of that year Jack underwent a cataract operation at the New York Medical Center and could not work for two months. He spent July and August recuperating in East Hampton, hoping his daughters would visit him, but they were unable to. Jackie stayed in Europe and Lee spent the summer on a ranch in Wyoming. By then the unacceptable fact was that Jackie and Lee, with no conscious intention of hurting their father, had successfully emancipated themselves from his influence and control. From now on, Jack's struggles for his daughters' time would lead to an unbroken succession of defeats.

The year 1951 was particularly critical for Jack in this respect. On returning from her year in France, Jacqueline did not reenter Vassar but chose George Washington University, in Washington, D.C., instead. Disliking the secluded, exclusively female, atmosphere of the Vassar campus, and hating Poughkeepsie, she found living and studying in Washington the next best thing to Paris and the Sorbonne. For Jack, however, the transfer was a severe blow. If Jackie had frequently chosen Merrywood over 125 East Seventy-fourth Street when she lived in Poughkeepsie, how would he ever coax her to 125 East Seventy-fourth Street again, with Merrywood now but a stone's throw from her new college? Jackie at George Washington University meant only one thing to Jack: her definitive, if unconscious, capitulation to the Auchinclosses. And the galling thing about it was that even though he was firmly opposed to her going to GW, he still had to foot the bill.

To Jack's surprise and delight, however, Jacqueline did make several trips to New York in the first half of 1951, for it was then that she became engaged to John G. W. Husted, Jr., son of a prominent New York banker. Like Jack Bouvier, the young man had gone to Yale and worked on Wall Street. For a while the couple took turns seeing each other in New York and Washington, with John spending a weekend at Merrywood and Jackie spending the next one at her father's apartment in New York. Jack was very pleased. If Jackie married a New York stockbroker, she would be removed from the Auchincloss orbit once and for all. She would settle with young Husted on Manhattan's East Side; she would be near Jack's apartment and he would run into her husband regularly on Wall Street.

But it was Jack's fate to have his daughter snatched from him at the last moment every time he thought he finally had her all to his own. Thus when Jackie and Husted called off their engagement, and Jackie returned to Washington, Jack suffered another keen disappointment.

As always, however, just when he felt his expectations for Jackie had been most cruelly thwarted, she would do something to renew his pride in her and give him hope that she would one day return to New York. This time it was winning *Vogue's* Prix de Paris contest. The 1,280 contestants in the 1951 competition had been asked to submit a plan for an entire issue of *Vogue* and write four "technical" papers on high fashion and an essay on "People I Wish I Had Known." Choosing three *raffinati*, Charles Baudelaire, Oscar Wilde, and Sergei Diaghilev, as the people she wished she had known above all others, and submitting discerning papers on high fashion, Jackie won the first prize—an opportunity to work for six months on Paris *Vogue* and for six months in the magazine's New York offices. Thus, Jack was again unexpectedly afforded the delicious prospect of having Jackie removed from the Auchinclosses for a whole year. Judging from the way things had gone the last time Jackie was in Paris, their relationship would again be a happy one while she was there, and after her stay was up he would savor the bliss of having her near him during her six months at *Vogue's* offices in New York.

But again his hopes were frustrated. After considerable discussion, Janet and Hughdie convinced Jacqueline not to accept the prize, on the grounds that she had been away from home too much in recent years. Later Jackie would confess to relatives and friends that she wanted very much to go but was afraid—in view of her temperamental affinity for the French, and her happy memories of her year at the Sorbonne—that if she returned to Paris she would find a way of staying there forever.

With the extraordinary *Vogue* opportunity eliminated, Jack made a last-ditch effort to lure Jackie to New York by repeating his offer of a job in his office after she left George Washington U. An acceptance on her part would have fulfilled what had become the last and only ambition of Jack's life, to have Jackie near him as he approached old age. But the man Jack regarded as his adversary was not dormant. Jackie had always toyed with the idea of going into journalism, and Hugh Auchincloss, through his friend Arthur Krock of *The New York Times,* managed to turn her inclination into a reality. At Hughdie's request, Krock got her an interview with Frank Waldrop of the now defunct Washington *Times-Herald,* and before long, Jacqueline Bouvier became the paper's inquiring photographer, at $42.50 a week. The job called for her to ask a specified question of several people each day, take their pictures, and record their answers, along with their photographs. Naturally she would have to remain in Washington.

Jacqueline plunged into her new job in late 1951 without a by-line. By March 26, 1952, her name headed her column. Her questions were as miscellaneous and unstudied as those of most twenty-two-year-olds. At the Washington Postgraduate Dental Clinic she asked doctors, nurses, and interns: "Are men braver than women in the dental chair?" Along "Antique Row" she asked dealers: "If you could keep one thing in your shop, what would it be?" In stores along Connecticut Avenue she asked women: "Can you spot a married man?"

On November 28, 1952, she was given another designation. From inquiring photographer she graduated to inquiring camera girl and in that new capacity asked the Treasurer of the United States, the Secretary of the Senate, an administrative assistant to the President, Perle Mesta, and the Attorney General what they would be doing after Eisenhower's inauguration. And shortly after the inauguration, on January 24, 1953, she asked the workers dismantling the grandstands in front of the White House whether they had received any complaints from the Eisenhowers about the racket they were making in front of their new home.

It was while Jacqueline was writing for the *Times-Herald* that she was first introduced to John F. Kennedy. The two were brought together by Charles Bartlett, a mutual friend and Washington correspondent for the Chattanooga *Times,* on May 8, 1952, at a dinner at the Bartletts' home in Washington. Although they got along well enough at the dinner, they did not begin to date regularly until several months later. Even then, Jacqueline did not appear to take Kennedy very seriously. I was a Naval officer at the time, on temporary duty in Washington, and had a chance to sound her out on her romance with the young congressman. Over lunch I asked Jackie if there was anything to the rumors I had heard that she was going to become engaged to Kennedy and was surprised to hear her dismiss him as quixotic because he had confided to her that he "intended to become President." Pursuing the subject failed to elicit confirmation of the engagement, although it was obvious from both the tone of her voice and her evasiveness that she liked Kennedy. Eventually Jacqueline put an end to my third degree by snapping my picture and interviewing me for her column. The question was: "Are men as inclined to fall for a line as girls are?" My fifty-word answer amounted to "yes."

Before long, however, Jackie began taking Jack Kennedy more seriously, despite his seemingly quixotic aspirations. In January 1953 the newly elected senator escorted her to Eisenhower's Inaugural Ball, and from then on, the two grew closer together as Jackie found excuses to make photographic inquiries on Capitol Hill and Jack came to look forward to her visits. A trip to London at the end of May to cover Elizabeth II's coronation for her paper provided the inevitable absence that makes the heart grow fonder; then, on June 25, 1953, Jacqueline Bouvier and Senator John F. Kennedy were formally engaged. Actually, Jackie had told her family of the engagement several days before the official announcement. Phoning the news to her Aunt Maude, she begged her not to tell anyone, "because it wouldn't be fair to the *Saturday Evening Post*," explaining that the Post was just about to come out with an article entitled "Jack Kennedy—The Senate's Gay Young Bachelor."

Knowing her father's ultra-Republican political inclinations, and the way he had opposed Joseph P. Kennedy's policies when Kennedy was head of the SEC, Jacqueline was understandably anxious about how he and her fiancé would get along. To her immense relief, they hit it off beautifully. The two Jacks had, surprisingly enough, a great deal in common: both shared a healthy interest in women and sports and a realistic, unhypocritical attitude toward life. Both came from Catholic families which had fought their way to prominence against the Anglo-Saxon

Protestant establishment, and both were decidedly men of the world. Still, it is always difficult for a father to see another man dominate his daughter's life. Jack Bouvier had already had the pain of having been partially replaced as a father by Hugh Auchincloss. Now another man was laying an even more enduring claim on his daughter's loyalties. And he was a senator who lived in Washington.

Two and a half months before Jacqueline's engagement to Kennedy, Jack had been forced to spend a day in the heart of Auchincloss country and it was not difficult for him to see why his daughters liked it so much. The occasion was Lee's wedding to Michael Canfield in Washington on April 18. Lee, who was twenty at the time, had known young Canfield for many years, having gone to scores of dances and parties with him in New York. Jack gave the bride away at the ceremony, then went with the twins to the reception at Merrywood. It was a rainy day, but the Virginia estate, with its great Georgian house and a distant view of the Potomac, looked magnificent. Jack was given a quick tour of the house and grounds, for it was his first visit, and he conceded reluctantly that it was every bit as beautiful as Lasata. As he inspected the estate and admired the rolling green hills and the woodlands, he was painfully aware of the comparison between what Hughdie had been able to give Jackie and Lee and what he had been able to give them during the past ten years. During the reception Jack had to summon all his strength to keep from breaking down. Standing there, in the midst of his rivals, he was compelled to be pleasant to Janet, Hughdie, and Mr. James T. Lee. Although he was immensely proud of Lee, who never looked more beautiful, it was still a terrible ordeal.

Now that Jacqueline was engaged, Jack had another ordeal awaiting him, another encounter with Janet, Hughdie, and James T. Lee. This time it would be at the Auchinclosses' summer place, Hammersmith Farm, in Newport, on September 12, 1953. It was billed by the press as the wedding of the year.

Having coped fairly successfully with the reception at Merrywood, considering the intense emotional strain he was under at the time, Jack was determined to make a brilliant impression at Jackie's wedding in Newport. During August he acquired a magnificent tan in East Hampton and began putting together a wardrobe for the big day, sparing no effort or expense. Just the right length of collar, vest, and cuff. Striped trousers just the right width. Cutaway made to order. His late father's pearl stickpin. A new pair of gray suède gloves. Yes, he was going to make Jackie proud of him on this the most significant day of her life. And he would make Jack Kennedy proud of him too. And all the other Bouviers and Kennedys. Most of all, he would show the Auchinclosses who Jackie's *real* father was.

And so Jack went to Newport the evening of September 11, with a stockbroker friend, and checked into the Viking Hotel, while the twins and their families traveled separately and took rooms in the Munchener King.

Once at his hotel, Jack found himself fussed over as if he were a maharaja. The management had been informed he was the father of the bride and treated him, accordingly, as the most important guest in the hotel. Thus did the valets turn somersaults to make sure his trousers were given knife-edged creases and his shoes blinding shines. Thus did room service rush his ice and drinks and cheese and crackers to his suite the minute he rang for them. And when he appeared in the dining room, John Vernou Bouvier III was given the best table in the house.

To everyone's relief, September 12, 1953, turned out to be a magnificent day. A bit windy, but warm and sunny, with hardly a cloud in the sky. Busily the Bouviers began pulling themselves together in their respective hotels. While Jacqueline, Lee, Janet, and Hughdie readied themselves at Hammersmith Farm.

Jack's feelings, as he began dressing for what he had come to regard as one of the most important events of his life, must have been terribly confused. He adored Jackie. For him she was the sun and earth and moon and "all things holy." And yet both the wedding ceremony and the reception to follow had been organized by his arch rivals, the Auchinclosses. Thus, he was faced with a situation so emotionally explosive he dared not think of it. To give Jacqueline away, with Janet there in the front pew, and all those stuffy Newport dowagers whispering to each other: "That's her first husband . . . it was a dreadful divorce"; and Hughdie standing by Janet's side. Oh, god! By ten o'clock it was evident from Jack's phone calls—to the Munchener King, to Hammersmith Farm—that he was not up to performing at the wedding.

After further telephone conferences, the twins' husbands were dispatched to the Viking to look after him while the twins and their children went off to St. Mary's.

It was a glorious wedding. Archbishop Cushing was there to officiate and bestow the Apostolic Blessing of Pope Pius XII on the bride and groom. Lee and the bridesmaids, in pink taffeta with claret sashes, looked beguiling as they marched slowly up the center aisle, casting furtive smiles to relatives and friends. Jack Kennedy and his best man, Robert Kennedy, were too tanned and handsome to be believed. When Jackie appeared, in cream taffeta faille and a yellow lace veil decorated with orange blossoms, all heads turned. She looked so beautiful that few people in the church, beyond her closest friends and relatives, paid much attention to the fact that she was not on the arm of her father but on the arm of Hugh D. Auchincloss. Triumphing over her embarrassment and disappointment at her father's inability to give her away, she dazzled the congregation with her bright charm and gracious manner. As for Hugh Auchincloss, a more stalwart, straight-backed father of the bride could not have been imagined. Performing his role with a grave and stately dignity, he sealed his final, if unwitting, victory over Jack.

Hammersmith Farm made a splendid setting for the bridal luncheon. The tables had been set up under a huge, striped tent on the lawn. From them the guests could see Black Angus cattle grazing on lush green meadows and admire a broad blue sweep of Narragansett Bay.

The crowd of 1,200 was a heterogeneous one. Newport socialites and Massachusetts politicians. Social Register friends of the Auchinclosses and the Bouviers, and a vast Kennedy following of congressmen, mayors, senators, and ward healers. The two worlds did not mix. When Meyer Davis, who had played at Jack's and Janet's wedding, began the dancing, the socialites danced and the politicians, for the most part, watched. Everyone was captivated by the bride and groom. Jack and Jacqueline made an incredibly glamorous couple. As the only Bouviers present, besides the bride and the matron of honor, the twins and their children found themselves deluged with compliments for Jackie. Not all the guests realized, however, the full extent of Jacqueline's courage. She had wanted her own father to give her away and be there in the receiving line at Hammersmith Farm. That he had been unable to rise to the occasion must have been a painful humiliation. She knew some people would be wondering what had happened, knew there would be whispers and half guesses at his expense. And yet she succeeded in appearing radiant and at ease as she greeted guests, smiled at photographers, and danced with her husband and stepfather.

Meanwhile, as the festivities at Hammersmith Farm advanced toward the throwing of the bridal bouquet and the departure of the bride and groom, Jack Bouvier folded his unused cutaway into his suitcase, checked out of his hotel, and retreated to his apartment in New York. How he felt can easily be imagined. Before leaving Newport he rationalized his loss of nerve by telling Maude's husband that he loved Jackie too much to bear seeing her "commandeered" by another man, even though he liked and admired Jack Kennedy.

But the true reasons for his inability to live up to what would have been one of the greatest moments of his life were probably unknown even to himself. His intense love for Jacqueline and his equally intense rivalry with the Auchinclosses undoubtedly confused him, and it was humiliating that *he* was not giving the wedding reception for his daughter, but these were merely aggravating circumstances. He could have gritted his teeth and endured them. The sad fact was that Jack Bouvier, in spite of his swashbuckling manner and appearance, had rarely lived up to what had been expected of him in life. With the sole exception of his erratic granduncle Eustache, the three generations of Bouviers before him had known all but unqualified social and financial success. But he and his brother Bud had clearly not been the measure of their forebears. And they had been told so, emphatically, by their father many times. By 1953 Jack Bouvier was accustomed to letting his family down. And so, when he failed his daughter in Newport, the lapse was not unexpected. For years JVB, Jr., had said he could not live up to his family's name and reputation. Perhaps, at Newport, Jack finally found a way of telling his father he was right.

Mr. and Mrs. John F. Kennedy spent their honeymoon in an idyllic pink villa overlooking the Pacific at Acapulco. Not long after they arrived, Jackie wrote her father a letter of forgiveness which Jack showed his partner, John Carrere, with tears in his eyes. Carrere does not remember the wording of the note but recalls that it was one of the most touching, compassionate letters he has ever read, one that only a rare and noble spirit could have written.

Jack Bouvier never fully recovered from his failure in Newport. Word of his "indisposition" during the wedding seeped into Newport, New York, and East Hampton society, and Jack found it difficult to hold his head up in his old haunts. As a result, he became something of a recluse after September 1953, seeing very few people and gradually fading from the New York-Long Island scene. With both his daughters married, visits from them naturally became rarer, and a chilly sense of loneliness and isolation gradually took possession of him. Perhaps he found consolation in the fact that at least his girls were no longer with the Auchinclosses. But it was, at best, a minor solace. Without a lasting relationship with a woman, and with his three sisters still smarting from squabbles with him over their father's will, Jack Bouvier was left with only two faithful, enduring companions: his clerk and his maid.

While her father was entering his last, lonely years, and the Bouvier family was becoming more and more fragmented, Jacqueline Bouvier Kennedy was adjusting to a new life and a new family. Even though the Kennedys were somewhat overwhelming, Jacqueline made the adjustment with relative ease. By then she had become an expert in adjusting to new family situations, having spent her life thus far coping with three other formidable families, the Bouviers, the Lees, and the Auchinclosses. As it was, Jacqueline found the energetic, united Kennedys a tonic after the contentiousness and disunity of her own families. Their deep inner strength, their lack of pettiness, their strong sense of mutual loyalty and comradeship gave her a warm feeling of assurance she had not known before. Now she was in a family situation analogous to that of the Bouviers of the second generation, that wonderful, vital time in the family's history when all ten of Michel, Sr.'s children were united, when there was no such thing as a Bouvier divorce, when the clan's financial fortunes were on the rise and their future appeared limitless. Now, also, she was in a family whose financial resources dwarfed anything she had known before. Both Jack Bouvier and Janet Auchincloss had kept Jacqueline on a very tight economic string. The most spending money she ever had before marrying was the $56.75 a week she eventually earned as inquiring camera girl for the Washington *Times-Herald*, combined with Jack's $50 a month allowance and an occasional largess from Janet. Once she was in the Kennedy clan, however, there were no more money problems. Not since the second generation's Lady Bountiful—Emma Bouvier Drexel—had a Bouvier daughter married into such wealth.

Although the Kennedys were very demanding of her time, Jacqueline actually saw more of the Bouviers after her marriage than when she had been living with the Auchinclosses. Every once in a while Jack Bouvier would visit his daughter and son-in-law in Washington, and when Michel Bouvier returned from South America in June 1955 to work for the Grumman Aircraft Corporation on Long Island, he and his wife became frequent guests of the John F. Kennedys. Occasionally Jack Kennedy would come to New York and his father-in-law would treat him to lunch at the Stock Exchange Luncheon Club, then take him down on the trading floor. One thing that drew Jack Bouvier and Jack Kennedy together was their sharing of a common ailment: back trouble. Jack Bouvier had suffered from a slipped disc for many years, and he and Kennedy would often compare remedies and discuss potential cures. In time Jack became one of the most forceful advocates of Kennedy's lumbar-spine operation and a frequent caller at his bedside at the Hospital for Special Surgery in New York after the operation.

The years 1954 to 1957 were difficult ones for Jacqueline and Jack Kennedy. Jacqueline confessed to various members of the family that politics and politicians often bored her: she was much more interested in art and artists. Frequently she found it beyond her powers to make her restless, ambitious husband relax. His convalescence during the fall of 1954 and winter of 1955 was a particularly trying time. Then in 1955 Jackie suffered a miscarriage and the following year she gave birth to a stillborn child and her husband lost the Vice Presidential nomination.

For the Bouviers, one of the happier events of the period was the birth, on January 4, 1950, in Huntington, Long Island, of John Vernou Bouvier IV to Michel and Cathy. The baby's christening, in Remsenburg, where the Michel Bouviers had bought a house, brought Jack Bouvier, Jacqueline, Emmy Lou, Miche, Cathy, and the twins together for the first time in many years. At the ceremony Jacqueline was godmother to her godfather's son.

Three weeks after the birth of his namesake, Jack Bouvier sold his seat on the New York Stock Exchange for a mere $90,000 (seats in 1929 brought as much as $625,000 and in 1968 $515,000) and retired from business on a capital of approximately $200,000, or a fifth of what the first Bouvier had retired on. The next day, January 28, 1955, he executed his last will and testament.

Jack's will was an elaborate document that differed in one important respect from the wills of his forebears: he left no money to either servants or employees, or to any charities, three categories of legatees which Michel, Sr., MC, and JVB, Jr., had amply provided for in their wills. Although he had always scoffed at his family's dynastic ambitions, he left his nephew and family heir, Michel Bouvier, the third largest legacy, awarding him $3,500 in cash and all his "jewelry, clothing, furniture, furnishings, silverware, plate and china," and leaving $1,000 to each of Michel's two children. Other bequests included $2,500 to Edith; $1,000 to Phelan Beale, Jr.; $1,000 to "each grandchild now or hereafter born"; his desk to Lee; his "picture of Arabian horses by Shreyer" to Jacqueline; and a portrait of his mother to Michelle. The rest and residue of his estate was to be divided equally between Jacqueline and Lee, each of whom would receive approximately $80,000 after taxes.

After retiring from business and drawing up his will, Jack Bouvier became more of a recluse than ever. In bad health—in addition to the slipped disc, he suffered from an inflamed sinus and a diseased liver—he spent most of his time in his New York apartment. His maid, Esther, was by now his only steady companion, since after his retirement from the Stock Exchange he stopped seeing John Carrere and his former clerk, Paul Maricondo. A lean, weatherbeaten Swedish woman with a long, creased neck and protruding eyes, Esther cleaned Jack's apartment, cooked his meals, did his laundry and pressing, loaned him money, foregoing her salary at times, took care of his shopping, accompanied him on his occasional travels, and listened to his endless declarations of love for his daughters. Years later, Jackie would remember Esther's service to her father by contributing to her support in her old age.

Although he saw little of his family now, Jack remained generous to his children and to his nieces and nephews to the end, remembering each of them with a modest check, or a book such as *Forever Amber*, every Thanksgiving, Christmas, Easter, birthday, and graduation. In making out checks, he had the endearing habit of writing a message on the check itself. Thus, a $25 graduation check to a nephew might read: "Congratulations, I never thought you'd make it, but then you *are* my nephew." Or one to a recently engaged niece: "Good luck engaged girl, if we weren't related I'd have beaten him to it." For his nieces and nephews, there was something very touching about receiving a check on a holiday, or a milestone, from Uncle Jack. *His* holiday would invariably be spent alone. And so one had the vision of this lonely man, who would have loved having his family near him, sitting down at his desk in his apartment to write all these checks to relatives he wouldn't even have the enjoyment of seeing on the particular holiday or occasion.

After his retirement Jack and the twins finally became reconciled, burying the bitterness and resentment that had resulted from wrangles over their father's estate. Maude and Michelle sadly recall that during those inactive years Jack frequently had the air of a man who had somehow lost his way. At sixty-four, an age when most of his contemporaries were at the pinnacle of their careers and had large, united families around them, Jack found himself without a business, with very few male friends, and almost without a family. Consequently he came to feel very sorry for himself, confiding occasionally to his sisters that he considered himself a lifelong and undeserved victim . . . of his estranged wife. If Janet hadn't rejected him, forced him to leave her father's apartment, and divorced him, his life would have been far different. For one thing, he would have made much more money, for his divorce had taken a large bite out of his capital at a time when he could have put the money lucratively to work trading. For another, with his family around him he would have won the respect of his father and sisters and would therefore have been able to assume the role of head of the Bouvier clan after JVB, Jr., died.

But these, of course, were merely hypotheses invented to assuage his feelings of personal defeat. In his generation, he was fond of saying, the victors were all women. Jack's misfortunes, however, were due to causes much deeper than his discord with Janet, who certainly was not to blame for divorcing him. In a sense, Major Bouvier's three older children had always been somewhat lost; none of them ever adjusted to the society into which they were born.

When his health permitted, Jack Bouvier managed to squeeze some pleasure out of his retirement by taking an occasional trip to Florida or Cuba, but by March 1957, a little over two years after he sold his Stock Exchange seat, his liver condition had become so serious that he couldn't go far from New York for any significant length of time. Confined to his apartment, with only Esther to comfort him, he had only one joy in life left: a phone call, or a visit, from his daughters.

But phone calls and visits from his daughters were not always regularly forthcoming. Lee was living in London and Jacqueline was the wife of a dynamic young senator with Presidential ambitions; Jackie's first allegiance was naturally to her husband, and the obligations he imposed on her were very demanding.

It was with confused feelings of surprise and joy and pique, then, that Jack Bouvier first learned from the evening paper that Jacqueline was pregnant again (with Caroline). By then John Kennedy's press secretary was quicker than Jacqueline in giving out news of her life. But Jack took her failure to call him first as one more instance of her "neglecting" him.

When Jack took a sudden turn for the worse in midsummer and had to be admitted to Lenox Hill Hospital on July 27, it was Jackie's turn to be taken by surprise: she had no idea her father was so sick. Neither, for that matter, had Jack. His doctors had never told him he had cancer of the liver, so he was totally unprepared for his final torment.

That torment began shortly after he was admitted to the hospital and lasted until August 3, when, on a very hot, humid afternoon, two and a half months after his sixty-sixth birthday, he thought of his darling daughters for the last time.

Deeply shaken by her father's death, Jacqueline flew from Hyannis Port to New York with her husband and quickly took charge of the funeral arrangements. She stayed at her father-in-law's apartment and surprised her family with the decisive, detailed, way she handled everything, from the obituary to the burial.

Dispatching her husband and her Aunt Maude to select the casket, she went to one of her father's woman friends to obtain a favorite photograph for the obituary. Then, after Jack Kennedy and my mother got back from their mission, she sent Jack out again with my father to *The New York Times* with the photo and the text of the obituary, which she insisted Jack deliver *personally* to the managing editor of the newspaper. For the last rites in St. Patrick's she insisted on avoiding a funereal atmosphere by rejecting such standard flower arrangements as crosses of lilies and wreaths of chrysanthemums in favor of garlands of summer flowers in white wicker baskets. "I want everything to look like a summer garden," she told her twin aunts, "like Lasata in August." And so emphasizing that she could never associate her lively, handsome father with death, preferring to remember him gay and debonair, she had his casket festooned with daisies and bachelor's-buttons and set baskets of meadow flowers by the altar. And later, at the burial in St. Philomena's in East Hampton, she made the gravesite a veritable garden of bachelor's-buttons.

There were not many people at the funeral of John Vernou Bouvier III. Besides the family, and Esther, there were no more than two dozen acquaintances and associates. There was, however, one eloquently conspicuous group of mourners whose presence was both touching and appropriate. They were all together in the last pew, wearing long black dresses and impenetrable black veils.

When Jack was finally laid to rest in East Hampton, it was mid-afternoon. Walking away in the August heat from the great mound of blue bachelor's-buttons, the Bouviers began to feel their loss for the first time. Although they hadn't seen much of Jack in the last two years of his life, he had nevertheless been a presence everyone was grateful for. Particularly saddened by his passing were his nieces and nephews. For them, dashing Uncle Jack had been unique and irreplaceable, an elder who consistently outdid them in defying the conventions and respectabilities their parents took so seriously. And, of course, everyone would later regret that he did not live to see the birth of his first grandchild, Caroline Kennedy, and the accession of his beloved Jacqueline to the White House as First Lady of the United States.

# III

THE INAUGURATION OF JOHN F. KENNEDY AS THIRTY-FIFTH PRESIDENT of the United States brought almost all the Bouviers together for the first time since their last summer reunion at Lasata. During the 1950s the family had scattered considerably. Although the twins had remained in New York and the two Ediths in East Hampton, the others had ranged over half the globe. It took an extraordinary event to reunite them. Not even Jackie's marriage to Jack Kennedy had succeeded in doing it. But the inauguration did. On January 19, 1961, Bouviers arrived in Washington from all over the world. Only two members of the family didn't show up: Big Edie, who hadn't ventured from her home in ten years; and Lee Radziwill, who was still recuperating in London from the premature birth of her daughter, Anna Christina. Lee's absence was particularly regretted, for many members of the family had not seen her since her first marriage. Such, in fact, was Jack Kennedy's disappointment at her and Stas's inability to attend the inauguration that, in spite of his demanding schedule, he found time to phone them twice, once early in the morning and once late in the evening, to say how much he missed them.

On the day of the inauguration, Friday, January 20, Washington was cold and clear. Mounds of snow lined the streets, remnants of the blizzard that had prevented everyone from attending the inaugural concert the night before. The city's monuments stood out icily against a deep blue sky. The glare from snow and white marble, the brilliant sun and freezing temperature were exhilarating. The city was supercharged with expectation. Although the ceremonies were not to begin until noon, the streets were crowded with spectators by ten.

An elaborate program of events had been communicated to the Bouviers the day before, along with complex logistical instructions. White House cars were to take them from their hotels to the Capitol for the swearing-in ceremony, for which they had been assigned seats in front of the Presidential platform. After the ceremony, special buses were to take them to a luncheon at the Mayflower, given by Joseph P. Kennedy. After the luncheon, they were to be taken to the reviewing stand in front of the White House for the inaugural parade. A reception in the White House for the Kennedy, Bouvier, Lee, and Auchincloss families was to follow the parade, and then, later, White House cars were to escort all three families to the Inaugural Ball. Although the arrangements were precise in most respects, for some reason they did not include the time of each event. No specific hour was given for the start of the swearing-in ceremony, for instance, either on the official invitation or in the instructions. From the newspapers the Bouviers learned that the swearing-in ceremony was to start at noon. They were quite surprised, therefore, to be notified at ten that their White House cars had arrived. Downing their coffee and hurriedly putting the finishing touches on their clothes, the various family contingents pocketed their instructions and invitations and left their hotels. Our contingent was greeted by a blast of polar wind and an Army corporal from Minnesota who announced that he was our driver for the morning.

On the way to the Capitol we could not help but ponder with some dismay the prospect of sitting in that cold for two hours waiting for the ceremonies to begin. Through the windows of the overheated car—an elongated black Cadillac with jump seats and a partition window that partially screened off the corporal—Washington was an Arctic of icy white marble and glistening snow and the air seemed as frozen as interstellar space. On asking the driver what the temperature was, we received a laconic "Twenty, sir" in reply. When we asked why we were setting out so early, the corporal replied, "Orders." Then, after thinking it over a bit, he added, "Traffic." He drove at attention, never taking his eye off the center line. Only once did he display a trace of human weakness: after repeatedly glancing up at the rear-view mirror, and darting a backward look over his right shoulder, he felt compelled to apologize: "Some guy tailgatin' me." When he arrived in the vicinity of the Capitol and proceeded toward the platform area, he was stopped by a policeman, even though the car had a White House marker on the windshield. "Who're your passengers?" asked the cop. "The Kennedy family," replied the driver. "Ain't no Kennedys in there," snarled the policeman, peering through the rear windows. "Show me your papers." They must have been very convincing, for the policeman suddenly straightened up and waved the car on. "Why did you say we were Kennedys?" asked one of the family, knowing full well why he had. "Who ever heard of the Bouviers?" was the reply.

The corporal was bringing Mrs. Kennedy's twin aunts, together with their sons and daughters, who had just flown in from Rome and Arizona, to the ceremonies. Other White House cars were bringing the married sons of her Aunt Edith, and in another rode the head of the family, Miche Bouvier, with his wife and young son, Michie. It wasn't until we had arrived at our assigned seats that we all finally met, some for the first time in twelve years. A family reunion after twelve years is, under normal circumstances, an emotional event. To have one in front of the Presidential platform the day a close relative's husband is being inaugurated President of the United States was almost unbalancing. The Bouviers were elated, to put it mildly. Busy catching up with one another's activities, they were equally busy coping with the idea of Jacqueline as First Lady. Not that they had been particularly surprised when she finally made it. Ever since Jack Kennedy began dating her in 1952, they had been predicting that this would be her destiny.

While the family was getting reacquainted, the seats and stands in front of the Capitol were filling up, the television equipment was being readied, the Marine band was assembling, and the mercury seemed to be falling. No one was seated. Everyone was shifting from one foot to the other, rubbing gloved hands, pulling coat lapels up over their ears. The Capitol loomed as an immense igloo against an Alaskan sky. The grounds beyond the ceremonial area gleamed with fresh snow. By the time the first dignitaries began appearing on the Presidential platform, there had already been a few casualties. Aunt Michelle had to take refuge in an empty press car. She was so stiff and numb she could hardly walk. When asked by a policeman who she was and what she was doing in the car, she replied that she was Mrs. Kennedy's aunt and that she was cold. He dismissed her as an impostor and told another officer to keep an eye on her. Other guests had to abandon their places to walk up and down the aisles or return to their cars, parked a half mile away. The eventual appearance of some celebrities, however, perked people up a bit. "There's Nixon." "There's Warren." "Hey, isn't that Ike?" Before long the Senate, the House, the Supreme Court, and the incoming and outgoing cabinets had assembled, and only the principals were missing. Then Jackie appeared, wearing a sable-trimmed beige cloth coat and pillbox hat of very simple lines, with her hands in a sable muff. She stood slightly to one side and began chatting with Mrs. Nixon. The Marine band started up. Finally the President-elect arrived, in top hat and chesterfield, tanned and smiling.

There followed, as soon as the band had quieted, the long, monotonal invocation by His Eminence Richard Cardinal Cushing, a solo by Marian Anderson, prayers by ministers of the Greek Orthodox and Protestant faiths, and a poem by Robert Frost which he almost bungled because of the glare on his manuscript. The oath of office was then administered to the new President by the Chief Justice.

The oath taken, Kennedy removed his overcoat and his hat and advanced to the podium to give his inaugural address. And so there he stood, in his cutaway, with no scarf, bareheaded in that freezing cold, as if to forecast what he was about to say, that his was to be an administration calling for sacrifice and courage in the face of adversity. The address was a tonic to the numbed audience. As long as it lasted, they forgot the cold. While Kennedy spoke, Jackie's cousins shifted their eyes back and forth from him to the First Lady. They could not help but fondly recall the days when they were children together, running around their grandfather's estate in East Hampton. Or the birthday parties, Thanksgiving, Christmas, and Easter feasts they had together at Grampy Jack's apartment in New York. Now Jackie no longer belonged to them, but to the nation. Miche Bouvier was deeply moved by the honor Jackie was bringing his family. Little Michie, however, was only interested in when the band was going to play again.

The band played the National Anthem after the President's address and Rabbi Glueck's benediction. Then it was over, and the Bouviers were faced with the problem of getting to Joseph Kennedy's luncheon. Where were the buses that were to take them there? Miche tried to elicit some information from the police and got nowhere. Other members of the family approached the press, the ushers, anyone with a badge on, and were equally defeated. The crowd was heading for the parking area. The cold was paralyzing. Aunt Michelle was still in the press car. It was after one o'clock. Kennedy's luncheon would soon begin. Finally a soldier with a walkie-talkie was accosted. He radioed the Committee on Arrangements and came up with the word: three buses were parked at the East Wing of the Capitol to take President and Mrs. Kennedy's families to the luncheon. The Bouviers made for the East Wing.

When they got there, they had no difficulty spotting the buses. They were decked out with great signs over the windshield:

"Kennedy Family." "Is there a bus for the Bouvier family?" asked Miche, approaching a driver. "You mean Mrs. Kennedy's folks?" "Yes." "They go in the Kennedy buses," said the driver. Miche laughingly spread the word and some seventeen Bouviers filed into the one bus that was not already full. A few of JFK's cousins were in it, plus a group of Auchinclosses.

The trip down Massachusetts Avenue to the Mayflower had a surrealist aura to it. The entire length of the avenue had been cleared of traffic. There was not so much as a parked car along it. On either side, the crowd stood ten deep behind mounds of plowed snow, silently waiting for the President. Here were thousands and thousands of people lining one of the main arteries of Washington, yet there was almost complete silence. Slowly the three "Kennedy Family" buses rumbled down the silent, crowd-lined avenue, preceded by a police escort. Nothing in sight but the vast empty avenue, the endless, silent crowd, the white snow and white marble buildings, and the cold, clear sky. Bouvier Beale, to break the eerie spell, began waving at the crowd through one of the front windows, and the crowd waved back. The waving sent a ripple of movement down the long line of spectators, and before long they were all waving and then they were cheering and finally, by the time the buses stopped in front of the Mayflower, the noise was deafening. Kennedys, Bouviers, Lees, and Auchinclosses headed for the hotel through a corridor of klieg lights, television cameras, policemen, and onlookers, soon to find themselves in the hotel's rose and blue East Room, where a sumptuous buffet was spread over an immense center table. It remained for Rose Kennedy to make the introductions. Most members of the four families present had never met.

Between Rose and the other mother of honor, Janet Auchincloss, the introductions were made, more or less, and everyone was then free to turn to the buffet. For a while the four families, at least sixty people in all, milled around the enormous table examining the spread: hors d'oeuvres, hot soups, lobster Newburg, Alaskan king crab, blue points on the half shell, shrimp cocktail, roast turkey, duck a l'orange, roast beef, pheasant, whole baked salmons, varieties of salad . . . Several Bouviers stopped to chat with the host, who appeared incredibly blasé for a man whose son had just become President of the United States. He acknowledged congratulations with a slight nod and a faint smile and scarcely uttered a word. It seemed as if he were savoring his family's victory deep inside and was not about to cheapen it by an outward display of enthusiasm. A picture of humility, almost inconspicuous, he picked away at the buffet unassumingly, as if he were a fifth cousin of the President's maternal grandaunt.

Rose Kennedy too was extremely quiet and unassuming. She did not appear particularly at ease unless she was talking to a member of her own family. Between the Bouviers and the Kennedys there had never been any significant altercations and yet something intangible kept them from establishing a relationship.

Before long, as soon as everyone had helped himself to a first course and found a place at a table, the various families had separated completely. Rose and Joe and the other Kennedys were seated together at five or six tables to one side of the room, and the Bouviers, the Lees, and the Auchinclosses, who had banded together as one family, were seated at five or six tables on the other side of the room. The buffet table became a no-man's-land between the two camps, into which occasional forays were made by both sides. It was only over helping oneself to a lobster claw, say, or another slice of duck a l'orange, that an occasional exchange was made between a Kennedy and a Bouvier. Once served, each would retire to his corner.

Whether the Kennedys were conscious of the invisible barriers between the two families, it was hard to tell. The Bouviers assumed that the Kennedys, as hosts, would mix the two families at the tables, but not the slightest effort was made to do so. "The Montagues and the Capulets, that's who we are," quipped a Bouvier. "What about us?" put in an Auchincloss. "You can play Friar Laurence, if you want to." "Alack, alack, this marriage will never work," was the reply.

So there sat the Kennedys on one side of the room, minding their own business. The President's sisters, Pat and Jean, were as quiet as their mother and father. Was this the clan that had been so unbeatable in congressional, then senatorial, then national, elections? What did it take to put them in high gear? . . . Being out of office. Now that the prize had been won, they were resting. Gathering strength for Ted's campaign two years hence. After all, there was nothing to be won from the Bouviers or the Auchinclosses. What could one gain from a bunch of die-hard anti-New Dealers anyway?

In contrast, the Bouviers and the Auchinclosses were enjoying themselves immensely. They had not all voted against Kennedy, and those who had were not at all upset at the way the election had turned out. Several of them were prompted to order a toast to the new President, but the new President's family was so distant no one could get up enough nerve to do it. "By God," someone exclaimed, "a Bouvier should be toasting Jack Kennedy and a Kennedy should be toasting Jackie and all of us should be toasting . . ." ". . . an Auchincloss," interjected an Auchincloss.

Before long, Joe Kennedy announced to his own family that it was time to go. The parade was about to begin. The Kennedys then rose and filed out. The Bouviers, the Lees, and the Auchinclosses followed. Soon the three huge buses were filled and the four families under one banner were heading for the reviewing stands.

The stands had been erected along Pennsylvania Avenue in front of the White House. The buses entered the White House grounds through the South Entrance and let their passengers off by the South Portico at the rear of the Executive Mansion. Kennedys, Bouviers, Lees, and Auchinclosses were then escorted by an aide into the White House, and out again, and were finally brought down the front drive and out the main gate to the reviewing stand. A coffee bar had been set up under the Presidential stand, at which there was a lone customer, Robert Kennedy, who, as a member of the new cabinet, had attended not the family luncheon but the official luncheon in the Capitol building for President and Mrs. Kennedy and the incoming government.

By the time the four families reached the stands and took their seats, the afternoon sun was well into the Western sky and Washington had grown bleaker and colder. The parade had already begun. It was supposed to last until six. How to survive three hours of parade in near-zero weather with only an open-air coffee bar to counteract the cold? Kennedys, Bouviers, Lees, and Auchinclosses pondered the problem, but Jack Kennedy appeared oblivious to it. There he was, hatless, scarfless, in the center of the Presidential box, grinning, talking, cheering each new contingent that marched by, applauding outstanding performances, spending himself, enjoying himself, with his wife by his side frozen to the bone. *He* couldn't take time out for a coffee; *he* couldn't go warm up for a minute in the White House. Other dignitaries were coming and going from the stands, but he had to stay there to the bitter end and cheer each float, each regiment of drum majorettes, as it trooped by.

After a while the new First Lady was seen to rise, shake hands with Vice President and Mrs. Johnson, pat her husband on the shoulder, and leave the stands, accompanied by an Air Force aide. It was around 3:30. The parade was still going strong and President Kennedy was still cheering, smiling, applauding as the blue-kneed, blue-lipped majorettes pranced by. If they were cold, what about the immobile audience? Paralyzed, numbed to silent forbearance. It was only a question of who would give up first. Finally someone said, "Let's go into the White House," and everybody did just that.

The "Reception for Members of President and Mrs. Kennedy's Families" was the first Kennedy party held in the White House and was to start as soon as the parade was over. Instead, it started as soon as the members of President and Mrs. Kennedy's families arrived, which was around a quarter to five.

The party was held in the State Dining Room on the State Floor, and even though the guests were an hour early, everything was already set up for the festivities. Jackie's social secretary, Tish Baldridge, had done an excellent job. There, in a green-walled room with mahogany furniture, a brass chandelier, and Healy's portrait of Abraham Lincoln, was a large table laden with all that the freezing guests had been dreaming about for the past four hours. In addition to the great silver tea services and coffee urns, the trays of cocktails, the relishes, the sandwiches, the cakes and cookies, the tall bourbons and water, a special attraction was the immense punch bowl filled with Russian caviar, surrounded by plates of crackers, toast squares, slices of lemon, and mounds of chopped egg. It soon became the center of attention, the focal point around which the party revolved.

The culmination of the reception was, of course, to be the arrival of the new President and his First Lady. The First Lady was already in the White House, having left the parade some time before. Her husband was not due in until the parade was over. From inside the room, you could dimly hear the drums and tubas and cymbals. Most of Jack Kennedy's family had abandoned him, but he was still out there cheering the marchers on.

As at the luncheon in the Mayflower, Rose Kennedy and Janet Auchincloss handled the introductions and acted, in general, as co-hostesses. There were new additions to each family to be introduced. Janet's sisters' children, the Ryans and the d'Oliers, appeared, the Ryans having flown in from South America. Peter Lawford and Ted Kennedy showed up. Little Edie Beale arrived.

Since there were more Bouviers, Lees, and Auchinclosses at the function than Kennedys, Republicans outnumbered Democrats, and several of them lost no time in casting aspersions on the visible evidence of "government spending." The enormous bowl of Russian caviar, around which at least fifteen Bouviers and Auchinclosses were buzzing, became a prime target of conservative criticism. It was variously estimated that, at five dollars a half ounce, at least a thousand dollars' worth of caviar was in the bowl. "The grand they nailed me for on that rejected deduction." "Wonder how many tons of this they serve a year." "Oh, maybe it's a gift from Khrushchev." As they all helped themselves to more.

When six o'clock came and neither the President nor the First Lady had arrived, the guests began to wander around the White House. Pat Lawford and Jean Smith were among the first to begin exploring. They ambled through the vast, empty rooms, sampling the damasked walls, the French eighteenth-century furniture, followed by groups of Bouviers and Auchinclosses... Down the Cross Hall to the white and gold East Room with its gilt columns and enormous chandeliers. Then into the smaller Green Room with its charming portrait of Angelica Van Buren and its green silk damask walls. From the Green Room to the oval Blue Room, hung with blue and gold silk and furnished with gilded fauteuils. Then on to the Red Room, hung in cerise silk with gold scroll borders, and containing the usual French furniture and a convex mirror surmounted by a Napoleonic golden eagle. And finally back into the spacious pale green State Dining Room with its immense bowl of caviar . . . A Bouvier, attempting to walk up a stairway off the Entrance Hall after inspecting the State Rooms, was stopped by a Secret Service man and told that the second floor was out of bounds. "Mrs. Kennedy is resting up there," said the agent. "But I'm her cousin." "I don't care . . . She left instructions she was not to be disturbed." When was Jackie coming down? Everyone was asking the same question.

By now the party was in full swing. The White House had been thoroughly explored, with the exception of Jackie's forbidden areas; almost all the guests had arrived, and everyone had had a drink. Peter Lawford was looking terribly busy and important, shaking hands with everyone as if he had just been elected

President. Ted Kennedy was coming and going, going and coming from the reception room as if he were on the alert for something. Was he checking to see if the President was coming? Where *was* the President? Still out in the cold. You could still hear the drums and the tubas and the cymbals in the distance. Would the parade never end?

At a certain point Janet Auchincloss disappeared, then returned to announce that Jackie "was still resting." "She's up in the Queens bedroom, trying to relax," she said. "She's taken a pill. I don't know if she'll be down." The disappointment was acute. Several Bouviers and Ryans had flown thousands of miles to see her. After a while Miche decided to see for himself. With Janet Auchincloss's authentication, the Secret Service man let him up. He returned fifteen minutes later to report that Jackie was in the Queens bedroom trying to get some rest so she would be able to face the five Inaugural Balls that evening. "Will she be down at all?" everyone asked. "I don't know," replied Miche.

It now appeared that the party might not be attended by the two people everyone had come to congratulate. To compensate for this possible disappointment, the caviar and cocktails were assaulted with renewed vigor. People began to loosen up. Little Edie Beale approached J. P. Kennedy, who was looking his usual unassuming self, and reminded him jokingly that she had once almost been engaged to his first-born son, Joe, Jr. And if he had lived, she probably would have married him and *he* would have become President instead of Jack and *she* would have become First Lady instead of Jackie! J. P. Kennedy smiled and took another drink.

Probably because she was upset about her daughter's not having come down, Janet Auchincloss redoubled her efforts as hostess. Ably she took charge of the party, ordering waiters here and there, introducing newcomers, apologizing to everyone for "Jackie's indisposition." It was grudgingly agreed that Jackie did have several good excuses for not attending. She had given birth to JFK, Jr., prematurely by Caesarian a little over a month before. She had been through a hard day, and she had to attend five balls that night. Still, it was disappointing. "Where's Jackie?" "Isn't she coming down even for a *minute* . . . for her first party as First Lady?" Janet Auchincloss was hard pressed. She had to do all the explaining.

Members of both families were congratulating Ambassador Kennedy on his son's accession to the Presidency, congratulations which he received with humility and grace, when all of a sudden the far-off band music stopped. Even though the parade was quite some distance away and the music was barely audible, everyone was conscious that it had stopped. The President would soon arrive. It was almost seven. The parade was an hour late in ending. According to someone who had just come back from the stands, everybody had left the reviewing box but JFK. Instinctively the guests moved toward the entrance to the room. A few expectant minutes . . . then suddenly there he was, the new President, entering the White House for the first time as President. His relatives moved forward to greet him. Janet Auchincloss ran up and kissed him on the cheek, saying he must be "so cold." Sisters, cousins, aunts, in-laws flung their arms around his neck. He greeted each with a smile, a hug, a pat on the back, a handshake. He looked marvelous. He had gotten up, reputedly, at 6:30, after only four hours of sleep, had gone through the swearing-in ceremony, had delivered his inaugural address, attended the inaugural luncheon, and reviewed a seemingly endless inaugural parade, and he looked as if he hadn't done a thing all day. Fresh. Vigorous. Smiling. Everyone was astonished by his stamina. Briskly he strode about the room saying hello to relatives and in-laws. Then he asked where Jackie was. "She's upstairs, resting," someone replied. Jack Kennedy acknowledged the news with a faint look of incomprehension, greeted a few more relatives, accepted a drink, and then announced he had better get ready for the ball. The first was due to start at ten. At this point Michel was suddenly summoned by Jackie and he spent the next half hour with her and Jack as they dressed for the evening's festivities. The reception broke up in a gay mood, in spite of Jackie's absence. "I don't blame her," said one of her cousins. "It's more important that she be rested for her TV appearance tonight than waste time with her relatives." "Still, she could have come down for a *second*," someone else insisted. "Just to say hello." Later, over dinner, the Bouviers concluded that it was probably easier for Jackie, who had always been shy with her relatives, to face the entire nation on TV than it was to confront her four families on that momentous day. To America she was the new First Lady. To the Bouviers, Lees, Auchinclosses, and Kennedys she was just Jackie. To play both roles required impossible shifts of emotional gear. Michel, who had seen Jackie upstairs, agreed with the interpretation.

Jackie looked exquisite at the Inaugural Ball that evening in her long white chiffon dress and Kenneth hairdo. Her family, her friends, the public, TV viewers throughout the nation had never seen her so radiant. After dropping in on the subsidiary balls, the Kennedys had finally arrived at the main one, the grand finale of the day's ceremonies. It was being held in the National Guard Armory, a vast, oval-shaped structure that resembled a covered football field. When the Bouviers arrived in their assigned box, near that of the President and the Vice President, the Armory was packed. The Kennedys, the Bouviers, the Lees, the Auchinclosses, and the distinguished guests were given seats on a balcony overlooking the Armory floor. Powerful searchlights were trained on the silk-draped Presidential box, so that JFK and Jackie were always looking into a blinding glare. Through the crisscrossing beams of light danced bits of confetti and billows of blue cigarette smoke. The TV cameras bore in from all sides and the orchestra blared from below midst a deafening tumult of voices and scuffling feet. Jack Kennedy had put in a twelve-hour day charged with excitement and great demands on his energies, yet he still looked fresh and vital. So did his wife. That rest in the afternoon had made sense. Now even Joe and Rose had come alive. Had they been storing their reserves of enthusiasm for this triumphant moment when the eyes of the nation were upon them? Suddenly the Kennedy family had awakened. They knew they were on stage and had to perform like the victors they were. Gone the unassuming indifference. Now they were smiling, greeting friends, shouting at friends, laughing, moving from box to box. It was an incredible transformation from the reception six hours before. Perhaps they needed Jack's presence to catch fire. Only one thing was certain. As soon as the spotlights were turned on, and the TV cameras began zeroing in, the Kennedys became the President's family for the first time that day.

It was impossible to dance at the Inaugural Ball. The dance floor was miles away and was always overcrowded. You couldn't hear the music. And waiters, taking short cuts through the dancers, were constantly in the way. The ball was not a party but a payoff, a way of thanking campaign donors, ward bosses, state committee chairmen, loyal employees, big fish and little fish, everybody who had the remotest hand in the Kennedy triumph. "I went to JFK's Inaugural Ball": that's what they wanted to say back home. And so the ball was impossible. The millions who viewed it on television got the best impression of it. There they were, Jack and Jackie, Lyndon and Lady Bird, Joe and Rose, Bobby and Ted . . . and who are those other people? They were Bouviers, Lees, and Auchinclosses anonymously basking in the fringes of the lights, wondering, among other things, what the future held in store for the couple who had unwittingly brought them into those lights, wondering what had been inaugurated. Later, after shaking Jack's and Jackie's hand, and wishing them well, everyone got lost. The family's Marine aides could not be found. The official cars were nowhere to be seen. Husbands got separated from wives and children from both. Almost everyone in the First Lady's family had to get back to his hotel on his own. And so the Bouviers dispersed once again.

# IV

DURING THEIR 150-YEAR AMERICAN ADVENTURE, THE BOUVIERS made many returns to France. The first great homecoming was, of course, Michel's long-delayed visit to his birthplace in 1853, when, as a local boy made good, he had proudly displayed his daughters and his success to his brother, sisters, and childhood companions. Subsequently, Louise Bouvier had made her novitiate at Conflans; Emma Bouvier and Francis Drexel had spent part of their honeymoon at Pont-Saint-Esprit; and in 1880. Mary, Zénaïde, and Alexine, with JVB, Jr., in tow, had made their breathless, spinster pilgrimage to the land of their forefathers. Many other homecomings followed: Emma and her daughters' in 1886; JVB, Jr.'s honeymoon in 1890; MC's reunion with his French cousins in 1916; Captain Bud Bouvier's service to France in 1918 and 1919; the twins' graduation present of 1923; and Jacqueline's year of study in 1949 and 1950. These, however, were preludes to the most triumphant *retour* of all: those three days in Paris in late May and early June of 1961 when Jacqueline Bouvier Kennedy came into her own.

The Kennedys' state visit to France in 1961 presented Jacqueline with the greatest challenge of her thirty-one years: representing her nation to Europe in a time of great international tension. In a country where faultfinding is almost a way of life, she, as an American of French descent, was particularly vulnerable. Her speech, her mannerisms, her clothes, her coiffures, her activities would be scrutinized and judged every minute of her stay.

It was with a great sense of relief, then, that she found herself both an instantaneous and an enduring success. Upon her arrival with her husband at Orly the morning of May 31, wearing the simple wool coat and pillbox hat that had become her trademark, she was greeted by an enormous crowd shouting "Vive Jacqui" which seemingly ignored the chief of state who escorted her and the chief of state who greeted her. And during the motorcade to Paris, crowds estimated at 200,000 reserved their loudest cheers not for the lead car but the car bearing Mrs. Kennedy and Madame de Gaulle.

Down the boulevard Saint-Michel, the section Jacqueline had known as a student at the Sorbonne; a 101-gun salute in the Place de la Concorde; and into the immense, cheering crowds at the

Quai d'Orsay, where the Kennedys were to occupy the state suite. A brief breathcatcher and a change of clothes; then, at the Elysée Palace, before luncheon with the de Gaulles, another mob scene of thousands shouting "Vive Jacqui! Vive Jacqui" Followed by still another demonstration, this time in front of the Child Welfare Clinic run by the Red Cross on avenue Brunne, where thousands broke through police lines to welcome "la jolie Jacqui." They even stood in the rain to greet Jacqueline that day, enduring a spring downpour before the Elysée Palace in the evening to applaud her as she arrived for de Gaulle's state dinner.

Among the thousands who greeted Jacqueline Kennedy the evening of May 31 was her cousin, Michel Bouvier, and his wife, Cathy. Michel had recently been appointed assistant to Grumman Aircraft's Director of Operations for Europe and the Middle East and had just moved his family from Long Island to Paris. It was at the state dinner for the Kennedys that Michel had his first opportunity to welcome Jackie to France. The event was a triumphant moment in Bouvier family history. One hundred and forty-six years after the defeated and penniless Michel Bouvier was forced to flee the vindictive aftermath of Waterloo, his great-great-grandson, Michel Bouvier, was greeting his cousin, First Lady of the United States, at a reception given by the President of France.

Although the event was momentous, its circumstances were far from solemn. After Jacqueline became First Lady, Bouviers began popping out of the woodwork of hundreds of French homes, scores of them, from Calais to Marseilles, claiming blood relationship to her. The U.S. Embassy and the U.S. Information Service were deluged by requests from her supposed cousins to be permitted to meet her. And so, when a man appeared before the receiving line at the Elysée, and was announced as Michel Bouvier, he received a glower from General de Gaulle and a look of embarrassed befuddlement from Madame de Gaulle: they were sure a spurious Bouvier had slipped past the palace guards. In the midst of the ensuing confusion, however, Jacqueline recognized her cousin and saved him from ignominious expulsion by stepping out of the receiving line and kissing him on the cheek. It was then that Michel said: "Bienvenue en France."

The following day, June 1, Jacqueline and her secretaries were gratified to learn from the French press that she had brilliantly passed her first inspection. Both the Greek-style toga gown by

Oleg Cassini and the medieval-princess coiffure she wore for the state dinner had won near unanimous approval from the fashion editors, and the papers were full of miscellaneous articles extoling her poise, her warmth, her superb Parisian accent.

Although a private fashion show had been offered her by the couturiers of Paris, political considerations prevented her from attending it. The American public was observing her as closely as the French, and it would not have pleased housewives in Kansas and Oregon if their First Lady had spent her time in Paris looking over Diors and Balenciagas. Thus, when she was asked at a reception for American and French newspaperwomen why she did not go to the Paris fashion shows, she replied: "I have more important things to do."

As it turned out, however, Jacqueline did make one important concession to the French fashion world, and that was the wearing of a Givenchy to the state dinner in the Galerie des Glaces at Versailles on the evening of June 1. It had been her original intention to wear another Oleg Cassini, but at the last minute, at the risk of angering the International Ladies Garment Workers Union, she decided to pay a tribute to the French couturiers by appearing in a Givenchy. The gown, of white satin embroidered with rhinestones, with a pale red, white, and blue bodice, won her and Givenchy immediate applause. With her Alexandre hair-do and diamond tiara, Jacqueline never looked more regal.

The dinner in the dazzling Hall of Mirrors was perhaps the most sumptuous state affair the Kennedys ever attended. Invitations to Versailles that evening were so highly coveted that scores of Americans and Parisians, whose sense of self-importance had led them to assume they should have been invited, were forced to leave Paris rather than face the shame of having been excluded.

Among those who had been honored with an invitation were two members of the First Lady's family, Lee Radziwill and Michel Bouvier. Michel recalls that despite enormous pressures, for the eyes of everyone present were constantly upon her, Jackie conducted herself with extraordinary assurance and grace, displaying remarkable stamina as she smiled warmly again and again and kept up a marathon stream of conversation with her hosts and their guests.

The culmination of the evening was the ballet performance in Versailles's exquisite Louis XV Theater, and once again Jacqueline rose to the occasion magnificently. Appearing in the royal box with her husband and the de Gaulles, she stood at dignified attention while the orchestra played "The Star-Spangled Banner" and "La Marseillaise," then charmed the audience with a wonderful smile as the guests turned toward the box and applauded the two first families after the national anthems.

The photographs of the Versailles evening which appeared in the papers the following day put the final seal on Jacqueline Kennedy's Parisian triumph. There she was in her sparkling white satin gown and diamond tiara looking more regal than any of the currently reigning queens of Europe. To the style-conscious French she was a revelation. An American girl with such dignity, such charm, such faultless taste. So overwhelmingly approving was her reception by both the general public and the leaders of taste and opinion that President Kennedy was moved to make the by now famous quip before the Paris Press Club at the Palais de Chaillot on the last day of his visit: "I am the man who accompanied Jacqueline Kennedy to Paris and I have enjoyed it."

From France, the Kennedys went on to meet with the Khrushchevs in Vienna and with Elizabeth II and Prince Philip in London. While in London, Jack Kennedy was godfather at the christening of Lee Radziwill's second child, Anna Christina, born the previous August 18. The tour concluded with a state dinner at Buckingham Palace, during which the Kennedys enjoyed still another unqualified success.

By the time the President and the First Lady returned to Washington, American prestige in Europe had soared to unprecedented heights. Europeans could relate to the Kennedys: they possessed qualities not always characteristic of American public figures. In one stroke they had annihilated the American stereotype. Now America would no longer be synonymous with bad taste and awkward manners. A fresh new image of their countrymen had been projected by the President and his wife which was to be of more benefit to the United States' interests in Europe than all the treaties supposedly holding the two worlds together. Reciprocally, a new appreciation of the Kennedys in America was launched by their European welcome which helped overcome much of the resistance they had encountered in their first four months in office. Now the First Lady could go on, with relatively little opposition, to accomplish her great work of restoring the White House and lending support to the best her country had to offer in the arts.

## $\mathcal{V}$

ON RETURNING TO THE WHITE HOUSE FROM HER STATE TOUR OF Europe, Jacqueline Kennedy found herself in a much more advantageous position than she had been in before. Having received unqualified praise from the European press and public, she could now act more confidently in her own nation. Although she would always have her critics, the widespread diffidence she had initially encountered from many of her fellow Americans would largely evaporate. Now, at last, she could enjoy the freedom of being herself. And in being herself she would create a new image of the American woman.

Not only did Jacqueline Kennedy win a new acceptance from the American public, but she also won a new acceptance from her husband. The state visit to Europe, especially, had made the President more aware than ever what an exceptional asset his beautiful young wife could be. In marrying her he had acquired what the Kennedys generally lacked: elegance, cosmopolitan appeal, and a link with their nation's past.

As the first First Lady of Southern European origins in United States history, and one of the few who had received training capable of fitting her for her high position, Jacqueline Bouvier Kennedy had a unique opportunity. Before this time, for the most part, a First Lady conformed to what the public expected of her, adopting the public's ideal as her own. Jacqueline, however, presented the country with a new concept of the role, a concept very much her own. Being of an artistic temperament, she had devoted herself more to self-cultivation than to social welfare. Thus, she was concerned with things not usually associated with Americans: with form, manners, ceremony, visual beauty— bringing an exquisite sense of appropriateness and elegance to her duties as First Lady. In keeping with her Latin temperament, she confounded the women of the nation by being self-centered, mercurial, and unpredictable; everything most American women were not but perhaps secretly wanted to be.

Jacqueline Kennedy's impact on the public was essentially a triumph of style, and the creation of that style is part of the story of her family. It took five generations of Bouviers to forge that rare combination of elegance, poise, *mystère*, sense of appropriateness, and sense of drama that made the new First Lady such a unique American. The foundations of her style were, of course, laid down by the first Michel and his wife, Louise Vernou. Michel had made the money that had allowed his children the time and freedom to cultivate their minds and sensibilities, and Louise Vernou had provided them with the guidance in manners and taste. Subsequently, fifty-four years of affluent, elegant living at MC's New York brownstone, and the marriages of Emma and John V. into families that had already attained a high style of their own, further refined the Bouvier taste. That taste was then transmitted to the family heir, John V., Jr., who finally brought it to maturity in the incomparable elegance and beauty of Lasata. It remained for JVB III to add a slightly theatrical flair to the Bouvier aesthetic and, in turn, to transmit his family's mature style to his daughters. It was Jack's posthumous triumph that Jacqueline would then project that style to the entire world.

Jacqueline Kennedy was fortunate to have three areas of activity open to her as First Lady in which she could express her style and personality to the fullest: redecorating the White House, entertaining visiting statesmen, and lending Presidential patronage to the best in the American performing arts.

Mrs. Kennedy's restoration of the White House was her most ambitious undertaking as First Lady. When Jacqueline first entered the White House she found it a dreary place whose vast halls and rooms were filled for the most part with solemn official portraits and furnishings that often clashed with the style of the rooms they occupied. Furthermore, the mansion had a singularly unlived-in look. No flowers in the vases. No ashtrays. No objects on the tables. To dispel this mournful atmosphere, Mrs. Kennedy conceived the project of restoring the mansion to its original state by refurbishing it with authentic pieces from the early 1800s, when it was originally built, and adding certain personal touches of her own. Her purpose was nothing less than to make the White House "the most perfect house in the United States," a source of inspiration to all Americans. It was ironic that she should address herself to this undertaking, when her father took almost no interest in history or tradition. Her inclination, then, insofar as we can attribute it to heredity and upbringing, must ultimately have stemmed from her grandfather, JVB, Jr., who spent a lifetime reconstructing his family's history and preserving its traditions.

To implement her plans, Jacqueline Kennedy asked Henry Francis du Pont, creator of the Winterthur Museum in Wilmington, to assume general advisory responsibility for the project. Subsequently, a White House Fine Arts Committee was organized, with David Finley as chairman; a bill was passed through Congress making the White House a National Monument; the position of White House Curator was instituted; and, in the autumn of 1961, the White House Historical Association was incorporated, "to enhance the understanding, appreciation and enjoyment of the Executive Mansion." Soon a campaign was begun for private donations which met with an enthusiastic response. Among the many contributions, Mr. and Mrs. Douglas Dillon gave a mahogany library table executed by Charles Honore Lanvier, a French-born cabinetmaker who worked in New York about the same time as Michel Bouvier worked in Philadelphia; for the Blue Room, George Wildenstein donated Jean Honoré Fragonard's "Apotheosis of Franklin"; and Dr. Ray C. Franklin of Mt. Kisco, New York, contributed a Hepplewhite mirror with Washington's likeness and a carved golden eagle that once hung in New York's Fraunces Tavern. Other gifts included furniture that had belonged to George Washington, Abraham Lincoln, James Madison, and Daniel Webster. Among the items loaned was a pier table that had belonged to Joseph Bonaparte at Point Breeze.

One gift that was particularly cherished by Jacqueline and members of her family was two maple chairs in Empire style, made by Michel Bouvier in 1820. They were donated by Mr. and Mrs. Henry T. MacNeill of Whitford, Pennsylvania, who had purchased them from a great-grandson of Michel's, John Vernou Bouvier Patterson. Eventually the chairs were installed in the Presidential living quarters. The old cabinetmaker would have been pleased.

Among the many changes effected in the White House, a few are of particular interest. The hanging of a Cézanne landscape in the Green Room. The almost total redecoration of the Red Room in French and American Empire (the styles Michel Bouvier worked in); the restoration of the Blue Room to the way it looked at the time of James Monroe, using copies of the Bellangé fauteuil the fifth President had ordered for the room. And the redecoration of the Diplomatic Reception Room, using some unusual scenic wallpaper by the early nineteenth-century French designer, Zuber. Almost all the principal rooms of the White House received at least a new touch, if not a thorough refurbishing. Some rooms were fortunate to have a bright Mary Cassatt replace a stuffy official portrait. Only one room was left untouched: Lincoln's bedroom. When the work was finally completed, about $2 million had been spent, mostly from private donations.

When Jacqueline was a young girl, she visited the White House as a tourist with her mother and lamented the fact that no written guide to the mansion was available. To remedy this lack, and also to enshrine the changes she had brought about, she asked John Walker, director of the National Gallery, to assist her in the preparation of a guidebook. She was further assisted by the National Geographic Society, which provided all the photographs for the book. The result was a volume that became an immediate best seller and is still the standard guide to the Executive Mansion. Five months before its publication, Mrs. Kennedy took the American public on a guided tour of their partially restored White House in an unprecedented telecast, over three major networks, viewed by more than 56,000,000 people. It was the first of two occasions when the eyes of almost the entire nation were upon her.

In keeping with her wish to promote her country's best, Jacqueline Kennedy was determined to raise social life in the White House to a new standard of excellence, to make both formal state receptions and informal parties occasions of good taste and warm hospitality which those who attended would never forget. The Roosevelts had not emphasized entertaining at the White House because of the Depression and the war. Under the Trumans, parties were homespun and folksy—as American as Thanksgiving in Missouri. And under the Eisenhowers, White House functions, though friendly and well organized, were generally uninspired. For years the best parties in Washington were given by people other than the President and First Lady; by professional hostesses like Gwen Cafritz or Perle Mesta or foreign diplomats like the French Ambassador. The Kennedys decided it was time the White House assumed first place in the social life of the nation. The number-one hostess in Washington should not be a private citizen with no official status but the First Lady of the United States.

Jacqueline Kennedy was literally bred to be a great hostess. Lavish entertaining was in the Bouvier tradition. The John V. Bouviers, Jr., had been famous for their sumptuous parties at Lasata, affairs at which Jacqueline was often pressed into service to pass canapés and drinks. And the John V. Bouviers III, before they were divorced, had also entertained in high style in New York and East Hampton. Jacqueline had also been exposed to the Auchinclosses' functions and to rounds of debutante parties in Newport, New York, and Long Island. By the time she became a senator's wife she had received an education in entertaining second to none.

As Washington's first hostess, Jacqueline passionately believed that in the White House the best food possible should be served, the highest standards of dress maintained, and the finest performing artists in America be seen and heard. She applied the same high standards to her guest lists. For the first time in decades, Nobel Prize winners, leading writers, outstanding scientists and composers found themselves invited to the Executive Mansion. What made Jacqueline Kennedy's White House parties the wonderful occasions they were, however, was not solely her insistence on quality but the marvelous way she and her husband combined haute cuisine, haute couture, and haute culture with gaiety and informality, thus preventing their gala affairs from becoming stiff or intimidating.

Among the great Kennedy parties, the most unusual, and also the most controversial, was the state dinner given for the President of Pakistan, Mohammed Ayub Khan, at Mount Vernon on July 11, 1961. Inspired by the French government's use of historical monuments such as Versailles for such functions, Jacqueline conceived the idea of holding the dinner at Washington's home on the Potomac, and quickly won the approval of her husband. The affair was an enormous success. Kennedy's yacht, the *Honey Fitz*, and two smaller boats borrowed from the Navy, each equipped with a band, transported the guests down the Potomac. Before dinner, mint juleps in silver cups were served on Mount Vernon's veranda, as in Washington's time. The dinner itself was served on small tables grouped under a green and yellow marquee on the lawn, overlooking the river. Display decorators from Tiffany's and Bonwit Teller's provided the décor; René Verdon prepared the food at the White House and shipped it down the Potomac in Army field kitchens. After dinner, the National Symphony held a concert on the lawn.

Other noteworthy parties included the state dinner for President Abboud of Sudan on October 4, 1961, which was followed by recitations from Shakespeare by members of the American

Shakespeare Festival Theatre; the state dinner for Governor and Mrs. Muñoz Marín of Puerto Rico, followed by a concert by Pablo Casals and attended by such distinguished American composers as Samuel Barber, Elliot Carter, and Walter Piston; and the state dinner for the Shah and Empress of Iran, which featured a performance by the Jerome Robbins ballet.

An altogether unique occasion was the dinner given on April 29, 1962, for Nobel Prize winners of the Western Hemisphere at which Fredric March read selections from the works of earlier American Nobel Prize winners in literature and John F. Kennedy made his famous remark: "I think this is the most extraordinary collection of talent, of human knowledge, that has ever been gathered together at the White House, with the possible exception of when Thomas Jefferson dined alone." The party was followed, on May 11, by another remarkable gathering, the dinner for André Malraux, Minister of State for Cultural Affairs of France, at which Isaac Stern, Leonard Rose, and Eugene Istomin played trios for violin, cello, and piano—a dinner attended by Saul Bellow, Elia Kazan, Robert Lowell, Arthur Miller, and Andrew Wyeth, among others.

In addition to serving as hostess for innumerable parties for world leaders and distinguished figures in the arts and sciences, Mrs. Kennedy presided over five musical programs for young people held on the White House lawn, opened an exhibit of Egyptian art at the National Gallery, and helped establish the National Cultural Center on the east bank of the Potomac, now named for her husband.

Through the charm of her public personality, Mrs. Kennedy was able to win widespread approval of her activities as First Lady, but she was not without occasional critics. Generally speaking, the criticism reflected a provincial disapproval of "extravagance" in the name of art. Thus, the president of the American Institute of Interior Designers of New York chided her for the installation of the Zuber wallpaper. Jacqueline had greatly admired the wallpaper in a home in Maryland. Accepting it as a gift to the White House, she had it taken down and put up in the Diplomatic Reception room at a cost of $12,500. Evidently the process of removing the faded antique paper from plaster walls was extremely painstaking and time consuming. According to the president of the American Institute, the paper could easily have been duplicated, since the original printing blocks were still in existence. "I don't know how faded the paper is," he stated, "but some people like old, broken-down things because they are old and broken down. Maybe Mrs. Kennedy is one of them."

The Mount Vernon dinner for President Ayub Khan also earned Mrs. Kennedy considerable criticism. Why go to the trouble and expense of ferrying poulet chasseur couronne de riz clamart and framboises à la crème Chantilly fifteen miles down the Potomac when steak and ice cream could have been served in the White House just as well?

Perhaps the most vehement criticism of Mrs. Kennedy as First Lady stemmed from her extended foreign travels unaccompanied by her husband. Here again Jacqueline was unique. Few First Ladies in United States history had ever undertaken a trip comparable to the Asian journey she made in March and April 1962. It had been scheduled for November 1961, but since Thanksgiving and the birthdays of both her children fell in that month, Jacqueline was persuaded to postpone the trip. The American public could accept, reluctantly, framboises à la crème Chantilly being ferried down the Potomac, but not the First Lady of the United States missing Thanksgiving and her children's birthdays for a journey through India and Pakistan without her husband. As it was, the journey provoked considerable controversy. While Americans read of their First Lady being lavishly entertained in Udaipur by the Maharani Shiri-Bhaget, feted in the pink city of Jaipur, guided through the Shalimar Gardens of Pakistan by Ayub Khan, congressmen and journalists demanded to know how much of the taxpayers' money was being spent on servants, transportation, gifts, and Secret Service men to make the trip possible and why Mrs. Kennedy was making it alone. Similar criticisms were leveled at her when in August 1962 she made another long trip, again unaccompanied by her husband, to Italy—a trip it was widely rumored, but never confirmed, either publicly or privately, that she made in order to petition the Vatican to annul her sister's first marriage.

Such was Jacqueline's sense of identity, however, such was the strength of her self-hood, that she was left largely unmoved by these criticisms. No narrow interpretation of her duties and position was going to affect her or make her change her style.

During her reign as First Lady, Jacqueline's relations with her family remained friendly but meetings with her relatives became, understandably, less frequent. Since Bouviers, Lees, and Auchinclosses did not share the President's political philosophy, there was an inevitable coolness to their relations with the Kennedy family. Also, if the Kennedys practiced nepotism on a truly Medicean scale, the opposite was the case with Jacqueline's three families: no Bouvier, Lee, or Auchincloss either asked or was offered a favor while Mrs. Kennedy was in power. And while the Kennedys seemed to court publicity, the Bouviers, Lees, and Auchinclosses, with the exception of Lee Radziwill, shunned it as much as possible.

Still, in spite of obstacles, there was some contact between Jacqueline and her three families while she was First Lady. Lee Radziwill remained her closest confidante, even though she spent most of her time in London. Janet and Hugh Auchincloss, who succeeded in avoiding the limelight almost completely, were frequent guests at state receptions. Michel Bouvier was invited to one of the first White House parties and, of course, he saw Jacqueline during her state visit to Paris. And the twins were invited to the White House on two occasions. Perhaps the most conspicuous absentee among Jackie's relatives during the Kennedy years was James T. Lee, who never saw his granddaughter as First Lady.

The twins' first invitation to the White House after the inauguration was to a luncheon for senators' wives given on May 23, 1961. Maude and Michelle took advantage of the occasion to present Jacqueline with a memento of Bouvier family history, John V. Bouvier, Sr.'s Civil War flag, a tattered old standard which had been flown by General Patrick and which Maude and I had rescued from Lasata in 1949. Since Jack Bouvier had spurned all relics of the Bouvier past, his daughters had inherited nothing relating to the history of their family. Yet, of all people, Jacqueline should have owned something associated with her family's past.

Maude and Michelle had expected the luncheon to be a stuffy, solemn affair, and were agreeably surprised to find it lively and entertaining. With great tact, Jacqueline had not put place cards on the tables but had had each guest draw her place out of a silver bowl. Thus, no one would have hurt feelings about where she sat, the senator's wife on Jacqueline's right and the senator's wife on Jacqueline's left having landed in their privileged places wholly by chance.

The twins were also impressed by the dignified informality of the luncheon, the Kennedy "casual grandeur." The flowers were not conventional arrangements of gladioli or tulips in vases, but mixed spring field blossoms in small wicker baskets. Each table was hosted by a cabinet member's wife who had also drawn her table by lot. Jacqueline ambled among the tables, greeting people she knew. But the fare was haute cuisine from first to last: demoiselles de l'océan en Bellevue, supreme of capon Demidoff, potatoes Parisienne, green beans with almonds, pineapple sherbet with petits fours. After lunch, demitasse was served in the Green Room. And after coffee the twins presented Jackie with the flag and Jackie showed her aunts some of the changes she had already made in the White House. In the end the flag became a favorite possession of the President, who, in turn, gave it to his son.

The next day the twins went to the Kennedys' Virginia retreat, Glen Ora, to see Caroline and John, Jr. For this visit they were joined by Michelle's daughter, Shella, who was married to a New York investment banker, William M. Crouse, and had four sons. When the three Bouviers arrived at the estate, they found Caroline in blue jeans and a riding derby, ready to show them her ponies, Macaroni and Tex, and her mother's horses. The twins recall that their six-year-old grandniece was fearless with horses, just as her mother had been at that age.

Two years later, on March 26, 1963, Maude and Shella made another visit to the White House, this time accompanied by Maude's daughter, Maudie, who had graduated from Smith and was teaching at the Brearley School in New York. As a schoolteacher and former colleague of Alice Grimes, who at the time was Caroline's teacher, Maudie wanted to inspect the school that had been set up in the White House for the President's daughter. It turned out, however, that her love of music almost prevented her from seeing it. While breakfasting she had turned on the hotel radio, and had heard for the first time the Mozart G major Piano Concerto. Captivated by it, Maudie forgot all else and almost missed the 11 A.M. departure. Arriving breathlessly but on time for their appointment, the two Maudes and Shella were greeted by Caroline, who promptly showed them her desk, her locker, her notebooks, her finger paintings, and Robin, her pet canary. While it was being displayed, the canary escaped from its cage and Caroline and her grandaunt and cousins spent the next ten minutes chasing it around the room. Maude and Shella, being the tallest, stood on chairs to try to snare the bird on its more ambitious flights, while Maudie and Caroline scurried around trying to catch it on an occasional swoop. The scene was pandemonium, with everybody colliding and the bird eluding everyone's grasp. Finally Caroline snared it on the wing in a deft cloaking maneuver with a towel. During the visit the two Maudes and Shella found Caroline very serious and mannerly—the only time she lost her dignity was when the canary escaped—and John, Jr., irrepressibly lively and gay. After an informal luncheon in the upstairs dining room, during which young John dominated the conversation with tales of his White House adventures, Jacqueline took her relatives on a tour of her living quarters, showing them the latest improvements she had made. The visit culminated in a group photograph taken in Lincoln's bedroom.

Most Bouviers who saw Jacqueline during her years as First Lady felt that she had blossomed in the White House as never before. As a senator's wife she had often seemed restless and vaguely dissatisfied. The rough and tumble of congressional politics was not at all to her taste, the small-time politicians she had to entertain often bored her, and she frequently felt frustrated because she could not be herself. But in the White House she came into her own. Above the vulgar contentions and ambitions of politics, she could finally call her own tune, be herself and get away with it. Thoroughly enjoying her eminence, she now had only one misgiving: the persistent intrusion into her privacy that accompanied it.

As Jacqueline Kennedy went from one triumph to another, unwittingly impressing her style upon the nation, the Bouviers bemusedly watched her apotheosis. So flattering were the tributes that poured off the nation's presses, so frequently did the First Lady's picture appear on the covers of *Look*, *Life*, and *McCall's*, so exalted was her reputed ancestry, that it seemed the public was bent on deifying her out of some deep, inarticulate need. Thus it was reported in countless newspaper and magazine articles that Jacqueline Bouvier Kennedy was descended from a French royalist nobleman who had fled his country during the French Revolution. And thus it was also reported that her mother's family stemmed from the Lees of Virginia (the Robert E. Lees, that is) or, as misstated in several publications of nationwide circulation, the "Lees of Maryland—an aristocratic offshoot of the Lees of Virginia." Did the Great Democracy, in the last analysis, need a queen goddess all men and women could look up to as the ideal of American womanhood? To the Bouviers it seemed so. Although they were proud of Jackie's achievements and renown, they, however, could not share the public's awe of her. To them she always remained Jackie, a pretty young girl in jodhpurs and pigtails trudging down to Lasata's riding ring to give Danseuse a workout, or one of ten boisterous grandchildren blowing whistles and snapping snappers at a family birthday party.

And so it was a bit with tongue in cheek, and sometimes with a smile on the lips, that Jackie's aunts and cousins watched America metamorphose her into a goddess and her family into a paragon of virtue and success. To read Mary Van Rensselaer Thayer's "official" biography of Jacqueline Bouvier Kennedy, one would conclude that the Bouviers had never known anything but wealth, health, extraordinary achievement, and uninterrupted terrestrial bliss. Not to mention a thoroughbred pedigree worthy of the Almanach de Gotha. What the public seemed to need, and want, was a sacrosanct figure, like the Pope, who was above criticism. This was to make Jacqueline perhaps the most vulnerable woman in the world.

There was a positive side to all this, however, for it enabled the rank and file of the American people to accept certain things it had been reluctant to accept before. The country had been founded, in part, out of rebellion against the concept of aristocracy. For this reason, lowest-common-denominator standards of dress and manners and artistic taste had come to dominate American life. Somehow, high aesthetic values and aristocratic ideals of excellence were "undemocratic." By means of the favorably received image Jacqueline Kennedy projected, however, the great mass of the American people were now freer to accept these long-rejected values and ideals, and haute couture, haute cuisine, and haute culture would no longer seem quite so un-American as before.

As John F. Kennedy approached the last months of his third year as President, he and his advisors were forced to concede that although his popularity had remained unbroken, his political effectiveness had slightly diminished. In spite of such noteworthy accomplishments as the successful resolution of the Cuban missile crisis and the signing of the Nuclear Test Ban Treaty, blunders like the Bay of Pigs invasion and the sabotaging of the Diem regime in Vietnam, combined with poor relations with congress, and growing division within his own party, particularly in Texas, had undermined many politicians' faith in the wisdom and competence of his leadership. Jacqueline's reputation, however, saw little, if any, deterioration in her third year as First Lady. Nationwide sympathy went out to her when, on August 9, 1963, she lost her two-and-a-half-day-old son, Patrick Bouvier Kennedy, the one child to whom she had given her family's name. And when, shortly thereafter, she made an extended tour of the Aegean Islands on Aristotle Onassis's yacht, accompanied by the Franklin D. Roosevelts, Jr., and the Stanislaus Radziwills, but unaccompanied by her husband, scarcely a word of criticism was breathed against her, even though Onassis was heavily in debt to the U.S. Maritime Administration at the time. By then Jacqueline Kennedy had become inviolable, as sacred as the Bill of Rights. He who dared criticize her publicly would run the risk of near-universal condemnation.

On returning to Washington from her trip to Greece, after a brief stopover in Morocco as the guest of King Hassam II, the First Lady plunged into her fall social schedule with vigor and enthusiasm. Among the engagements on her agenda were a Black Watch Tattoo on the White House lawn for 1,700 children, a reception honoring the judiciary, a trip to Texas, a state dinner for Chancellor Erhard of West Germany, and a birthday party for her son. Of the last two events, both of which fell on November 25, only one was observed—John's birthday—for by then the man who was to be Ludwig Erhard's host was dead.

# $\mathcal{V}I$

DURING THE THREE AND A HALF DAYS THAT SHE PRESIDED OVER THE nation's final tributes to her husband, Jacqueline Bouvier Kennedy was transformed into a national folk heroine. It would now be almost impossible to regard her as a mere woman. Even her relatives would find it difficult to think of her in strictly human terms.

A few weeks after the assassination, Michel visited Jacqueline and found her still very much shaken. The remarkable stamina she had displayed the day of the funeral had ebbed in the weeks that followed. Once she had fulfilled her immediate duties to her husband and her nation, the inevitable letdown had occurred. Later she would confess to members of her family that in the days between the assassination and the funeral she had felt imbued with superhuman strength, a power she never knew she had. With so many decisions to make, and so many relatives, friends, and world leaders to receive, she had had no time to feel her enormous loss. It wasn't until she had moved out of the White House and into the home Averell Harriman had made available to her in Georgetown that the full impact of the tragedy struck her. On November 22, 1963, in the space of a few minutes, she had lost everything: an incomparable husband and a position of power and influence few women in her nation's history had ever known. At thirty-one, "the cloud-capp'd towers, the gorgeous palaces . . . the great globe itself" had been given her, and at thirty-four they had been taken away.

During their meeting Michel was deeply moved by Jacqueline's disjointed account of the assassination and its aftermath and was repeatedly struck by how cruelly it had affected her. Both the clarity of her thinking and the stability of her emotions had been temporarily undermined. It was a wonder, Miche thought at the time, that she had retained her sanity in the face of her overwhelming tragedy.

As it was, Jacqueline's sanity was to undergo trials during the post-assassination period that were almost as severe as those that she had undergone at the time of her husband's murder. With her temporary home in Georgetown assaulted by tourists, with her face on the cover of almost every issue of almost every movie magazine, with the entire world talking about her, and with the world's press steadily molding her, against her wishes, into a national monument, she found herself raised to an impossible position, a level of renown even higher than that which she had known as First Lady. Yet, since her new eminence was partially based on near-hysterical emotionalism, she was extraordinarily defenseless. Uneasy is the head that wears the crown of Dowager Queen, especially in egalitarian America.

Now everything she did or said, or didn't do or say, gave some busybody an excuse to criticize her. And since her personality and style aroused such a wide spectrum of emotions, there was no lack of busybodies ready to cut her down to size. After the assassination she found herself unjustly reproached for being the first widow of an American President to have Secret Service protection, an office, and a secretarial staff at the taxpayers' expense, for having lunch with Marlon Brando, for taking a cruise in the Adriatic on the Charles Wrightsmans' yacht, for not attending the dedication of the Jacqueline Bouvier Kennedy Garden at the White House, and for not voting in the 1964 Presidential election. Then, after her year of mourning was over, she found herself being criticized for not attending President Johnson's inaugural, for going to Manhattan discothèques with the stage director Mike Nichols, for appearing at the Seville Fair in Spanish costume, for appearing in Manhattan restaurants in miniskirts, and for trying to rectify a mistake she had made, in reposing too much confidence in William Manchester, by insisting that portions of the author's book on her husband's assassination be censored. In the end Jacqueline was forced to concede that her every action, and omission, had become a matter of public concern, that she no longer belonged to herself but to all Americans. It was, at best, a grudging admission.

For her fame and vulnerability inevitably resulted in her victimization, her commercialization. Since the appetite for news of her had become insatiable, magazines could not resist the temptation to exploit the public craving. This would not have been so deplorable, for, after all, she *had* become a historical personage, if the magazines had maintained a respect for the truth, had given the public accurate information. But most of the "news" the public received of Jacqueline Kennedy and her family was either unverifiable backstairs gossip or sheer invention. Looking over a newsstand's rack of movie and pulp magazines, dozens of which would have Jacqueline's photograph on their cover, together with a blazing headline on her latest "escapade" or supposed loves, the Bouviers would often have the feeling that the other America, the America responsible for killing her husband, was now committed to degrading her.

What made Jacqueline's position so confusing was the fact that, along with the criticism and the sensationalism, the process of her idealization, begun during her years as First Lady, continued unabated. Thus, even after the furor caused by the Manchester dispute, during which she was criticized widely and sharply, a Gallup Poll still found that she was the "most respected woman in America," and writers for *The Saturday Evening Post, Ladies' Home Journal,* and *McCall's* still referred to her in their incessant stream of articles about her as "the most elegant New Yorker," "America's queen," and "the First Lady of the Western world."

Such notoriety inevitably bred a conflict in Jacqueline between her need for attention and her desire for privacy. It was only natural that after occupying the center of the world's stage she would miss the attention she had once so easily attracted if she didn't receive it. It was consoling, therefore, as well as gratifying, after her period of mourning was over, to receive as much publicity as she did when she visited Spain as guest of the Duke and Duchess of Alba, when she visited the Spanish Ambassador to the Holy See, Señor Garrigues, in Rome, and had an audience with the Pope, and when she traveled to Cambodia to meet with Prince Sihanouk and inspect the jungle ruins of Angkor Wat. Yet at the same time these appearances, which inevitably landed her on the cover of *Look* or *Life,* would arouse more hunger on the part of the public for news of her intimate existence, provoke fresh attempts to invade her privacy. And Jacqueline, reluctant to accept the more unpleasant consequences of her fame, would naturally resent them. Thus a nurse who would write about her experiences with Caroline and John, or a friend who would write about his friendship with her late husband, or a cook who would reveal that her boss had been dieting, would be dismissed from her favor forever. It was, all things considered, an extremely irritating situation. She who had not sought her eminence, she who had had it literally handed to her as a gift of circumstance, but who nevertheless enjoyed it once she had it, was now forced to pay for her unsolicited celebrity by having to endure, and repel, repeated threats to her privacy. The only way she could now lead a normal life would be to disappear from the public ken completely. But that would conceivably intensify curiosity rather than discourage it. She had become the prisoner of her fame.

It was in an attempt to lead as normal a life as possible, under the unique circumstances fate had ordained for her, that Jacqueline Kennedy moved to New York City in the fall of 1964. There, in the most callous, nonchalant, unimpressible city in the world, she might succeed in combining the two irreconcilables, fame and privacy.

The apartment Jacqueline chose at 1040 Fifth Avenue was nine blocks from her Aunt Maude's, eight blocks from her stepbrother, Yusha Auchincloss, and equally near both the Radziwills and the Robert F. Kennedys. It was also within walking distance of the school she had selected for Caroline, the Convent of the Sacred Heart, on Ninety-first Street and Fifth, which three generations of Bouviers had attended, including the twins. Farther downtown, at 400 Park Avenue, she established a four-room office, with her faithful secretaries, Pamela Turnure and Nancy Tuckerman, in charge.

Although New York by no means accorded her the total privacy she desired, it did allow her more freedom of action than she would have known in any other major city. There, at least, she could carry on, with a minimum of interference, what had become her mission in life and what would be one of her most significant achievements as a world figure: the glorification of her husband's memory.

She had begun this mission shortly after her husband's death by giving him the most elaborate and spectacular funeral in U.S. presidential history, by placing an eternal flame over his grave, and by placing under the Lincoln plaque in the Lincoln bedroom a plaque of her own: "In this room lived John Fitzgerald Kennedy with his wife, Jacqueline, during the two years, ten months, and two days he was President of the United States—Jan. 20, 1961-November 22, 1963." (Mrs. Richard Nixon had the plaque removed soon after she and her husband moved in.)

But there were other, far more spectacular ways of glorifying the memory of her late husband. Not long after the funeral she took a major step in the glorification process by persuading Lyndon Johnson to change the name of Cape Canaveral to Cape Kennedy.

When Lyndon Johnson was informed Jacqueline wanted to see him in the oval office, not long after he moved into the White House, he feared the worst. What would she have to say to the usurper of the throne? But when she simply asked him, in that childlike, whispery voice of hers, to name Cape Canaveral after Jack, Johnson was so relieved that was all she wanted, he gushed: "Why sure, Jackie, sure, we'll get it done right away." And so it was done. (In 1973 Cape Kennedy was renamed Cape Canaveral.)

It was around this time that Jacqueline first expressed to Theodore White, the ardently pro-Kennedy journalist and historian, her conception of President Kennedy's reign as resembling the mythical realm of Camelot, telling White that as a boy Kennedy was often sick and used to lie in bed and dream of performing valiant deeds like one of King Arthur's knights, and that his favorite music, the music he used to play before going to bed at night as President, was Lerner and Lowe's Camelot. And so the Camelot association with Kennedy and his administration was made, and Teddy White wrote about it in an article for *Life* magazine. Soon it was picked up by others in the media and it gained general acceptance. In time the Camelot metaphor would be used to epitomize the entire Kennedy Presidency, as if that brief, turbulent era, marked by the Kennedy brothers' secret wars against Castro and the Mafia, had been one thousand days of beauty and light.

Not long after the birth of the Camelot myth, Mayor Robert Wagner of New York changed the name of Idlewild International Airport to John F. Kennedy International Airport. And then, not long after that, Congress changed the name of the planned national cultural center in Washington to the John F. Kennedy Center for the Performing Arts, and appropriated $15.5 million in federal funds to match an equal amount to be raised privately for the new national monument.

Meanwhile, Jacqueline Kennedy vehemently pursued what had become her major personal contribution to the glorification, the John F. Kennedy Memorial Library in Boston. Here, in the city whose establishment the Kennedys felt had rejected them, she and her collaborators were to raise a monument to a Kennedy surpassing in grandeur that of any other son of Boston.

There was more to come. The U.S. Treasury minted a Kennedy half-dollar. Queen Elizabeth of England set aside three acres at Runnymede, where King John had signed the Magna Carta, as a

Kennedy shrine. A huge John F. Kennedy Memorial Park was created in New Ross, in southern Ireland, near the Kennedy ancestral homestead in Dunganstown. Canada named one of its tallest peaks Mount Kennedy. Kennedy plazas, places, schools, boulevards, streets, and hospitals sprung up all over the globe. One could not escape the name Kennedy anywhere on the planet. In a very real sense, John F. Kennedy's murder had multiplied the Kennedys' power. With the name of Kennedy so universally glorified in stone, and bronze, and institutional lettering, it seemed certain that, sooner or later, a Kennedy would avail himself of the power of his name to regain the Presidency.

Along with the glorification of John F. Kennedy, there went also his continued idealization and sentimentalization. If the press had gushed over John Kennedy before, now it became downright maudlin. The canonization had begun.

Unfortunately, what proceeded from all this was a monstrous distortion of the truth. A myth was created that could not possibly serve the interests of anybody but the Kennedy family. Jacqueline Kennedy's efforts at glorifying and mythologizing her late husband inadvertently did much to cloud what might have been behind her late husband's assassination.

The key elements in the myth-making process were the suppression of the truth about John F. Kennedy's past, the discouragement of any serious inquiry into the circumstances of his assassination, the lifelong inclination of Jacqueline Kennedy to construct and dwell in fairy tales, and the concerted attempt by the Kennedys and their court historians to manipulate history, including the suppression of books, such as William Manchester's *Death of a President*, they did not like.

All of these elements, however, would have been to no avail in building a Kennedy myth if the American people were not already emotionally disposed to accept one. In an America conditioned by the fabrications of Hollywood and Madison Avenue, the Camelot tale found fertile soil in which to grow.

Along with the sense of guilt, Jacqueline was also tormented by a sense of What Could Have Been Done to prevent the tragedy in Dallas. They should have heeded all the warnings and not gone to Texas. They should have spent more time at the Love Field airport shaking hands with the crowds: that would have delayed the motorcade considerably and the assassins might have lost nerve. She should have insisted on the bubble top. The driver of the presidential limousine should have speeded up after the first shot. There were so many things that could have been done, and weren't. However, reflecting on these once in the presence of her secretary, Mary Gallagher, Jacqueline showed she understood one facet of her late husband's character only too well. Turning to Mrs. Gallagher one day, after reciting a long litany of What Could Have Been Dones, she said, "Oh, well, I guess Jack would only have gotten more reckless as time went on anyway."

It is interesting to note that Jacqueline, despite her desire to glorify her husband's memory, seemed not to take any apparent interest in the official investigation of her husband's murder. Possibly this was because Robert Kennedy had encouraged her not to for the same reason he had adopted the policy of withholding vital information from the Warren Commission: He did not want certain things ever to come to light.

Jacqueline, in fact, in the immediate post-assassination period, often appeared to her Bouvier relatives to be strangely withdrawn and inhibited in regard to the assassination. Certainly there was little in her attitude that bespoke wanting to get to the bottom of the crime and see justice was done to those responsible for it.

The assassination left Jacqueline terribly vulnerable. She was vulnerable to the tabloids that exploited her, and she was vulnerable to those she had either snubbed, mistreated, or ignored. She no longer had the President of the United States to protect her. She no longer had her position as First Lady to protect her.

However, there were compensations. Jacqueline emerged from the assassination as a world celebrity. The entire globe had seen her leading the world's heads of state in the funeral procession. She had come out of this tragedy with virtually unlimited prestige.

The trouble was she didn't seem to know what to do with all the prestige she had. Since she had derived almost her total identity from a man, her husband, she had no real bedrock of selfhood to fall back on when he was gone, no selfhood that could successfully harness the immense prestige she had attained by force of circumstance. And so it seemed to many that she began to squander her prestige in aimless self-indulgences as she continued spending inordinate amounts of money on *haute couture*, frequented almost exclusively people of fashion, and jetted all over the world.

Then there was the problem of money. Kennedy had left Jacqueline well enough off, but not enormously well off, and all the money he had left her was tied up in a trust fund over which she had been given no control. Jackie's spending habits since childhood had been extravagant, and her living costs were now astronomical because she felt she had to keep up a standard of living appropriate to a former First Lady, her brand of First Lady. After the terms of Kennedy's will were made known to her, she wondered how she would ever make ends meet.

Fully cognizant of her extravagant ways, Kennedy had left his wife only $25,000 in cash. His major bequest was making her the beneficiary of a trust fund that would assure her an income of $175,000 a year, before taxes, not a vast income by any means, given her spending habits. It will be recalled that while she was in the White House Jacqueline spent over $100,000 a year on clothes alone.

There was also some money from the federal government, but not very much. From the government her husband had led she received only $43,229, representing civil service death benefits and salary owed the President from the period November 1-22, a widow's pension of $10,000 a year, and $50,000 a year in administrative expenses. So, in terms of actual cash she could lay her hands on, all she had was around $68,000.

Since she had long ago run through the $69,000 left her by her father, she was left with very little money she could call her own. And she was given no control whatsoever over the trust fund that had been established for her. The trustees were all members of the Kennedy family and business staff, and part of the trust agreement stipulated that if she ever remarried, her trust fund would automatically revert to her children.

It was this feeling of being in relatively difficult straits that caused Jacqueline to be somewhat stingy with her employees, thereby creating resentments that would later find expression in critical books. The U.S. government had awarded Jacqueline $50,000 a year in expense money to maintain an office and a staff capable of handling the considerable official work left over from her husband's administration, including the assembling and organizing of his Presidential papers. At first she balked at paying her secretary, Mary Gallagher, $12,000 a year out of her $50,000 allowance. Later she let Mary go. Mrs. Gallagher would tell the world about it in her book, *My Life with Jacqueline Kennedy.* Jac-

queline also balked at paying her maid, Providencia Paredes—
"Provi"—overtime, even though this faithful retainer had
worked herself to the bone, usually late into the night, both before
and after the President's murder.

Then, when President Kennedy's secretary, Evelyn Lincoln,
was asked to leave, and she complained bitterly, Jackie told her,
"Oh, Mrs. Lincoln, all this shouldn't be so hard for you, because
you still have your husband. What do I have now? Just the
Library." Before this episode, which Mrs. Gallagher related in her
book, Jackie had asked Mrs. Lincoln why she needed such a big
office, and Mrs. Lincoln had replied that she needed the space for
all the President's things she was working on, the papers, the
mementos, etc. To this Jackie replied, "But these things are all
mine!"

Finally, there came the move to New York in the summer-fall
of 1964, to the $200,000 apartment at 1040 Fifth Avenue. Much
was made of this at the time, as if abandoning Washington was
some kind of a mortal sin: the First Widow was supposed to be
making daily visits to Arlington for the rest of her life. But for
Jacqueline, living in New York was the most normal thing in the
world. The Bouviers had been living in New York since 1869.

The move to New York brought a fresh rash of publicity. Once
again Jacqueline was at the center of attention of an entire city,
the city that had become, by the mid-sixties, the financial and
cultural center of the western world.

But despite all the attention Jacqueline received she was nevertheless a lonely, unhappy woman. Every member of the Bouvier
family who saw her during this period, including myself, was
struck by her unhappiness and was deeply moved by her plight.

The first Bouvier, besides her sister, to visit her after the assassination was our oldest cousin, Michel Bouvier, who had grown
up with Jackie as a brother, and was her godfather as well. (Jackie
was, in turn, godmother to his son, John Vernou Bouvier IV,
named after her father.) Unable to get to the funeral, Michel had
paid a call on her at the Georgetown home she had moved into
after moving out of the White House. There Jackie gave him a
long, somewhat disjointed account of the assassination and the
funeral that moved Michel deeply. He observed that the highstrung Jackie seemed unusually overwrought, so much so that he
feared for the stability of her emotions and wondered whether
her sanity would hold up under the terrible strain of the adjust-

ment she was having to make. His heart went out to her, but he realized there was absolutely nothing he could do to assuage her grief or compensate for her loss. It was a feeling everyone in the Bouvier family would share.

My turn to see Jacqueline came in March 1966 upon the death of my father in New York. I was living in Italy at the time and flew from Rome to New York for the funeral. After the funeral Jackie came up to my mother's apartment to pay us her condolences. I had not seen her since I had gone to the White House after President Kennedy's burial to pay her my condolences.

When Jacqueline came in the front door I immediately noticed a startled expression in her eyes as she glanced here and there around the hall of my mother's apartment, as if on the lookout for a threat. Evidently my father's death had brought back childhood memories of her Uncle John, who had shared an office with her father on lower Broadway near the Stock Exchange, for she kept repeating "Uncle John" over and over, until we sat down on a couch in Mother's living room. There we reminisced for a while, and then she began staring into space and said, "Now they're all dead; they're all dead; they're all dead, all of them, all of them, all dead."

I nodded, and tried to change the subject by telling her how magnificent she had been at President Kennedy's funeral. She shrugged my compliment off in her customary unassuming way, and our conversation drifted back to our childhood days in East Hampton. I mentioned that I had been down in East Hampton the previous summer to take a look at Lasata, after not having seen it in ten years, and had found the old place much changed under its new owner, whereupon she remarked that she had been down there too, incognito, and the house had struck her this time as being "so small."

After talking a while about my father, Jackie got up to leave. As she was putting on her coat in the hall, glancing around with that startled, threatened look again, she appeared very vulnerable and alone, and, feeling suddenly protective, I decided to escort her down the elevator and through the apartment building lobby to her waiting limousine. Even walking through the lobby she looked guarded and tense. As she was to tell me several years later at the funeral of our Aunt Edith, "There are some things you never get over."

The consensus among the Bouviers, at least, seemed to be that Jackie should remarry. She was simply too exposed and unprotected on her own. But who could possibly deliver her? This was the unanswerable question. There seems to be an unwritten law of nature that a woman does not marry below her rank. Because Jackie had been married to the President of the United States, this narrowed the field of prospective husbands to zero. Jacqueline Bouvier Kennedy, the President's widow, had become the prisoner of her status.

# VII

DURING THE YEARS IMMEDIATELY FOLLOWING HER HUSBAND'S ASSAS-
sination, the man Jacqueline Kennedy came to rely on most
heavily for guidance and moral support was her brother-in-law,
Robert F. Kennedy. There were, in fact, no other men in her
several families to whom she could turn. Her father was dead.
Michel Bouvier lived in Paris. Hugh D. Auchincloss, though he
had always been an exemplary stepfather, was nevertheless very
far removed from the spirit of her generation. With two young
children to bring up and scores of complex problems to contend
with, Jacqueline was in desperate need of someone, preferably a
contemporary, who could fully understand her predicament,
provide advice and assistance, and in whom she could repose
absolute trust. With remarkable gallantry and unselfishness, considering the scope of his other responsibilities, Robert Kennedy
came forth to fill this need.

As the father of nine, soon ten, children, and as Attorney
General, then United States Senator; as the leader of a large,
internationally known family that had recently sustained a staggering loss, and as a prospective candidate for the Presidency,
Robert Kennedy had enough claims on his time and energies to
exhaust the strength and resolve of the most heroic of men. And
yet he gave of himself unstintingly to his sister-in-law and her
children in their time of acute privation, becoming, as best he
could, a substitute father for John, Jr., and Caroline and an unfailing source of comfort and moral support to Jacqueline.

It was he who had been Jackie's principal helper in planning
the state funeral, and her mainstay immediately after her
husband's death. It was he who had been her most frequent and
welcome caller while she was living in Georgetown before her
move to New York. It was he who had defended her most
vigorously in her dispute with William Manchester, he who
became her closest collaborator in planning the John F. Kennedy
Memorial Library at Harvard, he who became her children's
favorite adult relative and friend.

After Robert Kennedy declared his candidacy for the Presidency on March 16, 1968, reconstituted the Kennedy political organization, and launched his assault on the primaries, it
appeared, for a brief two and a half months, that John F.
Kennedy's assassination might be vindicated and the ideals and

aspirations for which the slain President had stood would be returned to the nation's highest office. The prospect for the Kennedy family was almost too wonderful to contemplate. What a day the Restoration would be! There on the inaugural platform, behind the new President, would be Rose Kennedy and Jacqueline and JFK, Jr., and Caroline and all the other Kennedys. And later, after the inaugural parade, they would all enter the White House together for the reception for President and Mrs. Kennedy's families. And so there they would be, eight years after the reception for the first President and Mrs. Kennedy's families, back in the high place from which they had been so brutally toppled in November 1963. Nothing, and no one, could, of course, take the place of John F. Kennedy for Jacqueline; nevertheless, the restoration of her husband's spirit to the Presidency in the person of the man who had been her greatest ally after her husband's death would be a consummation beyond her most fervent hopes.

Then, on June 5, in another explosion of envy and hatred, the possibility of that historic consummation was repudiated. The nation lost both a proven statesman and an incalculable potential. A great family lost its leader. A wife and ten children lost their husband and father. And Jacqueline lost the man who had done so much to alleviate her own sense of loss four and a half years earlier. For her the unimaginable had happened again. Fourteen years of devotion to the hopes, ideals, and ambitions of the Kennedy family had ended in two senseless murders. Where, in whom, in what faith, would she find her consolation now?

It did not take long after the murder of Robert Kennedy for the press to begin referring to the late senator in much the same terms, and tones, it had been using to portray his slain brother John during the past four and a half years. Thus, in the days immediately following his burial in Arlington, Robert Kennedy underwent yet a third metamorphosis of personality, changing, in the press's view, to a "martyred hero," "a martyr to freedom," and "a knight fallen in battle." The second Kennedy glorification had begun.

Granted, the glorification of Robert Kennedy was not nearly as intense and exaggerated as that of John F. Kennedy. Still, it was sufficiently hysterical and widespread to cause the name Kennedy to be bestowed on several more landmarks and institutions and to inspire a fresh new rash of adulatory Kennedy books.

As the tumultuous Democratic convention of August 1968 approached, the journalistic apotheosis of the slain Kennedy brothers intensified to such an extent that the 36-year-old surviving Kennedy brother, Edward, could probably have ridden the public mood and captured the Democratic nomination himself had be chosen to fight for it, which, as it turned out, he was not prepared to do.

And if the American people had felt irrational mass guilt over the murder of John F. Kennedy, now, after the murder of Robert F. Kennedy, they were thrown into a veritable frenzy of self-laceration. A widespread feeling began to arise among the people that they now owed the Presidency to the Kennedys. Consequently it soon became a matter of virtual certainty that young Edward Kennedy would be handed the Presidency one day, as a kind of grant from the people, most likely in 1972 or 1976.

However, in order to win the presidency back, the Kennedys had to keep aloft the inflated image. They could not reveal themselves to be more human beings with human frailties, who occasionally got into accidents or made unseemly marriages. The Presidency would be granted to the last of the Kennedy brothers only if he and his family did not destroy the illusions about themselves they had so pointedly built up.

But with both John F. Kennedy and Robert F. Kennedy gone, a lot of restraints had been removed from the Kennedy field of action. Both Jacqueline Kennedy and Edward Kennedy had to hold themselves in check for the sake of Bobby's political ambitions. Now they no longer had to behave quite so virtuously. They could finally let themselves go.

Ironically, the first Kennedy to let go, and in so doing cause a puncture in the family image, was the Kennedy who had done so much to inflate the image, who, in fact had been the main force behind the glorification of John F. Kennedy, and that was the late President's widow, Jacqueline.

On October 18, 1968, barely four months after the assassination in Los Angeles, Jacqueline Kennedy made an announcement that so deflated the Kennedy image it has never been quite the same since. She announced that she was going to marry the divorced Greek shipowner and multimillionaire, Aristotle Onassis, a man twenty-nine years older than she, with an unsavory reputation, who was so unlike the late John F. Kennedy in looks and manners and values, that her marriage to him suddenly raised disturbing questions about the nature of her marriage to her first husband. Had that union also been just for money and power?

On the few occasions in the mid-sixties that I had a chance to talk with Jacqueline Kennedy, I was always struck by the aura of loneliness, vulnerability, and insecurity that seemed to envelop her. Then she became Mrs. Aristotle Onassis and changed dramatically, becoming much more cheerful, outgoing, and sure of herself. Noting the tremendous difference, I came to the conclusion that, for a while at least, the marriage to Onassis had been good for her, and hence made some sense.

But to the world at large it made no sense at all. Rather, it was widely regarded as some sort of incredible disaster. A worldwide negative reaction to the marriage of Jacqueline Kennedy and Aristotle Onassis resulted. The American public had conceived of Jackie as the loving wife of an American hero, as a radiant, queenly First Lady of unimpeachable virtue, and then as a grieving widow devoted to her slain husband's memory and ideals. They had thought of her as a sacred American legend, as a living saint.

When this paragon of American womanhood virtually eloped with a disreputable old man who seemed to have no ideals whatsoever beyond piling up enormous sums of money and collecting yachtfuls of celebrities, people were stunned.

"Jackie—How Can You?" headlined a London tabloid. "The Reaction Here Is Shock and Dismay," headlined *The New York Times*. "America Has Lost a Saint," headlined the West German *Bild-Zeitung*, adding in a subtitle, "All the World Is Indignant," "John Kennedy Dies Today for a Second Time," headlined Rome's *Il Messagero*.

In France news of the marriage broke as a national tragedy. *Le Monde* opined that Onassis represented "the antithesis of President Kennedy's dream of a less cruel world," and went on to observe that "Mr. Onassis is concerned more with dominating this world than reforming it." "Is it this appetite for power, with all that it reveals of a quasi-animal energy that charmed the widow of John Kennedy?" *Le Monde* asked. In conclusion, the French paper observed that "the second Mrs. Onassis will cause to be forgotten the radiant Snow White who contributed so much to the popularity of her husband."

Even the Vatican's ultraconservative *L'Osservatore della Domenica*, normally reticent, leveled a broadside at the former

First Lady, declaring that, as a result of her remarriage, Jacqueline was in "a state of spiritual degradation" and was now "a public sinner," an assertion that showed how hysterically unfair the reaction to the remarriage could be.

Along with this journalistic castigation of the marriage went a near-universal condemnation of Onassis. Italy's *L'Espresso* was particularly severe on the Greek shipowner, describing him as "this grizzled satrap, with his liver-colored skin, thick hair, fleshy nose, the wide horsey grin, who buys an island and then has it removed from the maps to prevent the landing of castaways."

But not everybody was shocked by the Kennedy-Onassis marriage. Those who knew Jackie best saw nothing especially unusual about it. Most members of the Bouvier family, for example, were surprised by the marriage, but hardly shocked. Those of us who had grown up with Jackie felt that Onassis was precisely the type of man we thought she would marry. She had always liked older men, much older men, even as a teenager. And we all knew that her mother and father had relentlessly coached her to marry a very rich man. Furthermore, Onassis was, in many ways, a man very much like Jackie's father, whom she had adored. Like Black Jack Bouvier, Onassis was very masculine, protective type who loved to indulge women. Both men were totally materialistic. Both were very "worldly." And both had a way of making a woman feel very appreciated and secure. Security was what Jackie needed after Bobby's murder.

Jack Bouvier, had he lived to see the marriage, would have no doubt been delighted with Onassis. Over and over again he had drummed it into Jackie's ears that she should marry a very rich man. Jackie's mother used to urge her to do the same thing. In marrying Onassis Jackie was doing exactly what she had been brought up to do—which brings up the question of money. In marrying Onassis, Jackie was finally able to break her financial dependence on the Kennedys and indulge her extravagant tastes at whim. To Jackie's Bouvier relatives this was reason enough for her to wed Onassis.

There was also another good reason for Jackie to marry Aristotle Onassis: escape. Jackie had been very close to Robert Kennedy. He had been her confidant, her adviser, and her most devoted male friend. When he was murdered she was shattered. Some say she became incoherent. The whole Kennedy adventure had ended in horror. Her husband had been murdered. And now her brother-in-law had also been murdered. In the weeks following Bobby Kennedy's assassination Jackie was seized with a desperate desire to escape the Kennedy nightmare. What more sublime escape could there be than a shimmering island in the Aegean sea and one of the most luxurious yachts in the world? For Jacqueline, after what she had gone through, the beauty and serenity of Skorpios and the luxury of the Christina were heaven-sent.

Finally, she could also realize her childhood "dream of glory." With a 68-year-old shipping emperor by her side she could finally be "la fille naturelle de Charlemagne," with Camelot replaced by a new fairyland on an enchanted Greek island.

Nevertheless, despite Jacqueline's quite valid personal reasons for marrying Aristotle Onassis, the marriage was, in a larger perspective, a mistake. For Jacqueline had become a world figure whose conduct was watched and copied everywhere. This was a considerable responsibility. By all rights, Jackie should have weighed the possible public reaction to marrying a man like Onassis, but she did not. In fact, she resented the limitations on her freedom being a public figure imposed.

I remember being shocked, when I returned to Italy in 1972 to write a book on Venice, by my European friends' reactions to Jackie's marriage. I was, in fact, much more shocked by these reactions than I had been shocked by the news of her remarriage. Everywhere I went—Paris, Rome, Naples, Venice—I was compelled to defend Jackie's marriage. "She threw it all away, didn't she?" was a typical remark. "We all thought she would marry someone like André Malraux," a Polish writer friend told me, "and here she goes off with a gangster."

It was astonishing how many European friends of mine had totally misread Jackie. Malraux was the last type of man Jackie would marry. Marry a man of no independent means, who lived off royalties from books and the modest salary of a French government official? That wasn't Jackie's cup of tea at all. But what about her supposed intellectualism and devotion to the arts? Wouldn't that have brought her closer to a Malraux than to an Onassis, many inquired? Jacqueline was never particularly interested in the world of ideas. And her interest in the arts was never more than superficial. Although she was endowed with a sense of history, she was never concerned with history as a search for truth. For Jackie history was a kind of aesthetic antiquarianism. It was being concerned that a James Monroe pier table be rescued from the White House storage bins and placed in the Red Room where it belonged. The idea that Jackie would marry a man of ideas was preposterous. Jacqueline needed to be married to a man of material power. It had been power that had attracted her to Kennedy, and it was power that attracted her to Onassis. Jacqueline had always derived her sense of identity from association with a powerful man. When she was young she was Daddy's best girl. Then she was a senator's wife, and then the President's wife. For Jackie being someone's wife was very important. Now she was Mrs. Aristotle Onassis, the wife of one of the richest men in the world. This status gave her a tremendous satisfaction. You see, she seemed to be telling the world, you thought I had lost everything, but look at me now, married to one of the richest men on earth!

Still her reputation suffered grievously from the marriage, especially in Europe where Onassis was emphatically not liked. It wasn't long before the former Mrs. John F. Kennedy, widow of the late President of the United States, was reduced to being called "Jackie O." As if to give her a monument appropriate to her new status, a new disco off the Via Veneto in Rome was named "Jackie O."

Then there was the problem of her much-coveted privacy. One of the reasons she had married Onassis was that he was in a position to guarantee her privacy with his yacht and island. As it turned out, Onassis's fortune, yacht, and island failed to bring her the privacy she craved. As the marriage wore on she drew more attention and harassment than ever and became the unwitting star of a seemingly never-ending media circus. The paparazzi became merciless in their exploitation of her. It wasn't long before fourteen photos of Jackie sunbathing nude on Skorpios appeared in an Italian magazine.

Unflattering books became another unpleasant consequence of the Onassis marriage. Before Jacqueline married Onassis, she had received nothing but praise from biographers, historians, and memoirists. After the marriage she began receiving abuse from them.

Jackie's marriage to Onassis also put her in the annoying position of no longer being able to criticize people (such as writers) convincingly for exploiting the Kennedy tragedies, for, in a sense she had, in marrying Onassis, profited from them herself. It is safe to say that if she had not been the widow of the assassinated President, Onassis, the celebrity collector, desirous of enlarging his fame, would not have married her and shared his vast wealth with her.

If Jacqueline's reputation suffered from her marriage to Onassis, the Kennedy reputation suffered from it also, by extension. The Kennedys, both blood and honorary, did not, in fact, like the idea of the marriage at all. Realizing full well that it would damage the image they had labored so mightily to inflate, the Kennedys had first tried to talk her out of her marriage plans. Ted Kennedy was understandably wary of the effect the marriage might have on public opinion. However, Jackie held firm and succeeded in getting him to give her his reluctant public blessing. Rose Kennedy also gave her a reluctant public blessing, conceding that the marriage made some sense in that it should finally give Jackie the financial independence she so desired. But the "honorary Kennedys" were less hypocritical about the whole affair. Dave Powers, for example, told me in Boston that he never could understand why she married the shipping magnate, allowing that it certainly did not do John Kennedy's memory any good.

The marriage, according to what Jacqueline told certain Bouvier relatives, worked until the death of Onassis's son, Alexander, from an air accident, in January 1973. After that tragic event the marriage turned sour. A dispirited Onassis began regretting he had not married a younger woman who could have given him another son. He reputedly told Jackie, who could no longer have children, that she was "bad luck."

Onassis had his good points but he was also a cruel and vulgar man. He had married Jackie for prestige and had proudly displayed her in public as he would an old master or a jewel. He enjoyed making Jackie jealous and went out of his way to be photographed in public with old flames like Maria Callas, knowing Jackie would see the pictures in the papers. And it was said that he took a perverse delight in taking guests on whale hunts where they would watch the whales being harpooned and taken aboard the ships of his whaling fleet, a pastime that certainly did not endear him to his sensitive, animal-loving wife. It was, all things considered, a tense ménage. Onassis's children did not care for their new stepmother, and John F. Kennedy, Jr., it has been reported, came to regard his stepfather as "a joke." As might be expected, Jacqueline's extravagance bothered Onassis not a little, as it had bothered her father and John F. Kennedy. It was widely rumored that she spent some $1.5 million of Onassis's money in the first year of her marriage alone.

Jacqueline had naturally expected to inherit an enormous fortune from Onassis some day, but after the death of Alexander that hope was extinguished. As soon as he began to recover from the shock of his loss, Onassis drew up a new will, creating the Alexander Onassis Foundation and bequeathing a substantial share of his fortune to it. He also added to daughter Christina's share. The foundation was designed to promote "nursing, education, literary works, religious and scientific research, and journalistic and religious endeavors" and effectively put an end to Jacqueline's dream of one day possessing great wealth. During the last two years of Onassis's life, he and Jacqueline became more and more estranged; in 1974 the aging shipping magnate began contemplating divorce, calling his wife, according to biographer Lee Guthrie, "cold-hearted and shallow." To columnist Jack Anderson he complained of Jackie's extravagance and the complaint found its way into Anderson's column. As Onassis's health began to fail and his mood grew darker and darker, Jacqueline found herself being gradually excluded from his life. On March 15, 1975, he died in Paris with only his daughter Christina at his side.

After the funeral Jacqueline issued a statement to the press that probably contained a kernel of truth:

> Aristotle Onassis rescued me at a moment when my life was engulfed with shadows. He meant a lot to me. He brought me into a world where one could find both happiness and love. We lived through many beautiful experiences together which cannot be forgotten, and for which I will be eternally grateful.

The estate of Aristotle Onassis was estimated to be worth close to a billion dollars, minus debts, which were considerable, and taxes. According to Greek law, Jacqueline's legal share of a billion-dollar estate would have been something in the neighborhood of $125 million. However, Onassis had arranged things so that she would get far, far less, even going to the extent to persuading the Greek parliament to change some of the inheritance laws to protect his fortune. In the end, as all the world knows, executrix Christina settled $26 million of her father's estate on Jacqueline. Thus, since she had to renounce her Kennedy trust upon marrying Onassis, Jackie ended up with not a great deal more money than she would have had she not married Onassis. By the mid-seventies the Kennedy trust, worth $10 million in 1963, would have probably grown to be worth at least $20 million, or roughly the same amount Onassis had left her.

And so it was that Jacqueline's marriage to Aristotle Onassis failed to enrich her significantly beyond her condition under the Kennedy trust, yet it damaged both her reputation and the Kennedy image. It was, in fact, the first major blow to the Kennedy image that, in the summer of 1968, had seemed absolutely unassailable. But this was no great calamity. As certain members of the Bouvier family observed at the time, Jackie had done more than her duty by the Kennedys; she had done quite enough for them. Where would they have been, who would they have been, without her?

Although criticism of Jacqueline for her marriage to Onassis has persisted, I believe it is basically unfair. That Jacqueline kept her sanity through two assassinations and was able to begin a new life was an achievement that far outweighed her apparent failure to protect the vanity of an inflated image.

# VIII

ABOUT TWO YEARS AFTER ONASSIS' DEATH I HAD A CHANCE TO TALK with Jacqueline at the funeral and wake of our Aunt Edith Beale at East Hampton. Like most extended American families in the latter decades of the twentieth century, the only occasions when the entire Bouvier family would get together were at family milestones: weddings and funerals.

In fact, the last time all my Bouvier aunts and uncles and cousins were reunited was at the funeral of President Kennedy.

During the intervening fourteen years Aunt Edie and her East Hampton estate, "Gray Gardens," on Lily Pond Lane, had steadily deteriorated. What had once been an unencumbered blue and gray shingled wooden house surrounded by a spacious lawn, a lush garden, and neatly trimmed hedges, was now a tent of ivy and morning glories, punctured here and there by protruding gables and chimneys, in a field of weeds, poppies, and black-eyed susans, that looked something like the House of the Seven Dwarfs. A broken-down black Cadillac was rusting in what used to be a bluestone driveway and now was a bed of tangled weeds. It had rested there, undriven, for over twenty years.

Edith Beale, known as "Big Edie" in the family, had been living as a virtual recluse in "Gray Gardens," along with her daughter, "Little Edie," and some forty moth-eaten cats, for the past twenty-seven years.

So run down did "Gray Gardens" become that in 1971 the Suffolk County Health Department brought condemnation proceedings against the Beales claiming that their house had become a menace to public health. The presence of forty cats running wild in and out of the house, leaving their excrement everywhere, had caused "Gray Gardens" to emit a constant stench. When the wind blew off the land "Big Edie's" neighbors could breathe. But when the sea winds prevailed the briny humid air of the nearby Atlantic would blow the stench of cat and raccoon manure and rotting vegetation into those neighbors' doors and windows. Mothers feared for their children's health for occasionally a child of the neighborhood would wander onto Big Edie's front lawn, now a tangle of bushes and weeds, and chase the forlorn cats, often getting badly scratched by them once they were captured.

Curiously the Beales were all but oblivious to their progressive deterioration. The picturesque squalor of "Gray Gardens" did not particularly dismay them. In contrast to their public-opinion-conscious relatives, they couldn't care less what other people thought. The immaculately manicured, parklike appearance of most East Hampton estates did not impress *them*. For Big and Little Edie, worldly success and social prestige had become as insubstantial as "hailstone in the sun."

Yet there had been a time when Edith Bouvier Beale had been regarded as a great beauty, living in splendor at "Gray Gardens" with her successful lawyer husband, Phelan Beale, and their three children, Bouvier, Phelan, and Edith Bouvier Jr., who, in her day was *the* belle of the Bouvier family. "Little Edie" had almost become engaged to Joseph P. Kennedy Jr. Joe Sr. had even bestowed his blessing on her at Palm Beach. If Joe Jr. hadn't been killed in the war, he might well have become President and Little Edie would have been First Lady instead of Jackie.

Now the Beales would sit on their decrepit front porch, listening to the ocean booming in the distance, the owls hooting in the hedges, and the sporadic rustling of their many cats, and wondering when the Suffolk County Health Department would throw them out on the street.

The countdown toward eviction was ticking away when, lo and behold, Aristotle Onassis came to the rescue. At Jackie's urging the Greek Midas agreed to clean up the house and grounds, repair the enormous hole in "Gray Gardens" ' roof, and install a new furnace and a new plumbing system. It took over a thousand tall garbage bags to contain all the trash that had accumulated in the house. For days workmen cleaned cat fur and cat excrement from the floor. The stench was so overpowering the workmen had to go outside every fifteen minutes for a breath of fresh air. But the job was done, at Aristotle Onassis' expense, and the Suffolk County authorities gave "Gray Gardens" a clean bill of health. At least Aunt Edith would be allowed to live out her last days in her home for the past fifty years.

The end came in early February, 1977, when she was rushed to Southampton Hospital, complaining she had difficulty breathing. She died three days later at eight-one.

Now her funeral would be held at St. Philomena's church, which had been the Bouviers' summer parish since 1915. Bouviers from far and wide, including Jacqueline Onassis and her sister Lee, would descend on East Hampton for their first family reunion since John F. Kennedy's funeral.

"Big Edie," as we know, was an accomplished soprano who enthralled her nieces and nephews with her passionate renditions of such sentimental songs as "Indian Love Call," "Smoke Gets In Your Eyes," and "Stardust." A large woman of operatic girth and Mediterranean features and complexion, she was a born actress who demanded, and received, the full attention of her audience. Seated at the grand piano in her decaying livingroom, she would shake the dust off the piano and rattle the windowpanes with the power of her voice. I remember the twelve year old Jackie in Jodhpurs and riding boots, listening to "Big Edie" singing "Because God Made You Mine, I'll Treasure Thee" with rapt attention, her large, wide-apart eyes full of wonder and admiration.

"Big Edie" had made recordings of her favorite songs and it was decided to play them at her funeral.

The small church was packed with relatives and friends and a huge crowd of photographers and journalists was kept at bay outside.

Jacqueline, looking very subdued, even demure, was wearing a black veil and a below-the-knees black dress. She was sitting across the aisle from me with her sister, Lee.

All of a sudden the distant voice of "Big Edie" reverberated throughout the church. She was singing "Because God Made You Mine." Jerome Kern's "All The Things You Are" followed and then came everyone's favorite, Kern's "Smoke Gets In Your Eyes."

> They asked me how I knew
> That our love was true
> I of course replied
> Something here inside
> Cannot be denied.

I looked at Jackie. She was crying. Thirty-five years had gone by since she and I and our other cousins had crowded around Big Edie's dusty cobwebbed piano at "Gray Gardens" and listened enraptured to her singing "Smoke Gets In Your Eyes." So much had happened to us all since then. While Big and Little Edie were living out their long, monotonous days at "Gray Gardens" caring for their ever increasing brood of cats, battling the raccoons rummaging in the garbage cans outside the kitchen door, Jacqueline had become a world figure, dining at Versailles with Charles de Gaulle, being welcomed at Buckingham Palace by Queen Elizabeth II and Prince Philip, presiding over the funeral of her assassinated husband, President John F. Kennedy.

It was a rude shock to all of us when we emerged from the church, red-eyed and emotionally drained, to be confronted by a surging crowd of at least a hundred news photographers and reporters, all jostling for position, flashbulbs popping. And then the long line of spectators, calling out "Jackie! Jackie! Jackie!"

It was time for the burial. After a short drive the limousines pulled up by the Bouvier plot at St. Philomena's cemetery where the body of "Big Edie" would be lowered into the ground alongside her brothers Jack and Bud.

By now the crowd of photographers, television cameramen, journalists, and spectators had swollen to at least two hundred. As Jackie approached the graves of her father and grandfather the photographers closed in on her, blinding her with their flashes which seemed to go off every second. None of the photographers paid the slightest attention to Big Edie's sons and daughter. Soon it was pandemonium as the family reached the gravesite. The town police had to come in to restrain the surging crowd. It was then that I first understood what Jackie had to put up with since January 20, 1963. Her fame had exacted a terrible price. Even at so private an event as the funeral and burial of a beloved aunt she had to endure the intrusion of a merciless and unruly press. It was like that wherever she went, whatever she did. The press had absolutely no respect for her privacy.

After the burial the Bouviers and a few friends met for lunch, and sort of a wake, at John Duck's restaurant in neighboring Southampton. Despite the circumstances, it turned out to be a very festive occasion. Many of us had not seen each other in years. Present were Little Edie and her brothers, Bouvier and Phelan, the twins, Maude and Michelle, the last survivors of their generation, Michel Bouvier and his wife and sons, myself, my sister, Michelle's children, Scotty and Shella, and Jackie and Lee.

Before sitting down to lunch we milled around in a room adjoining the dining room having drinks and getting reacquainted with one another.

I gravitated toward Jacqueline who was standing alone at one side of the room. I did not know what to expect from her, since I had never received her reaction to my 1969 book, *The Bouviers—Portrait of An American Family*. Might she have found something objectionable about my portraits of her and her father in that book? To my surprise, and relief, she turned out to be very friendly and cordial. I remember we talked about Aunt Edie at length, especially about her singing to us in the old days and what an outrageous character she was. When I asked Jackie if she wanted a Bloody Mary she very firmly said, "no thank you, but you can get me a mineral water." After bringing her a Perrier we talked about the publishing world in New York. She was finding her editor's job at Viking very challenging and demanding. I was having a difficult time emotionally depicting the later years of Peggy Guggenheim in Venice in the book I was doing for William Morrow, *The Guggenheims—-An American Epic*. I had just returned from interviewing Peggy in Venice where I had stumbled across a terrible tragedy in her life that nobody knew about, the double suicide of her daughter and her lover, a young Italian painter. I was wondering whether I should include it in the book and asked Jackie's opinion. She reflected a moment, then came out with an extraordinary statement that seemed unrelated to the advice I was seeking from her. "There are some things you never get over," she said.

I let it go at that, dropping the matter of whether to mention Peggy Guggenheim's tragedy or not.

As we talked on I noticed that Jackie appeared to be far more relaxed and at peace with herself than she had been when she visited my mother and me in New York after the death of my father. Then she had seemed so vulnerable, so threatened, and insecure. Now she exuded confidence and high spirits. Onassis, I reflected, had been very good medicine for her. He had rescued her from the nightmares of Jack's and Bobby's assassinations. He had brought her to the nepenthean island of Skorpios in the Aegean where pain and sorrow vanish and all is forgotten. And he had given her financial security at last. All her life she had been bedeviled by lack of money she could call her own. Since her father had left her with next to nothing, she had become wholly dependent on the Kennedys for mere walking around money and what luxuries Jack Kennedy would tolerate. Even after Jack's death she was entirely beholden to the trustees who managed the trust Jack had left her. She had to ask them for everything. Now, however, she had that $26 million Onassis had left her safe and sound. It was hers and she could do what she wanted with it. She was beholden to no one. It must have given her a good feeling and it showed.

About a year or two later I had occasion to gauge at what price Jackie's new serenity had been purchased. I was introduced to Christina Onassis in a Manhattan nightclub by a friend who committed the indiscretion of introducing me as Jackie's cousin.

"Oh really," Christina said, squinting her eyes, and, without extending her hand, turned and walked away. After a while my friend brought her back. I noted how ungainly she looked. She was carrying a tremendous amount of weight on her thighs and derriere, but her upper body was actually quite trim.

"Why do you bring me back to *him*?" she asked our mutual friend.

"Because I thought you would be interested to meet him. He isn't at all like Jackie. He writes books."

Christina's eyes narrowed and her lips hardened into a thin unsmiling line. "I don't care whether he's like her or not. He has the same blood. It's deadly. It destroys everything it comes in contact with." And without extending her hand, she turned and disappeared into the crowd.

The next time I encountered Jackie was, as usual, at a funeral. This time it was the funeral of my mother's twin sister, my Aunt Michelle. She had died of emphysema and other ailments in 1987 at eight-two.

The funeral was held in the magnificent Gothic church of St. Vincent Ferrer at Lexington Avenue and 68th Street, which had been the Bouviers' preferred church in Manhattan for over seventy years.

An enormous throng had assembled for Aunt Michelle's funeral for Aunt Michelle had legions of friends and, of course, many had also come in hope of catching a glimpse of Jackie.

My mother, sister, and I took our places in the second row pew, Aunt Michelle's children and grandchildren occupied the front row, and Jacqueline was directly behind us in the third row.

Since Vatican II a custom has arisen in the Catholic mass whereby at a signal from the officiating priest the members of the congregation are invited to turn around to the occupants of the pews behind them and shake their hands saying "peace be with you." It has become one of the most moving and agreeable moments of the service, a gesture of love and brotherhood to one's fellow man.

At this solemn moment in Aunt Michelle's funeral I turned around and extended my hand to Jackie and said "peace be with you." To my dismay she made no effort to extend her hand to me and said nothing, looking past me. It was an act of enmity committed at the very moment the church had set aside for expressions of love and reconciliation.

What puzzled me later was that I never heard from Jackie that something I had done or said had displeased her. In fact, there had been no contact between us since Aunt Edith's funeral ten years ago. At that funeral our relations had been cordial and harmonious.

Granted, during that interval I had written a monumental, 859 page book on the Kennedy family called *The Kennedys: Dynasty and Disaster*, which was a national bestseller in 1985. In that book I consciously made an effort to demythologize the Kennedys, something I thought was long overdue. The Camelot image, which Jackie had so strenuously promulgated, was, in my opinion, anti-historical, a gross distortion of the truth. I therefore did not hesitate to delve into the Kennedy brothers' secret wars against Castro and the Mafia and some of their more dangerous liaisons with the likes of Judith Campbell Exner and Marilyn Monroe. I did this not to titillate my readers with gratuitous prurient gossip, but to set the record straight and bring the history of the Kennedys down from the empyrean skies of Camelot mythology to the bedrock of reality.

I bore no malice for anyone while writing the book, least of all toward Jackie.

And after the book was published and had received widespread attention, I did not receive any letters from the Kennedys, or Jackie, among the hundreds I received from readers all over the nation. Not the slightest hint of official Kennedy disapproval.

Not until that solemn moment during the High Mass For The Dead when the congregation is invited to embrace and shake hands with one another saying "peace be with you."

But it was not so much the vicious snub I received from Jacqueline that morning in the Church of St. Vincent Ferrer that bothered me. I rather expected that she would take some aspects of my book on the Kennedys badly.

It was what she did to an entirely innocent person, my mother.

For years my mother had always championed Jacqueline in the face of her friends' criticisms of her. She was always Jackie's staunchest supporter. And she had always been very devoted to Caroline and John. She had arranged for Caroline's christening in St. Patrick's cathedral in 1957 and had entertained her and John Jr. in her apartment when they were very young.

And yet Jacqueline saw fit to not invite my mother to Caroline's 1986 wedding to Edwin Schlossberg in Hyannisport. My mother was devastated. She was Jackie's oldest Bouvier relative. The last of her father's generation.

To all surviving members of the Bouvier family this was petty vindictiveness in the extreme. It represented a deep corruption of Jacqueline's character.

Jacqueline had erected her Kennedy-as-Camelot mythology hoping it would stand the test of time. Those who attacked it would be written off her list forever. The first to arouse her fury had been William Manchester, author of *Death of a President*. Then came *Washington Post* editor Ben Bradlee for his *Conversations With Kennedy*. One of Jack Kennedy's best friends, Red Fay, was stricken off her list for his innocuous *The Pleasure of his Company*. Robin Douglas-Home was put on her blacklist for writing a magazine article on Jackie. Truman Capote was dropped for *Answered Prayers*.

After Jackie's marriage to Onassis a spate of Kennedy books came off the presses that evaded her scorn. But, in the end, the only books on the Kennedys she approved of were written by Kennedy sycophants. Flatter the Kennedys and you won her approval. Criticize them and you would pay a price. Jacqueline even came to exercise a censorship role in regard to books on the Kennedys. When in 1977 she became an editor at Doubleday, which owned the Literary Guild book club, the Literary Guild, which had chosen my book, *The Bouviers,* as a Main Selection in May, 1969, ceased selecting books on the Kennedys. And at Doubleday she made sure that books published by the company unflattering to the Kennedys would not receive significant promotion and advertising. A case in point was *All American Mafioso—The Johnny Rosselli Story* by Ed Becker and Charles Rappeley. In their book the authors chose to write about President

Kennedy's affair with Judith Campbell, Judith Campbell's affair with mobster Sam Giancana, and the Kennedy sponsored CIA plots to assassinate Fidel Castro. That was too much for Jackie. She persuaded the brass at Doubleday not to promote the book and the book died.

In recent years Jacqueline has grown increasingly intolerant of books on the Kennedy assassination. Not necessarily because they were offensive to the Camelot-Kennedy mythology, but because they threatened to be. The Kennedys have always been worried that if investigators ever got to the bottom of the crime they would uncover things that would be damaging to John and Robert Kennedy's posthumous reputations. In 1977-79 The House Select Committee on Assassinations reinvestigated the assassination of President Kennedy, concluding that Kennedy was probably killed as a result of a conspiracy, and naming Teamsters boss Jimmy Hoffa and Mafia bosses Santo Trafficante and Carlo Marcello as prime suspects. Jacqueline had refused to cooperate with the investigation.

The House Committee's tentative solution to the Kennedy assassination case suggested the murder was in retaliation for Robert Kennedy's relentless campaign against the Mafia and their pawns in organized labor. It also vaguely suggested that President Kennedy himself was to blame for his own death. For he had done the inexcusable in the eyes of the Mafia. He had accepted favors from the mob, including the sexual favors of Judith Campbell, and had still continued to make war on them. In the eyes of the mob this was a doublecross, the worst infraction of the Mafia code of all, the penalty for which was death without trial.

If this assassination scenario was indeed the case, and the Kennedys themselves knew about it, Jacqueline's post-assassination glorification of John F. Kennedy may have been a gigantic smokescreen designed to thwart future investigators of the crime. Was Camelot the ultimate cover-up?

Fortunately Jacqueline had other more pressing concerns than protecting the Camelot image of the Kennedys. She had her new editor's job at Doubleday and the raising of her children, Caroline and John Jr., to think about. In both these tasks she would enjoy considerable success.

# IX

IN JULY 1988, TELEVISION VIEWERS ACROSS THE NATION WITNESSED the political debut of handsome, twenty-eight-year-old John F. Kennedy Jr., as he addressed the 1988 Democratic National Convention in Atlanta. Poised and charismatic, like his father, but displaying more the physical traits of his mother's family, this great-great-great grandson of Michel Bouvier disclaimed political ambition in his speech, but showed he could make a stunning impression speaking on his feet. The following year he graduated from New York University Law School and was appointed an Assistant District Attorney by Manhattan D.A. Robert Morganthau, who had received his first job in the Justice Department from President Kennedy in 1961. Then, in 1990, after two much-publicized failed attempts, he passed the New York State Bar exam. By then young John Jr.'s face, a perfect blend of his Bouvier and Kennedy genetic inheritance, had become almost as familiar as his father's had been during the White House years and his future seemed bright indeed.

By the time of young Kennedy's speech to the Democrats in Atlanta, his sister, Caroline Bouvier Kennedy, had graduated from Columbia Law School, passed the Bar exam, married Edwin Schlossberg, produced a daughter whom she named Rose Kennedy Schlossberg, and had begun working on a book for William Morrow, *The Bill of Rights in Action*, which eventually would become a national best-seller.

Much of the credit for the way John Jr. and Caroline turned out must go to their mother, who had overcome enormous odds in bringing up her children to be relatively normal, natural, and, above all, unspoiled, young professionals.

From their earliest years John and Caroline, as the children of an assassinated President, had received overwhelming attention, wherever they went, whatever they did. If that was not enough to spoil them there was all that money their father had left them, and the money Onassis had left them as well. As we know, when Jacqueline married Onassis the trust fund she had inherited from Kennedy automatically reverted to her children so that each one of them received trusts worth approximately $7 to $10 million depending on market conditions. Then when Onassis died in 1975 he left John and Caroline each incomes of $25,000 a year until their twenty-first birthday. That meant when Caroline was eighteen and John was fifteen each had an annual income of at least $200,000 a year probably more. Yet, miraculously, the money did not spoil them. Both Caroline and John graduated from college and law school, buckled down to work in New York City, and eschewed the jet set world of red Ferraris and weekend jaunts on the Concorde to Paris.

Yes, Jacqueline had brought up her children well. Even her most vituperative critics agreed she was an exceptionally good mother.

Realizing how spoiled young John Jr. could become, Jacqueline took steps early in her son's life to toughen him up. She told one of the Secret Service agents assigned her to give John boxing lessons. When the boy turned eleven she sent him to the Drake Island Adventure Center in Plymouth, England, for a demanding course in canoeing, sailing, and mountain-climbing that was supposed to build character. At thirteen she dispatched him to the Outward Bound program for the development of survival skills under extreme conditions of deprivation. John survived these rigors satisfactorily. Nevertheless, still fearing he would become too soft, Jacqueline packed him off to the National Outdoor Leadership School in Kenya, where he was compelled to learn how to cope with life in the African wilds with almost no creature comforts to fall back on.

John Jr. did not distinguish himself academically at the Collegiate School in Manhattan so Jacqueline enrolled him at the stricter Phillips Academy in Andover, the alma mater of George Bush. There he took an avid interest in the theater, acting in school plays. For reasons that have never been satisfactorily explained, upon graduating from Andover John entered Brown University instead of Harvard where his Kennedy grandfather, father, uncles, and some of his cousins had gone.

Again John Jr. did not distinguish himself academically at Brown but became increasingly interested in the theater, acting with success in a number of ambitious college productions.

Upon graduating from Brown John Jr. announced he wanted to be an actor and immediately drew the stern opposition of his mother. No, he could not become an actor. He had to enter a more dignified, respectable profession. Nevertheless, in defiance of his mother's wishes he starred in Brian Friel's off-Broadway play *Winners.* At his mother's express request there were to be no reviews of the play, lest a good one might encourage John to proceed further with his acting career. Soon, however, serious offers from television producers and Hollywood moguls began coming in. Some believed he stood a chance of becoming a major film star. He had dark, Mediterranean good looks, was charismatic, athletic, and had indisputable acting ability.

Jacqueline was a very conscientious mother, but she was also a very manipulative one. She has the ability to abruptly turn off affection and approval when she is crossed, then just as quickly she can turn it back on again when her demands are met. Disapproval from Jacqueline can be devastating. She can be so gracious and warm and affectionate when she wants to be, that it makes her withdrawal of favor and affection that much more withering. She exercises a form of emotional blackmail on people. Once you have been given the cold shoulder by Jacqueline you don't want to experience it again.

We do not know what actually transpired between Jacqueline and her son when the showdown occurred between them over John's desire to be an actor. But I can say from experience that his mother's scorn must have been insufferably painful to him. For at some point he capitulated to her and gave up his ambition to become an actor, deciding to enter law school instead.

That the law was not so congenial to his temperament and interests was proven when he twice failed to pass the New York State Bar exam. Perhaps now that he is an Assistant District Attorney he might get a chance to demonstrate his acting skills in a courtroom as a government prosecutor. Histrionics are a not inconsiderable part of a trial lawyer's offensive arsenal.

Then again it is not inconceivable that in discouraging John from pursuing an acting career Jacqueline prevented her son from realizing himself, from fulfilling his own personal destiny. And he may resent that and hold it against his mother.

In many ways John Jr. is more a Bouvier than a Kennedy. Certainly his complexion, features, and dark hair resemble those of his mother more than his father. And he bears a striking resemblance to his grandfather John V. "Black Jack" Bouvier when "Black Jack" was a young man. Correspondingly his face bears no resemblance whatsoever to his paternal grandfather, Joseph P. Kennedy. In temperament and interests he is also more a Bouvier than a Kennedy. He is much more drawn to the arts than he is to politics. Also a decidedly histrionic streak runs in the Bouvier family. John Jr. was made aware of that when he first visited his great aunt Edith Bouvier Beale at "Gray Gardens" in East Hampton and succumbed to her operatic personality as she sung to him "Smoke Gets In Your Eyes" and "Only Make Believe." It is worth noting too that since John Jr. became an Assistant D.A. in Manhattan he has been spending his summers in East Hampton, where his mother grew up, rather than in Hyannisport.

Caroline, on the other hand, is very much a Kennedy. Bearing a marked resemblance to her father, she took very little from her mother. Certainly she is completely bereft of her mother's sense of style. Devoted to her father's memory, she is the dedicated vice president of the John F. Kennedy Library Foundation in Boston.

A very conscientious young woman, Caroline worked hard at Radcliffe and did well academically, graduating near the top of her class in 1980. Upon leaving college she took a job in the Film and Television Development office of the Metropolitan Museum of Art, worked at it for four years, then surprised everybody by enrolling in Columbia Law School in 1985 at the age of twenty-eight. That same year she married forty-one year old Edwin Schlossberg, an inventor of electronic games and a designer of museum exhibits and amusement parlors, from an Orthodox Jewish family and moved into a 12-room $2.5 million apartment on Park Avenue and 78th Street. On June 24, 1988, she gave birth to her first child, whom she named after grandmother, Rose Kennedy Schlossberg. Another daughter, Tatania, followed, and then in 1993 she gave birth to a son whom she named John Bouvier Kennedy Schlossberg. Meanwhile she had graduated from Columbia law, passed her Bar exam and had co-authored, with Ellen Alderman a bestselling book, *The Bill of Rights in Action*.

While her children were beginning to establish themselves in New York Jacqueline pursued a part-time career as an editor, first at Viking, later at Doubleday. She had begun to tire of being known only as the rich widow of very rich men and had decided to become a woman of the eighties with a profession of her own. Her mission at Doubleday was to attract celebrity authors to the house. The biggest fish she landed turned out to be the pop star Michael Jackson, whose memoirs she edited. Later she brought the Nobel prize winning Egyptian novelist Naquib Mahfouz to Doubleday.

In time Jacqueline built for herself a 19-room Cape Cod house on 375 acres of oceanfront land on Martha's Vineyard, using $3.5

million of her Onassis inheritance. She also acquired a new companion. He was Maurice Templesman, an Orthodox Jew her same age, originally from Antwerp, who had made a fortune dealing in South African diamonds and precious metals. Although he remained married, Templesman became Jacqueline's closest companion. Soon they became inseparable. They took trips together. He stayed at her Fifth Avenue apartment and house on Martha's Vineyard. He also became a valued investment advisor and made her considerable amounts of money speculating on the international diamond and gold markets. According to one source Templesman increased the $26 million fortune she had inherited from Onassis to $100 million. Knowing Jacqueline, this must have contributed significantly to the success of her relationship with Maurice.

The 1990s found Jacqueline leading perhaps the most serene existence of her life. She was comfortable in her part-time editor's job at Doubleday, comfortable in her new house on Martha's Vineyard, and comfortable with Maurice Templesman, who made few demands on her, and was certainly not prone to run off with the likes of Maria Callas. Most of all she was financially secure at last.

At sixty-two Jacqueline is as trim and attractive as ever. With her facelift sharpening her profile and her sleek figure benefitting from her relentless dieting, she keeps fit by jogging regularly in Central Park and riding her beloved horses at her rented estate at Bernardsville, New Jersey.

Jackie's recent years have been somewhat clouded by the decline of her mother, Janet Bouvier Auchincloss, who came down with Alzheimer's disease in 1987. Concurrently her aunt Winifred d'Olier, Janet's sister, also succumbed to the disease. Janet's mind deteriorated to the point where she could not remember who John F. Kennedy was. Almost totally disoriented mentally, she died of complications resulting from the disease in 1991.

With both parents dead, and both husbands dead, Jacqueline was left with her two children, her fortune and her fame.

Her reputation is inevitably associated with her fame. Fortunately for her the damage her reputation sustained at the time of her marriage to Onassis has largely, but not entirely, been healed. Although the golddigger image remains, Jacqueline is still admired by many Americans. However, her inherent remoteness prevents her from being loved the way Eleanor Roosevelt and Barbara Bush were loved. For most Americans Jacqueline remains an inaccessible enigma: a radiant, stylish First Lady, who survived appalling tragedies with courage and dignity, who nevertheless remains unknowable.

But one thing is certain. During the two years, ten months, and two days Jacqueline was at the center of the world's stage her conduct was always, in the words of the Bouvier family motto, "Sans Peur et Sans Reproche."

# X

As WE SURVEY THE 178-YEAR HISTORY OF THE BOUVIER FAMILY IN America we come to the inescapable conclusion that although Jacqueline Bouvier Kennedy Onassis is unquestionably the most famous of the American Bouviers, the greatest Bouvier, in terms of character and achievement, was the first one, Michel, the veteran of Waterloo, who, arriving from France as a penniless refugee, became a respected Philadelphia cabinetmaker while raising a family of twelve, then a successful furniture manufacturer, and finally an adroit builder and real estate investor leaving a fortune to his heirs of what in today's dollars would amount to around $10 million.

Jacqueline, in the end, was the creation of three extraordinary men, Joseph P. Kennedy, John F. Kennedy, and Aristotle Onassis—all of whom gave her substantial sums of money. No one had ever given Michel Bouvier a cent. He had created himself. In Napoleon's words, he was his own ancestor.

Michel Bouvier's career was the quintessential American success story. America was built in the nineteenth century by ten thousand Michel Bouviers. They came from Europe with nothing but their abilities. They worked hard. And in reaching their goals they built a nation.

Yes, Michel Bouvier was a giant of a man. His descendants number in the upper hundreds. His works, some of which are in the White House, are prized as antiques. One of his sons was wounded at Gettysburg. A great-great-granddaughter, wife of the 35th President of the united States, gave an example of dignity and courage to an entire nation in November, 1963. A step-granddaughter was beatified by Pope John Paul II at St. Peter's in 1988. Six generations later his name lives on. A great-great-great-great-grandson, Michel Bouvier V, was born in 1977.

Michel V is the grandson of Michel Bouvier III, "Bud" Bouvier's son, a first cousin to me and Jacqueline, and also the godfather of Jacqueline.

In keeping with America's growing international involvements throughout the second half of the twentieth century, Michel III has spent as much of his adult life abroad as he has in the United States. He speaks fluent Spanish, Italian, French, and German and is equally at home in Madrid, Rome, Paris, and Bonn as he is in Washington and New York.

After serving for three years as Assistant to the Director of Operations for Europe and the Middle East of Grumman International, Michel was made Director in 1964, thereby assuming responsibility for all Grumman business in that vast area. The job turned out to be a particularly congenial one at which he was very successful. His primary mission was to sell military aircraft to the armed forces of European and Middle Eastern nations and to supervise, in turn, the delivery and maintenance of the aircraft sold. This involved, among other things, frequent meetings with defense ministers and Air Force generals from Bonn to Beirut. As one who had been raised on tales of Bouvier military valor, and as the stepson of a career Army officer, who had spent much of his youth at Army bases, Michel felt very much at ease with the military and enjoyed dealing with them. Moreover, he liked traveling and could think of no more pleasant business trips than those his job repeatedly required him to take to the capitals of Europe and the Middle East.

In September 1966, Grumman aircraft, reacting to the unfavorable business climate generated by de Gaulle's anti-American policies, decided to transfer its European headquarters from Paris to Bonn, and so the Michel Bouviers were compelled to move to the West German capital, settling in the suburb of Bad Godesberg.

During the late sixties and early seventies Michel Bouvier was a well-known and much respected figure in the major cities of Europe, his tall, hulking frame being particularly familiar in the defense ministries and restaurants. Sympathetic to Europeans, and appreciated by them, he carved out a social world for himself that bore little resemblance to the milieu in which the Bouviers of New York, from JVB, Sr., to JVB III, lived and worked for over ninety years. One of the most significant things about him is his disregard of, and disdain for, the status game the Bouviers had always taken so seriously. Joining none of the exclusive clubs JVB, JR., and JVB III belonged to, staying out of the Social Register, taking little interest in the patriotic associations JVB, Jr., assured him hereditary membership in, and finding socialites, in general, uninspiring, Michel—in sharp contrast to his class-conscious forebears—couldn't care less whether he was in society or out of it. Likewise, he has never attempted to capitalize on his name or his relationship with the former First Lady, preferring to make his way in the world entirely on his own merits.

A forthright, down-to-earth family man, possessing the same fatherly talents as the first Bouvier, Michel prefers the company of his wife and sons to any other and has successfully prevented the opening of a generation gap in his household. A more united and affectionate family would be hard to find in this era of irreconcilable parent-child conflicts. Michel is convinced that one of the reasons his children have been unaffected by the contemporary youthquake is that they were brought up as exiles. Living in foreign countries for most of their lives, they were not exposed to the ferment of their generation in American and at the same time were removed, by nationality, from the tensions of their contemporaries in the countries in which they lived.

If Michel's life has differed greatly from that of his Bouvier forebears, his sons' lives promise to be even more different. For while Michel grew up in New York and Long Island, and absorbed some of the Eastern seaboard's style and outlook, Michel IV spent most of his youth in Peru, France, and Germany, and JVB IV's first five years of schooling took place in Paris.

John Vernou Bouvier IV, known as Jayvee, thirty-eight in 1993, speaks fluent Spanish, French, and German, whereas the three forebears after whom he was named never spoke anything but their native tongue. A very bright young man who has consistently been at the head of his class, he first attended the American School in Paris, then, upon his father's transfer to Bonn, entered a German "Gymnasium" where he took all his courses in German, having learned the language in less than a year. Although he bears Jack Bouvier's name and is the godson of Jacqueline Onassis, JVB IV has little in common with either. Physically he seems to take more after his mother's family, having blond hair, fair skin, and a droll, whimsical expression. In intelligence he is in a class by himself. Early in his life he settled on a career in oceanography and aerospace, professions far removed from that in which the three previous John Vernou Bouviers earned their living. Ninety years of stockbrokering should therefore remain the Bouviers' definitive contribution to Wall Street.

After taking a master's degree in mechanical engineering from the University of California, Jayvee worked for two California concerns, Deep Ocean Engineering Inc. and Oceanic Products, designing one-man submersibles and a variety of commercial underwater products such as breathing air regulators, underwater video camera housings, and Diver Maneuvering vehicles.

He then went East and joined Grumman Aerospace Corp on Long Island, where he worked first on flight test data acquisition on advanced military aircraft, including the F-14, and then Grumman's Space Station Program Support Division.

Eventually Jayvee ended up in Washington with Oceaneering Advanced Technologies, where he was responsible for the work of thirty-seven engineers engaged in designing robotics for NASA's Space Station Freedom and providing support to the Goddard Space Flight Center Telerobotic Servicer project. Today he is president of John V. Bouvier & Associates, an engineering/management consulting firm providing specialized consultation in the areas of robotics and controls technology to NASA headquarters, Office of Space Flight, Space Station Freedom.

In 1986 Jayvee married a young woman from Shanghai who had a scholarship to Mt. Holyoke College, by the name of She Xi, who bore him a daughter they named Jassica. She Xi Bouvier recently opened up a jewelry store in Washington's Union Station which she called "The Bouvier Collection." The store has been a great commercial success.

Michel's oldest son, known in the family as Michie, is the fourth member of the American Bouviers to bear the name Michel Bouvier, a name that has been in uninterrupted existence in the family, if we include the uncle from Grenoble after whom Michel the first was named, for over 247 years.

Michie, in contrast to his younger brother, is very much a Bouvier, both physically and mentally. His long, exuberant eyebrows, his eyes, nose, and chin are reminiscent of both the first Michel and his own father, and there are resemblances also to Bud Bouvier and Jacqueline Onassis. More athletic than his brother, but not as studious, Michie is an excellent swimmer and deep-sea diver as well as a talented guitarist. Like his father, mother, and brother, he speaks fluent Spanish, French, and German and gets along exceptionally well with Europeans.

Michie graduated from Schiller College near Stuttgart, then spent five years in the U.S. Army including a tour of duty in Vietnam, during which he was severely wounded in action, making him the third Bouvier to be wounded in battle. His grandfather, William "Bud" Bouvier, had been gassed in World War I, and great-grandfather, John V. Bouvier, had been wounded in the Second Battle of Bull Run and at Gettysburg in the Civil War.

After leaving the army Michie took an engineering degree from the University of Florida, then got a job as an Acoustics Engineer with the Electric Boat Company in Groton, Connecticut. For five years he worked in the Navy's nuclear submarine program trying, in his own words, "to make submarines quiet."

From Electric Boat Michie took a job as an Aerospace Engineer with the Department of Defense at the Redstone Arsenal in Huntsville, Alabama. Recently he was transferred to the Department of Defense offices in London. Michie is married and is the father of three daughters and a son, Michel V.

Michie, now forty-five, has led an adventurous life. I asked him what the most memorable experience of his working life has been to date. Preferring to forget Vietnam, he told me about an expedition in the Red Sea he participated in the summer of 1966, under the direction of the French scientist Olivier Gonet, just before he joined the army. His father had helped get him into the expedition through Jacques Piccard, who, in addition to his many other positions, was, at the time, a consultant in oceanography for Grumman. Olivier Gonet's specialty is determining the contour and composition of the ocean floor, but he is also interested in coral and in undersea photography. One of the many purposes of the Red Sea expedition was to test a new device he had invented for finding oil in sea beds. As a member of his expedition, Michie was apprenticed to one of Gonet's oceanographers, Max de Rham, and served as crewman and deep-sea diver.

Michie's summer on the Red Sea turned out to be the most exciting of his life . . . Riding a Russian plane, an Egyptian army jeep, an oil truck, and trekking miles over open desert to reach Gonet's ship at Al Qusayr. Diving for coral off headlands with such exotic names as Raz Abu Fatama and Marsa Halaib. Discovering two-thousand-year-old sunken cargoes of Roman amphoras. Being stranded in the desert for three days without water. Fighting seas so rough his ship could make no more than a few feet headway an hour. Being shot at by Egyptian PT boats whose officers later accused him and Gonet of smuggling. Gliding along the floor of the Red sea and encountering green-haired shipwrecks and enormous sea turtles. Swimming through showers of silver sardines. . . to be suddenly confronted with their pursuers, twelve-foot sharks and schools of as many as forty barracuda. Battles with dragon-snouted moray eels . . .

After it was over, Gonet wrote a book about the expedition, entitled *La Mer a Coeur Ouvert—corail, mers chaudes et adventures*, in which he gave this description of Michie: "On board we had the de Rhams, a cook by the name of Bechir, myself and a young American apprentice, Michel Bouvier. Very engaging, and gifted with a subtle and charming sense of humor, Michel was only seventeen years old and had all the qualities and defects of that age: at times very courageous and independent, at times a bit touchy and mercurial. Often it was necessary to protect him from dangers he would underestimate. Aside from that, he was very pleasant companion, amusing and, above all, intelligent."

Courageous, independent, mercurial, intelligent, adventurous . . . the description could well have been made 180 years ago of a young recruit from Pont-Saint-Esprit who had recently joined Napoleon's army.

# Epilogue

IN PONT-SAINT-ESPRIT TODAY THE VILLAGERS—PARTICULARLY THE
oldtimers—still enjoy talking over the Bouvier saga. The appearance of Jacqueline Onassis on the cover of a magazine, or a
newspaper article about one of her recent trips, is enough to start
the discussion going again. A group of Spiripontains might be
sitting around a table in the sycamore-shaded Café du Midi,
sipping their evening apéritifs, when a friend joins them,
magazine in hand. "Ah, c'est la jolie Jacqueline, encore!" one of
them explains. And it begins anew. Wild are the rumors concerning "les Bouviers d'Amérique." The first Bouvier who emigrated
to America was an illiterate farmhand who worked for a daily
wage. Some of his descendants live on two acres up in La Mirandole. In America he made a hundred million dollars. Each one of
his twenty children inherited over a million dollars from him.
One of his sons became a banker and supported all his French
cousins, except those at La Mirandole, sending them monthly
checks all their lives. Madame Onassis is his granddaughter. She
has two hundred million dollars and apartments in all the capitals
of Europe. Her first husband was murdered by a vast conspiracy
that included the heads of several Texas oil companies, the director of American Intelligence, Fidel Castro, and the Premier of the
Soviet Union. De Gaulle loved him like a son. One of the Bouviers
of La Mirandole was killed on her way to see Jacqueline in Paris.
Jacqueline was going to bring her back to America to make her
rich. In America even an illiterate farmhand can become rich.
Look at the first Bouvier . . . But here things are different. Here
things never change. Two thousand years ago Julius Caesar
marched through town and hardly anything has happened since.
Here there is no industry, no commerce. Nobody can make any
money. All one can do is talk. You can talk in the cafés all day
long if you want to, and you might as well, for you won't make
any money if you work. However, a Spiripontain Bouvier can go
to America and a hundred years later his great-great-
granddaughter is one of the richest and most influential women
in the world. If he had stayed here, she would be hoeing potatoes
up in La Mirandole . . .

Although their version of the saga is preposterous, the old-
timers of Pont-Saint-Esprit somehow get closer to the truth than
one might think. That a family like the Bouviers of Philadelphia

and New York should have originated in the torpid village by the Rhône *is* extraordinary.

Pont-Saint-Esprit has certainly changed a great deal since Julius Caesar rumbled through town after conquering Provincia in 52 B.C., but it has not changed much since Michel Bouvier left it 178 years ago. Whereas Michel's Philadelphia mansion and MC's two New York brownstones have been demolished, the house Michel was born in is still standing, as are most of the landmarks he knew as a child. The seven-hundred-year-old Bridge of the Holy Ghost still spans the relentless waters of the Rhône. The eight-hundred-year-old Church of Saint-Saturnin, where Michel worshipped as a child, is still the main church of the town. Surviving also are the fifteenth-century Maison du Roy, where twelve kings of France stayed while on tours of inspection through their southern domains; La Villette, Michel Barry's country home; Pélagie Barry's house on the rue Gambetta; and the vault containing the remains of Eustache Bouvier and his two wives.

Not only has Pont-Saint-Esprit remained physically unchanged over the past three hundred years; the way of life of its inhabitants has not changed appreciably either. Many scenes one encounters in the village today duplicate those portrayed in eighteenth-century prints of village life: women washing clothes in open-air fountains; farmers passing through town in oxcarts; a gaunt old woman shepherding some goats down an alley; some men playing *pétanque* in a dusty yard.

On warm days the villagers take to lounging in the cafés and squares, the men wearing their jackets over their shoulders like Spanish capes, the women clustered in circles, gossiping endlessly. There are still a few cabinetmakers in town. Although his sons left him, Eustache has had successors. Their shops are usually on the ground floor, opening onto an alley, with several pieces of furniture, and perhaps a pile of lumber, or upholstery, out on the pavement. Most of the buildings in the village, rarely more than three stories high, seem to be in a state of permanent disrepair, their bleached stucco façades slowly crumbling to dust. The architecture is typically Mediterranean—irregular shapes with arched doorways and windows haphazardly spaced. Terra-cotta jugs on windowsills and stoops, bursting with red geraniums, redeem the decrepit houses, give them, effortlessly, a second youth. Market days bring spurts of activity to the otherwise sleepy town, the main square filling up with stands of vegetables, fruit, cloth, toys and utensils, and crowds of shouting, gesticulating buyers and sellers. On other days, the quiet, dusty squares are inhabited principally by chickens and dogs. An almost tangible smell compounded of olive oil, plaster, sewage, warm red wine, and drying laundry lingers in the streets and alleys. The atmosphere is wholly without tension, as calm and uneventful as the surrounding countryside.

Frédéric Mistral, the Provençal poet, referred to Pont-Saint-Esprit in one of his works as the gateways to Provence. "C'est la porte sainte, la port triomphale," he wrote, "de la terre d'amour!" To many travelers the region is more typical of Italy than of France. There is the same feeling of antiquity, the same illusion of space, the same incandescent light. One has a feeling of liberation in this open, shining land, a sense of boundlessness, of inexhaustible beauty. South of Pont-Saint-Esprit, toward another town on the Rhône, Arles, where several of Jean-François Bouvier's children eventually settled, the countryside becomes so colorful and vibrant as to seem imaginary. Stands of green-black cypresses, bent permanently to the wind, bordering sunny fields. Silvery olive trees, clinging, like tiny clouds, to the hillsides. Clumps of blazing sunflowers. Oleanders and laurier roses lining the roads. Slim poplars and fresh oaks along the river banks. And in the distance, the orange-tiled roofs of villages perched on the summits of lilac hills. This is the landscape Van Gogh lovingly preserved. Where one looks, his orange skies and blue fields, his vine pickers with hats of yellow straw, his pear and peach blossoms, claim the eye. Throughout this bright region are scattered many isolated vestiges of Rome. Remains of aqueducts, triumphal arches, temples, and arenas. An empty Gallo-Roman sarcophagus in the shade of a cypress tree. A two-thousand-year-old wall, sprouting violets and dandelions, embedded in the façade of a gargoyled Romanesque church. In the autumn, at harvest time, rustic carts laden with crimson grapes make their way to wine presses established by Roman consuls. Although the natives will not admit it, even the celebrated Vins du Soleil, like so much in Provence, ultimately come from Italy.

Farther south, in the region known as the Camargue, where several of Jean-François's grandchildren settled, and where the Rhône empties into the Mediterranean, we come upon another ancient landscape. Swamp plains. Salt lagoons. Sand flats.

Streamlets, canals. Solitary farmsteads. An area populated by wild flamingos, wild horses and bulls, and painted gypsy caravans. There is a silence and desolation to this countryside that again recalls the Roman campagna, or the Ionian coast of Sicily.

This sense of antiquity, this timeless quality of a region that has known over two thousand years of civilization, joined to a landscape so gay, so sensual as to seem the home of eternal youth, has given the Provençaux a very specific attitude toward life, which the foreign visitor, if he or she stays long enough, easily absorbs. In essence it is a sort of hedonistic fatalism, the philosophic stance of a people who have seen and experienced everything and who have, in the face of two thousand years of history, come to the conclusion that the only things worth living for are the pleasures of the moment, that the warmth of the April sun on one's face, the taste of a rare Vin du Soleil, the sight of a solitary fisherman going down the Rhône on a brilliant summer day, is fulfillment enough for anyone. In Provence one does not want, or need, to strive, for it is too easy, and delightful, to enjoy.

Eustache Bouvier has many descendants living in this luminous region today, but only two who actually reside in, or near, Pont-Saint-Esprit. The two Spiripontains are both descended from his eldest daughter, Elizabeth, and are contemporaries of Michel Bouvier III and Jacqueline Onassis. One of them, Régis Flandin, lives alone in Mon Plaisir, a villa on the outskirts of Pont-Saint-Esprit that has been in his family for over eighty years. He works in an insurance agency. A lively man with the same swarthy complexion as Jack Bouvier, he once took a trip to the United States, hitchhiking from New York to San Francisco, during which he wanted to look up his American cousins, but the only one he knew about was the nation's former First Lady and he felt she was "beyond reach." Although he loves the relaxed atmosphere of the Midi, Regis would nevertheless like to find a way of living and working in the United States. However, he admits he has little chance of realizing his ambition. "I suppose I shall have to remain here," he says somewhat wistfully, "where your family's great adventure started . . . I don't think there will be much adventure in my life."

Christian Divôl, Eustache's other Spiripontain descendant, has a somewhat different outlook. Fully satisfied with his life, he has little desire to leave the Midi, least of all emigrate to America. He and his wife and one-year-old daughter live in the hamlet of Issirac, not far from the Rhône, and farm an old family property there, only a few kilometers from Pont-Saint-Esprit. Using modern agricultural machinery and techniques, Christian Divôl cultivates the vine and raises asparagus, plums, peaches, and pears. The farm is profitable and allows him and his family to maintain a comfortable standard of living. Situated on a plateau overlooking the Rhône Valley, the fifty-*hectaire* property is typical of the farmland of the region. The yellow fields are divided by stands of poplars and oaks. Sunflowers and poppies brighten the vineyards with splashes of gold and vermillion. In the spring the pear and peach trees are a feast of white and pink blossoms. In the fall the vineyards glow copper and gold . . . Along with a sense of timelessness there is a wonderful feeling of space. On clear days one can see Petrarch's Mount-Ventoux, hovering, like a lilac cloud, in the East. Although the land has been under cultivation for over two thousand years, it still seems an Eden, as fresh and inviolate as the New Jersey shore must have seemed to Michel Bouvier in the summer of 1815.

Christian Divôl's ancestors have lived in, or near, Pont-Saint-Esprit since 1787. If their lives have been unspectacular, they have been serene. No vast fortunes won, or lost; no great honors; no great tragedies. Over the years their lives have flowed by as steadily and peacefully as the Rhône. When Christian Divôl talks of his American cousins, only one of whom he has met, he is liable to refer to them as if they were beings from another planet. Most of what he knows about them he has heard either from his mother or from the old-timers of Pont-Saint-Esprit. Wild are the rumors concerning "les Bouviers d'Amérique." The first Bouvier who emigrated to America was . . . In America he made . . . As he prunes his peach trees, Christian will tell you, with no trace of envy, that he wonders whether the American Bouviers have fared any better than their French cousins. "Look at us," he will say, turning his tanned face toward you and smiling modestly. "My ancestors didn't leave and yet we are not badly off. I have my farm. The soil is good and the climate mild. This fall, after we make the wine, we're going down to the Camargue to ride wild horses."

# Index